Lu Xun's Revolution

Lu Xun's Revolution

WRITING IN A TIME OF VIOLENCE

GLORIA DAVIES

HARVARD UNIVERSITY PRESS
Cambridge, Massachusetts
London, England
2013

To John Davies and Jessie Trinh

Library of Congress Cataloging-in-Publication Data

Davies, Gloria
Lu Xun's revolution : writing in a time of violence / Gloria Davies.
p. cm.
Includes bibliographical references and index.
ISBN978- 0-674-07264-0
1. Lu, Xun, 1881-1936—Criticism and interpretation.
2. China—Intellectual life—20th century.
I. Title.
PL2754.S5Z595126 2013
895.1'8509—dc23   2012031840

Contents

Note on Translation

Every translator of Lu Xun seeks to bring to life the unique qualities of his language in a foreign tongue. Lu Xun's erudite and inventive Chinese poses a formidable challenge in this regard. That he was also fond of using allusions and quotations, of which many are obscure, complicates the task further. Moreover, Lu Xun's essays are rich with intertextual references, and this is particularly true of his polemical writings, which frequently require a sustained engagement with his oeuvre as a whole.

For these various reasons, Lu Xun's *Selected Works,* translated by husband-and-wife team Yang Xianyi (1915–2009) and Gladys Yang (1919–1999), deserves special acknowledgment. First published in 1956, with subsequent reprints and a third and final edition appearing in 1980, this four-volume anthology has played an unrivaled part in shaping the reception of Lu Xun's *baihua* writings in English. Comprising a large majority of Lu Xun's best-known essays, *Selected Works* remains widely quoted, and it is no exaggeration to say that to this day, Lu Xun "speaks" in English mainly through the Yangs' elegant translation.

My own debt to *Selected Works* is enormous, for it was in these four volumes that I first encountered Lu Xun in my undergraduate years. The influence of the Yangs' English renderings of Lu Xun is reflected throughout this book, in the form of citations from *Selected Works* and the Yangs' many other single-volume translations of Lu Xun. In instances in which I have taken only some of the wording from *Selected Works,* I have cited both the original Chinese in *Lu Xun quanji (LXQJ)* and *Selected Works (SW).* Where my translation differs entirely from that of *Selected Works,* or where I have cited from a part of Lu Xun's corpus not previously translated, the reference is to *LXQJ* alone.

The complex cadences of Lu Xun's language are always open to interpretation, and over time many scholars have also diverged from the Yangs in their readings of Lu Xun. Their translations, where appropriate, have also been cited in this book. In my translation of Lu Xun, I have adopted an approach that draws on his notion of "hard translation" (in the sense of an unyielding translation), which, by according equal importance to the semantic and syntactic properties of the text, seeks to highlight its literary and constructed nature. I hope by this means to draw renewed attention to Lu Xun's approach to writing as a science and technology of reinvention. Above all, I seek to maintain a fidelity to the subtle rigor of his *baihua.*

Guide and Chronology

Lu Xun's published quarrels with his contemporaries were eagerly consumed by the literati of his day and have remained a source of fascination for Chinese readers ever since. The bite and verve of these polemical writings and ripostes, together with the critical essays, reviews, and published and unpublished correspondence that he produced from the mid-1920s onward, have come to define the later Lu Xun. While sympathetic readers see in these writings a heightened vigilance and sensitivity to the dangers of orthodoxy, the less sympathetic perceive an eminent writer squandering his literary talents in unproductive debate. Some even contend that he allowed himself to become an instrument of Communist orthodoxy.

To understand why Lu Xun continues to excite such passions, we must delve into the contextual intricacies of his later writings. To help in this process, the chronological outline below provides a selection of events and texts mentioned in or relevant to this book.

1902–1909

Lu Xun's years in Japan; in 1902 Liang Qichao coins the term "literary revolution"; Lu Xun produces literary translations and writes numerous critical essays in archaic *guwen* prose, including "On the Power of Mara Poetry" and "Toward a Refutation of Malevolent Voices" (1908); in 1906 Lu Xun's mother, Lu Rui, arranges his marriage to the illiterate, foot-bound Zhu An, who dutifully serves her mother-in-law from this time until Lu Rui's death in 1943. (Zhu An dies in 1947.)

1909–1911

Lu Xun lives and works first in Hangzhou, then in Shaoxing.

1912

January: Founding of the Chinese Republic, with Sun Yat-sen as president.

February: Sun Yat-sen cedes the office of president to Yuan Shikai.

May: Lu Xun works in Nanjing's Ministry of Education at Cai Yuan-pei's invitation, transferring to Beijing in the same month with the establishment of China's first Republican government.

1913–1916

Lu Xun devotes his time to research on premodern literature, Buddhist sutras, and the local history of his hometown, Shaoxing.

November 1913: Yuan Shikai forces Sun Yat-sen into exile in Japan.

1915: *Youth (Qingnian)* magazine is established by Chen Duxiu, with the name changed to *New Youth (Xin qingnian)* in September 1916.

August–December 1915: Yuan attempts to become emperor.

May 1916: Sun Yat-sen returns to Shanghai.

June 1916: Yuan dies.

1917

February: *New Youth* declares the start of its "literary revolution."

July: Zhang Xun leads the short-lived restoration of the abdicated Manchu emperor Puyi. Lu Xun resigns from the Ministry of Education in protest on 3 July, resuming his duties on 16 July when the restoration is aborted.

1918

May: Lu Xun publishes "Diary of a Madman" in *New Youth*, using Lu Xun for the first time as his nom de plume.

November: *New Tide (Xin chao)* magazine is founded at Peking University, inspired by *New Youth*.

1919

February: Lu Xun's essay "Dissatisfaction" is published in *New Youth*.

May: The May Fourth Movement is launched in protest against the treatment of China at the Paris Peace Conference.

October: Sun Yat-sen remodels the Nationalist Party along Leninist lines; Lu Xun completes the essay "How Should We Be as Fathers Today?"

1920

Sun Yat-sen establishes his new political base in Guangzhou; Beijing's Ministry of Education adopts *baihua* as the medium of instruction in schools; Mao Dun becomes editor of the *Short Story Monthly* in Shanghai; Zhou Zuoren becomes editor-in-chief of *New Tide;* Lu Xun begins lecturing at Peking University.

1921

January: Lu Xun completes the short story "My Old Home."

June: Founding of the Creation Society in Tokyo.

July: Founding of the Chinese Communist Party.

December: First installment of *The True Story of Ah Q* is published in Beijing's *Morning Post Literary Supplement* (of which Lu Xun's protégé Sun Fuyuan, founding member of *New Tide,* is editor from 1920 to 1924).

1922

Ah Q is published in subsequent installments, generating debate and public interest; Chen Jiongming, the southern warlord ruling Guangdong, attempts to kill Sun Yat-sen, who seeks temporary refuge in Shanghai.

1923

Chen is defeated and ousted from Guangdong by Sun Yat-sen; the Nationalist-Communist "united front" is inaugurated; Lu Xun begins lecturing at Peking Women's Normal College.

January: Sun Yat-sen concludes successful negotiations with the Co-mintern representative Adolf Joffe and issues joint manifesto; Sun Yat-sen publishes his seminal article "The History of the Chinese Revolution"; the Crescent Moon Society is formed in Beijing.

July: Lu Xun and his brother Zhou Zuoren sunder ties.

August: Lu Xun's first short story anthology, *A Call to Arms,* is published by New Tide Press.

November: Sun Yat-sen appoints Chiang Kai-shek commandant of the Whampoa Military Academy.

December: Lu Xun's Peking University lectures, *A Brief History of Chinese Fiction (Zhongguo xiaoshuo shilue),* are published by New Tide.

1924

Lu Xun translates Kuriyagawa Hakuson's *Symbols of Mental Anguish.*

April: Guo Moruo and other members of the Creation Society declare themselves Marxist.

September: Lu Xun begins work on several of his *Wild Grass* prose compositions, including "The Shadow's Farewell," "Revenge," and "Revenge II," all of which appear in *Threads of Talk (Yusi),* founded in Beijing in November.

November: Sun Yat-sen makes farewell speech at Whampoa Military Academy, praising Lenin as "a great revolutionary saint."

December: *Contemporary Review (Xiandai pinglun)* is founded by Chen Yuan in Beijing.

1925

Founding of Beixin Publishing House by Li Xiaofeng, *New Tide* founding member, with Lu Xun's assistance; Beixin publishes new editions of Lu Xun's *A Brief History of Chinese Fiction* and *A Call to Arms (Nahan).*

January–February: Lu Xun's "Chewing and Gnawing on Words" is published in two installments in *Beijing News Literary Supplement (Jingbao Fukan).*

March: Xu Guangping writes her first letter to Lu Xun; Sun Yat-sen dies.

April: "The Wayfarer" appears in *Threads of Talk;* Lu Xun cofounds the magazine *Wilderness (Mangyuan),* whose contributors include Xu Guangping and Gao Changhong.

May: "May Thirtieth Massacre" occurs.

June: Lu Xun begins a war of words with Chen Yuan over Zhang Shizhao's decision to close Peking Women's Normal College, with his three-part scathing attack on Chen, "No Mere Casual Chat," appearing in *Threads of Talk* between June and November.

July: Lu Xun's "The Tremor of Debased Lines" and "Seeing with Eyes Wide Open" are published in *Threads of Talk.*

August: Lu Xun is dismissed from Beijing's Ministry of Education; he establishes the Yet to Be Named Society (Weiming she) with his students, including Li Jiye, Tai Jingnong, and Wei Suyuan.

November: *Hot Wind (Re feng),* Lu Xun's first anthology of essays, is published by Beixin.

December: Lu Xun's "Such a Warrior" is published in *Threads of Talk.*

1926

Early to mid-1926: Members of the Creation Society travel to Guangzhou to support the Northern Expedition.

January: Lu Xun is reinstated at Beijing's Ministry of Education; Chen Yuan attacks Lu Xun in an open letter to Xu Zhimo published in Beijing's *Morning Post Supplement* (then edited by Xu); Lu Xun's "On Deferring Fair Play," a riposte to Lin Yutang aimed at Chen Yuan, is published in *Wilderness.*

February: Lu Xun's "A Bit of Metaphor" is published in *Wilderness.*

March: Chiang Kai-shek and the Nationalist right stage a takeover of Guangzhou; Lu Xun writes a eulogy for Sun Yat-sen; several of Lu Xun's students are killed in a Beijing street protest on 18 March.

April: Lu Xun writes "In Memory of Miss Liu Hezhen" to commemorate the dead students; he eulogizes his former students who had joined the revolution in Guangzhou in "An Awakening" (later included in *Wild Grass*).

May: Guo Moruo publishes "Revolution and Literature" in *Creation Monthly.*

June: Lu Xun's second anthology of essays, *Inauspicious Star (Huagai ji)*, is published by Beixin; Cheng Fangwu's "Revolutionary Literature and Its Immortality" is published in *Creation Monthly*; the Manchurian warlord Zhang Zuolin takes Beijing; Lu Xun publishes "Wu Chang: Life-Is-Transient" in *Wilderness*.

July: Launch of the Northern Expedition.

August: Lu Xun leaves Beijing and takes up appointment at Xiamen University; his *Lore of Chinese Fiction (Xiaoshuo jiuwen chao)* is published by Beixin. Lu Xun's second anthology of short stories, *Wandering (Panghuang)*, is published by Beixin.

Late 1926: *Threads of Talk* and Beixin are relocated to Shanghai.

November: Lu Xun publishes "My Father's Illness" in *Wilderness*; Stalin demands Chinese Communist obedience to Chiang Kai-shek at the Seventh Plenum of the Comintern's Executive Committee; Zheng Zhenduo publishes his review of *A Call to Arms*; Gao Changhong publishes a review of Lu Xun's "Autumn Night."

December: The Northern Expedition's headquarters are relocated from Guangzhou to Wuhan.

1927

January: Lu Xun leaves Xiamen for Guangzhou to become dean of studies and head of the Chinese Department at Sun Yat-sen University; Yu Dafu's exposé, "Guangzhou Affairs," is published in the Creation Society's magazine *Deluge (Hongshui)*; Zhou Zuoren's "The Shanghai Style" appears in *Threads of Talk*; Jiang Guangci's tale of revolutionary romance, *On the Yalu (Yalu jiang shang)*, is published in Shanghai.

February: Workers' strike suppressed in Shanghai; Lu Xun speaks on "Silent China" at the YMCA in Hong Kong; Cheng Fangwu's "Complete Our Literary Revolution" is published in *Deluge*; Yu Dafu's "Dictatorship of the Proletariat and Proletarian Literature" is published in *Deluge*; Chiang Kai-shek's speech of 19 February foreshadows the "Party purification" campaign.

March: Lu Xun's anthology of essays *The Grave (Fen)* is published by the Yet to Be Named Society; Cheng Fangwu's rebuttal of Yu Dafu's essays is published in *Deluge*; on 21 March Shanghai's General Labor Union organizes a successful but short-lived workers' uprising in

Chinese-controlled Shanghai; on 28 March Mao Zedong writes his "Report on the Peasant Movement in Hunan."

April: On 8 April Lu Xun delivers the lecture "Literature of a Revolutionary Age" at the Whampoa Military Academy; on 10 April Lu Xun writes "The Other Side of Celebrating the Recovery of Shanghai and Nanjing"; on 12 April Chiang Kai-shek launches "Party purification" in Shanghai, with the massacre of Communists spreading to Guangzhou and other cities over the next few days; on 28 April Communist Party cofounder Li Dazhao is executed in Beijing under Zhang Zuolin's orders.

May: Beixin publishes Lu Xun's fourth anthology of essays, *Inauspicious Star: A Second Volume (Huagai xubian)*.

June: The Guangzhou authorities accept Lu Xun's resignation from Sun Yat-sen University.

July: Lu Xun delivers his lectures in Guangzhou on "The Style and Prose of the Wei-Jin Epoch and Their Connection with Wine and Drugs"; *Lu Xun in Guangdong (Lu Xun zai Guangdong)* and *Wild Grass (Ye cao)* are published by Beixin; Guo Moruo's "After Leaving Chiang Kai-shek" is published; Deng Yanda denounces the Nationalists and leaves for Europe.

August: Lu Xun's Wei-Jin lectures are published in Guangzhou's *Republican Daily (Minguo ribao)*; Yu Dafu announces departure from the Creation Society; Guo Moruo takes part in a failed Communist uprising in Nanching, then flees to Hong Kong; the Comintern removes Chen Duxiu as the Chinese Communist Party's general secretary.

September: Lu Xun and Xu Guangping leave Guangzhou for Shanghai; Mao Dun completes *Disillusionment (Huanmie)*.

October: Lu Xun and Xu arrive in Shanghai; two open letters—one chastising Li Xiaofeng, the other to Shi Youheng—and the "Mixed Impressions on the Constraining of *Threads*," "On 'Intensity,'" and "How to Write" are all published in *Threads of Talk*; Cai Yuanpei is appointed director of Nanjing's Academy of Higher Education; on 25 October Lu Xun delivers the lecture "On the Intelligentsia" at Shanghai's Labor University.

November: Lu Xun's "Wei-Jin" lectures are reprinted in the Shanghai-based *Beixin* magazine; Jiang Guangci's fame as a revolutionary writer rises with publication of *A Sacrifice in the Wild (Ye ji)*; Lu Xun accepts Guo Moruo's invitation to participate in a leftist literary collective based in *Creation Weekly*.

December: Lu Xun's "Fleeting Mixed Impressions" *(xiao zagan)* appears in *Threads of Talk*; the first volume of Lu Xun's *Strange Tales from the Tang and Song Eras (Tang Song chuanqi ji)* is published by Beixin; Cai Yuanpei appoints Lu Xun to the Academy of Higher Education; Lu Xun lectures on "The Divergence between the Arts and Politics" at Shanghai's Jinan University; an advertisement for *Creation Weekly* is published in Shanghai; Cheng Fangwu returns from Japan, assumes leadership of the Creation Society, and rejects the *Creation Weekly* venture; the Crescent Moon Society is reestablished in Shanghai.

1928

January: The Sun Society's *Sun Monthly (Taiyang yuekan)* and the Creation Society's *Cultural Critique (Wenhua pipan)* are launched; Feng Naichao's attack on Lu Xun in "Art and Social Life" is published in *Cultural Critique*; Lu Xun's "Rousseau and Appetite" is published in *Threads of Talk*.

February: Cheng Fangwu's "From Literary Revolution to Revolutionary Literature" is published in *Creation Monthly*; Li Chuli's "How to Construct Revolutionary Literature" is published in *Cultural Critique*; the second volume of Lu Xun's *Strange Tales from the Tang and Song Eras* is published by Beixin.

March: Cheng Fangwu's "The Necessity of a Totalizing Critique" is published in *Cultural Critique*; Qian Xingcun's "The Era of Ah Q Is Dead" is published in *Sun Monthly*; Lu Xun's "The Haze of 'Drunken Eyes'" is published in *Threads of Talk*; *Crescent Moon Monthly* is launched in Shanghai; "The Attitude of the Crescent Moon" by Xu Zhimo et al. is published in *Crescent Moon Monthly*; *The Representative Works of Yu Dafu (Dafu daibiao zuo)* is published by the Sun Society's Chunye Press.

April: Lu Xun's "Literature and Revolution," "Ditties on Universal Peace," "The Prospect of Purging the Communists," and "Correspondence with Y" are published in *Threads of Talk*; a feature article on Lu Xun appears in Shanghai's *Young Companion (Liangyou huabao)*; "On the Chinese Literary World Today," by Ruo Shui (Pan Zinian), is published in *Battlefront Weekly (Zhanxian zhoukan);* on 15 April *Cultural Critique* publishes its anti–Lu Xun special issue including articles by Feng Naichao, Cheng Fangwu, Li Chuli, Peng Kang, and Guo Moruo (with Guo using the pseudonyms Mai Ke'ang and Du Quan).

May: Lu Xun's "My Attitude, Tolerance, and Age" is published in *Threads of Talk;* the Nationalist Party holds its first conference outlining the "Three Principles of the People" as the guiding doctrine of the national educational system.

June: Chiang Kai-shek's forces capture Beijing from Zhang Zuolin; Lu Xun and Yu Dafu establish *Torrent (Benliu)* in Shanghai; Fukumoto Kazuo begins a fourteen-year prison term in Japan.

July: "Partification" of the school curriculum is announced by the Nationalist Party's Central Committee; the Nationalist government introduces its "Temporary Law on the Punishment of Crimes of Counterrevolution" *(zanxing fan geming zhi zui fa); Sun Monthly* and *Cultural Critique* are banned; the Creation and Sun Societies establish several new magazines.

August: Yu Dafu's "Revolutionary Advertisement" and Lu Xun's "Revolutionary Café" are published in *Threads of Talk.*

September: Lu Xun's semiautobiographical anthology of literary essays, *Dawn Blossoms Plucked at Dusk* (including "Wu Chang: Life-Is-transient" and "My Father's Illness"), is published by the Yet to Be Named Society; Feng Xuefeng's "Revolution and the Intellectual Class" is published in *Trackless Train (Wugui lieche).*

October: The Creation and Sun Societies enlist the support of Zheng Zhenduo and other influential editors and publishers to found the Chinese Writers' Association, which never becomes active; on 6 October Chiang Kai-shek becomes president of the "reunited" Chinese Republic in Nanjing; Lu Xun's anthology of essays *And That's That* is published by Beixin.

December: Zhang Xueliang cedes control of Manchuria and pledges allegiance to Chiang's Nationalist government; Lu Xun establishes *Dawn Blossoms Weekly (Zhaohua xunkan)* with Rou Shi, Xu Guangping, and others.

1929

Lu Xun devotes most of his time to retranslating Japanese translations of Soviet literary theory, writing prefaces for new works, and assisting young writers and artists with their publishing enterprises.

January: The Nationalist government issues its "Regulations on the Investigation of Propaganda Materials," censoring all materials perceived as sympathetic to communism, internationalism, and anarchism. Over the next twelve months, some 270 periodicals are banned.

April: Lu Xun receives a formal apology from the members of Creation Society and Sun Society for their attacks on him the previous year; on 15 April the Nationalist government issues "A list of reactionary materials banned by the Central Committee."

May: Lu Xun visits his mother in Beijing and speaks at Yenching University and Peking University; his Yenching lecture, "A General Survey of New Literature Today," is published in the magazine *Yet to Be Named (Weiming)*.

June: Lu Xun returns to Shanghai and participates in the editing of a book series on Marxist literary theory; Li Helin's anthology, *A Debate over Chinese Literature,* is published by Beixin.

September: Lu Xun's son, Zhou Haiying, is born in Shanghai; Liang Shiqiu's "Does Literature Have a Class Nature?" is published in *Crescent Moon Monthly.*

October: Lu Xun's translation of Lunacharsky's essays is published as *The Arts and Criticism (Wenyi yu piping)* by Shuimo (Water-Ink) Bookstore.

November: Chen Duxiu is expelled from the Chinese Communist Party for supporting Trotsky.

December: Zhou Zuoren's "In Praise of Anesthesia" is published in the Tianjin-based *Social Welfare Supplement (Yishi bao fukan)*; Lu Xun's "*Threads of Talk* and Me: A Full Account" is published in *Threads of Talk.*

1930

January: Lu Xun's "The Evolution of Hooligans" is published in the inaugural issue of the left-wing magazine *Sprout (Mengya)*.

February: *Threads of Talk* ceases publication; Qian Xingcun's review essay "Lu Xun" is published in the left-wing magazine *Pioneer (Tuohuangzhe)*; Lu Xun attends the final preparatory meeting for the League of

Left-Wing Chinese Writers with Rou Shi and Feng Xuefeng; Lu Xun attends and joins the General Assembly of the Chinese Freedom Movement.

March: Lu Xun's "'Hard Translation' and the 'Class Character of Literature'" and "An Unrevolutionary Eagerness for Revolution" are published in *Sprout;* on 2 March Lu Xun delivers the inaugural speech to the League of Left-Wing Chinese Writers as its nominal head.

April: Lu Xun's "We Need Critics" is published in *Sprout;* he establishes and edits the left-wing journal *Partisan* and devotes his time to translating Soviet literary theory, published as *A Policy on the Arts* by Shuimo Bookstore.

May: Lu Xun meets with the underground Communist leader Li Lisan; Liang Shiqiu's "On the So-Called Policy on the Arts" is published in *Crescent Moon Monthly.*

June: Lu Xun edits and writes an epilogue to Rou Shi's translation of Lunarchasky's *Faust and the City.*

July: Lu Xun's translation of Plekhanov's essays, *On Art,* is published by Guanghua Bookstore.

August–December: Lu Xun devotes himself to reading and translating Soviet and Marxist works; in October Jiang Guangci is expelled from the Communist Party; in November Li Lisan is ousted as general secretary of the Communist Party; Nanjing issues "Publication Laws of the Nationalist Government" *(Guomin zhengfu chuban fa).*

1931

January: On 17 January Rou Shi and other Communists are arrested in Shanghai's International Settlement; Lu Xun and his family take refuge in a hotel in Shanghai.

February: On 7 February Rou Shi and others are executed in secret; on 28 February Lu Xun returns home with Xu Guangping and Haiying.

April: Lu Xun mourns the "slain warriors" in a special commemorative issue of the underground left-wing magazine *Frontline (Qianshao);* he presents the lecture "Hooligans and Literature" at the Tōa Dōbun Shoin (Tongwen shuyuan) in Shanghai; he writes the commissioned but unpublished essay "The Present Situation of Literature in Dark China" for the American magazine *New Masses.*

June: Jiang Guangci dies.

July: Lu Xun presents the lecture "A Cursory Look at Shanghai Literature" at Shanghai's Society for Research in the Social Sciences.

August–December: Japanese troops invade Manchuria in September and occupy the entire region by January 1932; in October Nanjing issues a supplement to its 1930 publication laws, titled "Particulars Pertaining to the Implementation of the Publication Laws" *(chubanfa shixing xize)*; Lu Xun writes numerous essays and continues to support the work of young writers and woodblock artists; and he is inducted as an honorary member of the Japan Proletarian Culture League.

1932

January: Japanese troops occupy northeast China; Lu Xun's advice to writers, "In response to Questions Put by *The Dipper*," is published in *The Dipper*; Zhou Zuoren's anthology of essays, *Cloud Gazing (Kan yun ji)*, is published; the Japanese air raid on Shanghai is followed by an assault on Shanghai's Chinese city.

February: Lu Xun takes refuge with his wife and son in the Uchiyama Bookshop; he puts his name to the collective "Letter to the World from Shanghai's Cultural Realm," addressed to all "proletarian and revolutionary cultural organizations," protesting the Japanese invasion; Wang Jingwei assumes leadership of the Nationalist government's Executive Yuan to negotiate peace with Japan, remaining in this role until November 1935; Chiang Kai-shek redoubles his assault on Communist bases in the form of "anti-bandit" military campaigns that continue until he is kidnapped in Xi'an in December 1936.

March: Lu Xun and his family return to their residence; Japan establishes the puppet state of Manchukuo.

September–October: Lu Xun's anthology of essays *Three Leisures (San xian ji)* is published by Beixin; a second anthology, *In Two Minds (Er xin ji)*, is published in October by Hezhong Press in Shanghai and promptly banned; he writes several essays and edits and writes prefaces to several works of Soviet literature in Chinese translation.

November: Lu Xun's essay "On the 'Third Type' of Person" is published in the magazine *Les Contemporains (Xiandai)*; he visits Beijing and presents lectures in which he further criticizes "the 'third type' of person" and mocks pro-Nationalist writers as producers of "helpful literature"; Nationalist censorship intensifies with the release of "Criteria for Investigating Propaganda Materials" *(xuanchuanpin shencha biaozhun)*, leading to a ban on publications by Lu Xun.

December: Qu Qiubai and his wife take temporary refuge in Lu Xun's home.

1933

January: Lu Xun joins the Chinese Alliance for the Protection of Civil Rights (Zhongguo minquan baozhang tongmeng), a non-politically affiliated organization headed by Cai Yuanpei, and is elected to its Executive Committee, which includes Cai, Soong Ching-ling (Sun Yat-sen's widow), Lin Yutang, and five others; Lu Xun begins to write regularly for *Shen bao (Shanghai News),* Shanghai's leading newspaper, producing some 130 articles for its *Free Discussion (Ziyou tan)* supplement between January 1933 and September 1934, utilizing forty pseudonyms in this period.

February: Lu Xun's "On 'Going into Battle' and 'Running Away'" is published in Shanghai's *Taosheng (Preachers Magazine)* under the pseudonym Luo Wu (a homophonic pun on "backward," *luowu*); he attends a lunch gathering at Soong Ching-ling's home for George Bernard Shaw; he is interviewed by the American journalist Edgar Snow.

March: At Snow's request, Lu Xun writes "An Author's Preface to the English Translation of *A Selection of Short Stories*"; he publishes "Human Language" in *Shen bao* under the pseudonym He Jiagan (who's done this).

March–August: Lu Xun completes several essays and prefaces for translated Soviet works and collections of woodblock prints.

April: Lu Xun's eulogy to Rou Shi, "Remembering in Order to Forget," is published in *Les Contemporains*.

June: Lu Xun attends the funeral of Yang Quan, a fellow member of the Chinese Alliance for the Protection of Civil Rights. He writes a classical poem to commemorate Yang, who was assassinated by the Nationalist secret police; Lu Xun's essay "How I Came to Write Short Stories" is published in a Shanghai publication, *Experiences of Literary*

Creation (Chuangzuode jingnian); "In Praise of Night" and "Pushed" are published in *Shen bao* under different pseudonyms.

July: *Selected Mixed Impressions by Lu Xun,* edited with a preface by Qu Qiubai (in which Qu calls Lu Xun an "iron broomstick") is published by Qingguang Bookstore (an alias of Beixin).

August–December: Lu Xun completes several essays and prefaces and coedits a volume on traditional woodblock designs for letter-paper, *Beiping Stationery (Beiping jianpu),* with Zheng Zhengduo; Nationalist troops begin a major campaign against Communist bases in Jiangxi and Fujian.

October: Lu Xun's "The Personal Essay in Crisis" is published in *Les Contemporains. Essays on False Freedom (Wei ziyou shu),* Lu Xun's eighth anthology, is published by Qingguang Bookstore.

November: Lu Xun's "In Perfect Awareness of Being Worldly Wise" is pseudonymously published in *Shen bao.*

December: Feng Xuefeng leaves Shanghai for Ruijin, the Communist hinterland base in Jiangxi.

1934

Lu Xun continues to support and publish the work of young woodblock artists.

January: Qu Qiubai travels to Ruijin; Zhou Yang assumes direction of the activities of the League of Left-Wing Chinese Writers; Lu Xun, who openly questioned Zhou's judgment in 1932, begins to distance himself from the League.

March: Lu Xun's "Forgetting the Taste of Meat and Not Knowing the Taste of Water" is published in *Shen bao* under the name Chong Xun (revering the wind); Pu Yi, the last Qing emperor, is enthroned as the Kangde emperor in Japanese-occupied Manchukuo. Lu Xun's ninth anthology of essays, *A Collection of Confused Accents (Nanqiang beidiao),* is published by Tongwen Press in Shanghai.

April: Lu Xun's "A Lease of Life for the Personal Essay," elaborating on issues raised in "The Personal Essay in Crisis" (October 1933), is published in *Shen bao* under the name Chong Xun.

May: Lu Xun's "Reply to Questions Put by the International Literature Society," praising the Soviet Union, is published in *International Literature* (republished in *Pravda* in July).

June: Lu Xun's "Appropriatism" is pseudonymously published in *China Daily (Zhonghua ribao)*.

August–September: Lu Xun's "Discussing Writing from the Outside" is serialized in *Shen bao* under the name Hua Yu, which can be read as implying the author is confined *(yu)* within China *(hua)* or that China is a prison.

September: Lu Xun founds and edits the first three issues of *Translated Literature (Yi wen)*, a monthly magazine.

October: Lu Xun's "Remembering Wei Suyuan" is published in *Literature Monthly (Wenxue yuekan)*; the Chinese Communists leave Jiangxi and begin their 6,000-mile Long March northward to Shaanxi. About 8,000 of the original 80,000 marchers survive the journey, reaching Shaanxi in October 1935.

November: Lu Xun reflects on *Ah Q* in "My Reply to a Letter from the Editor of *Theatre Weekly*," published in *Theatre Weekly*.

December: Lu Xun and Zheng Zhenduo produce a reprint of the Ming-era scholar Hu Zhengyan's woodblock designs, *Ten-Bamboo Studio Stationery Manual (Shizhu zhai jianpu)*; Lu Xun's anthology of essays *A Pseudo-Romantic Discourse (Zhun fengyue tan)* is published by Lianhua Book Company.

1935

January: Lu Xun translates Lyonka Panteleyv's novel *The Watch* from German (published in July in the book series associated with *Translated Literature*).

February: Lu Xun begins translating Gogol's *Dead Souls*. The first section is published in the *Translated Literature* book series in November, but he does not complete his translation of the book.

March: Lu Xun writes a foreword for a collection of Xu Maoyong's essays *(Da za ji)*.

April–September: Lu Xun completes a series of seven essays on the topic "Mutual Contempt among the Lettered." These are published pseudonymously in *Literature Monthly* between May and October.

May: Lu Xun's *Addenda collection (Jiwai ji)* is published by Books for the Masses Company (Qunzhong tushu gongsi).

June: Qu Qiubai, arrested in 1934 by Nationalist troops, is executed in Changting, Fujian Province.

August: Lu Xun completes his translation of children's stories by Gorky and publishes them as *Russian Children's Stories* with Cultural Life Press (Wenhua shenghuo chubanshe, an independent left-wing enterprise of which Ba Jin was editor-in-chief).

October: Lu Xun publishes a commemorative volume of Qu Qiubai's translations.

December: The new slogan "national defense literature" *(guofang wenxue)* is promoted by Zhou Yang's group in the Left-Wing League; Lu Xun completes several historical stories, including "Exit from the Pass," published in January 1936 in the anthology *Old Stories Retold* by Cultural Life Press.

1936

January: Factional divisions deepen in the Chinese Communist Party, but negotiations for a truce between the Nationalists and Communists, first initiated in the autumn of 1935 toward a "united front" against the Japanese invasion, are now further advanced. Mao Zedong's leadership of the Long March secures his power as the Communist troops progress across Shaanxi Province, settling for several months at Wayabao. Meanwhile Mao's rival, Wang Ming, currently in Moscow, relays instructions from the Comintern. Feng Xuefeng, Lu Xun's protégé, is allied with the Maoist cause, but Zhou Yang, as the Left-Wing League's leading Party figure, takes his orders from Wang Ming.

February–March: Lu Xun's health deteriorates rapidly as a result of advanced tuberculosis.

March: The League of Left-Wing Chinese Writers is dissolved under instructions from Wang Ming in Moscow.

April: Feng Xuefeng returns to Shanghai from Wayabao in Shaanxi; Lu Xun recovers sufficiently to write three essays, including "Written in the Deep of Night."

June: Lu Xun's anthology of essays *Fringed Literature (Huabian wenxue)* is published by Lianhua Book Company; Lu Xun refuses to join Zhou Yang's newly established Association of Literature and Art to promote "national defense literature"; the division between Lu Xun and Zhou Yang intensifies; Lu Xun and his friends present a counterapproach in their "Manifesto of Chinese Workers in Literature and the Arts" *(Zhongguo wenyi gongzyozhe xuanyan)*.

July: Lu Xun's condition deteriorates again, and Feng Xuefeng assumes the role of amanuensis. Feng transcribes Lu Xun's short polemic "On Our Literary Movement Today," published in *Literature of the Present (Xianshi wenxue,* a vehicle of Lu Xun's group) and *Literary Realm (Wenxue jie,* edited by Xu Maoyong); an open letter, "A Reply to the Trotskyists", is published under Lu Xun's name in the *Literary Gazette (Wenxue congbao)* and *Literature of the Present.* The letter, addressed to "Chen Zhongxian" (an alias of the Trotskyist Chen Qichang), praises Stalin, disparages Trotsky, and declares full support for Mao Zedong. Its wooden language, uncharacteristic of Lu Xun, is later revealed to be the work of Feng Xuefeng.

August: Lu Xun's "A Reply to Xu Maoyong," an angry rebuttal of Xu's denunciation of writers close to Lu Xun (Hu Feng, Ba Jin, and Huang Yuan), is published in *Author (Zuojia).* This Shanghai-based monthly carries several articles concerning the "debate of the two slogans" (that is, between Zhou's "national defense literature" and Lu Xun's "mass literature of the national revolutionary movement"). Lu Xun dictates the letter to Feng Xuefeng; Feng publishes his own excoriating criticism of "national defense literature" in September.

August–September: Lu Xun completes several essays, including "This Too Is Life," "Death," and "The Hanged Woman." All three are published in September in *Midstream (Zhongliu),* an influential fortnightly founded in September 1936 by Li Liewen, former editor of *Shen bao,* who in 1933 and 1934 commissioned Lu Xun to write for the paper's *Free Discussion* supplement.

October: On 1 October "A Manifesto of Fellows in the Literary Realm, United against Foreign Aggression and in Defense of Free Speech" *(wenyijie tongren wei tuanjie yuwu yu yanlun ziyou xuanyan)* is issued. The twenty-one signatories include several allied with Lu Xun, others allied with Zhou Yang, and several unaffiliated but influential authors and publishers: Lu Xun, Ba Jin, Mao Dun, Zheng Zhenduo, Guo Moruo, Zheng Boqi, Ye Shengtao, Wang Tongzhao, Feng Zikai, Xia Qizun, Xie Bingxin, Fu Donghua, Shen Qiyu, Hong Shen, Li Liewen, Zhang Tianyi, Lin Yutang, Zhao Jiabi, Bao Tianxiao, and

Zhou Shoujuan. The manifesto brings an end to the "two slogans" hostilities of the preceding months; on 8 October Lu Xun attends a touring exhibition of Chinese woodblock artists; on 9 October he writes "Two or Three Things about Mr. Zhang Taiyan"; on 16 October he writes a foreword to Cao Jinghua's translation of *A Collection of Works by Seven Soviet Writers;* on 17 October he begins work on "Two or Three Things That Came to Mind because of Mr. Zhang Taiyan." On 19 October Lu Xun dies at home.

December: On 12 December Nationalist commanders, in discussion with Mao Zedong, kidnap Chiang Kai-shek to secure the second "united front"; on 25 December Chiang is released, and negotiations for a truce with the Communists are finalized in the days that follow.

1937

Under a fragile "united front" of Communists and Nationalists, China's "War of Resistance against Japan" begins in July and continues till 1945; in July, three volumes of Lu Xun's essays, written from 1934 to 1936, are published by Three Leisures Press (San xian shuwu) under the title *Essays from the Semi-Concession Pavilion (Qiejie ting zawen);* on 19 October 1937 Mao Zedong delivers a speech commemorating the first anniversary of Lu Xun's death, hailing him as "the sage of modern China."

Introduction

The Sage of Modern China

Lu Xun's essays so influenced the minds of Chinese youth in the 1930s that Xu Maoyong famously declaimed: "How could anyone not love Lu Xun?"

YU SHICUN, *Extraordinary Sayings*

Every country has its founding heroes whose contributions, in word or deed, are regularly commemorated and celebrated as part of the nation's origin story. In the People's Republic of China, Lu Xun is the preeminent man of letters in that story, revered not only as a nation-builder but also, and perhaps most importantly, as the voice of the nation's conscience. A controversial figure throughout his adult life, he became even more so in death. Xu Maoyong's response to Lu Xun's writings, quoted above, highlights the intensity of emotion and engagement that Lu Xun has generated since the early years of the twentieth century.[1] In his international literary influence Lu Xun might be compared with figures such as Mark Twain, Shakespeare, Goethe, and Tolstoy in terms of stature, impact, and lasting veneration. Others will protest that such cross-cultural comparisons are not possible, and that Lu Xun is a unique figure who needs to be understood and read as such. Yet in his own lifetime Lu Xun was frequently compared to Maxim Gorky (1868–1936), whom he greatly admired, and, according to those who knew him well, the accolade both pleased and embarrassed him.

Comparisons aside, in the People's Republic, a state-funded discipline called "Lu Xun studies" *(Lu Xun yanjiu),* known more colloquially as Luxunology *(Luxue),* has supplied approved ways of reading Lu Xun since shortly after his death in October 1936 and has grown into a vast textual enterprise. Today it supports the livelihoods and careers of a large number of scholars, writers, editors, and publishers as well as archivists and curators. In Chinese alone, the articles and books published about Lu Xun would fill an entire library. In Japanese, Russian, English, and other European languages, studies of Lu Xun are generally considered a research area in their own right. The details of Lu Xun's life are readily available on the Internet in multiple languages, along with copious collections and examples of his writings in Chinese and in various translations.

Lu Xun was born Zhou Zhangshou in Shaoxing in 1881 to an influential scholarly family that suffered sharp financial reversals in the mid-1890s. His father was Zhou Boyi (1860–1896), a scholar barred from office by his father Zhou Fuqing's (1838–1904) imprisonment for bribery and whose poor health was worsened by drink and opium. The boy was close to his mother, Lu Rui (1857–1943), a self-taught woman whose surname he adopted in his best-known nom de plume. He was the oldest of four sons. Two of his siblings, Zuoren (1885–1967) and Jianren (1888–1984), would become prominent intellectuals in their own right. A third brother died very young. Lu Xun lived and attended school in Shaoxing until 1898, when he went to Nanjing to attend the Jiangnan Naval Academy. It was during this time that he ceased using his birth name and adopted the *hao* (or chosen style) Zhou Shuren, a name that he retained throughout his adult life. In 1899 he transferred to the School of Mines and Railways in Nanjing. In 1902 he traveled to Japan on a government scholarship and over the next seven years lived and studied there, first in Tokyo (1902–1904) and then in Sendai (1904–1906) before returning to Tokyo to pursue a career in translation and writing (1906–1909). In 1909 he returned to China and worked as a teacher, first in Hangzhou (1909), then in Shaoxing (1910–1911), and then briefly as an education official in Nanjing (1912). After Nanjing he was transferred to the Ministry of Education in Beijing, where he held positions of ascending seniority between 1912 and 1926. During this period he pursued a variety of literary interests and lectured on Chinese literature at several universities in Beijing. His students referred to him as Mr. Zhou.

The name Lu Xun first appeared in 1918 in conjunction with the publication of his first short stories in *baihuawen* (the modern written Chinese vernacular, of which he was one among several celebrated pioneers; hereafter *baihua*). These stories brought him both national and international fame. By the early 1920s, as Lu Xun, he was hailed as China's foremost modern writer. In 1926 he took up a teaching appointment at Xiamen University, resigning his post just three months later to teach at Sun Yat-sen University in Guangzhou, the then headquarters of the Northern Expedition, a war prosecuted and vigorously publicized as a revolution of national unity against the warlord regimes that controlled different parts of China at the time. Lu Xun lived in Guangzhou from January through September 1927 and then went to Shanghai, where he worked as a writer and translator from October 1927 until his death in October 1936. Lu Xun read and spoke Japanese and German, and from these two languages he translated a diverse range of foreign works into Chinese.[2]

In China, an extensive and still growing biographical literature on Lu Xun reveals the reading public's continued absorption with the particulars of his life and character. Several engaging biographical accounts have also appeared in English.[3] We know, for instance, that he was short—shorter than his second de facto wife, Xu Guangping (1898–1968), his former student and the love of his life—and according to a friend "was addicted to tobacco, alcohol and sweets."[4] We also know that in 1906, at twenty-four and a dutiful son to his mother, he accepted a loveless arranged marriage to his foot-bound first wife, Zhu An (1874–1947), a relationship he reportedly never consummated.[5] He was a leading advocate of modern ideas who, though he occasionally donned Western attire, preferred the traditional long Chinese gown for both everyday and formal wear.

His rise to literary fame after 1918 turned him into a magnet for aspiring young writers, and his fans thereafter were legion. While Lu Xun's biographers are wont to ponder the extent to which marital unhappiness shaped his early *baihua* writings, what we do know is that, upon becoming intimate with Xu Guangping in 1925, his criticisms of China's cultural and moral decline intensified.

From his friend Yu Dafu (1896–1945) we learn that Lu Xun spoke with a mild Shaoxing accent, had a wicked sense of humor, and enjoyed a good laugh. He was fond of smoking Hatamen cigarettes, a luxury brand produced by the British American Tobacco Company. Yu observed that when in company, Lu Xun had the habit of reaching into the pocket of his Chinese jacket to extract a single cigarette each time he wanted one, as if to prevent people from seeing the entire packet and finding out which brand he smoked.[6] He suffered from recurring bouts of tuberculosis that were exacerbated by periods of heavy drinking, incessant smoking, and the punishing pace he set himself with his numerous concurrent projects; tuberculosis eventually took his life.

Lu Xun's literary career spanned three decades during which he produced a wide range of essays (personal, critical, and frequently polemical), poetry, short stories, works on Chinese literary history, and translations. In 1938 the very first *Complete Works of Lu Xun* was published in twenty volumes, comprising all his extant publications. This was a major publishing project of the time. As David Pollard writes: "Glowing tributes were appended to the collection . . . the homage paid was to a great man of letters, an outstanding scholar, a 'genius.'"[7] The *Complete Works,* however, has had a checkered history. It was reprinted in 1946 with subsequent irregular print runs that were accompanied by gross distortions of Lu Xun's words during the Maoist years. In contrast, editions published from the 1980s onward have received extensive scholarly treatment, facilitating the post-Maoist revival of Lu Xun studies in mainland China. Today Lu Xun's influence on Chinese intellectual life remains refreshingly relevant and frequently profound. As the eminent historian Xu Jilin remarked in 2007, upon surveying the many controversies over Lu Xun's legacy that occurred between the 1980s and 2000s: "It's more than likely that people will never get to the bottom of what made Lu Xun tick, but this clearly hasn't stopped anyone from striving to have a conversation with him. Hence 'debates over Lu Xun' have ensued, through which he is continually 'reborn.'"[8]

This book is centered on the last phase of Lu Xun's career (1927–1936), often referred to as his "years on the left." It situates his writings in the context of the intellectual milieu and political intrigues of the day and presents him in both conversation and argument with his contemporaries. During this period Lu Xun frequently parodied the Marxist-inspired "revolutionary literature" of his leftist peers as the unfortunate confusion of guns with words. Against their propensity to figure "revolutionary literature" as a gun or cannon, Lu Xun commended the dagger and the javelin as his own preferred weapons. He regarded the act of criticism as akin to wielding a blade. He had a particular fondness for modern woodblock art, seeing its techniques as analogous to what he attempted to achieve in language. In 1929 he wrote that woodcuts projected a stark realism with imagination and simplicity: "What we call a creative woodblock artist is someone who neither imitates nor copies others. Gripping the blade with finger and thumb, the maker approaches the wood and simply starts cutting away."[9]

The idea of a revolutionary literature preoccupied Lu Xun throughout the last decade of his life, and provoked considerable ambivalence. On the one hand, he saw it as a sign of artistic decline through the subjugation of creativity to ideology. On the other, he discerned in it the potential for a genuinely committed literature, one that resonated with his own hope of fostering a mode of egalitarian writing in which the majority (as opposed to an educated and elite minority) would find their voice. But it was mostly what he considered the more negative aspects of revolutionary literature that dominated his thinking and writings. In late 1927 Lu Xun remarked that self-styled revolutionary writers had reduced literature to the repetitive crudeness of "hit, hit, hit, kill, kill, kill, revolt, revolt, revolt."[10] Indeed he regarded the revolutionary literature they produced as frequently mere fodder for the propagandizing of the Northern Expedition, which was then being fought under the banner of a "united front" (tongzhan) of Nationalists and Communists. Guangzhou was the headquarters of this united front, and it was from there that the Northern Expedition was launched in July 1926. Yet despite his disdain for much of this revolutionary literature, and indeed in response to it, Lu Xun was one among thousands of Chinese intellectuals who, as members of an emergent literary left, felt inspired to write in defense of the revolution. Prosecuted with substantial financial aid and strategic advice from the Soviet Comintern, this war was hailed as a Marxist revolution par excellence.

Upon assuming a figurehead role in the Communist-sponsored League of Left-Wing Chinese Writers in 1930, Lu Xun began increasingly to promote a "literature of the masses" but always with the caveat that what he defended was a common humanity born of empathy. His insistence on distinguishing committed writing from what he called "propaganda" was itself a response to the times. By the early 1930s the Communist Party had become much more adept at shaping cultural production to accord with its policies. It was a development that angered and dismayed Lu Xun, and the verbal wars in which he became embroiled in the League's final two years (1934–1936) were never resolved. In 1936, even as Lu Xun approached death, he continued to dictate angry missives from his sickbed against several Party theorists.

The august reputation enjoyed by Lu Xun in the People's Republic is largely a consequence of his transformation into a revolutionary paragon under the auspices of Chairman Mao Zedong (1893–1976). The speech Mao gave on 19 October 1937, the first anniversary of Lu Xun's death, set the precedent for the hyperbolic praise that would enshroud Lu Xun until Mao's death in 1976. On that first anniversary, Mao declared that the Party vanguard should emulate three qualities of Lu Xun in particular: his depth of political vision, as exemplified in his "microscopic" and "telescopic" observations of society; his uncompromising "fighting spirit," which Mao likened to "a great steadfast tree, not a blade of wavering grass, against the onslaught of dark and violent forces"; and his "spirit of sacrifice," which Mao extolled in terms of Lu Xun's "utter fearlessness of enemy intimidation and persecution," "total indifference to enemy enticement," and "ruthless destruction with his swordlike pen of everything he hated." Mao raised Lu Xun to the level of "a Chinese sage of the first order," declaring that "since Confucius was the sage of feudal China, Lu Xun should be re-garded as the sage of modern China."[11]

In short, Mao enlisted the posthumous Lu Xun to lend intellectual weight to his own political vision, which by the 1940s was fast becoming the canon known as Mao Zedong Thought. The fusion of Lu Xun's language with Mao's Thought gathered pace in the 1950s and 1960s with the transmutation of more and more of Lu Xun's words into Maoist aphorisms and slogans. Indeed, in a letter to his wife Jiang Qing (1914-1991) in July 1966 (coincident with the launch of the Great Proletarian Cultural Revolution), Mao wrote that he and Lu Xun were "of one mind" because they shared the same love of a rebellious inde-pendence.[12] A union was thus forged between Lu Xun's concerned so-cial criticisms and Mao's justifications of violence as "righteous rebel-lion." At the height of the Cultural Revolution (from the late 1960s to the early 1970s), "the Lu Xun spirit" was invoked time and again to sanctify the exercise of brute power. Thus were Lu Xun's words con-verted into a destructive weapon.

This political complexity surrounding Lu Xun's legacy demands a substantial contextualization of his writings to yield a clearer sense of why he wrote what he did, the way he did, when he did. Hence a key aim of this book is to explore the elegant ambivalence Lu Xun expressed toward the idea of revolution itself: he affirmed its necessity yet de-voted considerable energy to condemning the repressive forces it un-leashed. His unease, I argue, is central to his critical practice, for he was partial to presenting the act of writing as a state of heightened alertness against institutionalized truths and received opinions.

Moreover, Lu Xun held that affect was integral to insight. His re-marks in 1926 about the task of the writer offer a striking illustration of the importance he placed on feeling: "I still remember how three or four years ago a student came to buy a book of mine: he took from his pocket a few coins still warm with the heat of his body: that heat burned me like red-hot iron, and even today, each time I wish to write, the fear of leading young people like him into error paralyses my pen."[13]

Mao's valorization of Lu Xun as a fearless warrior hell-bent on de-stroying his enemies persists in much mainland scholarship today. Lu Xun's writings remain barnacled by the militant attributes formerly

ascribed to them by Maoist Luxunology. But in fact the "militariza-
tion" of Lu Xun had begun in the 1930s while the writer was still alive.
In 1933, for example, his friend, the essayist and leading Communist
Qu Qiubai (1899–1935), first praised Lu Xun as a latter-day Remus wielding an "iron broomstick" *(tie saozhou)* to rid the masses of a "slavish
herdlike nature."[14] That year Lu Xun had used the same term to criticize the Nationalist government's education system, which he likened
to the system in Germany, then newly under Hitler's grip, where "books
are being burned, writers are being ordered to eat their own manuscripts," and "group upon group of students are being incarcerated in
labor camps." Lu Xun said it was because the Nationalist government
favored "severity" that it sought to impose ever stricter regulations on
the school examination system. He concluded that the overall effect
was "just like an iron broomstick that keeps on sweeping and sweeping, and so it sweeps the majority of the educated youth right into the
midst of the people [*minjian*]."[15]

The dissonance between these two uses of the same metaphor is
striking. Whereas Qu used the "iron broomstick" to praise Lu Xun's
language as a formidable revolutionary force, Lu Xun used it to highlight the ruthless aggression of Nationalist rule and thereby to suggest
something far subtler: in excluding socially engaged students from
further education, the repressive state was inadvertently encouraging
their sympathy and identification with and for the masses. Yet it was
Qu's cruder positive figuration that prevailed. Among others, the Communist literary scholar Li Helin (1904–1988) reprised the metaphor in
1938 to extol Lu Xun's polemical writings as "an iron broomstick that
makes a clean sweep of the noisy chatter of his critics."[16]

Communist admirers of Lu Xun were undoubtedly in awe of his
international renown, which considerably enhanced the Party's profile
in intellectual circles. Moreover, Lu Xun's figurehead role in the League
of Chinese Left-Wing Writers coincided with a period of intensive Party
rebuilding, conducted under the straitened circumstances of Chiang
Kai-shek's (1887–1975) anti-Communist rule. The Communists, however, were by no means the only people to praise Lu Xun. He was revered
across the political spectrum of China's intellectual world and in death
was given the supreme accolade "the soul of the nation" *(minzu hun)*:

the phrase was reverently emblazoned on the white flag that draped his coffin.[17]

To understand Lu Xun's overall cultural significance, we need to consider his literary achievements in *baihua*. This fledgling experimental vernacular of the 1910s became the national language of the divided and rival Chinas: the People's Republic of China and the Republic of China (Taiwan). *Baihua* (ordinary language, or the language of common folk) was first proposed in the mid-1910s by Lu Xun and other prominent intellectuals who were associated with the journal *New Youth* based at Peking University. They envisaged an egalitarian language that would supersede *wenyanwen* (hereafter *wenyan*), the vehicle of the premodern elite culture, which was still the dominant written language in the early Republican era. *Baihua* was to appear first in written form (*wen;* hence *baihuawen*) and then to be progressively disseminated in speech and writing (that is, as both *hua* and *wen*) as a national mother tongue. Written *baihua* (progressively standardized as modern written Chinese) facilitated the development of *putonghua* (the common language), the spoken medium of the People's Republic. The *baihua* experimentations of Lu Xun and his contemporaries were radical but by no means new, for the language itself derived from early modern forms of vernacular prose widely used in the progressive newspapers and magazines of the 1900s and 1910s.

These styles were, in turn, developments out of *guanhua* (the language of officials), the lingua franca of dynastic officialdom in nineteenth-century Manchu-ruled China. For this reason, *baihua* shared many of the features of *guoyu* (the national language), the first official attempt to establish national standards of speech and writing out of these existing styles, introduced in 1913 (a year after the founding of the first Chinese republic). *Baihua*, like *guoyu*, was conceived first and foremost as an instrument of nation-building. What separated *baihua* from the contemporaneous *guoyu* and other vernacular forms was not grammar and syntax but its experimentations with content and style and the use of a highly Europeanized vocabulary that quickly became its defining characteristics.

Unlike the purposes of ordered education and government intended for *guoyu*, the repertoire of modern ideas introduced and debated in *baihua* (such as anarchism, democracy, humanism, individualism, liberalism, realism, romanticism, science, and socialism) was meant to inspire a conversion to the "new literature" *(xin wenxue)* and "new culture" *(xin wenhua)*. Accordingly, the advocates of *baihua* declared their fashionable enterprise a "literary revolution." By 1920, Beijing's Ministry of Education (in which Lu Xun worked) had formally named *baihua* as the medium of instruction in Chinese schools.[18]

Lu Xun's "Diary of a Madman," a short story that made extensive use of *baihua,* became, upon its publication in the 15 May 1918 issue of *New Youth,* something of a seminal work for the budding "literary revolution." Thereafter it became popular among *baihua*'s advocates to declare their radical enterprise as a necessary madness. Among them, Fu Sinian (1896–1950) eclectically lauded Jesus Christ, Socrates, Nietzsche, and Tolstoy as exemplary lunatics and lamented: "China is nearly dead today precisely because we have too few madmen."[19] Lu Xun's story has been described ever since as an inaugural moment for China's "new literature." It immediately captivated its readers and generated a clamor of enthusiastic responses. Lu Xun's audacious indictment of traditional Chinese values as a cult of cannibalism quickly became a catch-cry for the modern vernacular, with many echoing Lu Xun to call for an end to "cannibalistic Confucian mores."[20]

Lu Xun's unique authority in the world of Chinese letters and ideas makes him one of what Michel Foucault (1926–1984) called the "founders of discursivity":

> They are unique in that they are not just the authors of their own works. They have produced something else: the possibilities and the rules for the formation of other texts. In this sense they are very different, for example, from a novelist, who is, in fact, nothing more than the author of his own text.... they both have established an endless possibility of discourse.... These founders of discursivity (I use Marx and Freud as examples, because I believe them to be both the first and the most important cases) make possible something altogether different from what a novelist makes possible ... I mean that they made possible not only a certain number of analogies but also (and equally important) a certain number of differences. They

have created a possibility for something other than their discourse, yet something belonging to what they founded.[21]

Unlike Freud (1856–1939) or Marx (1818–1883), Lu Xun never produced (or had any intention of producing) a systematic account of his ideas as constitutive of a philosophy or theory. Yet there are recurrent themes, rhetorical devices, and modes of argumentation across his oeuvre that, taken together, form a sustained and cohesive critical inquiry guided by the question of what it means to be human.

Unlike most studies of Lu Xun, which are centered on his fiction, my inquiry deals mainly with his essays and in particular with his later polemical writings. Each of the following chapters examines Lu Xun's engagement with the relation between violence and language from a different perspective. Chapter 1 discusses Lu Xun as a witness to the growing authority of revolutionary discourse and situates his inquiry within the context of the Communists' ill-fated participation in the Northern Expedition in 1927. It explores his ambivalence toward revolutionary discourse in two ways: first, in contrast to the nation and Party-building utterances of Sun Yat-sen (1866–1925), whom Lu Xun admired; and second, as deeply at odds with the revolutionary propaganda of 1927 Guangzhou. To highlight the differences that divided Lu Xun from the writings of newly risen Marxist theorists such as Guo Moruo (1892–1978) and Cheng Fangwu (1897–1984), this chapter also examines his disavowal of prescient claims about a revolutionary victory. More broadly, it discusses Lu Xun's increasing apprehensiveness about the content and style of the revolutionary tutelage of his day.

Chapter 2 provides an account of Shanghai as China's new intellectual center with the establishment in 1928 of Chiang Kai-shek's Nationalist government in Nanjing. It examines the attacks on Lu Xun by Marxist theorists in relation to the precarious circumstances of Communists and leftists after 1927. This chapter is structured around the ambient word "haze" *(menglong)*, which Lu Xun used to characterize the intellectual politics of late 1920s Shanghai and the rise of revolutionary literature. While his contemporaries were keen to take sides either for or against "revolutionary literature," Lu Xun was more interested in criticizing Shanghai's enterprising writers and publishers for profiting (and thus cynically profiteering) from radical politics. He characterized "revolutionary literature" in Shanghai as the radical chic of a violent age. To provide a fuller engagement with Lu Xun's criticisms of revolutionary commerce, the chapter also considers his own comfortable economic circumstances. His ambivalence toward China's commercial metropolis was shared with numerous other elite pioneers of Beijing's "literary revolution," including the members of the Crescent Moon Society, for whom he repeatedly professed hatred. Accordingly, the chapter also discusses the origins of his intense dislike of this intellectual coterie, whose leading member, Hu Shi (also known as Hu Shizhi; 1891–1962), like Lu Xun, achieved fame as a pioneer of *baihua*.

The giddy speed of change in China from the 1920s to the 1930s was both a response to the violence of the age and a product of the new market-driven demand and commercial prospects for *baihua* publishing. Chapter 3 examines Lu Xun's reflections on the speed of change in the intellectual politics of post-1927 Shanghai in the context of his style of inquiry as a whole. Unlike his contemporaries, who valorized the speed and acceleration of revolutionary change, Lu Xun dwelt on the belated arrival of true insight as a tragic ordeal. Hence the chapter also explores Lu Xun's observations about living in dangerous times.

Chapter 4 provides an account of the polemical exchanges between Lu Xun and his critics and focuses especially on his quarrels in the late 1920s with individuals from the Creation Society, Sun Society, and Crescent Moon Society. Lu Xun's attacks on the Crescent Moon Society—which he regarded as an organization actively returning *baihua* into an elite tongue—are examined for what they reveal of his own vision of a language of the masses. As these quarrels predate the rise of the Communist Party's orthodoxy, they offer a lively contrast to the deepening doctrinalism of the left from the 1930s onward. This chapter also elaborates on Lu Xun's dislike of Marxist ideologues through a consideration of his troubled relationship in the mid-1930s with the League of Left-Wing Chinese Writers. Lu Xun's posthumous induction as a revolutionary saint is also examined in relation to the misfortunes that befell his former adversaries under Maoist rule in the 1950s and 1960s.

Chapters 5 and 6 deal specifically with Lu Xun's literary art *qua* art, with a focus on his formulations of the critical act. Chapter 5 considers the poetics of Lu Xun's *baihua* prose through an examination of key devices and tropes in his oeuvre. It begins with his figurations of criticism as a dagger or a javelin and follows him through his figurations of *baihua* as a moral journey; in the process it also explores his many rhetorical uses of a summoning voice. The chapter then considers the overall affective qualities of Lu Xun's prose and dwells in particular on his fondness for phrasing self-cultivation in terms of knowing what is good to eat. His was a modern and angst-filled form of self-cultivation. He regarded any aspiration to orthodoxy, no matter how well-meaning (and even when such orthodoxy presented itself as the radicalism of a revolutionary tutelage), as the path to oppression. Thus in writing against the lures of universal or utopian claims, he defended an aesthetics of emotion, describing his principal aim as one of fostering a visceral empathy for the suffering of others.

Chapter 6 considers Lu Xun's numerous invocations of ghosts, guardian spirits, and historical personalities in relation to his frequent denunciations of Daoist magic. It begins with his pejorative remarks about the language of China's educated elite serving as a Daoist talisman: an esoteric object designed to secure the power of the priestly elite over the illiterate majority. In this context it explores the renewed efforts Lu Xun made in the last decade of his life to vigorously defend *baihua* as the common property of the masses. A particular focus is Lu Xun's remarkable literary depictions of the ordinary Chinese appetite for supernatural spectacles, which he affirmed with sympathy as signs of a human need for community and an innate yearning for justice. These depictions allow, indeed invite, us to read his critical legacy as a form of second sight: an act of summoning plebeian spirits as champions to keep *baihua* safe from the clutches of power. The book concludes with Lu Xun's insights into language as a vehicle of empathic experience, contextualized in relation to his "afterlives" in the People's Republic.

As the synopsis indicates, this book is part biography, part history, and part literary analysis. In focusing on Lu Xun's observations of the world around him and the people he identified as foes, my intention is to highlight particular aspects of his writing that have long been a source of interest and fascination in Chinese scholarship. In the 1900s and early 1910s he wrote in *guwen*, the archaic prose of the ancient classics, and *wenyan*, the premodern literary language of dynastic China, of which he was an acknowledged and adept master. His career in *baihua*, which began in the mid-1910s, is typically divided into two periods: the early Lu Xun (roughly 1917–1926) and the later Lu Xun (1927–1936).

The later literary period of Lu Xun has posed a particular problem for mainland scholars in the post-Mao era because several of his later essays were particularly virulent, and had formerly furnished Maoist Luxunology with a convenient means of legitimizing acts of violence against "class enemies." The lingering influence of Maoist misreadings of these essays, in which Lu Xun was portrayed as someone prepared to kill as opposed to merely waging a war of words, has posed a challenge for those who now wish to highlight the writer's humanist qualities. Because of these various difficulties, the writings of the later Lu Xun have become marginalized in post-Mao times. In contrast, the fiction, prose, and essays of his early, nonpolitically affiliated period present few such obstacles and have been copiously cited as evidence of his intellectual independence. The early Lu Xun is also conveniently located in what is known as the May Fourth era, a phase commonly and fondly historicized since the 1980s as a prelapsarian period of democratic promise in modern Chinese history. Nonetheless, many Lu Xun scholars defend his later writings as a continuation of the themes of his earlier ones. Among them, Lin Xianzhi, author of *Lu Xun's Final Decade* and other major works on the maestro, has attracted notable attention and praise for his sustained efforts at distilling out of Lu Xun's later writings a holistic image of fidelity to freedom.[22]

These passions surrounding the later Lu Xun alert us to long-term anxieties that have pervaded Sinophone discussions about the impact of revolution on modern Chinese thought. In this regard, one question in particular has shaped Chinese intellectual discourse since the founding of the republic in 1912: what is the intellectual's role in society, and what path should the intellectual take? As this question carries the moral presumption of providing leadership and direction, one concern in particular has haunted intellectual thinking in modern China, namely, what type of guidance should the intellectual, operating under an authoritarian regime, give to readers? Should the advice be to speak blunt and oppositional truth to that power or to conduct a more pragmatic and nuanced dialogue? These compelling questions also exercised Lu Xun, although he took pains to reiterate that he had no answers.

By virtue of his extraordinary fame, Lu Xun was and remains burdened with the expectation of leading by example. This Sinophone investment in exemplarity has its roots in the premodern (classical) Chinese ethos of emulating a true sage in the hope that one may, in turn, guide others onto the (one) true path. And the fact of Lu Xun's canonization by Mao as "the sage of modern China" has ensured that evaluations of his legacy will continue to generate heated debate. As Xu Jilin observes, even in the twenty-first century Chinese intellectuals continue to look to Lu Xun more than to anyone else for answers, thereby transforming him into an enduring figure of "modern orthodoxy" (xiandai daotong).[23]

Lu Xun himself was equivocal about the idea of assuming responsibility for others. On the one hand, he expressed heartfelt admiration for people he regarded as working toward a just cause, in particular those who gave their lives in service to it. On the other, he was dismissive of the idea that he, or anyone else, should serve as a guide for society. He wrote in 1926 in typically self-deprecatory terms:

> I don't know myself what path to follow. The youth of China already have no shortage of "elders" and other "master thinkers": I am not of their number, and anyway these people do not inspire my trust. The one thing I see with certainty is our journey's end: the grave. But this is something anyone can perceive as clearly as I—no need for a guide to reach that. The problem is, what route to follow from here to there. There is not just one path, and for my own part, I do not know which is right.[24]

Similar statements abound in his essays and private correspondence. But notwithstanding his disavowal of "master thinkers," Lu Xun wrote and published with a clear intention of leaving behind his own textual legacy. First and foremost, he sought to leave a record of the violent age in which he lived. He made the memorable remark in 1933 that living in China was akin to being blinded by a sandstorm while knowing that "wolf packs and tigers are on the prowl."[25] Second, throughout his career as Lu Xun, he was keen to claim the destruction of *wenyan* as his guiding purpose. He regarded this language of the premodern elite as fatally corrupted by centuries-old dynastic rule and wrote that as the embodiment of ancient inequities, *wenyan* could only ever foster a disposition to genuflect to power. Indeed, he marked his entry into *baihua* with a series of concerted attacks on *wenyan*. For instance, in 1919 he accused those who defended *wenyan* of attempting to "murder the present" and rebuked them as "modern men, breathing modern air, who want to ram moribund Confucian morality and a dead language down people's throats."[26]

Against *wenyan*, Lu Xun valorized *baihua* as a "living vernacular," by which he meant a vehicle of both self- and collective transformation. Yet we must proceed carefully when referring to Lu Xun's "*baihua* writings," for he never wrote entirely in *baihua*. Instead he used an intricate blend of *baihua* and *wenyan* as if to enact, over and over, the drama of an ineluctable symbiosis between the two languages. The resulting discordances of ancient and modern created a rhetorical turbulence, as if his language was at war with itself. Moreover, for all his invective against *wenyan*, Lu Xun wrote more than sixty classical poems over his career.[27]

This heterogeneity is crucial to understanding Lu Xun's art and critical practice. In the very strangeness of his *baihua* there inheres a desire not merely to represent but to "perform" the struggle for free expression. This immanence is reinforced in the substance of his writing. He referred to his essays as *zawen* (miscellaneous writings) and *zagan* (mixed impressions), thereby privileging (through the word *za*) the complexities of human experience and by implication negating the exactitude of correct ideas. Thus, he frequently reminded his readers, somewhat Socratically, that he had no truth to propound beyond personal insights into concrete events as he experienced them.[28]

Yet his disciples felt compelled to distill an essential truth from his oeuvre, and the idea of a "Lu Xun aura" *(Lu Xun feng)* emerged shortly after his death and was popularized in 1939 with the publication in Shanghai of a magazine with this title.[29] The "Lu Xun aura," vigorously promoted by his widow, Xu Guangping, and intended to declare an emulation of Lu Xun's polemical style, soon morphed into the more capacious and combative attitude that Mao lionized as the "Lu Xun spirit." Because of these posthumous complications, it is all the more important to maintain a clear distinction between his art of critique and the conscious or unconscious ontologizing of Lu Xun as an "aura" or "spirit," however defined. There are two further issues to consider in this regard.

Terms like "aura" and "spirit" in present-day mainland scholarship on Lu Xun have become significantly depoliticized, and many now use them to liken the act of reading Lu Xun to a form of communion with his language. Undoubtedly he would have approved of such communion, understood simply as a compact between reader and writer. But in an environment with an entrenched Luxunology, "aura" and "spirit" continue nonetheless to pose the danger of an institutionalizing ambition: of ascertaining correct ways of knowing Lu Xun. Indeed, Luxunology has also produced a negative reaction to Lu Xun, with many making a point of disavowing interest in his legacy altogether. Among his present-day detractors is the highly popular Beijing-based writer Wang Shuo, who remarked in 2000 that the extent to which there is genuine pluralism in intellectual China can be discerned from the degree of tolerance for negative views of or even indifference toward Lu Xun.[30]

In this regard, Lu Xun's later polemical writings were, in many ways, attempts at setting the record straight about his role as an intellectual. He was clearly anxious about the prospect of being misunderstood by posterity. On this topic, he wrote in December 1935 that whereas "there is perhaps no harm in reading poetry as poetry," the same cannot be said of prose: "Prose, ideally, should be considered not only in relation to the author's entire oeuvre but in relation to his person as a whole. We must also include the state of the society in which he lived. This would lend a proper rigor to our considerations."[31] My own reading of Lu Xun in the following pages seeks to accord with his wish to be presented as a keen witness of his times.

Lu Xun noted of the journals of his day that, regardless of the perceived merits or flaws of the *baihua* produced therein, the journals themselves were a valuable source of instruction about the social conditions that propelled them into being: "this is the 'literature' of present-day

China or, at the least, of a certain group of people. Today it affords us an insight into our own times. In the future it will give others an insight into the past and, for this reason, ought to be preserved in the larger libraries." He then gets to the nub of the matter. Alluding to his many vitriolic exchanges with his detractors and rivals, he remarks: "a writer who lives among others and has something of a combative nature is bound to find enemies in society." He calls for due attention to be paid to how such a writer might fall prey to the "tricks" of those bent on slandering him, who would stoop to altering the historical record or to shifting their ground as opportunity or circumstance dictates. In discussing a writer's legacy, it is imperative to take into consideration the provocations that led him to write as if he were "fighting a war of resistance." Without the evidence of such provocations, the writer's warring words will be unjustly reduced to "mad ravings addressed to the sky."[32]

Here Lu Xun also hints at a systemic asymmetry, especially between himself and his adversaries. He implies that whereas his fame seems certain to guarantee the preservation of his writings, his lesser-known adversaries risk being forgotten over time. He offers his own studies of the Chinese literary tradition as an illustration and laments the prospect that posterity will be deprived of "the writings of the opposition because these have all perished."

He continues: "If these had been preserved, they could have cut through the muddled thinking of latter-day critics." Elaborating on this point, he writes that the style of combative essays of long-dead writers, whose opponents' writings no longer exist to provide the full context in which they were produced, are often unfairly negated through such dismissive circumlocutions as "the points and edges are too revealing" or "the sword is brandished and the bow fully drawn."[33]

These are poignant remarks when we consider Lu Xun's own posthumous fate. Contrary to his fear of appearing "too sharp or too emotional" because his lesser-known adversaries were no longer in print, Luxunology has ensured the meticulous preservation of published criticisms against Lu Xun. Moreover, precisely because such writings were directed against Mao's chosen exemplar, in the Party's successive purges of the 1950s and 1960s they furnished convenient evidence of punishable "thought crimes" committed by Lu Xun's erstwhile rivals. Given Lu Xun's revulsion toward the state violence he observed under Chiang Kai-shek, it seems likely he would have been all the more appalled by the Maoist abuse of his writings.

The later Lu Xun, more than any other modern Chinese thinker or writer, unsettles present-day scholarship in China. The "mixed impressions" his essays present of the politicization of intellectual life afford insights into the convolutions that have bedeviled modern Chinese thought ever since. And in this regard, despite his grotesque afterlife as Luxunology, the poetic qualities of his language have remained intact. Lu Xun's humanism, as I argue in Chapters 5 and 6, is carried by the force of his words, which impart a flesh-and-blood quality to his critical observations. For instance, in cautioning against essentialist representations, Lu Xun wrote: "Some collected works include a man's early writings but often revised in such a way as to stick a white beard on a child's face."[34] On another occasion he described the technique of characterization he utilized in his fiction as involving the "mixture of a mouth from Zhejiang, a face from Beijing, and clothes from Shanxi."[35]

In my undergraduate years, I was fortunate to be inducted into the compelling visuality of Lu Xun's language by the eminent Sinologist Pierre Ryckmans (a.k.a. Simon Leys). I recall in particular an instance when Ryckmans, a gifted teacher, told our class that it was necessary to "see" the phrase *heng mei* (fierce-browed) in Lu Xun's classical poem in order to properly understand it.[36] An adept sketcher, Ryckmans then drew what has since persisted as a vivid image in my mind of resolute anger: a planklike single thick brow above the nose, below which peered two beady eyes.

The singular vividness of Lu Xun's writings makes it all the more necessary for us not to confuse and conflate this authorial persona with Zhou Shuren (the name the author used throughout his daily adult life). Undoubtedly, the texts signed "Lu Xun" (or others that appeared under the some 140 pseudonyms he used over the course of his career) were drawn from lived experience, but they were nonetheless a highly selective distillation and refraction of the life he inhabited. As several sections of this book will show, Lu Xun frequently chafed over the problem of his relationship to the Lu Xun that was destined for libraries and archives.

In this connection, we must also note his fondness for figuring language as a "nonplace" *(wudi)* and as "darkness" *(hei'an)*.[37] This aspect of Lu Xun's language alerts us to his preoccupation not only with mortality but with the frailties of literature as the work of mortals and contingent on interpretation. On this issue, his critical insights resonate with George Steiner's remark that "we cannot devise a systematic theory of meaning in any but a metaphoric sense": "Meaning is, in terms of proof, no more decidable, no more subject to the arrest of experimental demonstration than is the purpose (if there is any such) or 'sense' of our lives in the unbounded script of time and the world."[38]

The unbounded nature of language preoccupied Lu Xun and led him, time and again, to present the act of writing as an attempt to wrest something meaningful from an otherwise infinite flux of the sayable and writable. The central problem, in his view, was to know whether one truly had anything important to leave to posterity. Thus, he remarked of himself in 1933 that he had "nothing more to say" after "having grown accustomed to stories of punishment by electrocution, death by shooting, beheadings, and assassinations."[39] This was an ironic statement insofar as he continued to write (mostly pseudonymously) of the torture and murder of Communists by the Nationalist government. But in making the statement, what he sought to drive home were the dangers of a withering away of humanness through the desensitizing effects of violence. The importance he accorded to defending the empathic properties of language resonates in the concluding line of an essay he completed three weeks before he died: "We have been born with human heads; let us speak like human beings."[40]

The human path that Lu Xun sought to forge in *baihua* is a critical bequest that has been variously appropriated and interpreted countless times since his death in 1936. Today his words have become an integral part of Sinophone polemics, in particular the growing cyber polemics that range from the ideals of universalized human rights to an entrenched and pragmatic national pride. To the extent that Lu Xun lives on in the Chinese language (and because of the Internet, he now haunts that language even more actively), the issues dealt with in this book are by no means dead or indeed buried. Rather, they bear testimony to the ways in which Lu Xun's gift of words remains, and no doubt will remain, perennially alive and vital to Chinese critical thinking.

I

Eyes Wide Open

On 15 May 1925 a Japanese factory foreman opened fire on striking Shanghai workers at the local Japanese-owned Nagai Wata Mill, killing one and wounding several others. Local students responded swiftly with demonstrations in the streets and were in turn arrested and arraigned to be tried in the International Settlement's courts. On 30 May some 10,000 Chinese workers and students gathered to protest the arrests and marched down the broad expanse of Nanking Road in the Settlement shouting anti-imperialist slogans and demanding fair treatment for the Chinese within the Settlement. In a brutal response, Sikh soldiers led by a British inspector opened fire on the unarmed demonstrators, killing thirteen protestors and arresting more than fifty others.[1] The rapidly reported killings fanned widespread public outrage culminating in a general strike in Shanghai, street protests in other Chinese cities, and further sporadic casualties elsewhere.

Having condemned the killings as a massacre, many Chinese intellectuals rushed to commemorate the "May Thirtieth Movement," eulogizing the mass protests it incited as harbingers of imperialism's imminent demise. It was a time when Leninism was in full vogue. Six weeks later, on 22 July 1925, Lu Xun wrote the essay "On Seeing with

Eyes Wide Open," in which he characterized this rising revolutionary clamor as the "praise of blood and iron."[2] Using Bismarck's famous phrase, he remarked that the militant rhetoric augured nothing but the onset of a blinding self-delusion among the aspiring revolutionaries themselves. This essay provides a good example of the critical art Lu Xun named *zagan* (mixed impressions).

In his essays, the *zagan* effect resides in the skillful assemblage of diverse images to illustrate a central idea. The assemblage typically consists of ancient and modern, Chinese and non-Chinese elements inventively combined to fashion a blurring or "mixing" of time and space. In this particular case, the central idea was straightforward and simple. It came from a statement he had read in a recent article: "we should have the courage to face things squarely."

The device of quoting from the media was one that he frequently employed: a quotation from a newspaper or journal would start the essay and serve as the point of departure for his disquisition. In the essay in question, Lu Xun begins with the quotation from the article, duly praises it for expressing a worthy sentiment, but then states that an even more pressing need exists, namely the need for the Chinese to stop fooling themselves.

He continues with a sweeping indictment of the literati of dynastic China, accusing his predecessors of having mastered the Confucian ability "to avert their gaze from all that is unseemly" *(fei li wushi)*.[3] He writes that centuries-old Confucian tutelage and a fastidious lack of attention to "the unseemly" had not only withered the ability of the Chinese to face "the unseemly" but had encouraged among them an unfortunate tendency toward "concealment and deception." He then offers examples in support of his contention, ranging from politicized uses of the Confucian classics (*The Analects* and *Mencius*), through the treatment of plot and character in the popular romances and historical novels of the Ming and Qing epochs, to his own reflections on historical and contemporary events.

On the basis of these examples, Lu Xun concludes that over time, people grew accustomed to avoiding unhappy truths, with the result that they not only became incapable of self-scrutiny but also acquired an enormous appetite for outlandish fantasies. As evidence, he then

cites several examples of impossible happy endings in Chinese literature, using them to clinch his argument against the revolutionary rhetoric of his time. He suggests that such rhetoric amounted to no more
than a fantastic diversion from real and present social misery, noting:

> The climate seems to have changed; we no longer hear the soulful
> odes to flowers and the moon that used to be everywhere, for these
> have now been replaced by the praise of blood and iron. But if we
> speak with a deceiving heart and a lying tongue, it hardly matters
> whether the subject is A & B or Y & Z, for both are equally phony. All
> that will happen is that those so-called critics who formerly dispar-
> aged compositions about the flowers and the moon will now be
> awed into silence, and content themselves with the prospect of Chi-
> na's imminent resurgence. He who wears a great big "patriotic" hat,
> who has once again shut his eyes, is to be pitied. But perhaps some-
> one like this has always had his eyes shut.[4]

The appeal for clear-sightedness (and the authorial perspicacity it
implies) is a hallmark of Lu Xun's essays. The perspicacity he sought
and claimed for himself was empirical and sensory, not conceptual or
theoretical. What he encouraged in the name of "seeing with eyes wide
open" was a scrupulous observation of contemporary life and, more
specifically, the gaps between published work and the actual lived social experience. In the passage above, he warns that the dramatic shift
under way in *baihua* from "soulful odes" to revolutionary calls means
nothing without a substantive change in the status quo, and implies
that the revolutionary outpourings he has read have struck him as false.

Similar disavowals of revolutionary dreaming appear in numerous
essays he wrote in the late 1920s and 1930s. Lu Xun, however, was never
comfortable about dampening his readers' enthusiasm for revolution
and hence frequently mitigated his criticisms with a rallying call to action. He chose to end this 1925 essay with the encouraging statement:
"China will not have a genuinely new literature without pathbreakers
prepared to destroy traditional ideas and traditional methods of writing in their entirety."[5]

Lu Xun's insistence on perspicacity developed out of his lifelong
ambivalence toward the idea of revolution. He supported the cause of

revolution in his teens and twenties and was hailed as a pioneer of the "literary revolution" in his thirties. However, during the mid-1920s, as an eminent intellectual in his forties, Lu Xun encountered a new problem. Publicly hailed as a radical innovator, he had deep misgivings about the speed and breadth with which revolutionary language was spreading around him. To appreciate his unease, we need to consider the complexions of the term "revolution" in 1920s China.

Of Blood and Iron

In the 1900s, revolution was promoted as the patriotic (and indeed racial) violence required for bringing the Manchu Qing dynasty to an end and restoring Han Chinese sovereignty in the form of a modern nation-state.[6] In 1912, with the founding of the first Chinese Republic, this idea of revolution entered the vocabulary of the state, where it became sacrosanct as the driving force of modern change in China. But despite the rhetorical authority of revolution, Sun Yat-sen, its leading proponent and the Republic's founding figure, was soon ousted from national politics. Sun had occupied the office of president for only forty-five days, from 1 January to 15 February 1912, before agreeing to cede it to Yuan Shikai (1859–1916), the former commander of the Qing imperial troops. By November 1913, Yuan had forced Sun into exile in Japan. The nascent Republic then witnessed two failed attempts to restore the dynastic system: first Yuan Shikai's bid to make himself emperor in 1915, followed quickly (after Yuan's death in 1916) by the extremely short-lived restoration of the abdicated Manchu emperor Puyi (1906–1967) in 1917, orchestrated by the archconservative militarist Zhang Xun (1854–1923).[7]

By the time Sun Yat-sen returned to China in 1917, he had revised his views to place a new emphasis on "revolutionary construction," an idea that became the centerpiece of his speeches and writings from the late 1910s until his death in 1925. For Sun, "revolutionary construction" meant, above all, revolutionary self-cultivation. He stressed the importance of self-knowledge to revolutionary success, encapsulating the idea as a four-character axiom, *yi xing nan zhi:* "to act is easy, to know is difficult." In his famous essay of this title completed in December 1918, he chastised the members of his party for failing to follow the initial work of "revolutionary destruction" (that is, the 1911 revolution that ended the Qing dynasty) with "revolutionary construction" (in the early years of the Republic). He claimed that this failure was a result of their failure to understand the foundational importance of his "Three Principles of the People" and that they had committed the fatal error of dismissing these principles (of people's rights, people's livelihood, and nationalism) as "too lofty." As a consequence, he averred, the revolution, having halted at "destruction" without the concomitant work of "construction," was hijacked by counterrevolutionary forces.[8]

Sun Yat-sen's political resurgence after 1917 at his new southern base in Guangzhou coincided with the rise of the "literary revolution" in Beijing. The basic goal of this literary revolution was simple but formidable. It sought to eradicate everything old *(jiu)* that was perceived to hold China back, and to create the new *(xin)*—in effect an entire New Culture—to hasten the arrival of a fully fledged modern society in China. The "soulful odes to flowers and the moon" to which Lu Xun referred were part of the modern romanticism that swept the New Culture into fashion: it was a revolutionary self-cultivation different from the one that Sun proposed. Its roots were in literature, not politics, and its pioneer was Liang Qichao (1873–1929), China's best-known intellectual activist and cultural entrepreneur of the 1900s.

It was in the numerous journals and newspapers established by Liang that the educated elite acquired and practiced their sense of living in a modern world. For instance, Lu Xun recalled that when he had attended the School of Mining and Railways from 1899 to 1902, its cosmopolitan director had asked his students to write compositions on George Washington and had read Liang's influential newspaper *Shiwu bao (The Chinese Progress)* as he rode to work each day in a horse-drawn carriage.[9]

Indeed, it was Liang who coined the term "literary revolution" in 1902, expressly to commend the powers of fiction in renovating human minds and shaping moral character. Liang insisted that "the reformation of the government of the people must begin with a revolution in fiction."[10] In the early 1900s Lu Xun, according to his brother Zhou Zuoren, was profoundly moved by Liang's description of "literary revolution" as an act of self-transformation. Liang outlined the process as based in what he called the "four powers" of fiction (to envelop the senses, to immerse the reader in the narrative, to stimulate new feelings, and finally to effect a spiritual elevation, which Liang likened to a Buddhist awakening). Zhou recalled his older brother resolving to emulate Liang in order "to touch society and stir the nation's spirit."[11]

The "literary revolution" launched in Beijing in 1917 was far bolder than what Liang Qichao had envisaged fifteen years earlier. Centered on the promotion of *baihua*, it included all varieties of publications, both literary and intellectual. The rules were simple and open-ended. As Hu Shi wrote in his 1917 position piece "My Views on Literary Reform," the user of *baihua* need only heed "eight injunctions" *(ba bu zhuyi)* against the use of *wenyan:* "speak only of matters of substance; don't emulate the ancients; pay attention to grammar; don't lament without cause; discard wornout stock phrases; don't invoke the classics; don't heed [the traditional poetics of] matching rhyme and sense; don't avoid the use of common words and popular sayings."[12]

The themes of politics and romance were intertwined in *baihua* from the outset. Candid self-expression and modern ways of loving—as aspects of the radically new and revolutionary—were regarded as integral to modern nationhood. And with the success of the Bolshevik Revolution, ideas and formulations derived from Marxist and Soviet works became a growing presence in this nascent literary vernacular. Sun Yatsen was so impressed by the success of the Bolshevik Revolution that in October 1919 he remodeled his organization, the Chinese Nationalist Party (Guomingdang), along the lines of the Soviet Communist Party. In 1921 the Chinese Communist Party was founded in Shanghai by two leading figures of the "literary revolution," Chen Duxiu and Li Dazhao.

In the early 1920s a Soviet-inspired discourse arose against the Republic's descent into warlord misrule, a worsening national economy, and widespread social unrest.[13] Moreover, the capitulation of several of China's warlord regimes to Japan's expansionist demands in exchange for financial and military aid further inflamed public anger. Patriotic sentiments burgeoned in the late 1910s and were volubly expressed during the May Fourth Movement of 1919. This movement was inaugurated by a student protest in Beijing against international disregard for China's sovereign interests at the peace conference negotiations in

Paris that year. It quickly spread to other cities. Chinese citizens demanded the rejection of the peace treaty's intention to cede to Japan, instead of China, Germany's former concessions in China. The protests continued for several months and developed in new agitative directions, including a boycott of Japanese goods. In the process, the symbiosis of patriotism and cultural radicalism in China's "literary revolution" became more pronounced: its much-vaunted New Culture thereafter merged with the aims of "May Fourth."

In the early 1920s, as banditry and armed conflict between rival warlords grew, Sun Yat-sen planned a new revolution with the aid of the Soviet Union. The alliance between the Nationalist Party and the Soviet Union was formalized in January 1923 by Sun Yat-sen and Adolf Joffe (1883–1927), the Comintern delegate to China. Thereafter Sun's idea of "the people" was frequently conflated with the Marxist concept of the proletariat, and his calls for "securing the people's livelihood" found effortless transposition into countless Communist slogans about achieving victory for the proletariat. Sun's attraction to Soviet-style politics only deepened with the financial and military aid he received from the Soviet Union.

Sun's goal, however, had never been to establish a Communist society. In the joint manifesto he issued in January 1923 with Joffe, Sun stipulated that "because of the non-existence of conditions favourable to their successful application in China, it is not possible to carry out either Communism or even the Soviet system in China."[14] But despite this skepticism about the prospect of Communism in China, Sun was canny enough to declare in December 1923 that "essentially, there is really no difference between the Principle of People's Livelihood and Communism."[15] With Soviet support, he declared a revolution against the feuding warlord regimes and pledged to reunify China under Nationalist rule with Communist support. Sun died of cancer less than two years later in March 1925 as initial war preparations were under way.

When Lu Xun wrote "On Seeing with Eyes Wide Open" in July 1925, his relationship with Xu Guangping had just begun through correspondence initiated by her. She was his student, seventeen years his junior, and, at the time, a regular visitor to his home, but it was in their frequent exchange of letters that the intimacy between them grew.

He became involved in student politics in support of her activism at the Peking Women's College. They left Beijing together in August 1926: she went to Guangzhou while he took up a teaching position at Xiamen University. Separated by over 300 miles, their feelings deepened through continued intense correspondence.[16]

Meanwhile the Northern Expedition, launched in July 1926 in fulfillment of Sun Yat-sen's vision, was gaining pace. The revolutionary government in Guangzhou was keen to attract prominent intellectuals. In October 1926 it invited Lu Xun to serve concurrently as dean of studies and head of Chinese studies at Guangzhou's Sun Yat-sen University, with the expectation that he would lend intellectual prestige to the revolution's headquarters. Lu Xun's letters to Xu indicate his pleasure at this invitation, but his tardy acceptance of it (over a month later) also reveals his misgivings about being recruited to support the cause of war.[17] Moreover, in writing to Xu, Lu Xun often expressed frustration with the rumors surrounding their relationship. In his final letter to her from Xiamen in December 1926, just before he joined her in Guangzhou, he declared he no longer cared what other people thought.[18]

His arrival in Guangzhou in January 1927 was greeted by a fanfare of publicity. He was hailed as a fighter and a revolutionary, together with such gushing statements as "Mr. Lu Xun will help us to shout, guide us when we shout, and he will also be shouting with us. . . . Let us shout! It makes no difference whether we shout with a gruff or a piercing voice; shouting is much preferable to silence." The author of this particular effusion was Bi Lei (d. 1927), a young student whom Lu Xun liked and befriended.[19]

In Guangzhou he faced the predicament of having to endorse a revolution about which he knew little and of which he saw scant evidence of social change on the ground. The fact that a crowd of aspiring revolutionaries sought his guidance only exacerbated the pressures he experienced. On the eve of his departure from Guangzhou in September 1927, Lu Xun wrote in an open letter to his publisher and former student Li Xiaofeng (1897–1971):

There were those who came to interview me, to conduct research, to discuss literature, to query my ideas, to ask me to write prefaces or inscribe a few words, or to invite me to present public lectures. They gave me no peace. What I dreaded most was public speaking, since the schedules for such occasions were fixed and could not be postponed. When the time came, a group of young people would arrive and I would be bundled off with much gusto. I spoke mainly on prescribed topics, and I am least expert in composing to a given theme. Otherwise, back in the days of the Qing era, I would have been awarded the *xiucai* [county-level imperial examination] qualification. Anyway, they left me with little choice but to mount the rostrum and say a few words. I did have my own routine, which was to limit myself to speak for no more than ten minutes. But I couldn't help feeling ill at ease, and before and after such occasions I would often say to friends, "Well who would have thought that I would be producing Western-style *baguwen* [octopartite compositions] in 'the hotbed of the revolution?' "[20]

In the spring of 1927 the Northern Expedition was etching a victorious path toward Shanghai, a key strategic target along the troops' northward march to Beijing. But as the calls for revolution grew louder, the Northern Expedition was fast departing from its original conception as the common cause of the Nationalists and Communists.

As a war prosecuted with Soviet aid and spurred on by Leninist rhetoric, the Northern Expedition's stated twin goals were to complete Sun Yat-sen's unfinished revolution and to advance the great socialist world revolution. It was a war of national unification *(Bei fa tongyi)* formally declared as a two-party revolutionary bloc of patriotic "petty bourgeoisie" (the Nationalists) and "workers and peasants" (the Communists).[21] In practice, however, this was an asymmetric and unequal partnership in which the fledgling Chinese Communist Party, under instructions from Moscow, became subsumed under the Nationalist Party. In effect, Communists were required to join the Nationalist Party and submit to its authority. Hence the Nationalists referred to the relationship patronizingly as the "accommodation of Communists" *(rong gong)* within their ranks while the Communists, holding themselves equal, idealized the alliance as a "united front" *(tongyi)* or "united revolution" *(tongzhan)*.[22]

As the Northern Expedition advanced northward from mid-1926 to early 1927, accompanied by the burgeoning of peasant associations and labor unions across China, its propagandists hailed the defeat of imperialism and the impending arrival of a new socialist world order. The rhetoric, however, bore little resemblance to the realpolitik decisions that were shaping the course of war, in which Chiang Kai-shek, the Expedition's commander-in-chief, played the leading role.

Chiang Kai-shek had emerged victorious as Sun Yat-sen's successor in March 1926, after a year of factional struggles within the Nationalist Party following Sun's death. As the Nationalist right's leading representative, Chiang was determined to exclude the Nationalist left and Communists from power. He attacked their strongholds in Guangzhou on 20 March 1926 but was careful to disguise his coup as a mistaken raid sparked by ominous rumors of a leftist plot to oust him from Guangzhou.

Still very much dependent on Soviet aid, Chiang reassured the Comintern Executive Committee in September 1926: "The Chinese revolution is part of the world revolution. . . . The leader of the world revolution is the Comintern."[23] Nonetheless, it was clear to more than a few that he had achieved his aim of both undercutting the Chinese Communists and wresting control of Guangzhou from the Nationalist left. Having secured his leadership of the Nationalist Party by military force, he then forced his key rival, Wang Jingwei (1883–1944), leader of the Nationalist left, into a self-imposed exile in Europe.[24]

After March 1926, as one scholar observes, Chiang's public speeches changed in both tone and substance. There were now far more frequent mentions of "national revolution" than "world revolution" and scant reference to the Soviet Union.[25] From then on, the Nationalist right dominated the politics of the revolutionary "united front," with continued Soviet aid and acceptance. While Chiang consolidated his power in the remainder of 1926 and early 1927, he continued to accommodate the Nationalist left and the Chinese Communists. The latter in particular were proving very useful in organizing grassroots strikes and protests.

But despite these developments, which placed the Northern Expedition under Chiang Kai-shek's control from the outset, its propaganda was written in the language of the left. In 1926 and 1927 neither the

Communists nor the Nationalists had yet established a party ortho-doxy. Chiang would begin this process only after consolidating his power in 1928. In fact, as the leading Nationalist strategist Hu Hanmin (1879–1936) noted of the situation in Guangzhou in early 1926, such unison prevailed between the Communists and the Nationalist left that there was nothing to distinguish between their tasks and objectives.[26] Chiang's fears of a leftist-controlled Guangzhou were evidently not unfounded.

The propaganda of the Northern Expedition, which grew out of the very same revolutionary language that worried Lu Xun in 1925, marked a significant shift of perception: what had begun as a "literary revolu-tion" was now being celebrated as a tool of revolutionary violence. The "praise of blood and iron" he cautioned against was the work of converts to Marxism like Guo Moruo, leader of the Creation Society, a literary organization that first achieved fame in 1921 for its romantic poetry and prose. Guo, who became the Northern Expedition's chief propagandist in 1926, published an influential essay in May that year, "Revolution and Literature," in which he outlined the narrative of revolution that was taking hold in Chinese intellectual circles. The narrative rested on three simple rules that applied equally to history and literature: the events presented must show revolution as the force of history, class struggle as the law of social evolution, and "the oppressed" of each age as the inevitable victors over their oppressors. In Guo's words:

> In every period of revolution, there is in essence the opposition be-tween two social classes. When two such classes oppose each other, one will want to maintain the power it has always held while the other will want to overthrow it. At such a time, either class naturally has its own spokespersons: what you say will depend on which class you represent. If you stand on the platform of the oppressed class, naturally you will praise the revolution. If you are a person who is opposed to the revolution, then the literature you write or the litera-ture you appreciate is naturally antirevolutionary and speaks on behalf of the oppressing class. Such literature naturally cannot co-exist with the revolution, and naturally it will be despised and re-jected by revolutionaries. If you are a person who favors revolution,

then the literature you write or appreciate is naturally revolutionary literature that speaks on behalf of the oppressed class. Such literature will naturally become the vanguard of revolution and will naturally bring forth a golden age of literature during the era of revolution.[27]

Guo's repeated insinuations of class war in this passage exemplify the stridency and unbridled optimism of Chinese revolutionary discourse and the ease with which it could be and was turned into propaganda. The whole article is peppered with the adverbials *dangran* and *ziran* (naturally) to suggest the inevitability of eventual success for "the revolution." Moreover, such terms as "national struggle" and "class struggle" were conflated and used interchangeably, as if in tacit acknowledgment of the Northern Expedition's declared coalition of the (Nationalist) "petty bourgeoisie" and (Communist-led) "workers and peasants."

Thus when Lu Xun appealed for clear-sightedness in 1925, he avoided the term "revolution" altogether. Instead, he figured the idea as "blood and iron" to suggest that the resurgence of revolutionary rhetoric amounted to no more than a Bismarckian exaltation of violence. He expressed a similar apprehensiveness in an essay of November 1926 (coincident with his decision to travel to Guangzhou) by recalling the spurious revolution that had occurred in his hometown of Shaoxing in 1911. It was as if he were writing a cautionary analogy for the Northern Expedition he was about to serve:

> though outwardly all was changed, beneath the surface all went on as before; for this was a military government organized by a few of the old-style gentry. The chief shareholder in the railway company was head of the administration, the moneylender had become director of the arsenal. . . . And this military government did not last long, for as soon as a few youngsters raised an outcry, Wang Jinfa [the head of a secret society who joined the revolutionary cause in 1911] came in with his troops from Hangzhou. In fact, he might have come even without the outcry. After his arrival, he was surrounded by a crowd of idlers and new members of the revolutionary party, and reigned supreme as Military Governor Wang. In less than ten days most of his men in the *yamen*, who had arrived in cotton clothes, were wearing fur-lined gowns although it was not yet cold.[28]

In his attention to who was actually exercising power in the name of revolution, Lu Xun's observations resonate with Lenin's political question, "Who-whom?" of which Raymond Geuss offers the following useful elaboration:

What this means in the first instance is that the impersonalized statements that one might be inclined to make about human societies generally require, if they are to be politically informative, elaboration into statements about particular concrete people doing things to other people. The sign in the Underground that reads, "Nonpayment of fare will be punished" means that a policeman may arrest and fine you, if you fail to buy a ticket; "Unemployment has risen by x percent" means that certain people who have control of particular economic organizations have done something concrete, terminated the employment of certain other people.[29]

In stark contrast to Lu Xun's insistence on concrete observations, the revolutionary discourse of Guangzhou teemed with unqualified and impersonal statements about human societies, the purpose of which seemed less to inform than to instruct readers on the correct view of revolution. Guo Moruo's essays of this period reflect the zeal with which Marxism (as Marxism-Leninism) was being presented as a science of revolution. Hence, in "Revolution and Literature" Guo writes of an immutable dynamic of class struggle at work across centuries of historical change:

When a minority monopolizes the greatest happiness, social life simply cannot develop, and the existing society returns to a state of disintegration. In such a society, the unfortunate majority will clearly want to rise up and overthrow the regime of the minority, to found a new society that conforms to the principle of social organization. This is none other than the phenomenon of revolution in that society.[30]

To accentuate the "science" behind this proposition, Guo used Chinese notational characters (the equivalents of alphabetic letters like A, B, and C) to present the Marxist dialectic as a law of "unceasing substitution," expressing the idea in algebraic terms as a process whereby "A is replaced by B," which in turn "becomes replaced by C," then "by D," and so on. He extends this quasi-scientific formalism to include an algebraic theorem of the relation between revolution and literature. Having declared that the revolution of a given age constitutes its *Zeit-geist* or "the spirit of the times," Guo now asserts that revolutionary literature, by virtue of its function (F) as an instrument of "the spirit of the times," is reducible to revolution itself, namely:

Revolutionary Literature = F (the Spirit of the Times).

Literature = F (Revolution).[31]

Through such heady abstractions, the idea took hold that the growing presence of a revolutionary discourse was in itself a sign of revolutionary change at work. In an abstract yet fervent diction, Guo urged his readers: "know exactly where you stand" in relation to the "foundations of social organization and the form of social development." He called on aspiring writers to distinguish the texts they "ought to praise" from those they "ought to oppose."[32] The exhortations reach a climax in the conclusion of his essay: "Youth! Youth! . . . If you truly desire to become writers, you must quickly steel your nerves and make haste to grasp the spirit of the times. . . . Don't think that drinking a few glasses of wine shows that you have a romantic spirit or that quipping a few lines of bent verse means that you are some kind of literary genius. You must rejuvenate yourselves and hold on to the mainstream of literature. You should go to the soldiers, the people, to the factories, and into the vortex of the revolution." To assure them that he was at the vanguard of change, Guo added: "I am not making plans for you; rather, I am making plans on behalf of our masses."[33]

In Guangzhou, Lu Xun expressed his opposition to these febrile and formulaic pronouncements being proffered as a Marxist science. In his address at the Whampoa Military Academy on 8 April 1927, he observed of revolutionary Guangzhou:

There is still plenty of the old literature; practically all the newspaper articles are in the old style. I think it suffices to show that China's revolution has hardly changed society. It has barely affected those who defend the old ways; hence these people continue to act as if they are untouched by the world. The literature discussed in Guangdong's newspapers is also old, there's very little that's new, which confirms that this society has yet to feel the impact of revolution. With neither paeans for the new nor dirges for the old, Guangdong remains what it was ten years ago. What is more, there is nary a complaint or protest. We do see trade unionists taking part in demonstrations, but they do so with government permission, not because they are opposing oppression. Thus, this is but revolution by imperial decree.[34]

This speech is of particular significance because Lu Xun was then addressing the Northern Expedition's elite cadet corps. The Whampoa Military Academy was Chiang Kai-shek's brainchild. He was its commandant from November 1923, a position to which Sun Yat-sen appointed him upon Chiang's return from a three-month tour of Russia where he studied the Red Army's weaponry and techniques of organization and training.[35] Despite Chiang's antipathy toward Communism, he was deeply impressed by Soviet discipline and promptly adopted its methods and techniques at his own academy. Accordingly, the cadets at Whampoa received both military instruction and political education, with the latter designed to ensure their unquestioned obedience to Chiang.

When speaking at the academy, Lu Xun took considerable pains to caution against unthinking acceptance of revolutionary propaganda. Referring to the fashion of invoking a "people's literature" (pingmin wenxue), he observed that the currency of the term indicated nothing more than its successful appropriation by ambitious intellectuals seeking to promote their own literary wares. Moreover, he continued, "the people" had yet to find their own voice:

At present, some writers use the common people—workers and peasants—as material for their novels and poems, and this has come to be called people's literature when actually it is nothing of the sort, for the people have not opened their mouths yet. These works voice the sentiments of the onlookers, who put their own words into the mouths of the common folk. Although some of the lettered today are poor, they are nonetheless still better off than workers and peasants, for they have enough money to study, which in turn allows them to produce essays. At first glance, their works may seem to come from the people, but in fact they do not: they are not the real stories of the people. Now some writers have started transcribing mountain songs and rustic tunes as if these represent the true voice of the people, for these are their songs. But the influence of the old books on the common folk is enormous. They are absolutely in awe of those country gentry who own 3,000 *mou* of land, and seek at every turn to adopt the gentry's ideas as their own. As the gentry like to recite five- and seven-syllable quatrains, the mountain songs and rustic tunes sung by the common people have taken mainly these two forms. That this folk art not only relies on classical prosody but presents ideas and meanings that are rather old and stale disqualifies it from being called a genuine people's literature. . . . The writers of our time are all scholars. If the workers and peasants are not liberated, their ideas will remain those of the scholars. We must wait until the workers and peasants have truly achieved liberation before we can begin to see a genuine people's literature.[36]

Two days later, in a short essay, Lu Xun quoted the following statement, ascribing it to Lenin (1870–1924), in support of his own appeal for clearheadedness: "The first thing is not to become intoxicated by victory and not to boast; the second thing is to consolidate the victory; the third is to give the enemy the finishing stroke, for he has been beaten, but is by no means crushed."[37] Lu Xun then concluded: "The repeated setbacks suffered by Chinese revolutionaries in the past were due, I think, to the fact that they overlooked this. At the slightest success, they grew so intoxicated by songs of triumph that their muscles relaxed and they forgot to fight on, whereupon the enemy seized the chance to strike back."[38]

On 12 April 1927 the revolutionary "united front" came to an abrupt end when Chiang Kai-shek's Nationalist troops, assisted by local gangster recruits, attacked Communist strongholds in Shanghai. Reported figures of union leaders and workers killed on that day alone range from 400 to 700.[39] The slaughter continued all day and into the next, with hundreds more arrested, wounded, or killed.[40] Three days later the Nationalists launched a similar attack against the Communists in Guangzhou, and the purge soon expanded to other parts of

Nationalist-controlled China. This was a startling and complete reversal of how the Northern Expedition had been presented and publicly understood as a revolution up to that time.

Four days earlier at his Whampoa Military Academy address, Lu Xun had told his audience that "during a great revolution, literature disappears and there is silence, for, swept up in the tide of revolution, all turn from shouting to action and are so busy making revolution that there is no time to talk of literature."[41] He cautioned against the spell of revolutionary rhetoric and urged his military audience to focus on doing battle instead:

> You gentlemen are actual fighters, you are revolutionary warriors, and I think you had better not admire literature yet. Studying literature is of no benefit to the war—at best, you might produce a battle song that, if it is well written, would offer some diversion to those who read it during a period of rest after battle. To put it more grandly, it is like planting a willow: when the willow grows and gives shade, peasants knocking off work at noon can eat and rest beneath it. The present situation in China is such that only the actual revolutionary war counts. A poem could not have frightened away [the warlord] Sun Chuanfang [1885–1935], but a cannon blast soon sent him fleeing.

In case they missed the point, he added that, to his ears "the sound of cannons rings more sweetly than the sound of literature."[42]

When Lu Xun promoted an ethics of seeing clearly in 1925, using "eyes wide open" to heighten the need for critical vigilance against hollow rhetoric, he was not encumbered by any obligation to defend the cause of revolution. In Guangzhou, however, he was required to serve the revolution as an intellectual mentor, and, as his speech at the Whampoa Academy indicates, he did so by rallying his audience to fight. But from 1925 through 1927, the revolutionary discourse that he initially mocked as self-deceiving had also grown fatally compromised.

As his remarks about Guangzhou's "revolution by imperial decree" indicate, Lu Xun maintained his distance from the celebratory rhetoric around him in the revolution's headquarters. But he failed to point out that Guangzhou itself was inhospitable to the perspicacity he encouraged. The anti-imperialist, antiwarlord discourse actively promoted in and outside Guangzhou in the mid- to late 1920s was an idealization of Soviet-inspired discipline. It was, in essence, a party-based faith: a higher purpose promoted initially as a "united front" before its decisive bifurcation, after April 1927, into the opposite aims of the Nationalist Party and the Communist Party (not to mention the other competing aims that informed subsequent factional struggles within either party). In this context, the capaciousness of this discourse—its reduction of all struggles to that of an oppressed majority righteously battling an oppressing elite—proved serviceable to left and right alike. As a language that demanded strict adherence to the authorized view (that is, the view of the revolutionary leadership), it was incommensurable with the critical rigor that Lu Xun sought to promote.

Ways of Seeing Clearly

From a longer historical perspective, the appeal of revolutionary discipline in 1920s China resonated with the anticipation of a true path that had long been inherent in discussions of ethics, morality, and politics in dynastic times. This was an idea encapsulated in the word *dao* (the Way) and its sense of a cosmic order, from which the language of state Confucianism derived the ideality of an enduring orthodoxy, expressed in the term the "kingly way" *(wangdao)*. Through linguistic inheritance, in particular through the continued authority of the word *dao* and its connotations of orthodoxy, this ancient hope of founding a lasting creed lingered in the modern Chinese idea of revolution. When Liang Qichao drew on the eleventh-century Neo-Confucian axiom "literature should carry the Way" *(wen yi zai dao)* in the 1900s, he was not only defending literature as an agent of change but presenting the words he published as a veritable blueprint for the correct way forward.[43]

When Lu Xun and his contemporaries advocated a "literary revolution" in the 1910s, it was often the presumption of a singular true path that fueled their quarrels over the direction and purpose of *baihua*. By the mid-1920s, intellectuals who cleaved to one or another ideal were further delineating their purpose in accord with their declared political position, whether of anarchism, communism, liberalism, a broader socialism, or other types of affiliation. A large number followed Chen Duxiu (1879–1942) and Li Dazhao (1889–1927) into the Chinese Communist Party. With Sun Yat-sen vowing to complete his unfinished revolution in 1923, these competing purposes found common cause in his vision of a reunified republic to be born out of the defeat of the warlords.

Although Lu Xun was deeply opposed to the warlord regimes, he did not express support for Sun Yat-sen's cause per se. In the early to mid-1920s, literary representations of human experience, what he called "the human path" *(ren dao)*, occupied his attention, and in this regard he expressed a particular interest in pre-Soviet Russian literature. In 1926 he remarked of his translation (from German) of Mikhail P. Artsybashev's 1906 novella *Worker Shevyrev* that the protagonist, who was possessed by an all-consuming desire for revenge and destruction, led him to wonder about the absence of such characters in Chinese literature. He observed that Chinese forms of destruction tended to be contingent on pragmatic considerations of power that were of a distinctly different variety from the unconfined rage portrayed in *Shevyrev*.[44]

Lu Xun's criticism of Chinese-style destruction as the result of calculated rather than honest rage was predicated on his view of state Confucianism as a vehicle of repressive power that benefited the wily and penalized the guileless. Yet implicit in Lu Xun's disavowal of Confucianism was his own fidelity to the ancient idea of edifying the young and equipping them with true knowledge. Thus in his writings he tended to prevaricate, alternating between an eagerness to instruct and an equal alacrity to refuse a guiding role.

In any case, by the early 1920s, with the rise of the Nationalist Party, this Confucian-inspired form of moral tutelage about which Lu Xun was deeply ambivalent had been modernized and reworked into a Soviet-inspired "political tutelage" *(zhengxun)*. This was a concept synonymous with "party tutelage" *(dangxun)* and one that Sun Yat-sen actively promoted in the form of benevolent one-party rule. He argued that this form of authoritarianism was vital to revolutionary construction insofar as it would efficiently cultivate a citizenry capable of active participation in China's future multiparty democracy. According to Sun, the creation of effective national organizations and the nationalization of key industries would further strengthen the nexus between citizenship and popular sovereignty, such that Chinese citizens would come to internalize China's sovereign rights as their own rights. Hence, he argued, they would instinctively defend the Republic against the encroachment of other nations with the same fierceness with which they would defend their own homes. In other words, Sun regarded authoritarian rule in a period of political tutelage as a necessary transitional stage to a multiparty democracy.

Sun set out the historical and practical reasons for this "revolutionary strategy" in his 1923 article "The History of the Chinese Revolution."[45] This was a piece he wrote for a special commemorative issue of *Shen bao (Shanghai News)* on the occasion of that august newspaper's fiftieth anniversary. It is no accident that Sun chose this occasion to deliver a comprehensive account of his latest political program. After all, it was the print media that had brought international attention to bear on his cause and his political organization. Programs and visions of reform and revolution had first appeared in the pages of socially engaged newspapers and journals like *Shen bao* and Liang Qichao's *Shiwu bao* before being translated into actual uprisings and military campaigns.

A year later, in 1924, Sun delivered a speech in which he stated that it was not only "excellent ideas" that had contributed to the Russian Revolution's "thorough success" but an unquestioned obedience to Lenin's vision as well.[46] Among other things, Sun declared:

[Lenin] organized a revolutionary party, proposing that this revolutionary party should have liberty [while] opposing liberty for party members. All the members of the revolutionary party supported his views, and each of them proffered his personal liberty to the party, committing himself to total obedience to the orders of the revolutionary party. Because the revolutionary party could collect together the strength of many party members, and they could with freedom of action act in unison as one body, the effect was huge. Consequently the success of the Russian Revolution was attained very swiftly. This revolutionary method of the Russian Revolution should serve as an excellent model to us.[47]

The Chinese Communist Party, as a new political organization in the mid-1920s, showed a greater diversity of opinions and political preferences. As Tony Saich and Benjamin Yang observe, "seven of the nine original members in the Communist Party group in Canton [Guangzhou] were anarchists," but the situation quickly changed: "Such members had to be purged from the organization, and the notion of the party as the focus of loyalty had to be substituted for the personal loyalty ties that dominated a number of the early party groups."[48] Hence, over the course of the Northern Expedition, the demand for unquestioned obedience to the party leadership also became strictly enforced in the Communist Party.

In 1924, when Sun Yat-sen was hailing Lenin as a revolutionary saint and praising the genius of one-party rule, there was also a growing demand for translations of Russian and Soviet works. Lu Xun's translation of *Shevyrev* was part of this thriving commerce. In April that year, he composed his famous prose poem "The Shadow's Farewell," in contemplation of the utopian claims of his contemporaries. The poem opens with the one-sentence prologue, "When one sleeps until a time when one no longer knows time, that is the moment when one's shadow will come to bid one farewell," followed promptly by the shadow's declaration:

> There is something I dislike in your heaven. I do not want to go there. There is something I dislike in your hell. I do not want to go there. There is something I dislike in your future golden world. I do not want to go there.

The shadow then voices its contempt for the self from which it has become dislodged:

> It is you, though, that I dislike. Friend, I'll no longer follow you; I don't want to stay here. . . . Ah no, I don't want to. I prefer to wander in emptiness [*kongxu*].[49]

In this critical response to the revolutionary visions then crowding into Chinese public culture, Lu Xun takes pains to stage the shadow's *address to the self*—to avail himself of a voice proximate to yet nonidentical with the self. This interplay of shadow and self enacts the predicament of being divided between support for the revolution and dislike of its accompanying propaganda. As such, the shadow's speech is an appeal for fidelity to one's conscience and critical judgment. It offers a way of affirming the cause of revolution but without endorsing the false prescience of a final destination.

The shadow's declared preference for emptiness offers a further clue to Lu Xun's renunciation of prophetic claims. His use of *kongxu* has often been mistranslated as a secular "nothingness" that deprives the term of its suggestive Buddhist connotation as a key to spiritual enlightenment. Given Lu Xun's keen interest in Buddhist sutras (he once told his friend Xu Shoushang that in the sutras he found the answers to several "big questions"),[50] it seems more than likely that he intended *kongxu* to resonate not with nihilism but with the transcendent Madhyamika Buddhist sense of *sunyata* (infinite emptiness as salvific truth). The fact that *sunyata* is soteriologically cognate with *nirvana* (as a final liberation and release) calls attention to mortal finitude, implicit in the suggestion of death in the poem's opening line about "a time when one no longer knows time."

As such, "The Shadow's Farewell" also invokes the transcendence of art against the brevity of human life. This is clearly signaled toward the end of the poem when the shadow declares in despair:

> You want a gift from me, but what can I offer you? There is simply nothing other than darkness and emptiness. I wish you nothing but darkness though it may disappear in your daylight. I wish you only emptiness because it will never possess your heart.[51]

The shadow—as the voice of immortal art outliving the authorial self—avails Lu Xun of an opportunity to affirm writing as belonging to *yet* departing from life. In other words, the written text mediates between the living and the dead. The shadow's gifts of darkness and emptiness are thus a counsel against orthodoxy: the reader is warned not to become possessed by or hold others captive to a particular form of words. In this reading, the poem alerts us to our own finitude and warns us not to treat finite concepts as eternal verities. Language, as the shadow suggests, is ultimately an inky darkness.

Lu Xun's affirmation of a salvific emptiness in disavowal of revolutionary visions is so starkly at odds with Sun Yat-sen's enthusiasm for "total obedience to the orders of the revolutionary party" as to present us with two incommensurable ways of seeing. Published in the same year, these two texts indicate the progressive eclipse of the critical independence that Lu Xun defended. It is hence no accident that Sun and Lu Xun had starkly divergent ways of emulating a Russian exemplar.

Unlike Sun, who enthusiastically embraced the tutelage of "the old man" (*starik*, the nickname Lenin was given in his twenties, in acknowledgment of his intellect and wisdom), Lu Xun sought solace from reading Artsybashev (1878–1927), from whom he acquired the posture of disavowing "a future golden world" (a key motif in Artsybashev's two best-known works in Chinese, *Sanin* and *Shevyrev*).[52] As Mark Gamsa observes, Lu Xun acknowledged his debt to Artsybashev in his 1920 short story "The Story of Hair," in which the protagonist, Mr. N., challenges the narrator: "Borrowing the words of Artsybashev, let me ask you: you subscribe to a golden age for posterity, but what have you to give these people themselves?"[53]

By 1927, the obedience that Guangzhou's revolutionary leadership demanded effectively transformed independent thinking into a threat, with the consequence that the anticipated "golden age" was not meant to be examined but to be heralded in unanimous chorus. Among the intellectual luminaries gathered in Guangzhou, Lu Xun and Yu Dafu, the writer and Creation Society cofounder, stood out as strident critics of blind political obedience. Yu's indictment of Guangzhou was in fact far more pointed than Lu Xun's. In January 1927 Yu, who had recently returned to Shanghai after living in Guangzhou, published "Guangzhou Affairs," in which he presented his observations of the abuse of power in the revolution's headquarters.

Yu wrote that the revolutionary discourse in Guangzhou had become nothing more than a tool of control. He observed that there was rhetorical unison insofar as "Everyone claims to be working toward the benefit of the masses and everyone shouts the same slogans." The effect, however, was to obscure "actual points of divergence" between the right and the left, and thereby to suppress concerns raised that were in disagreement with the views of the revolutionary leadership. Hence in Guangzhou "the government continues to speak the language of government and the oppressed class remains unable to do more than to spit out one or two drops of the misery crowding their bellies."[54]

He observed of Guangzhou's revolutionary youth that they had become so cowed by "the language of government" that they fall silent when the right used revolutionary rhetoric to attack the left:

> When the government says "horse," the students "horse" along, when the government says "deer" the students have no choice but to "deer" along, to the extent that students and society alike are unable to raise one word of criticism against the high-handed methods adopted by the government in its treatment of students and schools. Consequently, one sees the expulsion of students who came from the Communist training center, the screening of students at the Sun Yat-sen University, and the removal of teachers and principals who are somewhat more intense about their ideals. What is more, with the hullabaloo of moving the seat of government [from Guangzhou to Wuhan in December 1926] everything is in a state of limbo. At present, education in Guangzhou is in hibernation. Everything has come to a standstill; nothing has been achieved.[55]

Mikhail Bakhtin's (1895–1975) observations about the compelling force of an authoritative discourse are helpful for understanding the situation that Yu described. With an emphasis on obedience as the primary objective of an authoritative discourse, Bakhtin writes that it "demands that we acknowledge it, that we make it our own," since "it binds us, quite independently of any power it might have to persuade us internally."[56] In short, allegiance to the discourse took priority over knowing and mastering it. Indeed, the more authoritative the discourse grew, the less important the substance of its argument became while the importance of allegiance to the faith increased exponentially.

Thus, with each successive victory of the Northern Expedition, growing numbers of people rushed to join the revolution. Zhang Guotao (1897–1979), a founding member of the Chinese Communist Party, recalled: "Speechmaking was not only in vogue, but the more leftist the content of such talk, the better. . . . Even the big bosses of industry and trade would shout, 'Long Live the World Revolution!'"[57] Broadly speaking, this rhetorical exuberance reflected the success of the pragmatic alliance forged between the Nationalist Party and its Soviet sponsor. More specifically, it indicated the ability of Chiang Kai-shek and Joseph Stalin (1878–1953) to command obedience to their disparate aims, voiced in a common language of revolution.

What mattered most to Stalin was the Soviet Union's national interest and international influence: specifically its guidance of the Northern Expedition as *the* Chinese Revolution. Indifferent to the left's political predicament in Guangzhou, Stalin focused instead on the need for an initial tactical alliance of all groups, united in the cause of a war of national liberation. Viewing the formation of this multiclass united front as the immediate task, Stalin relegated the "dictatorship of the proletariat" to a future time, claiming that it would evolve out of the progressive ousting of bourgeois elements from the united front. As he so famously put it just one week before Chiang's coup of 12 April 1927, this eventual Communist victory would see the Nationalist Party, having outlived its purpose, being "squeezed out like a lemon and then flung away."[58]

Within Soviet circles, Leon Trotsky (1879–1940) strongly opposed this model of a gradual transition from nationalism to communism that required the Chinese Communists to submit to the Nationalist Party's leadership. Accusing Stalin of betraying communist principles with his conciliatory approach to China's Nationalist right, Trotsky demanded that the Chinese Communists be released immediately from political subjugation. These differences between Trotsky and Stalin sharpened from mid-1926 onward. Against Stalin's concessions to Chiang Kai-shek, Trotsky demanded renewed fidelity to class struggle and Lenin's internationalist vision. Faced with Trotsky's opposition, Stalin became even more insistent that the immediate goal of the Chinese Communists was to achieve national unification under Chiang Kai-shek.

At the height of Stalin's and Trotsky's disagreement in November 1926, the Comintern held the Seventh Plenum of its Executive Committee. On that occasion, Stalin was at pains to reiterate the urgency of liberating China from imperialism. He argued that it was imperative for the Chinese Communists to fight under the Nationalist banner and that class struggle should thus be suspended in the interim.

According to Stalin, this "unique" path of the Chinese revolution accorded with Lenin's vision of national liberation as a necessary historical stage of the world revolution. Highlighting the national aspect of
the Northern Expedition, Stalin claimed that "the advance of the Canton [Guangzhou] troops" was none other than "a blow aimed at imperialism, a blow aimed at its agents in China." Elaborating on the Chinese revolution as a key link in the chain of events that would destroy
the imperialist world order and its capitalist system, Stalin continued:

> In China, it is not the unarmed people against the troops of their own
> government but the armed people in the form of its revolutionary
> army. In China armed revolution is fighting against armed counter-
> revolution. This is one of the peculiarities and one of the advantages
> of the Chinese revolution. . . . What is important is not the bourgeois-
> democratic character of the Canton government, which forms the
> nucleus of the future all-Chinese revolutionary power. The most
> important thing is that this power is an anti-militarist power, and
> can be nothing else, that every advance of this power is a blow
> aimed at world imperialism and is therefore a stroke in favor of the
> world revolutionary movement.[59]

Stalin's authority ensured that, despite their misgivings, the Chinese
Communist leadership accepted and obeyed the "bourgeois-democratic"
leadership of the Nationalist Party. In response to Stalin's remarks,
Tan Pingshan (1886–1956), the Chinese delegate to the Comintern's
November 1926 Plenum, noted warily: "We must safeguard the interests of the peasantry, but on the other hand, we must maintain and
solidify the united front of the national revolutionary movement. In
so contradictory a situation, it is not easy to maintain a correct tactical line."[60] Chen Duxiu, then general secretary of the Chinese Communist Party, later bitterly recalled that, despite mounting evidence of the
Nationalist right's hostility, in early 1927 Mikhail Borodin (1884–1951),
the Northern Expedition's chief Soviet adviser in Guangzhou, instructed
him: "The present period is one in which Chinese Communists should
do coolie service for the Kuomintang!"[61] In May 1927, as the violence of
the Nationalists' anti-Communist campaign widened, Trotsky commented sardonically: "From the theses of Stalin, it follows that the

proletariat can separate itself from the bourgeoisie only after the latter has tossed it aside, disarmed it, beheaded it and crushed it underfoot."[62] In November 1927 Trotsky was himself expelled from the Communist Party and in January 1928 forced into exile.

Meanwhile, in early 1927 Chiang Kai-shek was planning the expulsion of the Communists from his national revolution. In a speech delivered on 19 February, he foreshadowed his intention to end the "united front." Among other things, Chiang reminded his audience that Sun Yat-sen had frequently lamented the failure of his fellow Nationalists to fully submit to his tutelage as the cause of party disunity. Chiang stated that the Northern Expedition was faced with a similar problem because "reactionaries and counter-revolutionaries" were now undermining the party's foundational aims from within. In the following passage, he invokes Sun's tutelage specifically to justify the violence he was then planning against the Communists:

> Of these people, there are still too many. The time has come to expel them since they are not true comrades. . . . No more differences or tendencies among us! Being known as a faithful believer in the doctrines of Sun Wen [Sun Yat-sen], I have the right to say that every true member of the party must be just that and nothing else. Whoever goes against the aims and methods indicated by Sun Wen will not be a comrade but an enemy who must not remain among us.[63]

When Chiang initiated the purge on 12 April 1927, he did so in a language of revolutionary unity. The fact that the Communists were admitted into the National Party under the rubric of a "united front" enabled him to legitimize the purge as a process of "Party purification" *(qingdang)* aimed at cleansing the party of the enemy within.

The fact that Stalin's and Chiang's speeches were intended purely as instructions qualifies them as examples of what Bakhtin called authoritative discourse. In effect, Chiang's words demanded hatred for Communists as a sign of allegiance to the Nationalist cause while Stalin's utterances ensured that the Chinese Communists took their orders from Chiang. Indeed, despite rising alarm among Chinese Communists about Chiang's intentions in March 1927, following their capture of Shanghai's Chinese quarters from warlord control, Stalin continued to issue explicit orders forbidding any preemptive action against the Nationalists.[64]

Hence there were two opposite representations of Chiang Kai-shek when he entered Shanghai on 26 March 1927. The Communists, bound by party loyalty and obedience to the Comintern, welcomed him as the undisputed Soviet-backed leader of the Northern Expedition. Conversely, the treaty port's Chinese and foreign bosses viewed Chiang as their potential savior from these same Communists. This was a time when the rise of organized labor and its declared links to Communist and Soviet goals was a growing concern in the treaty port. Shanghai's newspapers published frequent alarmist reports about workers' strikes. For instance, an article in *The Constitutionalist* of February 1927 noted that "peaceful foreign residents have been driven from their homes, their property destroyed" and that "many foreign firms . . . are now facing ruin" but went on to claim that "these are really trivial matters" when compared to the urgency of "the struggle against a political idea whose avowed aim is to destroy present world civilization . . . hampered by no scruples of conscience." An editorial on 28 March in the British-owned *North China Daily* indicted communism even more explicitly, stating that Chiang Kai-shek and his generals "remain now the only protection of China south of the Yangtze from being submerged by the Communist Party. . . . But if General Chiang is to save his fellow-countrymen from the Reds, he must act swiftly and relentlessly."[65]

Against these anti-Communist appeals to Chiang Kai-shek by Shanghai's Anglophone expatriates, the Sinophone discourse of revolution continued to rise in authority but did so with a concomitant degeneration in meaning. As Harold Isaacs (1910–1986) wrote, "every local satrap" became a member of the Nationalist Party and thereby "part of the 'armed revolution.'" Hence,

> his land became theoretically inviolate, along with the land of his satellites, his relatives, his supporters, i.e., all of the local owners of land for whom he ruled. Peasants in Guangdong, Hunan and Jiangxi were already discovering this as they reached out to take land for their own. Protection of "officers' land," sanctified by the Comintern and enforced by the Communists, became a noose for the revolution

on the land. It meant in effect defense of the landlords against the peasants.[66]

Isaacs's retrospective insights, published in his 1938 account of the Northern Expedition, resemble Lu Xun's gloomy recollections of the façade of revolution in Shaoxing during 1911. But despite the actual dominance of the Nationalist right and its opportunistic use of Soviet propaganda, the Communist idea of revolutionary class struggle was also gaining ground. Hunan in early 1927 was a shining example of organized peasant activism. In January 1927, registered membership in Hunan's peasant associations totaled over two million.[67] Not surprisingly, the optimism of imminent triumph in Mao Zedong's "28 March 1927 Report on the Peasant Movement in Hunan" sits at odds with Isaacs's retrospective wisdom. The report was produced just two weeks before Chiang Kai-shek began the grisly process of "Party purification" to put an end to all mass movements.

In his report, Mao praised the peasants of Hunan for venting their anger on the "bad gentry" and applauded the public humiliation and physical abuse of landowners as just and righteous. He made a point of noting that the seizure of land and property was class struggle at work, and a process by which the oppressed were achieving justice for themselves.[68] It was in this 1927 report that Mao sanctified violence with the quip commonly translated as "A revolution is not like a dinner party." What he actually wrote was: "A revolution is not like inviting people to dinner, or writing an essay, or painting a picture, or doing embroidery: it cannot be so refined, so leisurely and gentle, so 'benign, upright, courteous, temperate and complaisant.'"[69] With this witty derision of Confucian temperance using a quote from *The Analects,* Mao dignified revolutionary violence as existentially authentic because it liberated people from all such "refined" contrivances.

But whereas Mao lauded the peasantry's commission of violence in rural Hunan, at the Northern Expedition's headquarters in Guangzhou (and, after December 1926, in Wuhan as well), the same euphoria turned obedience into a necessary corollary of revolutionary success. Since obedience demonstrated adherence to party discipline it signaled by extension a complete dedication to the stated revolutionary purpose. It also helped to obscure the repression of the left by the right. Months after the launch of Chiang Kai-shek's anti-Communist purge, the prominent author Ye Shengtao (1894–1988) remarked, "The Nationalist Party and the Communist Party were all mixed up in our minds. Anybody, it seemed to us, could have joined both—or so we thought in our ignorance."[70]

For self-styled Marxists like Guo Moruo who perceived themselves as a vanguard, the fact that it was the anti-Communist Chiang Kai-shek who led the war did not make the discourse of revolution any less authoritative. They presented themselves as instruments of an already perfected science that required no further interrogation. Consequently, they judged criticism voiced against the unfolding developments as a transgression against the longer-term good.

Not surprisingly, Yu Dafu's criticisms of Guangzhou, which appeared in two articles in January and February 1927 in the popular Creation Society journal *Deluge,* effectively ended his friendship with Guo Moruo and Cheng Fangwu. The three men were close friends who had studied together in Japan and later achieved literary fame together as cofounders of the Creation Society. At the time that Yu's essays were published, Guo and Cheng were working as war propagandists. Guo, in fact, was traveling across China as part of Chiang Kai-shek's entourage. Yu recorded their reactions in his diary (which he published later the same year).

Among other things, he wrote: "Got a letter from Guo Moruo . . . reprimanding me for my bad inclinations. I am afraid that he will be reined in by the rightists. We shall probably go our separate ways." Yu noted that Cheng Fangwu had also written to berate him for undermining the war effort, accusing Yu of failing to consider that "Moruo, because of his position, had to echo Chiang Kai-shek." Yu wrote that he was deeply saddened by the rebukes he received from his former confidants. He added: "I think it's time to speak out for the people rather than echo the warlords and bureaucrats or the new warlords and new bureaucrats who are struggling for power."[71] In March 1927, when Cheng Fangwu's severe rebuttal of Yu's essays was published in *Deluge,* the journal's readers became spectators of the deepening rift between these former close friends.[72]

In October 1927 Lu Xun recalled that while he lived in Guangzhou "euphoric cries" of revolutionary commitment had become so obligatory that the author of an article, fearing criticism, included a postscript begging his readers' forgiveness for not having adequately mentioned the revolution.[73] While such examples evince the authority of the discourse, they indicate little about its binding force. On this point, Lu Xun's notion of "seeing with eyes wide open" also reveals itself as overly simplistic. When he criticized the "praise of blood and iron" two years earlier in 1925 using this phrase, he assumed that perspicacity would be restored if people were prepared to take a long hard look at the gap between ideal and reality. The same premise informed his criticisms of revolutionary euphoria in Guangzhou. What he failed to consider was the discursive potency of revolution itself. For those who felt that the declared revolutionary goals clarified the purpose of their own lives, his criticism was at odds with their experience. After all, from their perspective, their eyes were well and truly open.

Between Ethics and Aesthetics

What set Lu Xun apart from the revolutionary faithful was his flat refusal to elevate political belief over personal ethics. In this regard, his notion of "seeing with eyes wide open" was also a self-injunction to resist the seductions of the collective will aestheticized in revolutionary word, image, and song. His defense of revolution, accordingly, never strayed outside the scope of an ethical obligation to take principled action. Yet what surrounded him in Guangzhou was a fully aestheticized form of political life in which propaganda not only produced the rhetorical fusion of "the people," "national unity," and "world revolution" but encouraged an ardent desire for the authority and direction of the revolutionary leadership.[74]

In Guangzhou, this conflation of desire and obedience found frequent expression in oaths and slogans of revolutionary commitment. Oaths of personal allegiance were a feature of the Revolutionary Alliance that Sun Yat-sen led in the 1900s, and he remained convinced in the 1910s of their efficacy. In January 1919, however, as part of his program of "revolutionary construction," Sun formulated a model oath, one that departed from his former insistence on having people swear their loyalty to him.

With his sights set on a nation reunified under his leadership, he elevated his "three principles" to a foundational doctrine, and became the first person to swear allegiance to it:

> I, Sun Wen, with right heart and sincere mind take this oath before the congregation that from this moment I will discard the old and build the new, dedicated to supporting the Republic of China, carrying out the Three Principles of the People, and adopting the five-power constitution so that the nation may be well governed and the people at peace and happy. Thus will the foundation of the nation be forever strong, and there will be peace throughout the land.[75]

Similar declarations of a nation-building will abound in the *baihua* publications of the time. Sun's death in 1925 facilitated the Nationalist Party's inauguration of its orthodoxy. His articles and speeches became mandated curriculum in the Nationalist Party's education system as a source of instructions to be studied, consulted, and followed. In 1934 Lu Xun referred to Sun's "three principles" as the "kingly way" *(wang dao)* of the Nationalist government. In figuring Sun's textual corpus in this manner, Lu Xun presented the Nationalist one-party state as a latter-day incarnation of dynastic Confucianism. He wrote that just like its ancient predecessors, China's modern dictatorship sought to sanctify its absolute rule by invoking a supreme exemplar, and reminded his readers that the "kingly way" and the "tyrant's way" were paradigms that enjoyed a "sibling relationship."[76] With reference to the censorship of his writings under Nationalist rule, he remarks sardonically: "I cannot help wishing that we had sung the praises of the Three Principles of the People. But now it is too late."[77]

Here we must distinguish Lu Xun's praise for Sun's revolutionary zeal from his apprehension over Sun's political doctrine. In the eulogy he wrote to commemorate the first anniversary of Sun's death in 1926, Lu Xun commended Sun's moral character with these words: "[Sun] rose to prominence as a revolutionary. In defeat he remained a revolutionary. After the founding of the Chinese Republic, he was neither satisfied nor complacent and continued to advance toward the completion of his revolutionary work. Even when he lay dying, he said, 'The revolution remains incomplete. Comrades, you must exert yourselves!'"[78]

Although Sun Yat-sen worded "revolutionary construction" as a moral pursuit, it was societal perfection that preoccupied him and on which he published copiously. In effect, "revolutionary construction," which was directed toward achieving the sublime state of (what Sun called) "millions united into one heart," became an aspiration that exceeded morality insofar as moral doubt had no place in this pursuit of perfect unity.[79] The editors of a collection of his writings point out that Sun's teleological vision was typical of twentieth-century Chinese political discourse as a whole. It centered upon "the primacy of a unique vehicle of leadership and power to purify, restructure and transform China, liberating it from foreign domination and the harmful effects of those pretenders to reform who were dragging China into the abyss." Sun's definition of a political principle as "an idea, a faith, and a power" reiterates the metaphysics of conversion implicit in his "three principles." It is through the ongoing clarification of a political idea that "a faith arises; and out of faith, a power is born."[80]

In contrast to the political faith that Sun extolled, Lu Xun wrote of his literary pursuit as guided by an ethical obligation, one that he worded in terms of "obeying my general's orders." The statement appears in his December 1922 preface to his first anthology of short stories, *A Call to Arms,* in which he figured his reason for writing in *baihua* as a response to "a call to arms" that led, in turn, to his "calling out" in the hope of encouraging true warriors to save China. In describing his *baihua* as action taken toward a better future, he remarked that he was unconcerned as to whether his cry sounded "brave and bold or sad and tragic," or even "repellent or ridiculous." This was because he had "no great urge to speak" in the first place but was compelled into action by a summons. In this connection, he remarked that he had "no qualms about distorting things every now and then" (to mitigate the harshness of his narratives with some optimism), because "the commander-in-chief at the time did not approve of pessimism."[81]

This prosopopoeia of a disembodied presence sits in stark contrast to the presentation of a program of action or an image of national perfection. By "personifying" social conscience as the voice of an unknown commander, Lu Xun turns the act of writing into an inward contemplation of how one should respond to its call. Hence, despite his use of a militant idiom, it was a self-reflexive practice that he described, a case of heeding an inner voice as opposed to swearing allegiance to an ideology. Lu Xun's figuration of "my general's orders" is consonant with Jacques Derrida's (1930–2004) view that ethics should be characterized as the compelling force of "the absolute other in me" (that is, as the work of heteronomy, "the other as the absolute that decides on me in me") and not as a matter of choice (that the presumption of individual subjective autonomy would have us believe).[82]

In this sense, Lu Xun's critical attentiveness to "the other *in me*" was an ethics constitutively resistant to the external demands of a political doctrine or a science of revolution. The positive remarks that Lu Xun did make about the cause of revolution were invariably directed to the work of individuals. In particular, he dwelt on the debt that the living owed to those who gave their lives to the cause. Reflecting in March 1927 on Guangzhou's public commemorations of the 1911 Revolution's martyrs, he wrote with reverence of their sacrifice:

> During the festivities on the evening of 12 March, the greatness of these revolutionaries moved me even more deeply. When two people find love and one dies, the other who lives on is left with nothing but grief. But when a revolution is successful, the revolutionaries who are killed bequeath to the living an annual occasion for merrymaking and even exuberant rejoicing. Revolutionaries alone, in life and in death, bring happiness to all.[83]

In these lines, and in the essay as a whole, he encouraged his readers to ponder the nature of the legacy bequeathed by the dead and to examine their own lives in this process. He concluded the essay with the humorous comment that the function of an anniversary date was to give everyone an occasion "to exhaust themselves in celebration, followed by a good sleep," such that "the next day, feeling reinvigorated, they would be able to apply themselves even more to the work they ought to be doing."[84] Couching the idea of a revolutionary legacy in these terms, Lu Xun encouraged his readers to ponder their own role in the cause.

In the late 1910s, Lu Xun's short stories proved so influential among the educated young that he became the undisputed pioneer of a socially committed literature in *baihua*. Despite his retrospective claim in 1922 that his narratives included some measure of optimism, his depictions were invariably of existential characters that were either inured to or brutalized by the bleak and unchanging circumstances of their lives. As Julia Lovell puts it, "Lu Xun publicly regarded his fiction as a kind of cultural medicine, designed to draw the poison out of the Chinese national character" and notes of his literary techniques that they produce the effect of "distancing the reader from the people and events described, bolstering our faith in the objectivity of our literary doctor."[85]

This critical distancing was a corollary of Lu Xun's view of socially engaged writing as a faithful chronicle of the author's personal observations. He was a voracious reader who cited a wide and eclectic range of authors and sources but who remained unaffiliated with any particular school or theory of literature. In 1923, when several Communist writers condemned romanticism in *baihua* literature as a bourgeois malaise, the idea of socially committed writing became identified with the politics of the left. These writers accused *baihua* poets of turning the modern vernacular into a vehicle for their "shallow and vulgar feelings" and "neurotic sentiments" and for purveying "sickly sentiments of love" and "nihilistic states of mind." They called for a new form of "serious scholarship" *(zhengjing xuewen)*, based in the materialist outlook of Marxism.[86] Among them, Xiao Chunü (1891–1927) explained that romanticism's elevation of art had produced a "dualism" that prevented the harmonization of "the material self" with "the spiritual self." The cure for this inner torment, Xiao proposed, was to discover and forge a common purpose with the oppressed, thereby turning literature into their vehicle. (Xiao was murdered in April 1927 when "Party purification" reached Guangzhou. He was then receiving treatment at the Sun Yat-sen University Hospital.)[87]

This emergent form of leftist aesthetics confined itself to presenting Marxism as the corrective lens required for a true social perspective and, in this context, urged the bourgeois writer to cultivate an acute sense of empathy for the downtrodden. In 1924 the Communist writer Li Qiushi (executed by the Nationalists in February 1931) invoked both ancient and modern exemplars in his impassioned appeal for a new sensory experience:

> You must carry out what you have learned for yourself. Like Tolstoy, you must go among the people. Like Buddha, you must descend into hell. You must follow the people wherever they are to be found. You must taste every form of human bitterness and undergo every kind of human degradation. Literature is nothing noble. . . . The aristocrat is the enemy of the common people; the aristocrat is the enemy of the true writer.[88]

By 1925 these Marxist-inspired calls for a politics of self-transformation were eclipsed by the "praise of blood and iron" that Lu Xun dismissed that year. Vera Schwarcz writes of the blood-suffused imagery of 1925 ("flowers of blood," "blood's earth," "blood's eyes," "blood's hands," and so on) that it reflected the exhilaration of the authors in identifying with the mass movement under way. Schwarcz notes of the intellectuals' newfound sense of community that "however fleeting" it was, it nonetheless gave them "voices they never thought they had before."[89] This sharpened intellectual militancy occurred in the context of a dramatic rise in workers' strikes (the General Labor Union in Shanghai reported that more than 156,000 workers were involved in the city's strike actions between 5 May and 13 June 1925) and in Communist Party membership (from 1,000 in May to 10,000 by November 1925).[90]

The gulf between this surge of revolutionary exhortations and Lu Xun's appeal for perspicacious self-reflection widened further with the launch of the Northern Expedition in 1926. By this time, and quite ironically, the leading exponents of a now widely proclaimed "revolutionary literature" included the members of the Creation Society: the very people criticized in 1923 for their romantic excesses. Guo Moruo and Cheng Fangwu now played a prominent role in defining what social commitment meant. Converted from romanticism to Marxism in 1924 and working as war propagandists by 1926, Guo and Cheng elevated literature to an ideological weapon in the revolution's service. The writer occupied a special importance in their scheme.

Praising writers whose "sympathies were with the masses and the national revolution," Guo claimed that their "automatic opposition to

imperialism" gave them a unique talent for inspiring righteous violence. As instruments of "the spirit of the times," he wrote, the vanguard
writer's role was both "to awaken the ideals of the proletariat" and
"give authentic expression to their anguish." Accordingly, he concluded
that it was the vanguard's "genuine revolutionary literature" that the
masses must emulate.[91] This valorization of the vanguard writer shared
a common discursive structure with Sun Yat-sen's attempts to found a
national creed on his "three principles." The difference was one of content: whereas Sun envisaged societal perfection under the Nationalist
Party's tutelage, Guo relied on a Marxist science to shape human ends.
Inherent in both projects was a yearning for a totalizing vision, as it
were, a theory of everything in which everything, finally, would be assigned to its rightful place.

To Guo Moruo's pronouncements on the vanguard writer, Cheng
Fangwu added instructions on how to cultivate the crucial vanguard
emotion: passion. In his influential article "Revolutionary Literature
and Its Immortality," published in June 1926, Cheng wrote that passion was the fruit of the revolutionary writer's self-realization: his awakening to "a great and startling knowledge." It was passion that enabled
the writer to transmit "the urgency of revolution," and passion that
endowed his literature with the power to transform others. Hence "We
must love humanity with passion. Thus in the consciousness we have
of ourselves, we must also cultivate a sense of collective consciousness.
When we feel as individuals, we must simultaneously feel as a collective. It is only by this means that we can produce revolutionary literature of immortal proportions."[92]

To distinguish this true passion from possible impostors, the writer
must experience "a leap of consciousness," which, regardless of "whether
it occurs in the collective or the individual," gave rise to a compulsion
to "feel as a collective."[93] These statements constitute a schema of self-
cultivation that present Marxism as a form of emotional tutelage. According to Cheng, the art of making oneself over began with the realization that one had encountered a "great and startling knowledge"
(that is, Marxism) capable of inspiring and fostering the necessary passion to transform society. He continued: "When revolutionary writers
become the first-awakened [xianjue] and share a common feeling [tongjue]

about the necessity of revolution, they will transmit their passion in an aesthetic literary form. Their writings offer a source of constant encouragement because they give expression to feelings deep inside people's hearts."[94]

In emulation of Guo Moruo, Cheng resorted to the following pseudo-algebra to present his argument as a science:

True human nature + aesthetic form = immortal literature.

True human nature + aesthetic form + passion = immortal revolutionary literature.[95]

Although Cheng's "theorem" may appear ludicrous to the unconvinced, it nonetheless conveys an acute longing for an axiomatic law—in this case, a law (or *dao*) of literature that elevates passion to an eternal engine of revolutionary change. This modern recourse to an equational formula bears a structural resemblance to the ancient axioms that declare a "kingly way" in state Confucianism: both are appeals to an absolute principle. In the case of Guo Moruo, this alignment was not accidental: as Xiaoming Chen points out, Guo read into Marxism a blueprint for actualizing the Confucian ideal of great unity *(datong)* not just in China but throughout the modern world.[96]

At this juncture it is useful to pause to consider George Kateb's general observation about ideal aims that are "ranked higher than morality" and are hence defended as undertakings to be pursued at any cost. He writes that such aims are often accompanied by "cravings for the elements of beauty." In the revolutionary discourse that pervaded Guangzhou, emotional and ideological unity became the desired state that justified the commission of violence. War, in this process, was also made beautiful. Hence it was no accident that Chiang Kai-shek chose to justify his purge of the Communists in terms of achieving an ideal political purity and to offer for emulation his own exemplary fidelity as a "faithful believer" committed to implementing the "aims and methods" of Sun Yat-sen. To quote Kateb again, when ideals are craved, their achievements "do not only please" but "provide intense gratification when they are imagined to exist, and often will be defended without mercy; and when they are thought possible, they often will be pursued without mercy."[97]

Chiang Kai-shek's "Party purification" produced a new form of organized violence in China that was denounced as a "White Terror" by the Communists. Using contemporary sources, Harold Isaacs in 1938 placed the number of suspected Communists arrested and imprisoned by the Nationalist government from April to December 1927 at 32,316. He reported that during this period, an additional 37,985 persons were known to have been formally condemned to death.[98] In reaction, the Communists launched a series of failed counterattacks that further escalated the death toll. The unaffiliated and the innocent were among those slain by both sides.

Lu Xun's protégé Feng Xuefeng (1903–1976) recalls his mentor telling him in 1929: "Needless to say, I went to Guangzhou carrying a 'beautiful dream'.... You could say that I've been around and know the ways of the world but none of what I knew was of any use.... I was clearly too naïve and too trusting of the 'ever-theatrical nihilist party' and was well and truly duped.... In the end, I was petrified with terror.... It was at the price of blood that I learned how I had been duped."[99] Feng quotes Lu Xun as saying: "My faith in evolution led me to think that the young were better than the old and that it was generally the old who oppressed the young.... But I learned otherwise. It was the young who betrayed, rounded up, and slaughtered the young. In the past when the warlords killed young people, I was grief-stricken and enraged. This time, I was utterly consumed by terror. It turns out that my views on evolution are totally bankrupt!"[100]

In his famous open letter of October 1927 to the young activist Shi Youheng, Lu Xun wrote an abject self-accusation. Reprising the trope of cannibalism that launched his literary fame a decade earlier, Lu Xun lamented:

> I have discovered that I am a ... what? I cannot give it a name at the moment. I once said, throughout the course of history China has laid out cannibalistic feasts; there are those who eat and those who are eaten. Those who are eaten, in their time, have eaten others, and those who eat now will, in turn, be eaten also. But now I have discov-

ered that I myself have helped to prepare such feasts. Sir, you have read my works, so let me ask you: does reading them numb you or make things clearer? Do they leave you feeling dazed or do they accentuate what you feel? If it is the latter, then my self-indictment is largely substantiated.[101]

Lu Xun's ambivalence in this passage is profound and moving. On the one hand, he blames himself for having inspired idealistic youth to wage a futile war against an ineradicable "cannibalism" only to hasten them to their deaths or to an ordeal of clear-sighted despair. On the other hand, as he clearly is not favoring numbness over perspicacity, he also implies that he felt compelled to open people's eyes to the social ills of the day. He continues, reiterating the sadism of the victorious oppressor:

Chinese feasts serve live shrimps steeped in wine. The friskier the shrimps are, the greater the eater's relish and enjoyment. I am one of those who helped to prepare this dish by clearing the minds and intensifying the feelings of honest and innocent young people, so that if by chance they land in trouble they will feel doubly wretched. At the same time, their enemies will experience an exquisite pleasure from the delectation of their extreme pain and suffering. Whether those being hunted are of the Red Army or the Revolutionary Army, I suspect that when they are captured by their enemies in the opposite camp, educated persons such as students will be subjected to greater torture than workers and others lacking education. And why is this so? Because in seeing their keener and subtler expressions of pain, their enemies will feel a particular joy.[102]

Here, in likening the enemy to an evil gourmand with a gruesome appetite for the pain of his victims, Lu Xun betrays a Confucian elitism by attributing to educated persons a superior sensibility to suffering. Despite accusing his peers of being latter-day literati who "put their own words in the mouths of the common folk," his remarks here echo the Confucian ideal of the educated elite as a moral aristocracy sympathetic to those in need. In this regard, he transposes the burden of Confucian altruism into a modern paradigm: namely, to become more fully human, one must foster a capacity for "keener and subtler expressions of pain" through an act of self-sacrifice. Between this tacit affirmation of Confucian altruism and other instances in which he disparaged Confucian propriety as self-deceiving, we can detect an unsettling equivocation.

In making a painful public confession in this letter, Lu Xun sought to point out that his frequent calls for critical vigilance against revolutionary bombast had proven utterly inept against the monstrous power of a doctrine capable of turning its young adherents into killing machines. As he wrote in the letter: "The game of blood has begun; the parts are taken by the young and played with gusto. At present, I cannot see an end to this show."[103]

Guo Moruo, despite his erstwhile position as the Northern Expedition's leading propagandist, did not dwell on the moral consequences of his own work. Instead Guo focused on his own feelings of desolation upon realizing the revolution had been stolen from the Communists. He wrote in his July 1927 autobiographical essay, "After Leaving Chiang Kai-shek," that he sensed on 4 April 1927 that the revolution had gone awry. He did not join in the celebrations of the Northern Expedition's newest victories then under way but felt instead "as if time had congealed and no longer flowed." On 4 April he noted in his diary:

> The tragedy of the revolution is probably about to begin. I feel as if I'm trying to hold back an overwhelming tide all by my puny self.... One's revolutionary spirit lives on, even after one has been recalled from a revolutionary occupation. The path I must take is clear. I will have to resign from office. After all, I'm but a tool, and I would rather be used as a tool for the correct path.... It's as if I have been tossed onto a deserted island, out of the angry tide of revolution.[104]

Lu Xun's most memorable response to the violence of 1927 took the form of an aphorism (what he called a "fleeting mixed impression") that he wrote in September 1927:

> As for the revolutionary, antirevolutionary, and nonrevolutionary: those who are revolutionary are killed by the antirevolutionary; those who are antirevolutionary are killed by the revolutionary. The

nonrevolutionary are mistaken for the revolutionary and killed by the antirevolutionary; or they are mistaken for the antirevolutionary and killed by the revolutionary; or they are not mistaken for any-thing but are killed anyway by the revolutionary or the antirevolu-tionary. Revolution; revolutionize the revolution; revolutionize the revolutionized revolution; revolutionize . . . [*geming gegeming gegegem-ing, gege* . . .][105]

The implied extension *ad absurdum* of "revolution; revolutionize the rev-olution; revolutionize . . ." has long since turned this famous parodic barb against revolutionary discourse into a popular jibe against rote-learned, unexamined political dogma generally. But read against the butchery he witnessed in Guangzhou, Lu Xun's "fleeting mixed im-pression" conveys less sardonic humor than his acute emotions during that time. In a 1926 explanation of what he meant by a "mixed impres-sion," Lu Xun wrote that his essays contained "nothing at all of uni-versal cosmic significance or life's true meaning." Rather, "It is simply that, every so often, I take up my pen to write down what I've come across, the ideas I've had or what I want to say, letting these things have their way no matter how shallow or extreme they seem." He then offered this analogy: "It is like the singing-crying noise one makes when in a state between grief and joy: simply a means of releasing an-ger and showing emotion."[106]

Few now remember that Lu Xun did not coin the sequence "revolu-tion; revolutionize the revolution; revolutionize . . ." Although he turned it into a grim parody of the Marxist dialectic, the formulation was in fact a popular way of endorsing Marxism around the time of the North-ern Expedition. The same sequence appears in Guo Moruo's seminal essay of May 1926, "Revolution and Literature," in the section where he outlined four historical stages in the "evolution of revolutionary litera-ture" in Europe.

Guo wrote that the revolutionary spirit expressed itself through an ongoing historical process of class struggle. He explained that it began with the overthrow of aristocratic rule in ancient Greece and Rome, continued with the rise and subsequent fall of Christian theocracy, and was followed, in turn, by the rise of bourgeois democracy after the

French Revolution of 1789. He described individualism as the revolutionary spirit of this third bourgeois democratic stage and argued that, as in each of the preceding stages, individualism grew corrupt over time to become the ideological core of an oppressive capitalism. Thus realism and romanticism, as cultural expressions of a once revolutionary individualism, also grew counterrevolutionary. He then described the contemporary moment in 1926 as one when "in Europe today, the age of the struggle between the [proletarian] fourth class and the [bourgeois-democratic] third class has arrived."[107] In summarizing this process, Guo offered the paradigmatic formulation: "If there is revolutionary literature in the preceding era, there will be a literature that revolutionizes that revolutionary literature in the following era, and the era after that will see, in turn, the emergence of a literature that further revolutionizes the revolutionized revolutionary literature."[108]

By the time Lu Xun turned this "essential truth" into a caricature, both he and Guo had witnessed the bloody violence of the Nationalists' "Party purification" at first hand. In stripping the Marxist dialectic bare of any presumption of historical inevitability, Lu Xun re-presents it as a chain of words teetering on the edge of nonsense: "revolution, revolutionize the revolution, revolutionize the revolutionized revolution." *"Geming, gegeming, gegegeming, gege . . ."* is produced by separating the Chinese word for revolution into its constitutive components of the verb *ge* (to cut) and the noun *ming* (fate or destiny). The further one progresses down this "revolutionizing" chain, the more remote becomes the "destiny" signified by *ming*.

In short, the aphorism de-aestheticizes the concept of revolution. It highlights instead an endless process of violent displacements that prevents the predicted future of national unity and societal perfection from ever arriving. We must not forget that Lu Xun himself had declared on 8 April 1927 that "the sound of cannons rings more sweetly than the sound of literature." He had uttered this war cry in a gesture of solidarity with the military cadets he was then addressing. His aphorism, written five months later, constitutes a desolate reversal of that earlier statement. The aphorism's ending in *"gegege . . ."* is a syntactic parody of the Marxist dialectic. As the Communists were being slaughtered in the name of the revolution that he had defended in Guangzhou, Lu Xun turned this onomatopoeic staccato stream of *ge*'s into a sound resembling machine-gun fire. The dialectic is hence recast as a vehicle of violence. In this way Lu Xun used his mordant wit to indict China's revolution as both tragedy and farce. The farcical aspect of this tragedy, he implied, is that the believers ultimately died for a form of words that projected the dialectical achievement of human perfection. What they failed to see, he suggested, was that these words were already welded to the power of guns.

2

The Shanghai Haze

On 11 September 1927, sixteen days before leaving Guangzhou for Shanghai, Lu Xun completed the essay "On 'Intensity.'" He wrote it as an oblique commentary on the daily terrors of "Party purification" and included "words of warning to the young": as if on the eve of his departure the author was fulfilling his final duties as a mentor. Using "intensity" to mean a display of revolutionary fervor, Lu Xun placed the word in quotation marks to highlight its ominous interpretability.

He advised his readers that as "the young seem especially prone to dying this year," they should take special pains to avoid appearing "too intense." This was so, he explained, because they lived in a society in which "what is praised as right and proper one day can turn overnight into a crime punishable by caning." Accordingly, it had become a risky liability to show intensity, and he urged the young "to proceed with the utmost care."[1]

These cautionary words present a bitter reversal of the expectations placed on Lu Xun by the Guangzhou authorities and the students at Sun Yat-sen University. They had hoped that he would play a major part in nurturing a revolutionary spirit among young writers and critics. Instead he now enjoined his charges to divest themselves of any desire for revolutionary change. In its place he offered erudite comments on discursive tactics inspired by the literary inquisitions during China's imperial past, using these to allude to the modern perils of "dangerous writing."[2]

In particular, he warned young writers not to imagine they could procure any modicum of safety by pretending that they were only "letting out a sigh of regret" *(ketan ye fu)*, and thereby ameliorate or in some way disguise their intense emotions. He wrote that while this tactic of "letting out a sigh" might have worked for their hoary predecessors in the Ming and Qing epochs, it was clearly unsuited for the treacherous modern age at hand. In this context, he advised: "the sighing of slaves might well be harmless, but the master will feel nervous all the same." Alluding to the self-censorship at work in his own writing, he instructed the reader to approach his essay as nothing more than "the letting out of a regretful sigh."[3]

In "How to Write," completed around the same time and published in October 1927, Lu Xun utilized a similar form of indirect yet profoundly affective language to commemorate Bi Lei, the student who had celebrated Lu Xun's arrival in Guangzhou by calling for an intensification of revolutionary shouting.[4] Bi was arrested with forty other students on the campus of Guangzhou's Sun Yat-sen University on 18 April 1927. At the time, Lu Xun had pleaded unsuccessfully with the local authorities for the students' release.[5] He never saw Bi Lei again. In this essay, he recalls Bi as an energetic young man whom he had suspected of being the author of several essays written in praise of Communism, each published under a different pseudonym, and that Bi had once presented him with a dozen issues of a local Communist journal, *Youthful Vanguard*. He writes that, from these memories alone, "one can surmise that Mr. Bi Lei was most probably a Communist Party member." He then mourns the seventeen-year-old with the simple words: "I suspect he has long departed from this world, that young man from Hunan, so slight and thin and with his wits about him."[6]

These elements from Lu Xun's essays of late 1927 indicate the parameters of criticism he felt he could allow himself while the Nationalists were systematically widening their anti-Communist purge. In this context, his sparse words of mourning offer a useful example of his tacit criticism. By calling attention to Bi Lei's slightness and alertness, he gestured to the ruthless barbarism that had extinguished this young life.

Lu Xun continued to live in Guangzhou from April to September 1927. In fact, even before the anti-Communist purge had begun, the exuberant welcome he received in January from Guangzhou's students had worn off. By March the more radically minded were already accusing him of lacking revolutionary zeal and shirking his duties as a mentor.[7] Lu Xun was also unhappy at Sun Yat-sen University: he sought to resign in March, when he had been there for less than three months. He did so because the university had appointed the historian Gu Jiegang (1893–1980), whom Lu Xun loathed.[8] He promptly announced that as he could not work in the same institution as Gu, one of them would have to leave. Nonetheless, because he still commanded enormous respect among the general student population, his request was initially denied. Contemporary observers speculated that the Guangzhou authorities feared his departure would inspire a student riot, and it was only in June 1927 that they formally approved his resignation.[9]

From July to September 1927, in his three remaining months in Guangzhou, Lu Xun devoted his energies to several writing projects. In the humid summer heat, he wrote numerous essays and prepared two personal anthologies for publication: *Wild Grass*, a collection of experimental prose poems; and *Dawn Blossoms Plucked at Dusk*, a series of literary compositions based on his childhood reminiscences. He also compiled and annotated a two-volume collection of premodern fiction, *Strange Tales from the Tang and Song Epochs*. *Wild Grass* and *Strange Tales* were published in 1927 and 1928 by Beixin Publishing House, Lu Xun's main publisher. *Dawn Blossoms* appeared in 1928 with the Yet to Be Named Press (Weiming she), which Lu Xun had helped to set up in Beijing.

In October 1928, twelve months after Lu Xun mourned Bi Lei in print, the Northern Expedition, prosecuted after April 1927 by the "Party purified" Nationalists, came to a triumphant conclusion. Flush with victory, Chiang Kai-shek established his government in Nanjing and was inaugurated as the reunified Republic's new president on 6 October 1928. From then onward, for the better part of what became known as the "Nanking Decade" (1927–1937), China's cultural and political centers moved to the south while Beijing fell into a steep decline. Following Chiang's capture of Beijing from the Fengtian warlord Zhang Zuolin (1875–1928) in June 1928, the capital's demotion to an ordinary city was formalized with a change of name.[10] After 1928, Beijing ("the northern capital") became known as Beiping ("northern peace," with the connotation of "the pacified north"). It was not until October 1949, following the Chinese Communists' defeat of the Nationalists, that Beiping reverted to Beijing and was reinstated as the nation's capital with the founding of the People's Republic of China.

Two decades earlier, in the bloody months that followed Chiang Kai-shek's first attack against the Communists in Shanghai on 12 April 1927, the Chinese Communist Party was in a perilous situation. Its leadership was deeply divided, and the intraparty logistical networks that the Communists had developed in Chinese cities from 1925 to 1927 were greatly undermined. Before 12 April 1927, the Communist Party boasted a registered membership of some 60,000. By the end of 1927 the figure had plummeted to below 10,000.[11] Moreover, the party's stronghold in Shanghai, the General Labor Union, was irretrievably destroyed after April 1927. At the height of its power in March 1927, the union's registered membership was 821,830.[12]

Despite these enormous losses and setbacks, the Chinese Communist Party was rebuilt over the "Nanking Decade," when Chiang Kai-shek was at the height of his power, but in a form quite different from its former incarnation during the "united front" period. After 1927, with the brutal repression of the urban mass movement, the Communist strongholds shifted from the city to the countryside. From 1927 to 1937 the Communists were driven underground and operated only clandestinely in the cities. Meanwhile Mao Zedong and Zhu De (1886–1976) rose to power through the "Red Armies" and guerrilla bases they established in the Chinese hinterland.

The separation and clarification of Communist goals from those of the Nationalists proceeded apace as the Nationalist campaign for "Party purification" widened after April 1927. The Comintern reversed its previous policy of pragmatic conciliation and ordered the Chinese Communists to wage open war on their formidable ally-turned-enemy. As a result the Chinese Communist Party leadership became divided when Chen Duxiu, the Party's general secretary and former *New Youth* editor-in-chief, challenged Moscow's new *Diktat* of militant class struggle. Chen argued that given the Party's dangerous circumstances, the new policy was a disaster that would put even more Communist lives at risk. In response, Moscow deposed him in August 1927 and, via the Comintern, entrusted its orders to the remaining members of the Party leadership, which included Qu Qiubai (who grew close to Lu Xun in 1932), Li Lisan (1899–1967), Li Weihan (1896–1984), Xiang Zhongfa (1880–1931), Zhang Guotao, Zhang Tailei (1898–1927), and Zhou Enlai (1898–1976). These men directed the work of the urban underground Communists from then on.[13]

Under Qu Qiubai, the autumn and winter of 1927 saw a sharp increase in Communist casualties resulting from ill-planned uprisings. Chen Duxiu's criticisms were vindicated, but he and his supporters were increasingly estranged from the party. Expelled in 1929 for opposing Moscow, Chen and his followers promptly became Trotskyists. Meanwhile the Comintern was forced to revise its insurrectionist policy. It now directed the Chinese Communists to rebuild the Party's bases in the cities and countryside but with a continued emphasis on preparing a full-scale assault against the Nationalist government. The discourse of Chinese Communism was by this time riven with opposing views, but it was the voice of the Comintern-endorsed leadership that prevailed. And it was in this authoritative discourse that the erstwhile compromised rhetoric of national unity before class struggle was changed, after April 1927, to focus fully on class struggle, with the stated aim of establishing a Communist China over the next decade.[14] The destruction of the proletariat's enemies accordingly became a rallying cry among the more radical members of the intellectual left.

In February 1927 Yu Dafu had observed of the "united front" that it merely gave the Nationalist right an opportunity to appropriate the language of revolution for itself. As he put it at the time, China now had "new warlords, bureaucrats, and capitalists" with "newer minds" and "more elegant ways of speaking" than "the old warlords, bureaucrats, and capitalists." He challenged his readers: "We should ask ourselves what is to be done if the sacrifices we make and the changes we want to achieve amount to no more than this."[15] In mid-September 1927, as the numbers of actual and suspected Communists arrested, executed, or killed in battle continued to climb while the Nationalists' celebration of their revolutionary victories grew, Lu Xun wrote from Guangzhou:

> Since the campaign for "Party purification" began, a kind of neurosis has crept into these "euphoric cries." Naturally, to revolt against the status quo is still mandatory, but it has become inadvisable to be too revolutionary. To be too revolutionary is to risk being seen as an extremist. To be seen as an extremist will lead to the suspicion that one is Communist and will, in turn, cause one to be identified as "antirevolutionary."[16]

Such remarks alluding to the grotesque manipulability of revolutionary discourse appeared frequently in his essays of mid- to late 1927.

In 1928 Lu Xun turned his attention to the commerce of "revolutionary literature" in Shanghai. In this context, unlike in his Guangzhou essays of September 1927, in which he advised self-censorship in the interests of self-preservation, by early 1928 Lu Xun was denigrating the self-censorship of his contemporaries in Shanghai.

Hence in March 1928 he wrote of a "haze" *(menglong)* that spanned the political spectrum and permeated Shanghai's cultural marketplace.[17] In using this word Lu Xun suggested that lurking beneath the fashionable certitudes circulating in post-1927 Shanghai was an unhappy commingling of fear of persecution and desire for fame. In this regard, he was as dismissive of leftist plans for the proletariat as he was of rightist celebrations of revolutionary triumph. "Haze" was also a word that marked his entry into the polemics of "revolutionary literature" in 1928.

A Postrevolutionary Haze

Lu Xun first used the word "haze" in his famous essay of 12 March 1928, "The Haze of 'Drunken Eyes.'" This was one of his longer essays and one that he had written as a riposte to his critics in the Creation Society. Of these critics, Feng Naichao (1901–1983), newly recruited into the society as a Marxist theorist in late 1927, was responsible for inspiring Lu Xun to write of Shanghai's "haze" in the first place.

Feng had published an article in January 1928 featuring the following remarks about Lu Xun:

> If I were to use literary language to describe this old man, Lu Xun, I
> would say that he looks out the window of a dark tavern and, with
> drunken eyes, observes life passing by on the street outside. Our
> contemporaries sing his praise even though he has nothing more
> than a few well-practiced turns of phrase. In fact, he's always pining
> for bygone days, filled with mournful feelings for waning feudal ways.
> As a result, he reflects the tragedy of someone who has fallen behind
> [luowuzhe] in an era of social change. Thus, in a state of dejection, he
> exchanges a few beautiful phrases about humanism with his younger
> brother [Zhou Zuoren]. Oh the joys of the reclusive life! Fortunately,
> he hasn't yet copied Tolstoy to become a despicable preacher.[18]

This was among the first published assaults on Lu Xun in 1928. Feng's
manifest disdain for the revered intellectual mentor attracted immediate public attention. In response, Lu Xun observed that Shanghai's
flourishing publishing scene seemed enveloped in an intellectual
"haze" pouring forth from a "spate of new periodicals" that had appeared between the solar and lunar New Year celebrations of early 1928.
Of the contributors to these periodicals, he wrote: "They seem to have
exhausted themselves by thinking up great and lofty topics but with
no thought for the deadly dull content that follows."[19] He was referring to the leftist periodicals newly established in January 1928 such as
the Creation Society's *Cultural Critique (Wenhua pipan)* and the Sun Society's *Sun Monthly* and *Modern Stories*.

Lu Xun then remarked that although Feng's caricature of him as a
washed-up carouser rather missed the mark, it was true that a form of
haze beclouded the public discourse of the day. In suggestive language,
Lu Xun presented this haze as an unfortunate by-product of life under
a dictatorship. He wrote that intellectuals, as producers of public discourse, were trapped in a bind. Using the words "bureaucrats and warlords" as a coded reference to the power elite who stood with Chiang
Kai-shek, Lu Xun implied, like Yu Dafu, that the oppressors had become well versed in the language of revolution. He concluded that in
these complicated circumstances, individuals who sought to attract

attention as revolutionary writers were evidently consumed by ambition. Alluding to the murky mix of desire for fame and fear of violence
that he discerned in the proliferating claims and counterclaims about
revolution, Lu Xun remarked:

> To my mind, the source of this haze—although Feng Naichao attri-
> butes it to my "drunken eyes"—remains those bureaucrats and war-
> lords loved by some and loathed by others. Those who are or want to
> be entangled [*guage*] with them often pen jolly sentiments to demon-
> strate to everyone how amiable they are. But being farsighted too,
> they have fearful dreams of the hammer and sickle and dare not
> flatter their present masters too openly. Thus, they are a bit hazy in
> this regard. As for those who are no longer entangled with them, or
> who have never been mixed up with them—those who want to ad-
> vance and join the masses—they should be able to speak without fear.
> Yet, although they seem so imposing in print and present themselves
> as heroes, few are foolish enough to forget who actually wields the
> commander's sword. Thus, they are a bit hazy too. As a consequence,
> those who want to be hazy end up revealing some of their true colors
> while those who want to show their true colors cannot avoid being a
> bit hazy. All of this is happening in the same place at the same time.[20]

In this passage, Lu Xun suggests that Shanghai's "haze" is none
other than the dissembling effects caused by the exploitation of revolutionary rhetoric for personal gain. He disparages this concentrated
activity as the work of anxious schemers on both the left and the
right, accusing them alike of adjusting their prose and hedging their
bets so as to remain within power's unsteady orbit. To Lu Xun, their
revolutionary sentiments are entirely guileful and the very opposite of
the honest intensity he wrote about in September 1927. To understand
his assault on Shanghai's intellectual culture in 1928, we must first
consider several pertinent events in 1927.

Throughout 1927, despite his evident dislike of revolutionary propaganda, Lu Xun had sought some form of practical collaboration with
the Creation Society. Indeed, on 7 November 1926 he confided in a letter
to Xu Guangping that his plans for Guangzhou included forming "a
battle front" with the Creation Society in order to "intensify my assault

on the old society."[21] He reiterated the same idea in a letter to his student Li Jiye (1904–1997) in late September 1927, just before he and Guangping left Guangzhou for Shanghai, noting that he had "lately enjoyed good relations with the Creation Society." He also told Li that, with the Communists under siege, it was all the more urgent for the left to maintain a strong presence in print.[22]

Lu Xun recognized the enormous appeal of the Creation Society among young Chinese radicals. His eagerness to be associated with the Creationists is all the more striking given that in early 1927 Cheng Fangwu had labeled him and other leading lights of Beijing's "literary revolution" as petty-bourgeois dilettantes. Unusually for Lu Xun, he did not retaliate then. He later explained his reluctance to criticize the left as a case of refraining from "casting stones" at the young.[23] Throughout 1927 he maintained a general level of criticism against "revolutionary literature." It was only in 1928, when several members of the Creation Society attacked him in concert, that he began publicly to ridicule their organization.

Meanwhile Guo Moruo's and Cheng Fangwu's roles as propagandists for the Northern Expedition had ended with the launch of Chiang Kai-shek's "Party purification" in April 1927. Guo traveled first to Nanchang, where he took part in a failed Communist uprising in August 1927. He then fled to Hong Kong, where he formally joined the Chinese Communist Party through the recommendations of two leading Party members, Zhou Enlai and Li Yimang (1903–1990). Li in turn became an editor at the Creation Society headquarters in Shanghai.[24] Meanwhile Cheng Fangwu traveled to Japan, where he met with several young Chinese students who were admirers of Fukumoto Kazuo's (1894–1983) brand of "us-or-them" Marxist fundamentalism. Historian Arima Takeo described Fukumoto's argument thus: "The gist . . . was that the Japanese Communist Party should separate the genuine Marxists from the fellow travellers and social democrats and then crystallize them into a well-organized party. Hence the well-known slogan: 'Break away first before we unite.' He saw that 'for the time being, the struggle is to be limited to the realm of the theoretical struggle.'"[25] Fukumoto's Chinese converts, who now included Cheng Fangwu, read this message as highly pertinent to the straitened circumstances of the left after April 1927.

In November 1927 several Creationists asked Lu Xun for assistance in establishing a leftist literary collective. He readily assented when three of the Creation Society's members, Zheng Boqi (1895–1979), Duan Keqing (1899–1994), and Jiang Guangci (1901–1931, who cofounded the Sun Society in January 1928), went to discuss the proposal with him. With Lu Xun's approval, a notice was published in the 3 December 1927 issue of the Shanghai-based *Current News (Shishi xinbao),* announcing the revival of the *Creation Weekly* (a then-defunct journal of the Creation Society) under the auspices of a literary collective consisting of more than thirty members.[26]

According to Guo Moruo, of the first five names on the membership list, Lu Xun's was at the top, followed by "Mai Ke'ang" ("I the Maker," Guo's self-aggrandizing pseudonym), then Cheng Fangwu, Zheng Boqi, and Jiang Guangci—an order suggestive of their relative importance in the hierarchy of the intellectual world. Cheng Fangwu, however, was strongly opposed to the project. He had played no part in the discussions. When the notice was published, he was in Tokyo absorbing Fukumoto's ideas and recruiting Fukumoto's young Chinese admirers (Feng Naichao, Li Chuli [1900–1994], Li Tiesheng, Peng Kang [1901–1968], and Zhu Jingwo [1901–1941]). A week after the notice appeared, these five new Creationists arrived in Shanghai, followed shortly by Cheng.[27]

Despite Lu Xun's frequent criticisms of revolutionary literature, the ever-pragmatic Guo Moruo, living under cover in Shanghai in late 1927, recognized the enormous value of collaborating with China's best-known writer. At the time Guo had become an identified target of the Nationalists and was no longer publishing under his own name. He had planned to visit the Soviet Union but never made the trip. As he was about to set sail for Vladivostok en route to Moscow, he contracted typhoid.[28] His illness coincided with Cheng Fangwu's return from Japan in mid-December and resulted in Cheng's assuming leadership of the Creation Society.

By the time of Guo's recovery in early January 1928, Cheng had already reorganized the Creation Society. Cheng, now equipped with a Fukumoto-inspired agenda, declared the necessity of initiating a theoretical struggle in China's intellectual circles to bring clarity of purpose to the left. According to Zheng Boqi, who had earlier supported

Guo's proposed cooperation with Lu Xun, Cheng's newfound militancy and his leadership of the Creation Society during Guo's illness were key factors that led to abandonment of the already publicized *Creation Weekly* venture. As a result, Creation Society members unanimously supported Cheng's proposal to transform their organization into a center for Marxist studies. They were keen to present themselves as an active vanguard waging an ideological war against the enemies of Marxism. Accordingly they redefined their mission as one of theoretical purification, and this would remain the Society's guiding premise until it was disbanded in late 1929.[29]

With Guo Moruo choosing to live in Japan upon recovering from his illness in early 1928, Cheng became the organization's leader in the last two years of its existence. In recalling these events, Guo wrote:

> When the fire of Japan came up against the waters of Shanghai, a stalemate occurred in no time.... Fangwu was resolutely opposed to the revival of the *Creation Weekly* and saw its mission as a thing of the past. He supported the proposal of the returned students and wanted to publish a militant journal with the title *Currents of Resistance* [*Kang liu*]. In the end, they settled for *Cultural Critique* [*Wenhua pipan*]. They were all very cold to the idea of cooperating with Lu Xun. As we had reached this impasse, I had to choose what attitude to adopt. It was painfully clear that if I were to proceed with my proposal, from the way things were turning out, the Creation Society was at risk of splitting up, and this was something I wanted to avoid at all costs. In any case, because I was about to leave the country, Fangwu had to shoulder enormous responsibilities for the Society. If things accorded with his plans, everyone would be happier, and there would be greater efficiency all around. Besides, who could say at the time that the new proposal—even though it seemed somewhat dangerous—would not turn out to be the better plan? Lacking concrete evidence, I felt I had no grounds to oppose them and so gave in to their proposal.[30]

Wang-chi Wong cautions that the Creationists' recollections of this period were produced in a time when the posthumous Lu Xun was beyond reproach: hence deliberate omissions or distortions were likely.[31]

Feng Naichao's mocking remarks about Lu Xun appeared in the inaugural issue of *Cultural Critique* on 15 January 1928, just one month after the announced revival of the *Creation Weekly*. From Lu Xun's perspective, the Creation Society not only abruptly canceled its already publicized collaboration with him but added insult to the injury by calling him a "petty bourgeois" has-been and a drunkard. The Creationists' denigration of Lu Xun as a melancholic pessimist became a key aspect of their "theoretical struggle." By accusing prominent intellectuals of hindering the advance of revolution (and none was more prominent than Lu Xun), the Creationists ensured they had plenty of publicity for their new cause.

This use of controversy as a self-promoting tool had long been a key feature of the Creation Society's *modus operandi*. From the Society's inauguration in 1921, its founding members (including Yu Dafu) actively sought notoriety. In their initial romantic phase, they produced frequent diatribes against influential pioneers of the Beijing-centered New Culture movement, accusing them of creating a literary monopoly for themselves. Following their conversion to Marxism in the mid-1920s, however, the Creationists began labeling these same individuals as "petty-bourgeois" dilettantes. Hence, when Feng Naichao mocked Lu Xun in his January 1928 article, he was largely repeating disdainful remarks that Cheng Fangwu had published about Lu Xun and Zhou Zuoren a year earlier. But Feng's insinuation that Lu Xun was a drunkard was something new.

Lu Xun had been a periodic heavy drinker. We know from the letters he exchanged with Xu Guangping in the first year of their relationship from 1925 to 1926 that she (then writing as a student) expressed frequent concern about her teacher's health. Lu Xun replied reassuringly that he was "well aware of the dangers of drink" and did not consider his consumption excessive.[32] In his first year in Shanghai, he was drinking heavily again. This was a time when he grew close to Yu Dafu.

In mid-1927 Yu, then already married, was beginning a new life with the famed beauty Wang Yingxia (1908–2000), who remains commemorated to this day as "Miss Hangzhou," a nickname she was given in high school that followed her into adulthood. Her willingness to cohabit with a celebrated writer who, despite his wife and two children, had pursued her relentlessly and publicly declared his love, ensured that the celebrity press in Shanghai provided a steady supply of gossip about their relationship.[33]

In Shanghai, Lu Xun finally set up home with Xu Guangping. When they lived in Guangzhou in 1927, they had shared a house with Lu Xun's old friend Xu Shoushang to maintain the appearance of a platonic friendship between teacher and student. It was in Shanghai that they abandoned this decorum and began living openly as a couple. Like Yu Dafu, Lu Xun was living out of wedlock. Unlike Yu, he had no wish to publicize his private life but attracted constant gossip because of his enormous fame. Xu Guangping effectively became Mrs. Lu Xun, thereby displacing Zhu An, Lu Xun's unloved first wife.

It was well known among Lu Xun's contemporaries that he was deeply unhappy about his arranged marriage of 1906. He ignored Zhu An but faithfully met his obligations to her as a provider. To his friend Xu Shoushang (1883–1948), he described his illiterate traditional wife as an unwanted present from his mother whom he would look after.[34] Zhu An, for her part, lived with and stoically tended to her mother-in-law in Beijing. Her reported response to the news of Lu Xun's open cohabitation with Xu Guangping in Shanghai reflects an old-school poise: Zhu An expressed unhappiness "but acknowledged her husband's right to take a concubine." In present-day scholarship, Zhu An is best remembered for having confided in a family friend that "she had always tried to be a good wife to Lu Xun despite his coldness to her, hoping that he would come to accept her. She compared herself to a snail, climbing slowly but steadily up a wall, but it was hopeless and she was not strong enough to keep climbing."[35] She was clearly no match for Lu Xun's "little devil," the nickname Xu Guangping gave herself when she first wrote to him in 1925.

Lu Xun and Yu Dafu had first met in Beijing and were now drawn together by their shared dislike of Guangzhou's revolutionary discourse and what they had experienced there. The fact that in Shanghai they were living with their de facto partners while remaining married to their first wives undoubtedly brought them even closer.[36] They also shared an interest in encouraging new Chinese writings as well as the translation of leftist literature, and their short-lived journal *Torrent*

(*Benliu*), founded in June 1928 and defunct by December 1929, sought to promote both types of endeavors. In Shanghai the two writers and their partners often dined and partied together.

From the early 1920s, Yu Dafu had actively cultivated a bacchanalian reputation as part of his literary persona. It remains anyone's guess as to whether it was under Yu's influence that Lu Xun began drinking heavily again. Lu Xun never discussed it beyond making the occasional diary jotting about having consumed a large amount of alcohol. For instance, he noted that during New Year's Eve celebrations at the end of 1927, he drank so much that he threw up when he and Guangping returned home.[37]

Hence, despite his anguish about the slaughter he had witnessed in Guangzhou and the ongoing witch hunt against Communists, Lu Xun's arrival in Shanghai in October 1927 was, in many ways, the beginning of a relatively happy period in his life. For nine years thereafter, in Xu Guangping's company, Lu Xun enjoyed the pleasures of China's commercial metropolis. In the late 1920s the couple often ate out, attended parties, and frequented bookshops and cinemas.[38] In a letter dated 14 October 1927 to Li Jiye and Tai Jingnong (1903–1990), two of his favorite students in Beijing, he wrote: "I have been here for ten days and am amazed to discover so many people I know. Dinner parties are keeping me very busy."[39] Lu Xun's youngest brother, the eugenicist Zhou Jianren, worked as an editor at Commercial Press. He found a house for Lu Xun and Xu Guangping in the Jingyun district, close to Baoshan Road, where the Commercial Press offices were located. Jianren, his wife, and their two children lived close by. Lu Xun thus found himself in the very hub of Shanghai's publishing scene, with family members, fellow writers, and friends like Yu Dafu, Ye Shengtao, and Mao Dun (pen name of Shen Yanbing, 1896–1981, then living under cover) as neighbors.[40]

Lu Xun's drinking and his busy social calendar in Shanghai did not pass unnoticed among his detractors on the left. Hence Feng Naichao's mocking of Lu Xun as an old man ensconced in "a dark tavern," gazing with "drunken eyes" at the world outside. There was, however, another barb in Feng's caricature of Lu Xun. Five months earlier in Guangzhou, Lu Xun had delivered two widely noted lectures that centered upon the topic of intoxication and drug-taking in ancient times. The lectures were presented in July 1927 at the invitation of the Nationalist authorities, as part of Guangzhou's summer lecture series that year. They were published as an extended essay in a leading Guang-zhou newspaper starting in August 1927, appearing over six install-ments under the title "The Style and Prose of the Wei-Jin Epoch and Their Connection with Wine and Drugs." In November 1927 the essay was reprinted in the fortnightly Shanghai journal *Beixin* (owned by Lu Xun's former student Li Xiaofeng).[41]

Lu Xun had delivered the lectures under the terrible duress of the anti-Communist purge then under way. Five days earlier, on 18 July 1927, the mayor of Guangzhou and the Education Bureau chief had de-nounced the Communists in their opening speeches for the summer lecture series.[42] Xu Guangping recalled that following the arrest of large numbers of students and teachers after mid-April 1927, several posters appeared on the Sun Yat-sen University campus naming Lu Xun as a subversive influence. Rumors quickly circulated that Lu Xun had "gone into hiding because of his Communist sympathies." More-over, several of Lu Xun's students who had followed him to Guang-zhou from Xiamen University (where he taught briefly in 1926) found themselves labeled as "the Lu Xun clique" and were expelled from Sun Yat-sen University.[43]

Lu Xun later remarked in his personal correspondence that his 1927 Guangzhou lectures on the Wei-Jin epoch were "suffused with emo-tion."[44] It is well known that he turned the lectures into an allegorical criticism of the Nationalist purge of Communists. Highly skilled in the uses of historical innuendo (*yingshe lishi*, a practice so pervasive in Chinese letters it is treated as a discursive tactic in its own right), Lu Xun spoke ostensibly about key personalities and events during an extended period of turbulence in China's ancient past, the Wei-Jin (220–420).

This was a historical period commemorated in numerous classical works of which three proved especially influential: the fifth-century compilation *A New Account of Tales of the World* by Liu Yiqing (403–444), consisting of 1,130 brief anecdotes about 626 personalities who lived in the period 150–420; the mid-seventh-century compilation *History of the Jin* (produced under the aegis of the second Tang emperor, Taizong, 599–649); and the fourteenth-century historical novel *Romance of the*

Three Kingdoms (by Luo Guanzhong, 1330–1400), based on events leading from the short-lived Wei (220–265) to the Jin (265–420).

These works ensured the Wei-Jin a unique place in Chinese culture.
It was not only renowned as a time of ruthless politics but became a
vivid repository of stories about exemplary heroes and archvillains, their
exploits, and their outlandish spiritual pursuits. The stories in turn
shaped the poetics of Chinese scholarship and literature. Generations
of authors would find in the Wei-Jin archetypes of courage and hubris
a perennial source of allegorical inspiration when writing about their
own times of chaos and violence.

In speaking of the Wei-Jin, Lu Xun was thus engaged in the time-
honored practice of tacitly comparing the villains of his day to those
of ancient yore. Summarizing the view presented in the memoirs of
Ouyang Shan, a student of Lu Xun's who attended his lectures on the
Wei-Jin, James Pusey writes:

> Lu Xun was surely "guilty" of "satirizing the present with the past."
> Through stories of the third-century despots, Cao Cao and Sima Yi,
> who killed Kong Rong and Ji Kang [also pronounced Xi Kang], he
> satirized Jiang Jieshi [Chiang Kai-shek]. Through stories of third-
> century "Confucians" who in Confucius's name trampled on the
> principles of Confucius, he satirized Nationalists who in Sun Yat-
> sen's name trampled on the principles of Sun Yat-sen. Conversely, he
> called those accused of opposing Confucius, or Sun Yat-sen, their
> "true followers." Ji Kang and his friends, he said, were like "true fol-
> lowers of Sun Yat-sen" who "scowl when they hear people talk hypo-
> critically" about Sun Yat-sen's Three Principles.[45]

Lu Xun's remarks on that occasion also reflected a certain confidence
that his fame offered him sufficient protection from persecution—so
long as he refrained from openly accusing the Nationalists. In coyly
comparing false praise of Sun Yat-sen to the hypocrisy of third-century
Confucian prose, he was careful to direct his accusations only at the
"warlords of the north," the militarist allies of Chiang Kai-shek (such
as Feng Yuxiang and Yan Xishan) and not at Chiang himself.[46] In 1932
he described his Guangzhou writings of mid- to late 1927 as "stumbling words, uttered indirectly and in fear."[47]

In the second of Lu Xun's Wei-Jin lectures, he commemorated the famous group of third-century literati retrospectively hailed as the "Seven Worthies of the Bamboo Grove" *(zhulin qi xian)*.[48] He praised them, in particular Xi Kang (223-262) and Ruan Ji (210-263), the best-known of the worthies and the personal favorites of lettered Chinese, for leading a rustic life and for favoring the delirium of wine and drugs over managing affairs of state in the metropolis. He claimed that their reclusive eccentricities such as "drinking while naked and hatless" reflected not only freedom from social niceties but fidelity to a cosmic truth. He urged his audience not to confuse such bizarre conduct with the mundane idea of "impropriety" *(wuli)* but to contemplate instead the necessity of cleaving to a higher morality in an age of chaos and violence. In this connection, he added that the difference between Xi Kang and Ruan Ji was that whereas the former was prone to expressing his views, which brought about his untimely demise, the latter "said very little concerning ethics and thus enjoyed a different outcome."[49]

Lu Xun's use of the word "haze" in 1928 marks a distinct complication of his earlier views on critical perspicacity. Whereas he had previously merely disparaged unthinking calls for "blood and iron," he now sharpened his criticism to identify revolutionary rhetoric as a smokescreen. In the passage cited earlier, he implied that to see clearly was to see an orchestrated "haze," one whose true nature was a tangled morass of undeclared intentions. In this context he used the compound verb *guage* (mixed up, embroiled, caught up) to draw attention to the dark or invisible forces he perceived as motivating intellectual and literary production in Shanghai.

Entangled in Shanghai

In his writings of 1928, Lu Xun often wryly described himself as utterly incapable of prescience. Reprising Feng Naichao's taunt in an open letter of April 1928, he stated that the horrors he experienced in revolutionary Guangzhou revealed that he was, indeed, "without foresight" and thus no different from someone who lived in a drunken haze. He went on to observe that because deficient foresight also affected "those revolutionary writers" in Guangzhou "who were then at a crossroads;

who were among the masses and the officials; who could transcend their age and see fifty years ahead," they too "did not embark on any 'theoretical struggle' just then." Hinting at the abrupt shift from a conciliatory "national unity" to an uncompromising "class struggle" in the discourse of the left, he wrote that if they had had the gift of prescience, "they might have saved several lives."[50]

In Shanghai, Lu Xun became preoccupied with the corrosive effects of commerce and politics on language. In his essays from 1928 through 1931, he made frequent mention of the problems that calculations of profit presented for literature and criticism. In particular, he scorned the advocates of "revolutionary literature" in the Creation Society as hungry for fame and claimed that, under cover of promoting Marxism, they were but catering to the clamor for all things revolutionary in Shanghai publishing. But the fact remains that the brutal exigencies of the time afflicted his language as much as his contemporaries', compelling him to make extensive use of innuendo and indirection (thereby generating a haze of his own) in the bid to avoid trouble. Moreover, although he accused others of currying favor with the new political masters in Nanjing, he benefited from having friends in high places in the new southern capital.

From December 1927 to January 1932, Lu Xun held the position of "writer by special appointment" *(teyue zhuangaoyuan)* at the Academy of Higher Education (Daxue yuan) in Nanjing. This was a title created for him by his mentor Cai Yuanpei (1868–1940), director of the academy, through the recommendation of Xu Shoushang, Lu Xun's close friend and the academy's secretary general.[51] Cai had been chancellor of Peking University in the late 1910s and was the undisputed patron of Beijing's New Culture. The luminaries of New Culture, including Lu Xun, were individuals whose careers Cai had fostered through academic and official appointments. There was a particularly strong bond between Lu Xun and Cai as fellow townsmen from Shaoxing. Shen Yinmo (1883–1971), a contemporary of theirs, noted that their closeness led Cai to invite Lu Xun's brother, Zhou Zuoren, to teach at Peking University in 1917.[52]

In October 1927, at Chiang Kai-shek's invitation, Cai went to Nanjing to become, in effect, the Nationalist government's minister of higher education. In appointing Lu Xun to his academy, Cai paid his famous protégé a generous monthly stipend of 300 Chinese silver dollars simply to facilitate his literary career in Shanghai. (The silver dollar was the closest to a standard currency at the time.) The funds proved very handy for building Lu Xun's personal library in Shanghai. More importantly, the position gave him some institutional protection from political harassment.[53]

Among the many epithets that the Creation Society created for Lu Xun in 1928, Feng Naichao called him a would-be "Robinson Crusoe," adding caustically that this castaway was unique, for his "drifter's life" was lived not in isolation but on "Nanjing Road of the twentieth century" (ershi shijide Nanjing lutou).[54] Feng's use of lutou, a compound word for "road" with the added connotation of "connections and cachet," was clearly aimed at Lu Xun's friendship with Cai Yuanpei and Xu Shoushang. Moreover, at the start of his essay, Feng had derided Lu Xun's comments about people's entanglements with power. And indeed Lu Xun's relationship with the Ministry of Higher Education was a highly privileged "entanglement," for he was required neither to visit Nanjing nor to undertake any work for his employer.

For Lu Xun to accuse his contemporaries of seeking opportunistic relationships from the vantage of his own extraordinary good fortune is not without irony. But it was also precisely the fact that he was not beholden to any political master that gave him critical distance from the highly compromised discourse of revolution. In this regard, his observations of the late 1920s resonate with his earlier condemnations of wenyan as a language fatally corroded by power.

In 1925 he had written that for all their wenyan erudition, China's premodern literati had little to offer posterity except the cautionary tale of what becomes of a language whose exponents are perennial servants of dynastic power. He observed that in a society in which the authorities had succeeded in creating rules for everything from "forced labor and payment of tax grain to ways of kowtowing and praising the sagely ruler," the lettered were reduced to wishing for either "the times when we longed to be slaves but couldn't" or "the times when we succeeded in becoming slaves."[55] By this he meant that wenyan was so thoroughly wedded to despotism as to encourage only an abject longing to serve either a present or a future master.

In 1928, however, it was the users of *baihua*, not *wenyan*, whom he accused of demonstrating these abject qualities. Hence, people who "pen jolly sentiments" to please their Nationalist masters to show "how amiable they are" were nonetheless preyed on by their "fearful dreams of the hammer and sickle and dare not flatter their present masters too openly." Similarly, those on the left who "present themselves as heroes" ended up producing a densely abstract discourse for fear of attracting the unwanted attention of the Nationalist authorities. He would have been sympathetic to the latter but for the fact that the Creation Society had turned him into a key target of its "theoretical struggle."[56]

In the mid-1920s, when he lived in Beijing, Lu Xun had already accused several of his contemporaries of perverting *baihua*. Chen Yuan (who wrote as Chen Xiying; 1896–1970) of the Crescent Moon Society was his bête noire. Lu Xun wrote that people like Chen were servile "helpers" *(bangmangzhe)* of the warlords and hence enemies of the left. Despite his own misgivings about the "praise of blood and iron," in 1925 Lu Xun was supportive of the young radicals who traveled to Guangzhou to join the revolution. But by the time he gave his Wei-Jin lectures in July 1927, he was deeply pessimistic about what he saw as an ingrained Chinese tendency, even among young radicals, to sacralize power.

As noted earlier, Lu Xun's discussion of Cao Cao on that occasion remains widely regarded as an allusion to Chiang Kai-shek's brutality. But this use of innuendo was only a small part of his critique. In fact Lu Xun devoted far more space to a melancholy exposition of how power had corrupted Cao Cao's use of language. He began his lecture by expressing admiration for Cao Cao (d. 220 C.E.), regent to the last emperor of the Eastern Han, who was posthumously honored by his son Cao Pi (187–226) as the founding emperor of the Wei dynasty.

Lu Xun said that Cao Cao ruled with an iron fist because he lived in a terrible age and noted that "even though I am not of his party" and despite the vilification of Cao Cao in subsequent centuries, the man had genuine talent and was "at the very least a hero." In particular, he praised Cao Cao for displaying and promoting an "unconfined spontaneity" *(tongtuo)* in a time of deadly rivalries and palace intrigues. He observed that this attitude was all the more remarkable when considered against the punctilious habits of Confucian moralists of the day, who, in fearful reaction to court-led purges, fetishized decorum and styled themselves as representatives of the "pure stream" *(qing liu)*. Of Cao Cao's essays, he noted that the few that were extant revealed an exemplary capacity "to write as he thought, without the least inhibition." Thus Cao Cao pioneered "a clear and austere style" *(qingjunde fengge)* characterized by "unconfined spontaneity."[57]

Lu Xun then observed that Cao Cao had betrayed these virtues when dispatching those whom he perceived as a threat. He claimed that in slaying Kong Rong (153–208, Cao's rival and interlocutor at the Han court) Cao showed no regard for Kong's candor and was alleged to have justified the killing on the grounds that Kong lacked filial piety. Lu Xun explained that Kong was known for favoring merit over blood ties and had once declared that during a famine a person ought to feed a deserving person rather than an evil father. As this was the type of thing Cao admired, it was ironic that he killed Kong for being unfilial. In musing about the deleterious effects of power on Cao Cao's character, Lu Xun noted that, despite Cao's insistence on recruiting individuals for their acuity and talent and not for their displays of loyalty and filial piety, no one would have dared to point out his dishonesty for fear of being sent to the gallows.[58]

Later in the lecture Lu Xun returned to filial piety and loyalty and their negative effects on Chinese culture. He observed that these two Confucian virtues were the staple justifications for dynastic rule in China but that the usurpation-prone epoch of the Wei-Jin leaned on the whole toward filial piety: "Why did they rule in the name of filial piety? This is because when people ascend to power through a forced abdication and other forms of trickery, they don't stand on firm ground if they start advocating loyalty as their style of rule. for it will only complicate what they say and do. Hence they must resort to the rule of filial piety."[59]

These remarks enrich our sense of what Lu Xun meant by "entanglements." He implied that the will to power unavoidably devolves into a demand for personal allegiance for which loyalty and filial piety supply the necessary justification and of which the latter proves the more binding. Toward the end of his second lecture, he observed that like their Wei-Jin predecessors, China's modern warlords, who declared themselves disciples of Sun Yat-sen, could now avail themselves of the "Three Principles of the People" as a weapon. He suggested that armed with the instructions of the Republic's founding father, they were able to accuse their critics as unfilial sons and daughters and thereby sanctify their murders.

In this instance, Lu Xun was gesturing to the coalition that Chiang Kai-shek formed in 1927 with the powerful northern warlords, Feng Yuxiang (1882–1948) and Yan Xishan (1883–1960), who between them controlled a vast region extending from Shandong in the northeast to Shanxi in the northwest. Feng and Yan were also dominant across Henan, Shensi, Gansu, and Qinghai in the west as well as Hebei and areas farther north. Chiang reached a similar accommodation with the southern warlord Li Zongren (1890–1969) and Li's ally Li Jichen (1885–1959), whose combined influence extended across Guangxi, Guangdong, Hunan, and Hubei.[60] As Communists were being slaughtered in the name of "Party purification," these alliances expedited Chiang's continued prosecution of the Northern Expedition and facilitated the capture of Beijing from Zhang Zuolin by June 1928.

In defeat, Zhang, who received Japanese aid, was advised to return to Manchuria, but as he was fleeing Beijing he was killed in a train accident. In December 1928 Zhang's son, Zhang Xueliang (1901–2001), ceded control of Manchuria and pledged allegiance to Chiang's Nationalist government.[61] In the intellectual discourse of the time, the militarists who shared Chiang's nationalistic goals became collectively known as "the new warlords."

In particular, Feng Yuxiang, nicknamed "the Christian warlord," had much in common with Chiang Kai-shek. Like Chiang, he had traveled and studied in the Soviet Union and had benefited from Soviet financial and military aid since 1926. Feng built his National People's Army in Soviet style, introducing a political department that extended into every level, thereby providing his troops with both military training and ideological instruction. Feng's powerful modern army, like those of the other "new warlords," contributed significantly to the Northern Expedition's victories.[62]

In July 1928, Chiang Kai-shek, in the company of Feng Yuxiang, Yan Xishan, Li Zongren, and the Muslim general Bai Chongxi (1893–1966), paid his respects to Sun Yat-sen at the Temple of the Azure Cloud, which housed Sun's coffin, in the Western Hills outside Beijing. In his biography of Chiang, Jay Taylor writes: "Chiang put his hand on the casket and wept openly. Feng and Yan also wiped their eyes. The five generals each proclaimed undying loyalty to the founder and to the Chinese nation."[63]

These were undoubtedly genuine quasi-filial emotions and, as such, have nothing in common with the disingenuous uses of filial piety that Lu Xun attacked in his Wei-Jin lectures. Lu Xun himself clearly revered his mother and was not opposed to filial piety as such. Rather, he saw this Confucian disposition to obedient reverence as open to abuse: it was because Confucianism fetishized filial piety that it turned from a simple moral obligation into an excuse for an oppressive compact. Thus in a society such as that of the Wei-Jin, which ostensibly "worshipped teachings of propriety," individuals perceived to be "destroying such teachings" were often "the very ones who actually cleaved to Confucius and regarded his code of propriety as a true treasure."[64]

Two years earlier, in 1925, he had used a similar argument to accuse Chen Yuan of toadying to warlord power under cover of defending social stability. Chen, as editor of the highly regarded *Contemporary Review (Xiandai pinglun)*, had published a mocking commentary in his magazine about students protesting in Beijing against the imminent closure of Peking Women's Normal College. Chen's haughty wit was a particular attraction of *Contemporary Review*, and he published a regular editorial column under the heading "Causeries" (*xianhua*, literally "casual chats"), in which he discussed a range of topical issues, including the fateful topic of the student protest.[65] On this occasion, Chen had supported the decision taken by Zhang Shizhao (1881–1973), minister of education under the then ruling Beiyang warlord Duan Qirui (1864–1936), to close Peking Women's Normal College on the grounds that rising student activism posed a threat to the college's proper functioning. The college's headmistress, Yang Yinyu (1884–1938), had earlier tried unsuccessfully to suppress student activism.[66]

Undoubtedly Lu Xun's deepening love for Xu Guangping, then a leading activist at the college, exacerbated his anger against these critics of student activism. In his verbal war with Chen, Lu Xun also attacked headmistress Yang; he accused her of projecting onto her students fears stemming from her own sexually repressed nature.[67] As hostilities escalated between Lu Xun and Chen Yuan, other Peking University academics entered the fray. On 18 August 1925 a group of academics including Lu Xun and Zhou Zuoren persuaded the university's policy-making council to sunder relations with the Ministry of Education in a gesture of solidarity with the protesting students. Lu Xun was promptly dismissed from the Ministry of Education as a troublemaker, and a fortnight later Duan Qirui's cabinet cut off all funding for Peking University.[68]

Public outrage at the university's closure forced Zhang Shizhao to resign as education minister in early December 1925, facilitating Lu Xun's reinstatement in January 1926. But even though Lu Xun emerged triumphant, he never forgave Chen and Chen's supporters. The Crescent Moon Society, to which Chen belonged, thereafter became a frequent object of Lu Xun's ridicule. His intense dislike of Chen is evident in remarks such as those published in December 1925, when he accused Chen of turning *baihua* into a cheap gimmick, describing him as "that kind of so-called 'man of letters' who fancies himself a critic but actually serves in the retinue of some royal personage: a bodyguard who calls out Tolstoy this, Tostolyena that, pointing and gesticulating everywhere he goes as if he were a moving screen for His Royal Highness."[69]

In February 1926 he broadened his assault to include other members of the Crescent Moon Society. He wrote that their complicity with power reminded him of a nimble-footed "goat wearing a little bell around its neck," with the bell serving as "the insignia of the educated class." He also accused the Crescent Moon members of elitist tendencies that betrayed the egalitarian purpose of *baihua*. Lu Xun likened them to the goats of northern farmers, noting that because these creatures were trained to lead their flocks of sheep to the slaughterhouse, they were themselves spared from the butcher's knife. He quipped that because his rivals were quick-witted and adept at making themselves useful, they proved more resourceful than their masters and better at survival than even the late Yuan Shikai and the reigning warlords who were his heirs.[70]

Chen Yuan replied in kind to Lu Xun's vitriolic caricatures. His open letter of January 1926, addressed to the celebrated poet Xu Zhimo (1897–1931), who had also been a target of Lu Xun's, remains widely quoted to this day as the first polemical attack against Lu Xun of a deeply personal nature. The letter was filled with such invective as:

> Mr. Lu Xun makes false charges against others as soon as he puts pen to paper. He subtracts and adds; if he's not quoting you out of context then he's concocting some story or other. Yet, as the "intellectual authority" in China, he is very quick to take offense. Someone told me: "What Mr. Lu Xun lacks is a great big mirror in which to see his great big face." I told him he was wrong; Lu Xun does have a great big mirror. You've no doubt heard the story about how Zhao Zi'ang [the famous Yuan-era artist Zhao Mengfu, 1254–1322] drew horses. To draw a particular posture, he faced the mirror and looked at the image of himself, lying on the ground, making that posture. And so it is with Lu Xun, whose essays are written facing the mirror. Each and every one of his denunciations can be leveled back at him. If you don't believe me, I'd be happy to bet on it.[71]

In Shanghai, Lu Xun continued to mock the Crescent Moon Society. He alternated between calling them "upright gentlemen" (zhengren junzi), using this Confucian epithet to deride them as sycophants of power, and reviling them more straightforwardly as "pugs." The Crescent Moon Society had relocated to Shanghai by 1927. Unlike the leftists who fled the Northern Expedition's command centers in Guangzhou and Wuhan to seek safe haven in Shanghai's foreign concessions, the Crescent Moon members traveled to Shanghai as intellectual refugees from Beijing, fleeing the brutal rule of the warlord Zhang Zuolin.

Many of Lu Xun's contemporaries and subsequent scholars have observed that his intense dislike of the Crescent Moon members bordered on the irrational, and that he was unfairly dismissive of their contributions to a cosmopolitan intellectual discourse in China. Yet he had his reasons for hating what they represented. He regarded their attempts at establishing new standards of art, criticism, literature, and theater as unconscionably congenial to the powerful in a time of violence. When he mocked them as "upright gentlemen," he implied that the universal values they invoked (whether of beauty, humanism, or rights) resembled the "pure stream" discourse of the Wei-Jin Confucian moralists. More fundamentally, he viewed them as people of an institutional bent who would turn *baihua* into the monopoly of the university-educated.[72]

The majority of Crescent Moon members had received their graduate training in the United States and England, and the society formed in Beijing in 1923 was named after the "Crescent Moon" poems of India's poet laureate, Rabindranath Tagore.[73] Led by Hu Shi, Xu Zhimo, and Chen Yuan, the society had operated mainly as a social club in its Beijing years. Its influence derived from the fact that its wealthy and erudite members were key members of the New Culture movement. Hu Shi, whose status was equal to Lu Xun's as a fellow pioneer of the "literary revolution," was widely regarded as China's leading liberal thinker. Chen, a professor of English at Peking University in the early to mid-1920s, was an influential essayist and social commentator, while the poet Xu Zhimo was admired for both his literary talent and his romantic liaisons.

The society's members enjoyed dining together and putting on plays and soirées for their own amusement. They had no intention of presenting a group identity but nonetheless acquired one by 1925. This was partly because of *Contemporary Review*, the Beijing-based journal that Chen Yuan founded and edited in 1925, and the *Morning Post Literary Supplement*, which Xu Zhimo began editing from October 1925. Both journals became publicly identified as the Crescent Moon Society's vehicles even though only some of the society's members were published in them.[74] After the society's relocation to Shanghai in 1927, its members sought to strengthen the group's public profile through the founding of the journal *Crescent Moon Monthly*, whose first issue appeared in March 1928.

In early 1929, at the instigation of the society's two leading political thinkers, Hu Shi and Luo Longji (1898-1965), the journal announced a shift of focus from art and literature to politics. Shortly afterward Luo published a lengthy article in which he accused the Nationalist government outright not only of blatant hypocrisy in its advocacy of "democracy and human rights" but of a "one-party totalitarian rule" more severe than "the Communist Party of Russia and the Fascist Party of Italy." This resulted in Luo's detention for a brief period and the temporary banning of *Crescent Moon Monthly* throughout Nationalist-controlled China.[75]

Despite these hardships suffered by his adversaries, Lu Xun remarked uncharitably in a letter of 17 August 1929 to his former student and confidant Zhang Tingqian (1901–1981): "There's been a sudden rush to action at Crescent Moon. They seem set to replace *Contemporary Review* in a new bid to serve the government as an honest friend [*zhengyou*]. This is understandable since *Contemporary Review* can now hardly come to the fore, having once served as Duan Qirui's honest friend."[76] In his ironic use of the term *zhengyou*—the classical ideal of candor in friendship—Lu Xun implied that the Crescent Moon members ultimately sought the patronage of a "court," whether that of the warlord Duan or of Generalissimo Chiang. Prejudiced as he was in scorning their advocacy of human rights as outright hypocrisy, Lu Xun was nonetheless attempting to highlight an important difference between himself and his former *New Youth* associate Hu Shi.

Jerome Grieder provided the useful observation that Hu Shi chose to live in Shanghai's International Settlement from 1927 to 1930 not only to avail himself of the legal protections of the city's foreign concessions to publish freely but to also be within proximity of powerbrokers in Chiang Kai-shek's government. As Grieder put it, Hu Shi "liked to think" of his position as one of "loyal opposition" despite his evident closeness to several of Nanjing's senior bureaucrats.[77] Lu Xun conversely regarded himself as a critic of Nanjing, and while he benefited enormously from his closeness to Cai Yuanpei, he did not share Hu Shi's desire to exercise political influence.

Lu Xun undoubtedly counted the urbane members of the Crescent Moon Society among those he mocked in March 1928 for attempting to please the authorities with their "jolly sentiments" and amiable demeanor. Even though the society's members had presented a scathing criticism of revolutionary literature in the manifesto of their *Crescent Moon Monthly* (discussed in the next section), Lu Xun regarded them as

irredeemably entangled with power and as enemies of honest communication. He had a very different and far more intricate view of the entanglements of the radical left.

Lu Xun was divided in his feelings about the Communists: there
were individuals whom he favored and others whom he despised as
dogmatists and opportunists. He seemed to have been largely unaware
of the bitter factionalism within the Chinese Communist Party after
April 1927. To a large extent, his support for the Party was based on the
camaraderie he enjoyed with several of its members. He was well acquainted with its founding figures Chen Duxiu and Li Dazhao, who
were fellow pioneers of *baihua* and with whom he exchanged ideas and
letters. When Chen left Beijing for Shanghai in 1920, he frequently
asked Lu Xun and his brother Zhou Zuoren for manuscripts to publish
in his journals. Of the short story "Storm" *(Fengbo)* that Lu Xun submitted to Chen's Shanghai-based journal *Weekly Review (Meizhou pinglun)*
in August 1920, Chen expressed his gratitude and remarked in a letter
to Zhou of 22 August that he was "fully prostrated in admiration."[78]

Lu Xun did not leave a written account of his impressions of Chen
Duxiu, but he did write a foreword for an anthology of Li Dazhao's essays in 1933. In it he expressed guilt for not having been as badly affected by Li's execution as he was by the deaths of his own students. Li,
who was Peking University's much-revered head librarian in the heyday of Beijing's New Culture in the early 1920s, was arrested and hanged
in April 1927 under orders from Zhang Zuolin. Commemorating Li's
death six years later, Lu Xun wrote that although Li's arguments "may
not be appropriate today, they are nonetheless immortal because they
are the work of a pioneer and a landmark in revolutionary history."
Against this praise of Li, Lu Xun contrasted "the piled-up tomes of
dead and living swindlers," and although he left the "swindlers" unnamed, he noted drily that their works were "beginning to totter so
that even bookshops have to make a sacrifice and sell them at a 20 or
30 percent reduction."[79]

It was Lu Xun's friendships with younger Chinese Communists, no-
tably Rou Shi (pen name of Zhao Pingfu; 1901–1931), Feng Xuefeng, and
Qu Qiubai, that defined his positive attitude to the Communist Party.
Of these three men, in 1928 Lu Xun knew only Rou Shi; he would meet

Feng in 1929 and Qu in 1932. Qu had corresponded extensively with Lu Xun in 1931, prior to their first meeting. Recalling the friendship between Lu Xun and Qiubai in her memoirs, Xu Guangping wrote that the chemistry between them was instant: "They were as intimate as close relatives; there was no ceremony between them."[80] Lu Xun's fondness for Qu is evident in the restrained yet emotional couplet he composed and presented to him in March 1933: "To find a true friend in a lifetime is contentment itself, and for as long as one lives, he will be looked upon as dwelling in one's heart."[81] Of the three men, only Feng would outlive Lu Xun. Rou Shi and Qu were arrested and executed by the Nationalist authorities, the former in 1931 and the latter in 1935.

Lu Xun's deep affection for these individuals stands in stark contrast to his disdain for his Marxist detractors in the late 1920s and those whom he regarded as opponents in the League of Left-Wing Chinese Writers in the 1930s. He had joined the League because he was keen to defend a "literature for the masses" but found himself wholly at odds with the doctrinal zeal that motivated the majority of his leftist peers.

Upon being theoretically "struggled against" by the Creation Society in early 1928, he wrote to his student Tai Jingnong in February that he felt "most unsettled." Recalling his highly publicized quarrel with Chen Yuan in 1925, he told Tai: "The situation in Shanghai is a good deal more complicated than in Beijing; the method of attack is different, and I am forced to mount a defense in each and every instance. It is a sorry business."[82] Six years later, in 1934, he made a similar comparison. By then Lu Xun's public quarrels with the Creation Society were long over, and he and they were fellow members of the Left-Wing League. Nonetheless he shared this confidence with the young editor Yang Jiyun (1910–1996) in a letter of 18 December 1934:

The pugs don't scare me. I find far more disturbing those so-called "comrades-in-arms" who say one thing while thinking another precisely because there is no way of defending oneself from their attacks. For instance, people of Shaobo's ilk [Tian Han, 1898–1968, the Creation Society's leading dramatist] remain a puzzle: I don't know what makes them tick. To protect myself from the rear, I cannot face such enemies head-on and hence must adopt a supine posture. It is truly exhausting to have to be ever alert to attacks from both the front and the rear. But these people have not caused my poor health, which is nothing but the result of old age. All the same, I can't help feeling a real sense of outrage every now and then. What a lot of my energy they have wasted that could have been better spent on doing something of real worth.[83]

In 1928 Lu Xun frequently accused his critics in the Creation Society and Sun Society of orchestrating a meaningless controversy and of exploiting his fame to attract public notice. In the inaugural January 1928 issue of the Creation Society's journal *Cultural Critique,* Cheng Fangwu and his radical Marxist recruits had written emphatically of the need to expose "bourgeois" and "petty bourgeois" elements hindering China's revolutionary literature. On 16 April 1928 Lu Xun published an open letter in which he mocked their "revolutionary literature" as nothing more than a "signboard" under which "writers talk up the essays of their mates while never daring to look directly at the present brutality and darkness."[84] The vanity of such "revolutionary writers," he continued, deprived them of basic honesty, and hence their "revolutionary literature" became "more poorly written than brief news reports." He ended the essay with a sardonic quote: "Let me illustrate this with the quintessential concluding lines of a play by Feng Naichao. 'Prostitute: I no longer fear the darkness. Thief: Let us revolt!'"[85]

This was one of numerous polemical texts by Lu Xun in which he described his accusers as imposters anxious to appear as heroes while failing to discuss the quotidian violence surrounding them. To highlight the vanity of the Creationists, Lu Xun also made several sardonic references to their fondness for the latest Western attire. In his memoirs, Lu Xun's protégé Feng Xuefeng recalled his mentor regaling him with stories about the fashion-conscious Creation Society and about how in Guangzhou its members "did not take part in any real struggles but swaggered about in high leather boots, looking very grand and acting like officials."[86]

To show that he was not merely trading insults with the Creation Society, Lu Xun published an essay on 30 April 1928, "The Prospect of Purging the Communists," in which he praised a recent news report about the public beheading of eight suspected Communists. He wrote that this unvarnished account surpassed "all the 'revolutionary' or 'realist' literature" he had come across.[87] Lu Xun undoubtedly intended the word *daguan* (prospect) in the title of this essay to echo the famous Prospect Garden *(daguan yuan)* in the classic Qing-era novel *The Dream of the Red Chamber,* by Cao Xueqin (d. 1763 or 1764) a work with which he was deeply familiar). In Cao's novel, Prospect Garden serves as a complex metaphor for the twists and turns of Chinese history, viewed from a panoramic perspective.[88]

Implicit in Lu Xun's use of *daguan* is a transposition of this same idea to suggest that the abnormal everydayness of public executions now offered the clearest *prospect* of the nation. The flesh-and-blood spectators at the execution ground had become thoroughly desensitized to the suffering of their fellow humans. In lamenting this brute indifference, he mourned the remoteness of "the people" as a transcendent idea. As for the literary merits of the report itself, Lu Xun highlighted its concise summary of the prisoners' genders and ages and the sparse account of the assembled crowd at their execution, noting that the use of a pared-down language compelled readers to exercise their minds and imaginations:

> As I read it, I felt I could see the head impaled at Court Gate and the three headless female corpses at the Teachers' Association. They must have been stripped to the waist at least too—or perhaps I am guessing wrongly because I'm just too full of darkness [*tai hei'an*]. . . . Let me add a few more fanciful details: the spellbound look on the faces in the crowd, with some already in a trance and others showing a sated expression. . . . I think it's the critic Rogachevsky who said, "Andreyev tries hard to frighten us but we're not scared in the least, while Chekhov, who doesn't even try, fills us with fear."[89]

He concluded the essay with the hyperbolic claim that decades of chronic warfare had produced a barbarous appetite among the Chinese such that "All they want to see are 'heads' and 'female corpses.'"[90] The corpse of the executed, as a recurring motif in Lu Xun's fiction and essays, testifies to the magnitude of the despotic state and is a figure around which he typically provided graphic descriptions of the scene of execution. Lu Xun regarded these spectacles of state violence as in-stilling not only fear but a fascination among the spectators with watching the slaughter of their fellow humans. For him, executions were merely the grotesque obverse of the same tyranny beatified as the belletristic orthodoxy of *wenyan:* two sides of the same coin.

In 1919 he had written that *wenyan* was a language that, having long served to laud imperial pretenders as "sagely and martial," had become constitutively oriented toward "bestial desires for power and prestige, progeny, riches and treasures" and accordingly bereft of any genuine vocabulary of "liberty and equality" to foster "mutual aid and coexis-tence." He added that *wenyan*'s antiquarian tendencies further encour-aged a narcissistic obsession with posthumous immortality.[91] In the early 1930s Lu Xun pondered the effects of this ancient inclination to power on those of his revolution-minded contemporaries who aspired to vanguard status.

In the essay "The Evolution of Hooligans," published on 1 January 1930, just two months before he assumed nominal leadership of the Left-Wing League, Lu Xun surveyed with biting wit an enduring cul-ture of bullying that had developed out of centuries-old dynastic rule in China.[92] He claimed that the educated elite in China could be roughly divided into the "disciples of Confucius who became priests [*ru*] and those of Mozi who became knights-errant [*xia*]."[93] Starting the essay with the remark that Confucius (551–479 B.C.E.) and Mozi (470–391 B.C.E.) were genuine reformers who used the idea of heaven *(tian)* to intimidate the mortal rulers of their day with the fearful pros-pect of being answerable to a higher power, Lu Xun wrote that, over time, their acolytes, in particular the "crafty ones," utilized the teach-ings of their masters to secure powerful patrons among the aristoc-racy and influential officials. To accentuate the longevity of this prac-tice, he observed that it was rife by the time of the Han dynasty (206 B.C.E.–220 C.E.).[94]

He devoted the remainder of the essay to an examination of how the Mohist knights-errant degenerated first into bandits (*qiangdao*) and then sank even lower to become hooligans *(liumang)*. By innuendo, he suggested that his Marxist accusers resembled hooligans. He noted that the bandits of yore were immortalized in the Ming-era novel *The*

Water Margin and that it was vital to note of this highly appealing work about noble outlaws that they restricted themselves to "fighting other bandits—namely those who were not 'carrying out the way of Heaven'" and were eager nonetheless to serve the dynastic state as personified in the emperor. He added: "They were slaves after all." With the founding of the Manchu Qing, the bandit archetype in literature was transmuted into the image of the loyal henchman who sits on the fringes of power. Lu Xun described people of this type as "obeying the orders of one side [the powerful] while availing themselves of the many opportunities to posture as heroes to the other side [the powerless]."[95]

He wrote that this henchman mentality was the genesis of hooliganism in late dynastic China. Of these early modern hooligans, he observed:

> In the interest of defending public morality, they beat up inebriated monks, arrest men and women for having sex, and humiliate prostitutes and black-marketeers. In order to show their disdain for the ignorant, they cheat and bully peasants who don't know the regulations of the foreign concessions. In the name of cherishing and upholding order, they taunt and berate women with short hair and show their hatred for social reformers.[96]

Lu Xun explained that these hooligans were able to throw their weight around because they had powerful backers and carefully chose their victims so that the people they bullied were "not the least formidable." Lu Xun clearly wanted his readers to know that he was implicating the Creation Society as he ended the essay with the remark: "If the present situation degenerates even further, people of this ilk will become the protagonists of our literature. I await the next work of the 'revolutionary writer' Zhang Ziping."[97]

This concluding remark carried a complex insinuation, for Zhang (1893–1959) was a founding member of the Creation Society who had parted ways with the group in 1925 to pursue fame and fortune as a writer of popular romances. Nonetheless, when "revolutionary literature" became fashionable in Shanghai in 1928, Zhang declared his revolutionary intent and published two successful novels that year about the agonies of love in a revolutionary climate.[98] By mocking Zhang, Lu

Xun used this former Creationist to exemplify the profit-driven nature of the group as a whole. Moreover, in his observations about hooliganism, he suggested that the Creation Society had brandished Marxism as a master weapon to attack their contemporaries as "petty-bourgeois laggards."

Eighteen months later, in a public lecture on 20 July 1931, Lu Xun produced a fuller exposition on the hooliganism of the Creation Society. By then the organization had been defunct for two years. Lu Xun's continued denunciation of the Creation Society provides some indication of how aggrieved he felt about the attacks on him and of the Creationists' erstwhile habit of tarring with the same brush *Threads of Talk*, the journal he edited in Shanghai, and *Crescent Moon Monthly*, the journal of his adversaries.

When the Creationists attacked Lu Xun in 1928, it was on their own initiative. Communist Party leaders played no part in these invented "struggles," for they were too preoccupied at the time with the Party's own internal conflicts. Nonetheless, the Creation Society and its ally, the Sun Society (founded in January 1928 by young Communist intellectuals), were keen to describe their own publications as an accelerant for the Marxist (Communist) cause and were anxious to occupy a position at the ideological forefront.[99]

According to the Sun Society's leading critic, Qian Xingcun (1900–1977, who later became better known by his pen name A Ying), it was Zhou Enlai who ordered the Creation and Sun membership to reconcile with Lu Xun in early 1929. He recalls that they did so by April 1929:

> The Sun Society and the Creation Society both accepted the Party's decision. Later, Pan Hannian [1906–1977] and others went to discuss this with Lu Xun as representatives of the Central Committee. Lu Xun agreed to be involved in setting up a literary collective. At this time I participated in two, possibly three such discussions with Lu Xun, all of which were held at the Gongfei Café on North Sichuan Road. These meetings took place in the afternoon, and besides myself there were Pan Hannian, Yang Hansheng [1902–1993], Feng Naichao, Xia Heng, and others. Feng Xuefeng also took part in these discussions. We criticized ourselves in Lu Xun's presence and acknowledged

that we had adopted the wrong attitude toward him. Lu Xun spoke
about the need for unity. In our conversations with Lu Xun during
this time, we showed him much respect even though we had not resolved the ideological differences between ourselves and him.[100]

Thus, by March 1930, Lu Xun's former accusers had formally acknowledged his leadership of the then newly established League of Left-Wing
Chinese Writers. With the exception of a widely noted sarcastic reply
from Guo Moruo, Lu Xun's merciless excoriation of the Creationists in
his July 1931 lecture did not elicit a barrage of abuse in return.[101] The
lecture was published a week later under the unassuming title "A Cursory Look at Shanghai Literature."[102]

Lu Xun began with a disquisition on *caizi* (genius), the disparaging
term that Beijing's New Culture elite had used in the early 1920s to
mock the authors of popular romantic fiction. He observed that the
educated elite in traditional China were "roughly divided into two
types: Confucian gentlemen [*junzi*] and talented littérateurs [*caizi*]."
Whereas the former were "wont to disdain things foreign, aspire to
rank and fame by following the proper channels, and hence never rush
about unless it is necessary," the latter were "broad-minded enough to
go anywhere." Thus, with the decline of dynastic China, "geniuses"
flocked to Shanghai's foreign concessions in search of a new path, in
line with the Confucian adage that "If the Way cannot be advanced,
one should board a raft and float out to sea."[103]

Lu Xun then described the "geniuses" of his day as shrewd operators
who churned out self-gratifying stories on the evergreen theme of "the
beauty and the genius" *(jiaren caizi)*. He noted that a process of evolution could be discerned in such works, for the male protagonist, formerly cast as the archetypal "genius + innocent fool," had now meta-
morphosed into a "genius + hooligan." This latter development had the
effect of turning Shanghai's pulp romance into "textbooks for whor-
ing," since the role of a "genius + hooligan" was to exploit the weak, including women trapped in prostitution, in order to advance himself.[104]

Lu Xun then proposed that the Creation Society members be viewed
as "geniuses + hooligans," explaining that they showed themselves adept at attracting the public's attention and making a successful career

out of denouncing others while talking up the revolution. In using "geniuses + hooligans," Lu Xun was also tacitly mocking the pseudo-algebraic formulations so favored by Guo Moruo and Cheng Fangwu in 1926 and 1927. Indeed, he explicitly mentioned the Creation Society's time in Guangzhou, noting that while they lived in "the cradle of revolution," they showed great ingenuity by "publicizing the phrase 'revolutionary literature,' in the absence of actual works" and parading as a vanguard at a time when "revolutionary literature" was not yet even known in Shanghai.[105]

He went on to note that upon their return to Shanghai in late 1927, the Creationists promptly capitalized on the trend for all things revolutionary to create "an upsurge of revolutionary literature." Lu Xun commented that the success of the Creation Society in promoting and selling "revolutionary literature" was all the more remarkable "because it was the result not of a revolutionary victory but because the revolution had been thwarted," adding satirically that this was "seemingly contrary to the situation in other countries." He then castigated the Creationists for failing to protest the horrors of war and the thousands of Communists murdered as part of "Party purification." Lu Xun concluded this damning assessment of his former critics with the remark that, because the rise of "revolutionary literature" in Shanghai offered little in the way of practical social criticism, it should be judged mainly as a vehicle for the authors' self-advancement.[106]

To deepen the insult, he added that in using the word "hooligan" he meant "someone who holds no definite theory; whose proposals for change are absent of logic and who, whenever he feels like it, grabs a theory from whichever school and turns it into a weapon."[107] In this connection, he parodied the linkage "revolution and literature" that Guo Moruo made popular as the title ("Revolution and Literature") of his seminal May 1926 essay. According to Lu Xun, the real relation between literature and revolution was not to be found in some law or theorem but in highly practical considerations of expediency and self-interest:

"Revolution" and "literature" seem distinct yet connected, like two boats close together. One boat is "revolution," the other "literature," and the writer stands with a foot in each. When conditions are fairly good, he puts more weight on the revolutionary boat and is clearly a revolutionary; but when the revolution is being crushed, he shifts his weight to the boat of literature to become a mere littérateur. Hence the advocates of revolutionary literature who, two years earlier [in 1929], were extremely radical and called for the total eradication of all nonrevolutionary works became mindful, a year later, of how Lenin liked to read the works of Goncharov to conclude that nonrevolutionary works were also very meaningful.[108]

Revolutionary Commerce

Lu Xun was by no means the first to deride the Creation Society's members as "geniuses" *(caizi).* In the early 1920s, Liu Bannong (1891–1934), a leading member of Beijing's New Culture elite, had called Guo Moruo "the poet of the Bund" *(Shanghai tande shiren).* Liu ridiculed Guo for "comparing himself to Goethe" and in this process likened him to a *caizi.* Used as part of the phrase "geniuses of the Bund" *(yangchang caizi),* the word *caizi* (literally, a "talented littérateur") refers to a writer without talent whose narcissistic delusion leads him to project onto the male protagonist of his stories the unhappiness of an unrecognized genius.[109] In the late 1910s the New Culture elite had used the expression to show their disdain for the producers of popular romantic fiction in Shanghai. The Creation Society, though founded in Shanghai, was clearly an avant-garde organization and not identified with these popular romances in any way. Nonetheless, the pugnacious attitude of the society's members and their self-aggrandizing proclivities earned them frequent ripostes from those whom they attacked and disparaged.

The fact that the society's headquarters were in Shanghai and its members were self-declared romantics made it irresistible for their critics to liken them to the *caizi* of pulp romances. Hence, in calling Guo Moruo "the poet of the Bund," Liu Bannong insinuated that Guo too might find solace in the love of a beautiful prostitute (in which role the tragic female protagonists of such stories were often cast).[110] A decade later, Lu Xun reprised this insult when he described the Creationists as "geniuses + hooligans," thereby implying that they had no qualms about wooing naïve readers with false revolutionary claims.

Understanding the significance of this insult requires a detour to explore the vituperative nature of New Culture attacks on Shanghai's romantic fiction. These attacks began around 1917 as the "literary revolution" was gaining momentum. The advocates of *baihua* described romantic fiction as the work of the "Mandarin Duck and Butterfly School," thereby denigrating two popular Chinese symbols of beauty and loving devotion to mock romantic fiction as abject enslavement to outmoded mores. The intensity of these attacks also evinced the determination of New Culture's proponents to attract the public's attention away from romantic fiction. Implicit in the stated moral reasons was a practical ambition to capture market share for "new-style" *baihua* from its highly successful "old-style" rival.[111]

Before the advent of New Culture, romantic fiction had enjoyed enormous respect as a staple of modern publishing in Shanghai. The New Culture elite purposely ignored the range of quality among works of romantic fiction to focus exclusively on the genre's more lurid and formulaic examples. In fact romantic fiction's role as a vehicle for new ideas had facilitated its ascendancy from the 1890s to the 1910s. The rise of romantic fiction in turn helped to accelerate the development of Shanghai's modern print capitalism.[112] In the early 1900s, when Lin Shu (1852–1924) translated *La dame aux camellias* and Liang Qichao was calling for a "literary revolution," romantic fiction was frequently linked to social progress and the spread of modern values such as the virtues of Western-style marriage and the importance of respecting the needs of men and women alike.

Consequently, the authors of romantic fiction often declared that one of their purposes was to promote modernization; they believed that their narratives were acclimating Chinese readers to the physical and social trappings of the modern age. As Xueqing Xu notes in her study of the genre, among its prominent authors, "Bao Tianxiao [1875–1973] summarized his aim as 'promising a new political system and preserving traditional morality,' and Zhou Shoujuan [1895–1968] his purpose as 'combining education with recreation.'"[113]

In the mid- to late 1910s this highly successful modern romantic fiction in Shanghai became an object of frequent mockery among the
advocates of *baihua*. As the majority of these New Culture radicals were
based in Beijing, they tacitly opposed a "high-brow" Beijing over a
"low-brow" Shanghai, and their moralizing served to obscure the commercial prospects that were just as vital to the success of their "literary
revolution" as they had been to that of romantic fiction. Indeed, the
"literary revolution" could not have succeeded without the substantial
capital investments of Shanghai's publishing magnates, for it was the
production of *baihua* works in mass quantities that ensured *baihua*'s
rapid rise in the marketplace. By the early 1920s, Shanghai's publishers
had acquired a considerable financial stake in New Culture and New
Literature merchandise and sought ever newer ways of marketing intellectual radicalism.[114]

But notwithstanding their growing investment in "new-style" fare,
these canny entrepreneurs also continued to cater to the well-established
traditional appetite for what was now being dubbed "old-style" romantic fiction. Mao Dun recalled of his time as an editor at the Commercial Press in the early 1920s that he and his fellow *baihua* advocates
were deeply unhappy about the press's continued publication and sponsorship of Shanghai's entertainment literature. But their denunciations met with indifference, since they were attacking best-selling
works with an extensive circulation and established readerships.[115]
Nonetheless, as the market for New Culture and New Literature expanded, the producers of *baihua* began to command rising manuscript fees and royalties.

The "literary revolution" was launched in the mid-1910s in deliberate contrast to official attempts at developing *guoyu*, the relatively
standardized speech and writing first introduced in 1913 as a proto-
modern national language. The advocates of *baihua* were dissatisfied
with the pedestrian pace at which they perceived *guoyu* to be circulating within the institutional confines of schools and government offices. They attempted instead to inspire the reading public directly
and conceived of *baihua*, unlike *guoyu*, as a language for immediate
mass consumption. Thus producers of *baihua* sought in equal measure to instruct readers and to gain market share for their particular

brand of racy "new-style" prose, poetry, criticism, social commentary, and treatises.[116]

But even as they had wanted their nascent language to succeed in the marketplace, they were just as keen to declare their enterprise as an altruistic mission. Indeed, the Peking University–centered journal *New Youth,* which first heralded the "literary revolution," remains commemorated to this day as an exemplar of selfless scholarship. This is because in 1918 (the year when *New Youth* published Lu Xun's "Diary of a Madman"), the journal announced that its editors and contributors were sacrificing their manuscript fees to hasten the nation's progress. But what is less frequently mentioned is that the people who made this generous gesture in 1918 were academics and senior officials earning handsome salaries in warlord-run Beijing. They could well afford to forgo their modest manuscript fees (which *New Youth* paid at the same rate as Commercial Press in Shanghai, then China's largest and most successful publishing house).[117]

To put this in perspective, a study of livelihoods in Beijing in the late 1910s indicates that an income of 11 ying yuan, or Chinese silver dollars, a month was just above the poverty line and sufficient to meet the living costs of a working couple with three dependents. In striking contrast, Chen Duxiu (the editor of *New Youth*) and Lu Xun each received a monthly salary of 300 dollars in their respective appointments as the dean of arts at Peking University and as a senior Education Bureau official. The monthly salaries of other *New Youth* contributors ranged from 100 to 300 dollars, with the majority earning over 200 dollars.[118]

The decision of *New Youth*'s contributors in 1918 to forgo their manuscript fees proved short-lived. By the early to mid-1920s, as the internecine feuds of rival warlord regimes eroded the economic situation in Beijing, salary payments became erratic, and the prospect of publishing new ideas gratis was no longer feasible.[119] Indeed, out of economic necessity, a large number of Beijing's intellectual elite traveled south to work for Shanghai's prosperous publishing houses.

By the early 1920s, a pecking order of "new-style" authors was well in place. At the Commercial Press, this hierarchy was determined according to a sliding scale of manuscript fees that normally ranged between two and five dollars per 1,000 characters depending on the author's

prominence. Thus, whereas Guo Moruo enjoyed an enviable reputation that earned him four dollars, he was outclassed by Lu Xun and
Hu Shi, who as acknowledged doyens of the "literary revolution" received the special rate of five to six dollars.[120]

Shanghai's laissez-faire commerce facilitated this intertwining of
published success and nation-building, and just as the *baihua* of New
Culture intellectuals was promoted as radical chic in the early 1920s,
Shanghai's thriving marketplace after 1927 witnessed the sensational
rise of "revolutionary literature." During this period of postwar recovery, Shanghai's major publishing companies also benefited from the
Nanjing government's tutelary ambitions: the institutionalization of
the Nationalist doctrine necessitated the production of vast numbers
of new textbooks.[121]

This intricate concatenation of commerce, politics, and personal ambition in intellectual and literary publishing was vividly captured in
the essay-length manifesto published in the *Crescent Moon Monthly*'s
inaugural 10 March 1928 issue (just two days before Lu Xun's essay on
Shanghai's haze appeared in *Threads of Talk*). Authored by Xu Zhimo in
consultation with other contributors to the journal, "The Attitude of
the Crescent Moon" describes the "marketplace of ideas" in post-1927
Shanghai as "crammed with stalls, shops, signage and advertisements"
for "no fewer than a dozen or more recognizable trades, each with its
own character and allure."[122]

In one breathless stream, Xu disparaged "sentimentalism, decadence,
aestheticism, utilitarianism, didacticism, aggressivism, radicalism,
pursuit of refinement, pornography, fanaticism, commercialism, slo-
ganism, and the pursuit of isms." Describing these as shoddy goods
that posed a grave danger to the overall quality of China's intellectual
marketplace, Xu made clear that he associated "revolutionary literature" with the majority of these denigrated properties.[123] In contrast,
he presented the Crescent Moon Society as a "loose coalition of friends"
committed to defending "health" *(jiankang)* and "dignity" *(zunyan)*. Offering these two virtues as the remedy for a world turned upside down
by violence and threatened with "the inversion of each and every value,"
the *Crescent Moon Monthly* thus declared as its raison d'être the restoration of order and reason to Chinese intellectual life.[124]

The manifesto's two English epigraphs—the first a quotation from the Bible ("And God said, 'Let there be light, and there was light'"), the second a line by Shelley ("If winter comes, can spring be far behind?")— were intended to enhance the journal's moral authority but served also to distinguish the *Crescent Moon Monthly* from its competitors.[125] Whereas leftist journals teemed with revolutionary sentiments, this Shanghai-based brainchild of a leading New Culture group invoked the themes of Western civilization. To elevate itself above the surging popularity of "revolutionary literature," the *Crescent Moon Monthly* boasted of offering a superior "broad road," based in the simple universalism of "human existence viewed in its entirety."[126]

The noble rhetoric of this manifesto also marked the Crescent Moon Society's new venture into commercial publishing. As displaced intellectuals who had left war-torn Beijing to take up academic or official positions in Shanghai and neighboring cities, the society's members established their own bookstore and journal in Shanghai in early 1928 (under the auspices of Crescent Moon as a holding company). In early 1920s Beijing, where institutional affiliation reflected the stature of an individual or a group, the Crescentists' association with Peking University and Tsinghua University enhanced their public image. None of the universities and colleges in Shanghai and Nanjing where they subsequently taught could compare with the reputation of these two illustrious Beijing institutions. Moreover, in commercial Shanghai, published success mattered much more than institutional affiliation.

Hence by 1928 the Crescentists were openly advocating market mechanisms as a safeguard for the freedom of expression. In "The Attitude of the Crescent Moon," Xu Zhimo argued that the solution was not to censor aberrant ideas but rather to protect the integrity of the marketplace through the promotion of "positive feelings" that would nurture love (against hatred) and community (against mutual destruction). By this means, he claimed, the "pollution" choking the flow of ideas would be gradually eradicated.[127]

In the less-complicated heyday of Beijing's New Culture during the early 1920s, the Crescent Moon members' message of "health" and "dignity" would have been sufficient as an indication of the organization's aspirations. But in the cut-and-thrust of Shanghai publishing in the late 1920s, the group chose to describe their journal as a product circulating and competing in the "marketplace of ideas," thereby drawing attention for the first time to their enterprise as a fusion of intellectual and commercial interests. In this regard, their bemoaning of their "ailing and aberrant" era and their condemnation of revolutionary literature as (political) "prostitution" and (ideological) "poison" served to cast *Crescent Moon Monthly* as a vital remedy to a polluted marketplace.

In short, the *Crescent Moon Monthly*'s manifesto was as much about the marketing of a distinctive literary brand as it was a statement of intellectual intent. The name "Crescent Moon" (used for both the journal and the bookstore that the group established) soon became synonymous with cosmopolitan sophistication, not least because the design of the *Crescent Moon Monthly* was handsomely modeled on the 1890s English literary journal *The Yellow Book*. This eye-catching design assigned an upmarket value to the journal, giving it an air of Euro-American stylishness. Moreover, the appeal of its contents, which ranged from topical articles on aesthetics, human rights, and civil liberties to regular review columns, poetry, and illustrations, was aided by the celebrity status of several key contributors.

Indeed, the success of the Crescent brand in Shanghai led Lu Xun to remark caustically in 1929 that just as "the Creationists have their revolutionary literature," the Crescent Moon Society appeared to be also vigorously marketing its wares. He wrote: "Liang Shiqiu has his Babbitt, Xu Zhimo has his Tagore, Hu Shi has his Dewey—oh yes, Xu Zhimo has Katherine Mansfield too, for he wept at her grave."[128] He sneered that, in advertising themselves as sole agents for their chosen foreign luminaries, the Crescent Moon members resembled the "cordon of interpreters, detectives, police, 'boys' and so on" who served their European masters in Shanghai's foreign concessions.[129]

Previously in Beijing he had taunted them as the "pugs" of their warlord masters. In Shanghai he now mocked their compradorial anxiety to secure foreign patents. Yet Lu Xun was himself engaged in a similar kind of intercultural agency and brokerage. By the mid-1920s he was widely associated with the Japanese literary theorist Kuriyagawa Hakuson (1880–1923) through his translations of Kuriyagawa's writings.[130] In 1928, when his Marxist critics pronounced him obsolete,

Lu Xun extended his translation activities to include the essays of Anatoly Lunacharsky (1875–1933) and Georgy Plekhanov (1857–1918), which he retranslated from published Japanese translations, and thereupon became an active producer in the then-expanding market for translated Soviet works.[131]

In the preface he wrote for his 1932 anthology of essays and speeches, *Three Leisures (San xian ji)*, he included a facetious vote of thanks to the Creation Society, noting that its denunciations of his bourgeois backwardness pressured him into reading Marxist literary theory. He noted that translating Plekhanov's *Theory of Art* taught him the limitations of his belief in social evolution.[132] In Shanghai's marketplace, such remarks, together with the fact of Lu Xun's involvement in the underground League of Left-Wing Chinese Writers, had the effect of reinforcing his new image as a leading leftist in intellectual circles. But while Lu Xun appeared to enjoy this new identity, he was also unusually preoccupied with defending his critical integrity in print.

On this point, Lu Xun's derision of "revolutionary literature" as the by-product of a crass marketplace reveals something of the unease he shared with his Crescent Moon adversaries about being perceived as profiting from writing. He and they alike, as leading members of the erstwhile New Culture movement in Beijing, were accustomed to presenting their literary endeavors as noble and selfless. Hence the fact that to remain relevant as social critics, they were forced to keep pace with the vogue for "revolutionary literature"—if only to ridicule it— would have caused them considerable discomfort. But whereas the Crescent Moon members were able to present themselves comfortably as agents of "health" and "dignity" in diametric opposition to "revolutionary literature," Lu Xun, who had been lauded as a revolutionary mentor in Guangzhou, was in the much more difficult position of defending a genuinely revolutionary literature (as yet to arrive) against the debased "revolutionary literature" he disparaged.

As a celebrated intellectual in Guangzhou, Lu Xun had been paid a handsome monthly salary of 500 dollars at Sun Yat-sen University. After resigning from the university in June 1927, he never again held a senior academic post. An open letter he published in *Threads of Talk* in April 1928 evinces an anxiety to assure his readers of his integrity:

At first I had no need to sell my words to make ends meet. I took up my writing brush in response to a friend's demand. But there must have been a bit of indignation lodged in my heart, for it seems that each time I used my brush, some angry and agitated words would slip out, almost as if it was my intent to stir up the young. I have no qualms in saying that when Duan Qirui was in power, we did not procure so much as half a ruble from overseas for the things we did. Neither was there a cent from some wealthy patron nor a trifling manuscript fee from some bookseller. Nonetheless there were those who spread rumors to this effect. Moreover, I certainly had no desire to fill the role of a "littérateur" and so never conspired with a gang of critics to sing my praise. I never would have thought that my few works of fiction would sell more than 10,000 copies.[133]

Lu Xun clearly had no need to encourage "a gang of critics" to write him up, for his name alone attracted a deluge of reviews and commentaries, whether in praise or criticism of his oeuvre. There were certain things that he understandably left a little hazy. For an illustrious author who disdained his adversaries as opportunists and toadies, the rewards that his own extraordinary literary success provided were complications best left out of sight.

In 1928, apart from the 300 dollars that he received each month from the Academy of Higher Education in Nanjing, Lu Xun was paid royalties and fees from his main publisher, Beixin Publishing House, and other publishers. He also received fees for commissioned essays and invited guest lectures. One study reports that in 1928 his average monthly income was 497.63 dollars. The figures rose dramatically to a monthly average of 1,281 dollars and 1,260 dollars in 1929 and 1930 respectively. This increase reflects the fact that he initiated legal proceedings against Li Xiaofeng, Beixin's owner, for unpaid manuscript fees and publishing royalties, prompting Li to settle the debt before the matter went to court.[134]

Lu Xun's earnings in Shanghai placed him comfortably in the category of the wealthy. According to a 1927 Shanghai survey, the monthly income of the average Shanghai household was 66 dollars per month (within a range extending from the working poor, who earned around

30 dollars per month, to the wealthy, who received monthly incomes exceeding 200 dollars).[135] In his famous essay of 1939, "Remembering Lu Xun," Yu Dafu wrote that the Lu Xun he knew in Shanghai was keenly aware that he now lived off his writings and that this led him "to break with considerations of face" when he hired a lawyer to retrieve the monies owed to him by his enterprising protégé. Yu reported that Li, who had blithely neglected to pay Lu Xun the greater share of his royalties for several years, was so alarmed by his mentor's resort to litigation that he entreated persons close to Lu Xun (especially Lin Yutang [1895-1976] and Yu Dafu) to intercede on his behalf. Yu, who was then in Hangzhou, received a telegram from Li urging immediate assistance. Yu also noted that when the matter was resolved, the greatly relieved publisher held a banquet for his mollified mentor and all persons who had assisted in the process of reconciliation.[136] Having paid the royalties he owed to Lu Xun, Li continued to enjoy a close relationship with his mentor in the 1930s.

Yu's account of this incident reveals the pangs of freelancer's anxiety that Lu Xun experienced in Shanghai. Despite his enormous stature and success, he was burdened by the thought of now having to "sell [his] words to make ends meet," and this economic necessity undoubtedly made him all the more defensive about his reputation as a social critic. Thus he projected a flattering self-image to stand against his repeated jibes at the Creation Society as comprised of "geniuses + hooligans" or of the Crescent Moon Society as "pugs whose lofty demeanor betrays an utter devotion to pleasing the master."[137] In effect, he presented himself as indifferent to self-advancement and as cutting an honest path through the haze that his adversaries produced.

The poet Zang Kejia (1905-2004) recalled Lu Xun telling him: "In a society preoccupied with turning a profit, it's always good to have a few more fools around."[138] Lu Xun evidently regarded himself as a champion of those whom he favorably perceived as indifferent to market competition. It was in this connection that Li Xiaofeng played an important part in Lu Xun's life, for Beixin Publishing House would employ and publish the young writers that Lu Xun recommended. For instance, Lu Xun negotiated a Beixin publishing contract in 1928 for Rou Shi that included a provision for royalties at 20 percent, the same rate that Beixin paid prominent writers like Zhou Zuoren. Lu Xun's royalties with Beixin were set at 25 percent: an extraordinary rate that he alone enjoyed.[139]

Lu Xun's income between 1932 and 1936 fluctuated as a result of tightened censorship. (Following the bonanza years of 1929 and 1930, his average monthly income in silver dollars was 742.44 in 1931, 399.04 in 1932, 858.48 in 1933, 473.30 in 1934, 472.61 in 1935, and 321.99 in 1936).[140] From 1932 onward his works were banned, and he was forced to publish under a variety of pseudonyms. Moreover, the monthly salary from Nanjing had ceased by January 1932. Nonetheless he earned more than enough in these remaining years of his life to enjoy a very comfortable existence, albeit amid state violence against Communists and increasing Japanese military incursions. Thus notwithstanding his unwavering opposition to Chiang Kai-shek, Lu Xun was a beneficiary of the economic regeneration that the Nanking Decade ushered in, which facilitated the resurgence of Shanghai publishing and with it his own prosperity.

In Shanghai Lu Xun also became a reluctant intellectual celebrity who found his name being used for a variety of advertising purposes. There was at least one case of an impostor in Hangzhou, which led him to publish a notice in April 1928 painstakingly refuting the scoundrel's spurious claims. His exasperation is plain in the repetitive phrasing of such statements as: "Since I've been in Shanghai, numerous papers have reported that I 'intend to open a bookshop' or that I've been 'traveling in Hangzhou.' In fact I have neither opened a bookshop nor traveled in Hangzhou. All I've done is to hide upstairs in my room to do a bit of translation."[141]

The local gossip papers annoyed him in particular, and he noted in a 1929 essay that when even the tabloids waxed lyrical about "revolutionary literature," it was a sure sign that this literature had become fatally sullied. As he put it: "Although many of the smaller papers dub themselves 'revolutionary literature,' so long as most of the advertisements are for restaurants or cures for venereal diseases, you know who the authors and readers are." He added scornfully: "The people running these papers are of the same ilk as those who used to specialize in talking about prostitutes and actors, except that they've now replaced the entertainers with authors, male and female, whom they praise or abuse so as to flaunt their own literary prowess."[142]

Although Lu Xun distanced himself from Shanghai's burgeoning celebrity culture, he could not prevent the smart set from lauding him as one of their own. A feature-length article about him appeared in the April 1928 issue of Shanghai's leading glossy magazine of the day, *Young Companion (Liangyou huabao)*, nestled among the fashion and lifestyle pages and society pictures. Hu Shi, Lu Xun's liberal rival, was similarly featured several issues later.[143] The magazine conflated modern glamor and intellectual radicalism, displaying a series of stylish "new women" on the monthly covers while bringing readers up to speed on intellectual icons and trends of the day. In the late 1920s, the magazine's celebration of revolutionary fashion presented a surreal contrast to the anti-Communist purge under way.

Lu Xun's distaste for this sophisticated cosmopolitan commerce is evident in the special loathing he reserved for the best-known member of Shanghai's high society, the debonair trend-setting poet and publisher Shao Xunmei (1906–1968). In Shao, Lu Xun discerned a frivolity that was poles apart from his own critical disposition. Shao was the son of a rich Shanghai family who had married the even wealthier Sheng Peiyu (1905–1988), the granddaughter of Shanghai's then-richest man. Shao's good looks (Lu Xun described him as "renowned for his manly beauty"),[144] together with his lavish parties and numerous romantic liaisons, ensured his constant appearance in Shanghai's tabloids. Shao's long-term affair with Emily Hahn (1905–1997) in the 1930s made him internationally renowned when she published a series of articles discussing him and his family in *The New Yorker* and fictionalized their relationship in her novel *Steps of the Sun*.[145]

Among other things, Lu Xun disparaged Shao as a rich dilettante who had bought his fame and accused him of using his wife's dowry to fund his publishing projects. In an article published in *Shen Bao* in 1933, Lu Xun mocked the *Golden Chamber Monthly (Jin wu yuekan)*, the first of several deluxe magazines that Shao published, with the following cruel remark about its title: "The old adage 'Within the pages one finds one's very own golden chamber' now reads, 'Amid the money one finds a littérateur' [*wenxuejia*]."[146] In his study of Shao, Jonathan Hutt observes that although his "persistence and generosity eventually won over many potential enemies," Shao "failed to make an impression" on Lu Xun. Hutt continues: "Lu Xun's campaign against the 'self-declared poet' took many forms. He refused to contribute to any journal edited by Shao and attacked the author's work both in his personal correspondence and in print."[147]

Lu Xun preferred a different kind of cosmopolitanism: one that favored the leftist perspectives he found in Japanese, Russian, and eastern European works. In Shanghai he frequented the Uchiyama Shoten (Neishan shudian in Chinese), a bookstore owned by Uchimaya Kanzō (1885–1959) that was the favorite haunt of Chinese intellectuals literate in Japanese.[148] As Shu-mei Shih points out, this bookstore not only became "the premier center for Sino-Japanese literary encounters" but constituted a space "where Japanese mediation of Western culture was encapsulated in physical form: it carried the largest collection of Japanese books in China and had in stock almost all the extant Chinese translations of Japanese works."[149] Lu Xun and Uchiyama became close friends, and from 1928 onward the store became Lu Xun's preferred venue for meeting with the many intellectuals and students who sought an audience with him.

The Uchiyama bookstore was on North Sichuan Road in the International Settlement, a busy commercial street with a concentration of Japanese-owned shops and buildings and where the Creation Society's headquarters were also situated. On 8 August 1928, *Shen bao*, Shanghai's leading newspaper, published a review-cum-advertisement of the Shanghai Café located on the same street. The reviewer recommended the café as a favorite haunt of intellectual celebrities, naming Lu Xun, Yu Dafu, and several members of the Creation Society among the people he had seen there. The reviewer noted in particular that "Mr. Feng Naichao, who advocates revolutionary literature, has often thought about opening a café but has so far been unsuccessful."[150]

For Lu Xun and Yu Dafu, these gushing remarks that elevated the radical Creationists to café society celebrities proved an irresistible object of lampoon. The two authors promptly responded with a short polemic each, with both essays published in *Threads of Talk* on 13 August

1928. The following excerpt from Yu's piece remains frequently quoted to this day: "I know an unrevolutionary old man, Lu Xun, and once discussed cafés with him. It seems he was trying to warn me not to enter cafés that belong to people of a different class. In his words, 'If you wish to enter, you should first ask to which class the café belongs. Otherwise, if you get the class wrong, things will not go well for you.'"[151] Lu Xun's equally mischievous text, titled "Revolutionary Café," featured a pastiche of quotations from both the review and the essays published in the Creation Society's journals. He wrote, among other things:

> Yonder there is a lofty foreign building standing on a broad street; a glittering neon sign illuminates its entrance. Upstairs you'll find "our literary celebrities of the day" engaged in high-brow talk or lost in thought. In front of each is a cup of steaming hot proletarian coffee while in the remote distance there's "the great unwashed—the peasants and workers." They drink, and think, and talk, and direct others, and obtain their objectives. This truly is an "ideal paradise."[152]

In particular, Lu Xun poked fun at Cheng Fangwu's influential essay "From Literary Revolution to Revolutionary Literature," published in January 1928, in which Cheng famously urged his readers to "overcome your petty-bourgeois nature, turn your backs on the class about to undergo *Aufheben*, and quicken your pace towards the great unwashed—the peasants and workers!"[153] Dismissing this as heady talk fueled by coffee fumes, Lu Xun turned the tables on his Marxist accusers and satirized their revolutionary literature as nothing more than a petty-bourgeois treat.

Of the term "revolutionary," he wrote that it had become a byword for commercial success, since those who were identified with it (such as the Creation Society and Sun Society) were well known for publishing multiple journals simultaneously. He opined that in a competitive marketplace where bookshops now wooed customers with complimentary gifts of silk stockings with the purchase of multiple books, the free stockings might prove a greater inducement than the books themselves. He remarked that the review of the Shanghai Café likewise indicated a new trend: whereas café advertisements had previously tantalized the

male voyeur with a visual feast of female dancers and pretty wait-
resses, the vista of "literary celebrities engaged in high-brow talk or
lost in thought" (a line quoted from the review of Shanghai Café)
now appeared to hold a similar allure. He then corrected the reviewer
who claimed Lu Xun as one of the "literary celebrities" frequenting
the Shanghai Café, asserting that he had never set foot in this
establishment.[154]

But one particular café did become a regular meeting-place for
Shanghai's leftists. In 1929 and 1930 numerous discussions about the
founding of the Left-Wing League were held in a room on the upper
floor of the foreign-owned Gongfei Café on North Sichuan Road. As
the café was frequented by Shanghai's Western expatriates, it did not
attract police interest; hence the underground Communists were able
to organize gatherings of around a dozen people there unnoticed.[155]
The entry in Lu Xun's diary for 16 February 1930 reads: "Fine weather.
Ji Shi's letter arrived this morning. In the afternoon I went out with
Rou Shi and Feng Xuefeng to have coffee."[156] It was at the Gongfei
Café that Lu Xun took coffee with his two Communist protégés, in the
company of several other Party members and leftists who included his
former adversaries in the Creation Society and Sun Society such as
Feng Naichao and Qian Xingcun. The occasion was the final preparatory meeting for the inauguration of the Left-Wing League, which was
founded in secret two weeks later on 2 March. It was obliquely reported in the leftist journal Sprout (Mengya) as "a seminar of the participants of the modern literary movement in Shanghai."[157]

Thus advertisements such as the "review" of the Shanghai Café that
Lu Xun and Yu Dafu parodied had the unintended positive effect of
shielding leftist activism by presenting it as harmless "high-brow"
consumerism. In other words, Shanghai's revolutionary commerce was
not entirely an odious haze: it also provided much-needed cover for
political engagement in a violent climate. In April 1928 Lu Xun had
quipped that China's revolutionary discourse had become so manipu-
lable that it was a matter of *intuiting* the position of the "revolutionary
writers" in question: "whether they belong to the group which thinks
the revolution a success, or to the group which thinks it not yet accom-
plished."[158] With his involvement in the Left-Wing League, Lu Xun

made it known that he stood with the latter despite his open unhappiness with the "geniuses + hooligans" he saw in this group.

This context illuminates the negatively inflected term *guage* (mixed up, embroiled, caught up) that Lu Xun used in March 1928 to characterize the networks and alliances of intellectual Shanghai. In deliberate contrast to such neutral words as "connection" *(guanxi)* or "association" *(laiwang)*, he used *guage* to imply that the more ambitious among his contemporaries, despite carefully hedging their political bets, would inevitably be dragged down by the bad company they kept. His use of this particular connotation of *guage* also hints at the gangster violence that pervaded Shanghai and, more crucially, the unholy alliance between Chiang Kai-shek and Du Yuesheng (1888–1951), Shanghai's leading gangster and head of the Green Gang. It was Du's gangsters who helped Chiang launch his grisly "Party purification" campaign in April 1927, and it was Du's gangland network that effectively became an extension of the Nationalist state's powers of surveillance and repression during the Nanking Decade.

The fact that Shanghai's French concession, adjacent to the Chinese city, was Du's operational base exacerbated the dangers for the Communists, whose many safe houses were located there. Du's services to the French authorities and local persons of influence in breaking workers' strikes in the mid- to late 1920s had made him a respectable figure in Shanghai society. With Chiang Kai-shek as the nation's president, the assistance Du had rendered Chiang in butchering Communists in 1927 further boosted his social standing. In 1931 he was publicly lauded as a philanthropist for his generous donations to public causes and institutions.[159]

In aiding Chiang, Du not only hunted Communists but also terrorized wealthy Chinese, turning them into captive financiers for the Generalissimo's plans. Du in turn exacted unique privileges to expand his narcotics operations beyond the Nanjing government's control.[160] Du is not mentioned in any of Lu Xun's writings, but Shanghai's highly visible arch-hooligan was undoubtedly a shady presence in the writer's many representations of Chinese politics as organized hooliganism.[161] That Chiang's liaison with Du was a Faustian pact highlights the affective force of Lu Xun's words. To paraphrase: Power is a sinister dynamic that binds its subjects to an expanding web of competing yet interdependent interests. In the Republican era of Lu Xun's China, these entanglements generated a haze of fear and apprehension from which not even the one "wielding the commander's sword" could extricate himself.[162]

Lu Xun (second from left) and Zhou Zuoren (far left) in Beijing with the blind Russian writer and esperantist Vasily Ereshenko, 15 April 1923. Lu Xun Memorial Hall, Shanghai. See Lu Xun's diary, 15 April 1923, *LXQJ* 14:451.

Lu Xun (left) with Xu Guangping (middle) and left-wing thinker and transla-tor Jiang Jingsan (right) in Guangzhou, 11 September 1927. Jiang sought Lu Xun as a mentor in Guangzhou and thereafter enjoyed a close friendship with him. Lu Xun Memorial Hall, Shanghai. See Lu Xun's diary, 11 September 1927, *LXQJ* 14:670.

Group photo taken 4 October 1927 in Shanghai. Front row, left to right: Zhou Jianren, Xu Guangping, Lu Xun; back row, left to right: Sun Fuxi, Lin Yutang, Sun Fuyuan. Lu Xun Memorial Hall, Shanghai. See Lu Xun's diary, 4 October 1927, *LXQJ* 14:673.

Group photo taken 6 August 1930 at the Gong De Lin Buddhist Vegetarian Restaurant in Shanghai. This was one of numerous salon discussions *(mantan hui)* on the arts, organized by Lu Xun's close friend and bookstore owner Uchiyama Kanzō (back row, far right) and attended by members of the League of Chinese Left-Wing Writers and Japanese intellectuals. Among the League members were (front row, starting from far left) Tian Han, Yu Dafu, Lu Xun, Ouyang Yuqian, and (front row, second from far right) Zheng Boqi. Lu Xun Memorial Hall, Shanghai. See Lu Xun's diary, 6 August 1930, *LXQJ* 14:834.

Lu Xun with son Zhou Haiying, 25 September 1930, Shanghai. Lu Xun Memorial Hall, Shanghai. See Lu Xun's diary, 25 September 1930, *LXQJ* 14:839.

A portrait of Lu Xun on his fiftieth lunar birthday, 25 September 1930, Shanghai. Lu Xun Memorial Hall, Shanghai.

左翼文藝作家
魯迅五十生壽紀念
表示願爲無產階級文學而努力

九月十七，是左翼作家魯迅五十生辰、他的朋友柔石，畫室，乃超，蔡詠裳，董紹明，許廣平等，發起一個紀念會，參加的人除左聯，社聯 美聯，劇聯，代表外，有葉紹鈞，傅東華，茅盾，史特梅女士，羅佛，田漢，石民，蓮子，楊邨人，等等三十餘人。首由主席柔石致開會辭，接着是各左翼文化團體代表講演，都是很熱烈的希望魯迅在兩個政權對立的現在，更勇敢的寫擁護蘇維埃政權而戰文學上的活動。體由各來賓德國新聞記者史梅特女士演講，德國社會民主主義的醜亂以及廣大無產階級鬥爭的發展與德國文壇現狀，希望魯迅堅決的爲無產階級文學運動而努力。末由魯迅致答辭，道先批評他自己過去沒有在革命中抱着犧牲精神，走上實際行動，表示對革命的慚愧。次說明他過去生活史的發展，最後表示將努力完成朋友們的希望云。

Article published 21 September 1930 in the underground Communist newspaper *Hongqi (Red Flag)* about Lu Xun's fiftieth lunar birthday celebrations. The dinner party, presided over by Rou Shi, was held on 17 September 1930 at Surabaya, a Dutch restaurant in the French concession, and was attended by prominent writers and Left-Wing League members. The headline states Lu Xun's avowed commitment to the proletarian cause. Lu Xun Memorial Hall, Shanghai. For details, see Lu Xun's diary, 17 September 1930, *LXQJ* 14:838; Wang-Chi Wong, *Politics and Literature in Shanghai: The Chinese League of Left-Wing Writers, 1930–1936* (Manchester: Manchester University Press, 1991), 99.

Photo taken 17 February 1933 at Soong Ching-ling's residence in Shanghai. From left to right: Agnes Smedley, Bernard Shaw, Soong Ching-ling, Cai Yuanpei, Harold Isaacs, Lin Yutang, Lu Xun. In the reprint of this photo in the Shanghai-based journal *Wenyi xindi (New Literary Land)* in September 1951 to commemorate the seventieth anniversary of Lu Xun's birth, Lin and Isaacs were airbrushed out—the former for his "compradorial" ways and the latter for being a Trotskyist. Both were deemed unworthy to share the same space as Mao Zedong's revolutionary sage. Lu Xun Memorial Hall, Shanghai. For details, see Lu Xun's diary, 17 February 1933, *LXQJ* 15:65; "Song Qinglingyu Lu Xun deng heying zhaopiande beihou" (The story behind the group photo of Soong Ching-ling, Lu Xun and others), at http://news.xinhuanet.com/zgjx /2008-07/30/content_8836941_1.htm (first published in *Wenzhai bao*).

Family portrait, dated 13 September 1933. From left to right: Lu Xun, Zhou Haiying, and Xu Guangping,. Lu Xun Memorial Hall, Shanghai. See Lu Xun's diary, 13 September 1933, *LXQJ* 15:99.

Group photo taken August 1931 in Shanghai with participants of the week-long woodblock printmaking workshop sponsored by Uchiyama Kanzō and held at his bookstore. Lu Xun is fifth from the right. Lu Xun held several discussions with Chinese woodblock artists at this venue from 1931 to 1936. Lu Xun Memorial Hall, Shanghai. For details, see Lu Xun's diary, 17 and 22 August 1931, *LXQJ* 14:889–890; Christopher T. Keaveney, *Beyond Brushtalk: Sino-Japanese Literary Exchange in the Interwar Period* (Hong Kong: Hong Kong University Press, 2008), 39.

Lu Xun's final meeting with woodblock artists, 8 October 1936, at the Second National Woodcut Travelling Exhibition, held at the YMCA, Baxian Bridge, Shanghai. From left to right: Lu Xun, Lin Fu, Cao Bai, Bai Wei, Chen Yan-qiao. This is one of eight photos taken that day by then aspiring photojournal-ist Sha Fei. Lin Fu, killed in 1942 at the Nationalist government's Shangrao concentration camp, was said to have treasured this photo, carrying it with him to his death. Photograph by Sha Fei, provided by his daughter Wang Yan. The exhibition is noted in Lu Xun's diary, 8 October 1936, *LXQJ* 15:315; informa-tion on Lin Fu appears in Wang Yan, "Lu Xun xiansheng zuihoude liuying" (The last images of Mr Lu Xun), at *Sha Fei Research Centre for Chinese Image,* http://www.shafei.cn/center/treatise/myfatherC/myfatherSF_006.htm.

Lu Xun in conversation and enjoying a cigarette at the exhibition, 8 October 1936, Shanghai. Physically frail and in the advanced stages of tuberculosis, he died at 5:25 A.M. on 19 October. Photograph by Sha Fei, provided by Wang Yan.

Front cover of *Ye cao (Wild Grass)*, Lu Xun's collection of experimental prose compositions, published in July 1927 by Beixin Publishing House. Lu Xun Memorial Hall, Shanghai.

絲 語

Front cover of the 17 December 1927 issue of *Yu si (Threads of Talk)*, relocated to Shanghai and edited by Lu Xun. Lu Xun Memorial Hall, Shanghai.

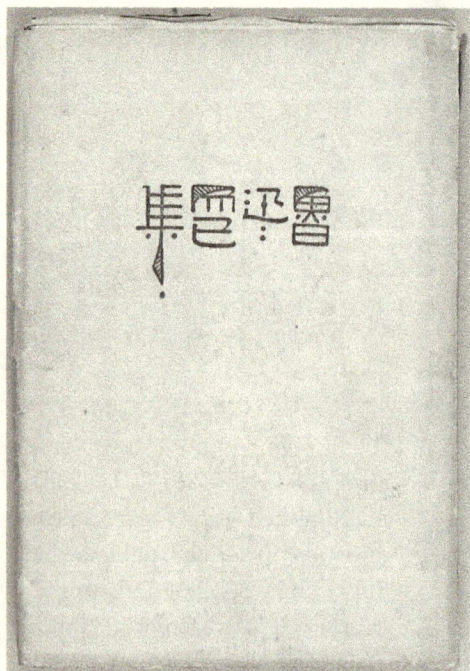

Front cover of *Eryi ji (And That's That)*, an anthology of Lu Xun's essays published in October 1928 by Beixin. Lu Xun Memorial Hall, Shanghai.

Front cover of the monthly *Benliu (Torrent)*, featuring Tolstoy, December 1928. Cofounded and coedited by Lu Xun and Yu Dafu in Shanghai, the journal published Russian literature in translation and articles on Marxist and Soviet theories of art and literature. Lu Xun Memorial Hall, Shanghai.

Front cover illustration of the weekly *Zhaohua xunkan (Dawn Blossoms)*, cofounded by Lu Xun in December 1928 and edited by Rou Shi. Lu Xun Memorial Hall, Shanghai.

Front cover of *Sanxian ji (Three Leisures),* an anthology of Lu Xun's essays published in October 1932 by Beixin. The title mockingly commemorates the Creation Society's attacks on Lu Xun in 1928. Lu Xun Memorial Hall, Shanghai.

3

Guns and Words

History, as Paul Virilio observed, moves at the speed of the weapons systems in use.[1] Modern firepower accelerated the collapse of the Qing dynasty in 1911 and the establishment of the Republic in 1912. Armored vehicles and bomber aircraft vastly enhanced the military might of China's feuding warlord regimes after 1917, while Soviet military technology and the counsel of over a thousand Soviet advisers rapidly expedited the prosecution of Chiang Kai-shek's Northern Expedition in 1926 and 1927.[2] In 1927 an article in the Tianjin-based American-owned newspaper *North China Star* claimed that China's importation of foreign arms had exceeded $100 million.[3] But it was the Expedition's Leninist propaganda—its calls for the simultaneous completion of Sun Yat-sen's "unfinished revolution" and advancement of "world revolution"—that gave meaning and purpose to mechanized warfare and the modern power of destruction.

Revolutionary violence was extolled and articulated at every opportunity with such propagandistic zeal during the Expedition's "united front" phase that one contemporary observer was led to remark: "Never before in China has the march of an army to victory been paved with so much paper."[4] Reflecting on this copious and euphoric propaganda three years later, Lu Xun wrote that those who promoted the idea that "all the fighters in a great revolutionary army" must share the same set of "absolutely correct and clear ideas" were producing not merely hollow rhetoric but also "a sugared pill to poison the revolution." These were the opening remarks of an essay he published in March 1930 under the title "An Unrevolutionary Eagerness for Revolution," in which he observed that two kinds of people embodied this disposition.[5]

Calling the first type "the decadent," he wrote that such a person seeks instant gratification and novelty to the extent that his "excitement about the revolution" is no different from that of "a glutton of jaded palate and ruined appetite" who "must eat things like pepper or chillies, causing his forehead to break out in a fine sweat, just to get down half a bowl of rice." Of the second type, although such people are "hard to classify," they share the key trait of "lacking any definite view" while nonetheless "feeling that everything in the world is wrong but they are always in the right." He concluded of the latter that their eagerness to declare themselves "the sole exponents of the golden mean" indicates that what they want is not revolution but rather "the status quo" in which they get to play the vanguard and have the last word.[6]

In the years that followed Chiang Kai-shek's bloody coup of April 1927, Lu Xun became more than ever before a critic of revolutionary doctrine. This is quite contrary to received accounts of Lu Xun's "Marxist turn" in mainland scholarship, which typically present him as a committed propagandist for the Communist cause. Indeed, the advocacy of a literature of the masses in his later writings was always broadly presented as egalitarian progress and never as part of a political ideology. If anything, his later writings reveal his deepening despair about the threatened future of *baihua* under the twin assault of Nationalist doctrine and Communist dogma.

Lu Xun's critical reflections on the speed of discursive change were situated in the interrelated contexts of authoritarian rule, leftist resistance, and commercial publishing. In the demands that each of these contexts imposed he discerned the advance of repressive forces, moving at an unforgiving pace to supplant social goals with military and business objectives. From the late 1920s onward he paid particular attention to the assumed relation between revolution and literature that was dominating Chinese intellectual discourse. In one celebrated instance in 1928, Lu Xun observed that the Creation Society's members were so impatient for success that they were in real danger of believing their own rhetorical ruses about turning "the weapons of art" (literature) into an actual "art of weapons" (guns).

Revolutionary Speed

The fashion for figuring revolution as pure speed took hold during the Northern Expedition. In February 1927, while the "united front" appeared still intact, Yu Dafu had observed: "It is impossible for an express train or an airplane to catch up with the leap of our ideals. Hence at the present moment we need more cultural critics and political critics who will painstakingly examine our ideals to compare the present and future situations of politics and culture. This will allow us to know the distance between our present situation and the type of politics and culture we idealize."[7]

In warning that war propaganda was blinding people to the widening gulf between their expectations and their actual circumstances, Yu nonetheless revealed himself as vulnerable to the thrill of racing toward an ideal future. He claimed that, armed with the correct insight, it might be possible "to see the limitations that hinder our rate of progress" and hence "to speed things up."[8]

In contrast, Deng Yanda (1895–1931), a prominent figure of the Nationalist left, lamented the futility of pitting mere ideals against the sheer power of militarist ambitions. He made this dismal observation in March 1927: "The result of this Northern Expedition is that military influences have outpaced the development of the party, have outpaced the government, have outpaced everything. This is an extraordinary danger for our party and an extraordinary danger in the future path of the Chinese revolution."[9] Deng concluded that the pragmatic arrangements and self-serving pacts between the Nationalist right and its warlord allies had made a mockery of the Nationalist Party's founding goals.

By July 1927, with the wholesale liquidation of Communists under way in the name of "Party purification," Deng, together with Sun Yat-sen's widow, Soong Ching-ling (1893–1981), and several leftists in the

Nationalist Party, denounced their own organization for attacking the masses and announced their separation from Chiang Kai-shek. Deng and Soong promptly left for Europe to live in temporary exile. After returning to China in 1930, Deng was arrested and executed under orders from Chiang.[10]

Lu Xun made several oblique remarks about the sudden change of revolutionary tack in his essays of mid- to late 1927. The series of aphoristic "Fleeting Mixed Impressions" that he completed in Guangzhou in September that year includes the following cryptic lines: "What we have are collections upon collections of speeches. What a pity they don't explain why the speakers' utterances are now totally unlike what they previously said, nor do the speeches indicate whether the speakers believe their own words."[11] Lu Xun was referring to the volumes of speeches by Nationalist leadership figures that were then being published in defense of "Party purification." This flood of anthologies included statements from the leader of the Nationalist left, Wang Jingwei, with whom Chiang had effected a pragmatic reconciliation in July 1927. The Nationalist left promptly joined the "Party purification" campaign of the Nationalist right and proceeded to arrest and kill Communists in Wuhan. In February 1928 Chiang's power was further strengthened with the dissolution of Wuhan as a revolutionary base. From then on, this city in central China, which had been the official seat of the Soviet-aided revolutionary government during the "united front's" final months in early 1927, ceased to pose any threat to Chiang of a rival Nationalist stronghold.

Lu Xun used the phrase "collections upon collections of speeches" to draw attention to the torrential outpouring of new Nationalist propaganda. His next remark to the effect that the speakers might not even believe their own words archly suggests that no amount of justification could paper over the massacre of Communists then under way. According to Yu Dafu, Lu Xun likened his own oblique attacks on the Nationalists' altered discourse to the "raised comb and beating wings" of a fighting rooster but one that sought nonetheless to "maintain a considerable distance from its opponent." Lu Xun told Yu that this tacit resistance was a practical necessity. He regarded it as a way of fending off the advances of those who sought either to co-opt or to harass him, explaining to Yu that "at the slightest sign of weakness, one's opponent would resort to the basest methods to coerce one even more."[12]

In late 1927 Lu Xun praised the Russian writers Sergei Esenin (1895–1925) and Andrei Sobol (1888–1926) as moral paragons in a time of violence. In October he wrote that the suicides of these two writers revealed a contradictory truth. On the one hand, "in an age of revolution, only those with the courage to declare they 'cannot go on living' are capable of writing revolutionary literature." But on the other hand, the fact of their suicides showed they were "not revolutionary writers after all." A genuine revolution must exceed the expectations of its prophets and in this process render their ideals obsolete.[13] Referring again to Esenin and Sobol in a Shanghai lecture in December 1927, he remarked: "They sang paeans to the revolution but met their end when they collided with the rock-hard reality they once eulogized. At this time, the Soviet Union came into being!"[14]

In these references to Esenin and Sobol, Lu Xun made no mention of the rising rate of suicide in the Soviet Union during the mid-1920s, nor to the copycat suicides that Esenin inspired.[15] Although he would have been aware of growing intellectual repression in the world's first Marxist state, he chose not to comment on it. He was conscious of viewing the Soviet Union from afar and in his occasional references to it maintained the respectful attitude of an outsider. To Lu Xun, the suicides of Esenin and Sobol mattered primarily as an ethical lesson about facing one's own illusions. In the exemplary honesty he ascribed to them, he found a loose analogy for his own despair about the thwarted cause of revolution in China. After 1927 he never again endorsed violence the way he did in Guangzhou when he referred to the sweet ringing of cannon fire.

Instead he focused on the tragedy that befalls those who truly believe in an ideal society. In the same December 1927 lecture in which he extolled Esenin and Sobol, he reminded his audience that a writer of vision attracts persecution by virtue of being ahead of his time. Using the analogy of a military drill, Lu Xun evoked the rigors of revolutionary indoctrination he had witnessed in Guangzhou earlier that year to observe of such a writer:

He is simply sensitive, quick to feel and quick to express himself (too quickly, at times, so even society opposes and excludes him). Take military drill for example: in presenting arms the regulation command is "pre-s e e e e nt ARMS," and you damn well can't present them until the word ARMS is called. Yet some people raise the rifle as soon as they hear the word "present," causing the instructor to punish them for their error. That's exactly how it is with the writer in society; he speaks a little too soon, and the public hates him for it.[16]

He added that writers whom he considered true revolutionaries were fatally at odds with power: their ideals led them to "volunteer themselves" as a form of macabre entertainment, for they were "trussed up and beheaded or placed against a wall to be dispatched by a firing squad." Lu Xun followed this violent image with another of gawking spectators "gathering around whenever the police patrol in Shanghai's foreign concessions use their truncheons to beat someone up."[17]

The predatory crowd conjured up in both images is a recurring figure in his writings: one that evinces his admiration for Friedrich Nietzsche's (1844–1900) contempt for the unthinking herd. In this lecture, Lu Xun observed that ignorance begets the passive violence of *Schadenfreude,* because "no one wants to be beaten up, but people seem to get something out of watching someone else being beaten up."[18] Lu Xun also suggested that unthinking people are motivated by a craven fear—cowering before power while loathing those who refuse to be cowed.

In this connection, he implied that the speed of violence ultimately favors repression over revolutionary change. This bleak view was clearly opposite to the one favored by the majority of the left: that violence would accelerate the arrival of a communist society. Before surveying the dismissive remarks Lu Xun made about his Marxist accusers' exaltation of warfare, it is necessary to examine what critical thinking meant to him.

Belated Knowing

In his choice of pen name, Lu Xun made "speed" *(xun)* the very essence of his authorial persona, but his self-reflexive disposition led him to valorize speed in a distinctly different way from that of mere velocity. It was not a quick transition from the present to the future that he sought. Rather, what occupied his interest was the question of how to recognize the *rush* of true insight (as opposed to delusion) and what to do with it.[19] Lu Xun understood insight not as prescience but as an awakening to error. He was undoubtedly influenced by Buddhist soteriology, with which he had a deep familiarity and an abiding fascination.

Not surprisingly, he tended to figure true insight as an ordeal. This is vividly presented in his inaugural 1918 work of *baihua* fiction, "The Diary of a Madman." The story centers upon the madman's rising horror as he gains knowledge of his own predatory involvement in the cannibalistic practices around him, of which he has become belatedly cognizant. Lu Xun suggests that the protagonist realizes he is fatally doomed to live out his days as a cannibal but that the anguish of his belated insight could serve nonetheless as a salutary emotion. Hence the madman's final desperate words: "Perhaps there are still children who have not eaten humans? Save the children . . ."[20] This plea lends itself to being read as a modern experience of redemptive suffering (in the Buddhist sense of *dukkha*), of realizing that one's own belated arrival at the truth can nourish a desire to help others on to a better path.

As a corollary to Lu Xun's favorite counsel of "seeing with eyes wide open," this idea of knowing too late also expresses a modernist attentiveness to the alienating effects of self-knowledge. This insight of Lu Xun's finds a sympathetic resonance in Walter Benjamin's (1892–1940) critical retranscription of Friedrich Schlegel's (1722–1829) remark that "the historian is a prophet facing backward." Against the conventional understanding of this statement as meaning that the historian writes as if he had transported himself into the past, Benjamin argues, with an emphasis on the dynamic force of historical insight: "But the saying can also be understood to mean something quite different: the historian turns his back on his own time, and his seer's gaze is kindled by the peaks of earlier generations as they sink further and further into the past. Indeed, the historian's own time is far more distinctly present to this visionary gaze than it is to the contemporaries who 'keep step with it.'"[21] In Lu Xun's dwelling on the instructive tragedy of belated insight, we find a writer who sought, against the literary peaks of generations past that captivated him, to make his own time far more distinctly present.

As the May Fourth Movement unfolded in 1919, Lu Xun was thirty-eight and lauded everywhere by his young admirers as a mentor. He was sufficiently senior to the student protestors to regard them as "children" and hence to express paternal concern for their welfare. Indeed, the role of in loco parentis came easily to him, schooled as he was in the elite Confucian ethos that fused the roles of teacher and moral guardian. However, he was also deeply ambivalent toward this traditional ethos; though keenly aware that he owed his very identity to it, he saw it as irredeemably corrupted. Hence his essays of this early period often reprised the urgency of "the madman's" final plea to "save the children" as if to suggest that although he was tainted, "the children" (his students and readers) were innocent of predatory guile.

In this context, he wrote frequently in the late 1910s and early 1920s that, contrary to standard wisdom, "the old" often overtook (or moved faster than) "the new." By this, he meant that the ingrained social habits of China's dynastic past proved so enduring as to hinder and even incapacitate the production of modern values. For instance, in a 1919 essay published in *New Youth*, Lu Xun wrote that among ostensibly progressive Chinese people, many still remained trapped in thinking of reform as a process of "self-strengthening." In this negative use of the protomodernizing slogan of mid- to late nineteenth-century Confucian bureaucrats, he was expressing his unequivocal disapproval of all attempts to preserve China's cultural past and, in particular, *wenyan*.[22] These criticisms were directed at scholars who had begun espousing "national essence" a decade earlier, including his former mentor Zhang Taiyan (1868–1936), a much-revered radical intellectual of the 1900s and early 1910s. By the late 1910s, Zhang was dismissed as obsolete by the advocates of "literary revolution." He was deeply opposed to *baihua* and the New Culture movement in which his protégé was playing such a significant part.

Three years later, in 1922, Lu Xun leveled the same accusation at a Harvard-educated group of self-styled "new humanists." He wrote bitingly of *Critical Review*, a journal founded by former students of Irving Babbitt (1865–1933) of whom the two most prominent were Wu Mi

(1894–1978) and Mei Guangdi (1890–1945), that it "reflected the fake luster of the fake antiques in the vicinity of the Jubao city gate in Nanjing" (where the journal was based),[23] because the journal sought to promote cosmopolitan ideas through the use of *wenyan*. Lu Xun was equally withering about the "National Studies" movement initiated by Hu Shi. This movement sought to establish a science of national history by applying Western-derived methods of textual evaluation to the study of Chinese civilization.

In his many published criticisms of such endeavors, Lu Xun maintained an uncompromising stance. In 1919 he declared that any attempt at institutionalizing a national heritage was tantamount to "acquiring new knowledge in order to shut the door on further importations of new knowledge, in order then to return to our old ways.... In other words, we acquire Western capabilities to preserve old Chinese habits. So, we want to have new capabilities, but we also want our ideas to remain old."[24] In this regard he frequently directed his attacks on "the old" at the debased institutionalized forms of Confucianism and Daoism that he perceived as the cause of China's social ills. He accused both these "orthodoxies" of encouraging venal conduct through an entrenched hierarchism and of fostering a priestly culture aimed at keeping the majority of ordinary Chinese forever under the spell of the educated few.

Although Lu Xun never provided a historiographic alternative to the national heritage model, the type of inquiry he favored is evident from his masterly account of premodern popular literature in *A Brief History of Chinese Fiction*.[25] As John Y. C. Wang has pointed out, the pioneering nature of this scholarly work, based on Lu Xun's lectures at Peking University, derives not only from his erudite insights into styles of representation in premodern works but from the special attention he gave to the reception of literature among different audiences. As Wang notes, Lu Xun's observations about the habits of mind formed as a result of patterns of reception constitute a watershed moment in Chinese literary scholarship.[26]

More broadly, Lu Xun's emphasis on the *experience* of literature as an encounter between self and other was integral to his treatment of humanism, less as a concept than as a palpable encounter. His lecture of 8 April 1927 at the Whampoa Military Academy provides an interesting

instance of literature valorized as a moral experience in tacit appreciation of an ancient Chinese sensibility. On that occasion, Lu Xun
opined that a successful revolution ought to produce paeans and
dirges, and claimed that the revolution in Soviet Russia was successful
because paeans were everywhere evident together with the dirges of
those intellectuals who were forced to flee overseas.[27]

He concluded that China, which had produced neither paean nor
dirge, lagged far behind. This comparison, together with Lu Xun's deliberate use of musical metaphors, suggests a conscious evocation of
the moral insight (vividly presented in the story of Ji Zha in the fourth
century B.C.E. Confucian classic the *Zuo Commentary*) that the well-being
of a state and its people is embodied in the music of the land.[28] Hence,
in commending Soviet literature as writings "in praise of construction," Lu Xun mused optimistically that these happy soulful tunes
augured the true advent of "a people's literature," adding that even
though "we cannot yet predict what will come later," such writings conveyed the hope that, one day, "the world will belong to the people."[29]

The butchery sanctioned as "Party purification" brought an end to
his praise of the untainted hope of the committed young. As he wrote
in October 1927, he discovered all too belatedly that some of Guangzhou's revolutionary youth proved "even more pitiless" than the "old
people" he had previously condemned.[30] After 1927 he continued to
examine how "the old" devastated "the new," but with a sharpened
despair. The contrast is evident in the images of velocity he produced
in 1922 versus those of 1927.

Among Lu Xun's evocative figurations of "the new" as an urgent
undertaking, two of the most memorable (and still frequently quoted)
appear in his 1922 preface to *A Call to Arms*. In one instance (noted in
Chapter 1), he called his prose a *cri de coeur* in aid of "true warriors as
they galloped on alone." In the second instance, he described "traditional China" as a hermetically sealed "iron house." Reprising the
theme of belated cognition, he asked whether people should be allowed to die peacefully or be awakened to their imminent death by
suffocation in the iron house. He wrote that he was heartened by his
friend Qian Xuantong's (1887–1939) reply that the awakened inhabitants
might actually succeed in destroying the iron house. In this manner,

Lu Xun likened the process of unlearning the received Chinese past to a slow ordeal of critical reflection.

In presenting "the new" as a self-unraveling akin to the death agonies of one's former self, Lu Xun sought to encourage among his readers a *speedy* resolve to undergo this *slow* ordeal. Hence, in contrast to his peers, who produced blueprints for the future home of Chinese being, Lu Xun explored the modern condition as a state of dispossession or homelessness (a state evoked in the two publishing projects he established for his acolytes in 1925: Yet to Be Named, a book series; and *Wilderness*, a journal). He was also partial to figuring *baihua* as a wounding of the Chinese language from within, in which the writer identifies himself as an integral part of the very thing he seeks to destroy. As he wrote in 1926, he was someone who, having "emerged from the fortress of the old," was better equipped "not only to see the situation more clearly but to turn his weapons against a formidable foe to deal it a deathblow."[31]

In his Shanghai lecture of December 1927, he expressed a more complex sentiment when he praised those of his students who went to Guangzhou to fight rather than write. He remarked that the letters he received from them over time showed "the rusting of their words and phrases."[32] It was in this lecture that he praised the suicides of Esenin and Sobol and spoke of the truly committed writer as destined to suffer. In a similar vein, he implied that his students' linguistic deterioration was proof of their genuine intention to serve the cause of revolution.

This was an echo of the poignant eulogy he wrote for the same students on 10 April 1926. Then still living in Beijing, Lu Xun praised them not only for risking their lives for a just cause but for doing so at the cost of their own happiness, noting that their prospect of success was remote. To express how moved he was by the letters and manuscripts they sent to him, he wrote: "One by one, the souls of these young writers who refuse to embellish their prose stand tall before me. They are graceful and pure, but oh how frustrated, sorrowful, and enraged they have become. In the end, their souls became rough, these young people whom I adore." Extolling their roughness with sensuous empathy, Lu Xun continued: "Their souls have grown rough from being constantly hammered by wind and dust. But I love these souls because they are human souls. Theirs is a roughness I want to kiss: formless and colorless but dripping with blood."[33] When Lu Xun wrote these lines in April 1926, Zhang Zuolin's warplanes had bombarded Beijing daily in a bid to wrest control of the capital from his rival, Duan Qirui. Lu Xun wrote that the bombing missions were as regular as "a classroom schedule" and noted an unusual quietness in the air one morning after the bombs fell, as he wiped "the pale dust" off his writing desk.[34]

Using "pale dust" as an allegorical trace of violence, Lu Xun created a resonance between it and the "pale bloodstains" he had evoked nine days earlier (1 April 1926) to commemorate several of his students who had been killed by Duan Qirui's troops in Beijing. In this earlier essay, "In Memory of Miss Liu Hezhen," he lauded the students' selfless courage as an inspiration for everyone, declaring: "Those who drag on an ignoble existence will catch a vague glimpse of hope amid the pale bloodstains, while true fighters will advance with greater resolution."[35] In these two eulogies of April 1926, the word "blood" is transposed from a sign of human biology to a shining symbol of shared humanity.

Profitable Words

While Lu Xun heaped generous praise on the untimely killed, he was conspicuously frugal in commending the living. As the 1920s progressed and as he continued to prosper as a radical thinker and writer, he grew increasingly pessimistic about the prospects of positive change. In an essay written in Guangzhou on 15 September 1927, twelve days before he set sail for Shanghai, Lu Xun noted that the news of the day featured an item about the banning of *baihua* in Zhang Zuolin's Beijing on the grounds that it encouraged vulgarity.

This was Zhang's attempt to unseat *baihua*'s nascent authority as the medium of instruction at new-style Beijing schools since the early 1920s. Lu Xun wrote of "the obligatory statements of profound sorrow" that would appear in the pages of *Threads of Talk* (the journal he cofounded) in protest against this ban but added that for his own part, he felt "truly indifferent."[36]

Contemplating the lethal duplicities of revolutionary *baihua* discourse in the south and the archaic despotism of Zhang Zuolin in the north, Lu Xun remarked that "since intellectual discourse is everywhere stifled, it really doesn't make much difference whether we call it 'white' or 'black.'" Here he played on the literal senses of *baihua* and *heihua* as "white speech" and "black speech" respectively, to suggest that in Guangzhou, although *baihua* was fashionably revolutionary, it had become no different from the "argot of thieves" (the figurative sense of *heihua*).[37]

But despite Zhang Zuolin's efforts to eradicate the effects of the "literary revolution," by 1927 *baihua* was already a permanent fixture in Chinese publishing, and the warlord's attempted ban proved as short-lived as his own regime. Meanwhile the urgent diction of revolutionary *baihua* that had been harnessed as propaganda for the Northern Expedition was fast spreading out of Guangzhou into commercial Shanghai and acquiring an aggressive commercial speed in this process. To Lu Xun and many other pioneers of Beijing's "literary revolution," the "revolutionary literature" that flourished in Shanghai's newspapers, books, and magazines after 1927 was a far cry from the people's tongue they had heralded a decade earlier.

Lu Xun regarded his active promotion of the work of young writers, translators, and critics as an integral part of his lifelong cause to regenerate Chinese culture. For those in whom he saw promise, he devoted considerable energies to hastening their success and widening their influence. On the whole, however, the individuals he mentored disappointed him. In a letter to Xu Guangping from Xiamen on 28 October 1926, Lu Xun confided that he was utterly disheartened that his wish to "lend a bit of strength to others" ultimately had borne only "bitter fruit."[38] In this instance he was alluding to the quarrels that ensued among his students in Beijing and to one individual in particular: Gao Changhong (1898–late 1950s), founder of the Hurricane Society (Kuangbiao she) and Lu Xun's most fractious acolyte.

In 1925 Lu Xun founded the Yet to Be Named Society (Weiming she), a literary organization that published its own book series, and established *Wilderness (Mangyuan)*, a magazine. These two Beijing-based literary enterprises were intended as vehicles for the publications of his protégés.[39] Because he was suspended from the Ministry of Education between August and December, 1925 was a year when circumstance and choice led Lu Xun to throw himself into his literary pursuits. In addition to writing essays, short stories, and experimental prose compositions (most of which first appeared in *Threads of Talk*, with the experimental compositions subsequently republished as the *Wild Grass* anthology in 1927), Lu Xun edited and contributed to *Wilderness* and oversaw the publication of Soviet works in Chinese translation under the Yet to Be Named imprint. He told Xu Guangping that he composed *Wild Grass* in a state of near delirium; he was so preoccupied with these various literary projects that he often "forgot to eat and took drugs to cut back on sleep."[40]

But despite lamenting the "bitter fruit" of his efforts as a literary mentor, Lu Xun enjoyed a lasting friendship with several members of the Yet to Be Named Society, notably Li Jiye, Tai Jingnong, and Wei Suyuan (1902–1932). In a moving eulogy he wrote for Wei in 1934, he noted that Wei always adopted a "special attitude" of solemn respect toward him. In attributing Wei's conduct to the difference in their ages, Lu Xun also expressed regret about being venerated as an elder. His desire for close friendship on an equal footing with the young people he liked is heartfelt and telling in the remark: "It's a pity that I can't change into a young man to show that it is possible for all of us to forget this difference between self and other."[41]

Among those who disappointed him were his successful protégés Li Xiaofeng and Sun Fuyuan (1894–1966), whose entrepreneurism he found deeply irritating. On the whole, Lu Xun's criticisms were fairly general, with only occasional references to specific individuals. Nonetheless, even among those he chastised in print, Lu Xun's enormous fame ensured their keenness to maintain his friendship.

Gao Changhong, however, proved the exception. He attacked his erstwhile mentor in print after their friendship ended abruptly in late 1926. In October Gao had published an advertisement announcing that his magazine *Hurricane* had the support of "the intellectual pioneer Lu Xun." In December Lu Xun published a curt refutation of this claim and cut all ties with the *Hurricane* magazine and its controversial founder.[42] The final straw for Lu Xun came in November 1926, when Gao, who had been close to Xu Guangping, published a poem in which he wrote symbolically of the sun (himself) and the night (Lu Xun) competing for the affections of the moon (Xu Guangping), thereby boasting that he had once been Lu Xun's romantic rival. At the time, Lu Xun had also received the unpleasant news that several of his protégés (including Li Xiaofeng) were spreading false rumors that Xu Guangping was secretly cohabiting with him in Xiamen.[43]

These rumors added to his unease as he prepared to leave Xiamen to join Guangping in Guangzhou. As Leo Ou-fan Lee has observed, their courtship as documented in their correspondence from 1925 onwards "shows her active pursuit and his gradual loosening of defenses." But as Lee also notes, "their common-law marriage represents perhaps the happiest chapter of Lu Xun's story concerning literary youths."[44]

In October 1927, when musing about the contrary uses that his admirers and detractors made of his name, Lu Xun remarked exasperatedly: "I'm no Jesus, so why on earth would I want to bear a cross for others?"[45] Fame-hungry writers like Gao gained publicity by association with Lu Xun while influential publishers like Li Xiaofeng and Sun Fuyuan reaped enormous financial profit from publishing him.

Threads of Talk, the journal with which Lu Xun became most identified, was an enterprise in which both Li and Sun played an instrumental role. In December 1929, some three months before the journal closed for good, Lu Xun published an autobiographical essay, *"Threads of Talk* and Me: A Full Account," in which he expressed his ambivalence toward the profit-driven mentality of these two protégés. He had known them since their student days at Peking University in the late 1910s and early 1920s.[46] Both Li and Sun were former members of the leading student organization New Tide Society, whose journal *New Tide (Xinchao)* acquired a reputation for trendy iconoclasm during the heyday of the New Culture movement.

The pluralism of *New Tide* reflected the influence of its various mentors. Among them, Hu Shi commanded authority as a declared liberal, Li Dazhao guided students who were drawn to Communism, and Lu Xun and Zhou Zuoren were sought out by those who shared their humanist interest in fostering social empathy through literature. As *New Tide* gained notoriety for its unrestrained denunciations of Confucianism and traditional social values, it became the journal of choice among radical students. In 1919, as the May Fourth student protest in Beijing widened into a national movement, *New Tide* reached even greater prominence and was regularly hailed as a leader of social change.

In 1922, however, the journal closed down, as several of its key members had left or were leaving for graduate studies in the United States and Europe. Li and Sun remained in Beijing. They reorganized the New Tide Society as a discussion forum and introduced commercial publishing as part of the society's operations.[47]

Lu Xun secured the success of this business venture in its first year of operation. In 1923 he gave Li and Sun two of his books to publish: *A Brief History of Chinese Fiction,* the survey work based on his early 1920s lectures at Peking University; and his first collection of short stories, *A Call to Arms.* These two highly acclaimed and commercially lucrative books launched Li's and Sun's publishing careers. A year later Sun initiated the founding of *Threads of Talk,* which was also published by New Tide and which also became very profitable.

In his December 1929 retrospective, Lu Xun recounted the genesis of *Threads of Talk* in Sun's resignation as editor of Beijing's prestigious *Morning Post Literary Supplement (Chenbao fukan).* The paper's managers had vetoed a satirical poem by Lu Xun that Sun wanted to publish, leading Sun to resign in protest. Lu Xun wrote that he felt a burden of responsibility to his protégé and hence supported Sun's proposal to found a new journal, which promptly resulted in the inauguration of *Threads of Talk.* According to Lu Xun, *Threads of Talk* proved to be such formidable competition for the *Morning Post* that Sun's erstwhile employers went to make peace with him. Lu Xun recalled that when Sun told him triumphantly, "Little did they know they were trampling on dynamite!" he felt "as if doused with cold water, suspecting that by 'dynamite' he meant me." He continued: "So all my thinking and writing would serve merely to blow me to smithereens on account of their petty quarrel!"[48]

The first sixty-four issues of *Threads of Talk* were produced out of the New Tide Society's office in the basement of Courtyard Number One, a building on the campus of Peking University. Li Xiaofeng did most of the work himself, utilizing a campus printing press (normally used for printing lecture materials) to print and distribute copies of the journal. The profits generated from subscriptions enabled Li to expand his activities. In 1925 he founded Beixin Publishing House, which thereafter took over the publication of *Threads of Talk.*[49]

Largely through Lu Xun's active support, Beixin became one of China's most exclusive publishing houses of the day. The name Beixin was a fusion of the two institutional names Beida (Peking University) and Xinchao (New Tide; Renaissance). Lu Xun encouraged Li and ensured the success of his new enterprise by making Beixin his preferred publisher. Thus, in its first year Beixin published new editions of *A Brief History of Chinese Fiction* and *A Call to Arms*, both of which were guaranteed best-sellers.[50] Beixin published a total of twenty-four books by Lu Xun, each with multiple print runs: *A Call to Arms* was its all-time best-seller, with twenty-four reprints between 1924 and 1937.[51]

In his 1929 retrospective, Lu Xun, having written disapprovingly about Sun Fuyuan, turned to criticize Li for compromising the integrity of *Threads of Talk*. He wrote that the journal had begun its life as the work of "a few congenial spirits" and that this was evident in the first two years of its operation in Beijing (1924–1926), when the only advertisements allowed were book notices. Moreover, "if the members did not think well of a new book they would not print a notice of it." Lu Xun lamented that, under Li's management, the journal's high standards deteriorated upon its relocation to Shanghai.[52]

This relocation occurred in late 1926, shortly after Zhang Zuolin captured Beijing from Duan Qirui. Under the archconservative Zhang, *Threads of Talk* was banned, and Beixin Publishing House faced closure. Seeing a bleak future ahead, Li moved his business to Shanghai. A year later, upon Lu Xun's arrival in Shanghai in October 1927, Li invited his former mentor to take over the editorship of the newly relocated *Threads of Talk*, to which Lu Xun promptly agreed.[53] Zhou Zuoren edited the journal in Beijing.

Lu Xun wrote that the Shanghai version of *Threads of Talk* carried advertisements not only for book notices but for clinics, a stocking factory, and "even one for pills to cure involuntary emissions." He found this policy intolerable and noted that the advertisements stopped only after he wrote several complaints to Li.[54]

In his 1929 retrospective, Lu Xun also described the journal's operations. He wrote that the editorial board regarded all regular contributors as fellow members and that, after the journal's move to Shanghai, former contributors from the journal's Beijing days and more recent regular contributors were described alike as "old members." Lu Xun explained that because these "old members" had the privilege of guaranteed publication, they could send their manuscripts directly to Beixin Publishing House, bypassing any editorial scrutiny. As a result, his role as the journal's editor was effectively only titular. He had "no authority to refuse articles by the other members"; moreover, because new writers highly recommended by "old members" could also avoid being subjected to editorial veto, he had little say over their manuscripts as well. He wrote that when he served as editor in 1928, "nine out of ten of our members sent their manuscripts straight to Beixin Publishing House, which delivered them to the printers; I saw them only when printed and bound." He found himself confined to "deleting certain passages" and exercising editorial judgment over a very limited number of manuscripts by nonmembers.[55]

Nonetheless, these same loose arrangements had also made it possible for both him and Zhou Zuoren to be involved in the journal's founding in 1924, despite their estrangement the previous year. The rift between the brothers has always been attributed to the hostility of Zhou's wife, Hata Noboku (1887–1962), toward Lu Xun in 1923, allegedly over money and her claims of sexual impropriety on his part. At the time, the two brothers and their wives shared a home in Beijing. The sibling tensions grew so serious that in May 1924 Lu Xun moved his mother and his wife, Zhu An, into a new home. Both siblings, however, maintained silence over the details of their falling out. Even their mother, Lu Rui, professed ignorance about the cause, and Lu Xun chose not to discuss it with his youngest sibling, Jianren.[56] Leo Ou-fan Lee has noted that the rift coincided with Lu Xun's depressed state of mind in 1923 and 1924. Months after falling out with Zuoren, he became seriously unwell, and there were rumors that he contemplated suicide.[57] In the decades before their dramatic falling out, the two brothers had been very close. During their student days in Japan in the late 1900s, they collaborated on numerous translation projects. They shared the conviction that Chinese literature lacked a genuine humanism and made it their mission to furnish it with one. Lee concludes that Lu Xun "must have been profoundly shaken by his estrangement from his beloved brother, who had hitherto been his closest literary comrade."[58]

Although Lu Xun and Zhou Zuoren were never reconciled, in the latter half of the 1920s they maintained a literary alliance via *Threads of Talk*. When Zhou edited the journal in the mid-1920s and Lu Xun in 1928, the two brothers were regularly featured in the same issues. Lu Xun's editorship of *Threads of Talk* in 1928 proved crucial for his polemical exchanges with his adversaries on the left (in particular, the Creation and Sun Societies) and the right (the Crescent Moon Society). The journal not only became his warhorse but frequently carried essays, commentaries, and letters by other contributors who were equally irate about the "theoretical struggles" of the Marxist radicals. Indeed, most of the articles featured in *Threads of Talk* defended Lu Xun against the attacks of the Creation Society and Sun Society. His polemical exchanges with the Crescent Moon Society were less frequent and attracted far fewer commentaries, but, as Lu Xun noted in his 1929 retrospective, the "upright gentlemen" of the Crescent Moon Society were the first to taunt him as "commander-in-chief of *Threads of Talk*," lumbering him with an epithet he hated.[59] But it was Mao Zedong's 1940 description of Lu Xun as "commander-in-chief of China's cultural revolution" that ensured he was posthumously saddled with this pseudomilitary title for decades.[60]

Lu Xun himself used similar-sounding titles to mock his Marxist adversaries. For instance, in August 1928, eight months after the Creation Society and Sun Society first began describing him as a petty-bourgeois laggard, he noted wryly that as he had fallen so far behind, he had "no way of knowing the situation at the core or in the vanguard" of the revolutionary movement. In mimicry of his accusers' breathless declamatory style (and with tacit reference to their insinuations that *Threads of Talk* was a conspiracy of two siblings), he wrote that, as a laggard, his only recourse was to

> gaze at the derrières of such personages as Commander Cheng Fangwu, who's in charge of *Creation Monthly, Cultural Critique,* and *Flowing Sand;* Chief Officer Jiang Guang X (forgive me for not knowing which character he is now using), who runs *Sun Monthly;* Wang Duqing [1898–1940], who heads up *Our Monthly;* the revolutionary young artist Ye Lingfeng [1904–1975], who sings solo in the *Gobi Fortnightly.*

There's also that other revolutionary young artist Pan Hannian, who edits *Modern Story* and *Battlefront* and is trailed by older brother Pan Zinian [1893–1972], who "echoes his younger brother in saying beautiful things" in *Primal Chaos Fortnightly*.[61]

In this sardonic litany of the names of persons and journals associated with the Creation Society and Sun Society, Lu Xun suggests that the unseemly haste with which his accusers were declaring others obsolete was in reality a desperate bid to achieve a quick and undeserved fame for themselves.

At this point it is worth recalling that it was in mid- to late 1927, while the anti-Communist purge was under way, that "revolutionary literature" became fashionable in Shanghai. In the marketplace, a whirl of revolutionary sentiments and persuasions helped to obscure the differences between Nationalist and Communist goals (to the advantage of the left). What was beyond dispute was the enormous marketability of revolutionary rhetoric itself. As the erstwhile leading light at radical Sun Yat-sen University, Lu Xun became a revolutionary "brand" that Beixin Publishing House was quick to exploit.

The open letter that Lu Xun wrote to Li Xiaofeng, published in the 1 October 1927 issue of *Threads of Talk* upon his acceptance of Li's invitation to edit the journal, affords an insight into the mutual profitability and complexity of their relationship. The letter, which ranges from candid criticism of Li to chatty insights about events and personalities in Guangzhou, illustrates Lu Xun's ambivalence toward his entrepreneurial protégé as well as the new pressures he faced in attempting to control his public image in Shanghai. He was fond of describing Li as *hutu*, an ambiguous word that could mean either innocent or feigned "muddle-headedness."[62]

Lu Xun began by expressing his unhappiness about *Lu Xun in Guangdong*, a work that Li had published in July 1927 without consulting him. This was essentially a Festschrift consisting of twelve articles about Lu Xun, with an appendix featuring the transcripts of four lectures he had delivered in Guangzhou in early 1927.[63] Lu Xun told Li that he learned of this publication solely because it had been advertised in several issues of *Threads of Talk*. He felt compelled to protest in print because the most recent of these advertisements had the temerity to claim that Lu Xun was the author of this work. He demanded that Li withdraw and revise the volume, expressly noting that he had played no part in its production. He then asked Li to comply with three requests: namely, that all his texts be removed from the volume; that his name be removed and replaced with the name of the actual editor; and that the letter stating these requests be published forthwith in *Threads of Talk*. He then informed Li: "Once this has been done, only the essays of others will remain. I have no objections to this and nothing further to say. But I must tell you that what I've read of *Lu Xun in Guangdong* offers the reader no insight into Lu Xun's life in Guangzhou. If you were to add several dozen blank pages to the volume, it might be more deserving of the name 'Lu Xun in Guangdong.'"[64] Having dealt with this unpleasant matter in the opening paragraphs, Lu Xun filled the remaining pages of his letter with personal news and observations, conveyed with chatty warmth.

In several of his publications from 1927 to 1929, Lu Xun revealed a similarly self-conscious awkwardness about the revolutionary credentials he had acquired as a result of having spent time in Guangzhou. For instance, in the lecture "On the Intelligentsia," presented on 25 October 1927 at the anarchist-sponsored Labor University in Shanghai, he noted that intellectuals were prone to adulation-induced amnesia. He warned against the confusing of narcissism with revolutionary ardor, stating that since a writer lauded by the masses as their spokesperson was liable to forget his admirers, the risk was multiplied if the rich were to also embrace the writer and turn him willy-nilly into "a member of the elite class . . . to leave the masses far behind." By way of ironic illustration he jokingly told his audience, "Your applause will raise my status and lead me to forget what I'm saying."[65]

Violent Hope

In the diversity of styles that informed the Chinese discourse on revolutionary literature, Futurism was a notably strong current that filtered through from war-extolling avant-garde Japanese, Russian, and European literature. Filippo Tommaso Marinetti's (1876–1944) *Futurist*

Manifesto of 1909 (widely known in Chinese intellectual circles by the late 1910s) made violence fashionable with its call "to exalt aggressive action," to celebrate "the beauty of speed," and to glorify war as "the world's only hygiene."[66] Vladimir Mayakovsky (1893–1930), the celebrated Russian Futurist poet and a leading advocate of art as political propaganda, was also greatly admired and imitated. Mao Dun, who had fought in the Northern Expedition as a Communist, wrote critically of this Futurist disposition in *Disillusionment*, a novel that he completed in August–September 1927 while hiding in Shanghai. In it he portrayed intellectuals who joined the revolution as bellicose, reckless, and self-destructive. Hence the story's male love interest, Qiang Weili, an officer in the Northern Expedition army (whose name stands literally for power), declares his revolutionary zeal as follows:

> I adore Futurism in art. I go after strong stimulants. I sing hymns to bombs, cannons, revolutions—all that expresses violent destructive force. I became a revolutionary because I was tired of the everyday round and that is also why I enlisted in the army. The battlefield is the best setting for Futurism: strong stimulants, destruction, change, inane killing, worship of brute strength, everything you can think of is there.... To tell you the truth, I like to fight, not for any reason, but because I thirst after strong stimulants; I don't care whether I win or not.[67]

Not surprisingly, despite Mao Dun's Communist credentials, *Disillusionment* was widely attacked on the left. His grim caricature of exuberant war-glorifying rhetoric had clearly struck a nerve, and the leaders of "revolutionary literature" in Shanghai, the Creation Society and the Sun Society, promptly condemned him for it. For instance, Qian Xingcun accused Mao Dun of failing to express "the consciousness of the newly risen class" and of remaining mired in "the disillusionment and vacillation of the plummeting revolutionary petty-bourgeoisie."[68]

The rhetoric of these two organizations echoed the strident prescriptions of the Russian Association of Proletarian Writers (RAPP, transliterated into Chinese as *Lapu*), and the Creation Society's members were inspired in particular by the writings of Fukumoto Kazuo, Japan's leading Marxist theorist of the mid-1920s. But both groups were mindful of the Nationalist censors and avoided any explicit praise of Communism. They used "revolutionary literature" as a catchall to encompass the range of writings they published: from prose and poetry to book reviews, open letters, social commentaries, theoretical essays, and translations.

The members of the Creation Society and Sun Society styled themselves as an avant-garde, but their political didacticism rendered their writings inherently conservative. In the marketplace, it was their association with formulaic fiction of the "revolution plus romantic love" (geming jia lian'ai) genre that brought them fame and catapulted "revolutionary literature" into fashion. Jiang Guangci, the Sun Society's leading representative, was the most celebrated writer of this genre in late 1920s Shanghai.

Jiang had first attracted attention with his debut novel, The Youthful Tramp (Shaonian piaopozhe), published in January 1926. This tragic love story, set against the "united front" of the Northern Expedition, proved a winning formula that Jiang would repeat with variations in his subsequent works. In essence, the male protagonist, a cadet at the Whampoa Military Academy, undergoes the anguish of falling in love but dies fighting and fails to reunite with his beloved. A year later, in January 1927, Jiang published a collection of short stories, On the Yalu (Yalu jiang shang), which was followed in November 1927 with A Sacrifice in the Wild (Ye ji).[69]

By late 1927, Jiang was not only the leading author of stories of "revolution plus romantic love," but his popularity helped to boost the use of the phrase as a marketing label. In February 1928 his close friend and Sun Society cofounder Qian Xingcun boasted of Jiang's work that "Now everyone's rushing to write about revolution and romantic love, but it's clear that this genre did not exist before The Youthful Tramp."[70] Jiang's success derived from his tragic tales of lovelorn heroes and heroines, separated or killed in action, and the occasional happy story of a reunited couple. The libidinal choice between satisfying one's sexual desire or fulfilling one's revolutionary ardor that each of his protagonists encounters, with the latter invariably trumping the former, held enormous appeal for his youthful fans. As T. A Hsia noted in his study of Jiang Guangci, each of Jiang's books enjoyed multiple print runs.

For instance, between 1926 and 1930 there were eleven printings of his first novel alone.[71]

Jiang Guangci was at the height of his fame in 1928 and 1929, and his essays of this period exude confidence in his literary prowess. For instance, he prided himself on his sensitivity to "the forces of darkness and light" and scorned "old-style writers" *(jiu zuojia)* who "lack the true feelings that come of intimate contact with people involved in the social movements of the time."[72] Declaring his own "true feelings" *(shi gan)* about the revolution, Jiang stated his mission as one of inspiring others "to attain revolutionary emotions."[73] Jiang's self-aggrandizing ways and his evident commercial success ought to have qualified him for the "genius + hooligan" label that Lu Xun applied to the Creation Society's members. Yet Lu Xun was unusually generous toward Jiang and never described him as such. He confined his mockery of Jiang to occasional remarks and noted in a March 1930 publication that he found it a pity that Jiang, who had studied Russian, did not produce more translations of Soviet works for the edification of Chinese readers.[74]

The fact that Jiang had published cutting remarks about Lu Xun makes the latter's restraint all the more intriguing. In January 1929, Jiang wrote of Lu Xun:

> Oh he's the very picture of the "uncrowned king" [*su wang*] in the literary scene today, bandit chief and big brother to all.... Praised by all and opposed by none, he's truly the forerunner of the literary realm and the intellectual world's leading authority. Who would dare let off a fart in his presence or say no to him! But for some reason, people have now changed their minds, and so, in the spring of 1928, several journals had the temerity to publish a few disrespectful words about Mr. Lu Xun, stating that his ideas were obsolete and noting his inability to see which age he was living in.... This caused him to become so enraged that he could not help letting out an almighty roar.[75]

In using the reverential title for Confucius, "uncrowned king," and in references to "bandit chief" and "big brother" alluding to *The Water Margin*, the Ming-era classic on noble outlaws, Jiang insinuated that Lu Xun held an unfair and obsolete monopoly, but a monopoly no less, on *baihua* literature.

It is highly likely that Lu Xun pitied Jiang. By the time Lu Xun called the Creation Society "geniuses + hooligans" in July 1931, Jiang was dead and an object of ridicule on the left. In October 1930 Jiang had been expelled from the Communist Party. A report published in an underground Communist newspaper in Shanghai detailed the reasons for his expulsion, noting among other things that "his romantic nature as a petty-bourgeois was impervious to the injunction and education which the Party never failed to give him." Listed among his crimes were his unauthorized visit to Japan in 1929, his lack of participation in revolutionary activities, and the publication of works "for the sake of nothing but royalties."[76]

It was a time when the underground Party in Shanghai was led by Li Lisan, a zealous advocate of open revolt against Nationalist rule. Following his appointment as general secretary by the Comintern in 1929, Li proclaimed the advent of a "revolutionary high tide" and ordered Party members and supporters in Shanghai to distribute pamphlets and to take part in slogan-shouting street protests. His urban insurrectionism coincided with the aggressive action taken by the "Red Armies" to attack and occupy major provincial cities.[77] The result was that the urban Party membership attracted an increased risk of arrest, while the Communist forces in the countryside suffered a succession of defeats (made all the more painful because these came after momentary victories). The overall effect was the further erosion of already imperiled Communist bases.[78]

Jiang had been unwilling to obey the command to participate in street protests and had resigned his Party membership, a fact that the leadership obscured by publicly expelling him.[79] In his 1933 commemorative essay about Jiang, Yu Dafu wrote that despite Jiang's narcissism (he compared himself to Byron and Pushkin) he was deeply unhappy that his intellectual peers ridiculed his best-selling revolutionary romances and was anxious for their approval. Yu noted that after 1929 Jiang also faced growing disapproval from the Party leadership and that this combination of peer disdain and Party censure brought on his depression. Yu added that he was "among those who showed disrespect to Guangci's works" and regretted having regarded his books with "more contempt than admiration."[80]

Jiang's health continued to deteriorate. In Lu Xun's March 1930 remarks about Jiang's knowledge of Russian, he made a point of noting
that Jiang had produced only one work of translation "since his illness."[81] A contemporary observer reported seeing Jiang and Lu Xun
deep in conversation one day in late 1930 at the Uchiyama Bookstore.
This meeting took place just before the Party leadership's public condemnation of Jiang and his expulsion from the Party in October
1930. The same observer noted that Lu Xun appeared to be consoling
Jiang, who looked dejected and unwell.[82] Jiang succumbed to tuberculosis at the age of thirty-one on 30 June 1931. From Jiang's untimely
death and his less-than-canny dealings with the Party leadership, we
can surmise that Lu Xun found him unsuitable as a "hooligan," despite the fact that Jiang clearly postured as a "genius" in his meteoric
rise to fame.

As Yu Dafu wrote in 1933, notwithstanding Jiang's literary flaws his
success was so enormous as to assure him of a place in history as the
author who sparked the vogue for "proletarian literature" in 1928. Yu
noted that the genre took off mainly because of the "dramatic increase
in the number of people who read and idolized Guangci's works."[83]
Indeed, it was because Jiang far outstripped all other revolutionary
writers in his popular appeal that in 1932 the Creation Society was led
to insist somewhat defensively that it had played as important a part
in popularizing "proletarian literature." This was a defense put forward by the leading Creationist, Zheng Boqi. He claimed that by early
1928, the Creation Society and Sun Society had so successfully established "proletarian literature" in Shanghai that each acquired its own
unique approach in developing this genre. By 1932 the Creation Society
had been defunct for two years, but Zheng was nonetheless keen to
laud its erstwhile achievements. Using the Sun Society as a foil, he
wrote uncharitably of the recently deceased Jiang that his works were
"two-dimensional narratives about events and individuals of the past."
Zheng stated that Jiang's works paled by comparison with the superior
writings of the Creation Society's authors, who "embodied revolutionary principles in the characters themselves."[84]

Lu Xun seldom commented on the prose fiction published in the
Creation and Sun periodicals. It was their social and theoretical essays

with which he took issue, and it was the Creation Society's publications that offended him in particular. He disliked the group intensely
because in January 1928 the Creationists had not only abruptly changed
their minds about forming a literary coalition with him but had begun attacking him in print. Nonetheless, Lu Xun was also concerned
that the Creationists were eroding the idea of committed literature by
equating it with propaganda.

In April 1928 he wrote that the Creation Society's mindless repetition of Upton Sinclair's (1878–1968) statement "All art is propaganda"
posed a threat not only to artistic integrity but to the art of expression
itself. As he put it:

> I think we should look for rich content and skillful technique before
> we hurry to label a writer.... Revolutionary writers bridle at the
> mere mention of "technique." To my mind, however, though all lit-
> erature is propaganda, not all propaganda is literature; just as all
> flowers have color (I count white as a color) but not all colored
> things are flowers. In addition to catchwords, slogans, notices, tele-
> grams and textbooks, the revolution needs literature...just be-
> cause it is literature.[85]

What concerned him most was the Creationists' proclivity to compare revolutionary literature to the destructive force of a gun. The
Creation Society theorist Li Chuli, was among the first to intensify
this aesthetics of violence, famously declaring in "How to Construct
Revolutionary Literature," his position piece of February 1928: "Our
writers ought to be considered as revolutionaries, for they don't merely
'reflect social life' but actively change it. Their 'weapons of art' serve
the proletariat as an 'art of weapons.' Thus, quite contrary to what
Gan Ren [a pseudonymous critic of the Creation Society] has said, our
works are not of blood, tears, and whatever else. They are veritable machine guns and trench mortars."[86]

During their time as Northern Expedition propagandists in 1926
and early 1927, Guo Moruo and Cheng Fangwu, as the Creation Society's leaders, were mainly interested in promoting the "united front"
as part of "world revolution" as opposed to declaring a class war. With
the reorganization of the Creation Society into a center for Marxist

studies in January 1928, a flurry of essays like Li's sought to present the society's literary endeavors as class struggle in action, exposing and denouncing "petty-bourgeois" values in Chinese literature and scholarship. The Creationists now volubly declared their "revolutionary literature" as "proletarian literature." As Li wrote in "How to Construct Revolutionary Literature":

> Some people say that proletarian literature is a literature that depicts poverty. This is not true, because in bourgeois literature we can find several outstanding works of this kind. Some people say that proletarian literature is literature written by members of the proletariat themselves. This is not true, since before their liberation from bourgeois consciousness, what the proletariat have been able to write is nothing more than bourgeois literature. . . . Some people say that proletarian literature expresses the ideas of the proletariat and their sufferings. This is not true, and we should leave those self-styled proletarians to their own devices. Some people say that proletarian literature is literature that describes revolutionary feelings. In that case, why not go and read the poems and prose of Liang Qichao and Zhang Taiyan? As opposed to all of these, proletarian literature has the goal of completing the historical mission of the class it represents. It pursues this goal not from the perspective of an external observer but from within the class consciousness of the proletariat. It is the production of a literature of struggle.[87]

Following this passage Li presented the Creation Society's members as actively applying Marxist theory to the production of this "literature of struggle." It was in defense of the Creationists' vanguard status that he reiterated the vital importance of an author's class attitude over and above his class origins—claiming in essence that the Creation Society's theoretical guidance was essential for the production of proletarian literature in China. According to Li, an effective means of determining whether someone stood with the proletariat was to ask whether he wrote "for the sake of revolution" or if he was merely making a show of taking part in revolution "for the sake of literature." Implying that the latter was true of Lu Xun, Li singled him out for special mention with these questions: "To which class ultimately does Lu Xun belong?

For which class does he write? To date, which class of people has he represented in his so-called candid portrayals of suffering?"[88]

In his riposte to Li Chuli, Lu Xun praised revolutionaries as people who were "never afraid of self-criticism" and hence not only "see clearly but speak bravely and plainly as well."[89] Against this valor and integrity, he mocked Li's argument as "the talk of a sophist sent by the propertied class." He cast doubt on Li's notion of literature as an "art of weapons," asking: "Why can't we reach the 'art of weapons' straight away?" and then answered himself: "Because the other side has the art of weapons. That is why our side can only have the weapons of art." Lu Xun then discussed the Creation Society's increased stridency in the same mocking ambivalent tone:

> The weapons of art are really all that's left: a sign of breaking away from the illusion of nonresistance to succumb instead to the new illusion of waging war on paper. But this is the only way for revolutionary artists to keep up their courage—this is all they can do. If they sacrifice their art in an attempt to turn theory into practice, I'm afraid they will stop being revolutionary artists. So it stands to reason that they must sit in the proletarian camp, waiting for the "weapons of iron and fire" to appear. And when these appear, the "art of weapons" will also emerge. If by then the iron-and-fire revolutionaries have a moment of "leisure" to listen calmly to accounts of their exploits, the writers will have become warriors just like them: a final victory.[90]

Lu Xun's reference to "the illusion of nonresistance" is ambiguous and suggestive of the ill-fated obedience mandated by revolutionary tutelage in Guangzhou. Similarly, in the "new illusion of waging war on paper," he implies the futility of combative rhetoric against the military might of Chiang Kai-shek's dictatorship. He followed up with a characteristic appeal for clarity and concluded with this observation:

> Although the revolutionary writers and proletarian writers of the Creation Society have been forced to play with "the weapons of art," the unrevolutionary militarists who have "the art of weapons" are beginning to play the same game too: there's no other reason for

their various cheery periodicals. Perhaps they are not too sure either of their "art of weapons." Into whose hands, then, has the highest art—"the art of weapons"—fallen today? Once we discover that, we shall know what China's immediate future is to be.[91]

In asking rhetorically who wielded "the art of weapons"—the undisputed power of guns—Lu Xun recalled his advice of the previous year to the elite cadets of the Whampoa Academy that "studying literature is of no benefit to the war." But he also implied that the published word nonetheless commands a different power: that of persuasion. As he pointed out, the "unrevolutionary militarists" (meaning Chiang Kai-shek and his allies) were also busy producing cheery propaganda to legitimize the new Nationalist regime.

Lu Xun was also fond of observing that the Creationists' impatience for revolution reflected a talent not just for politics but for commerce as well. For instance, at the height of their assault on him in April 1928, he wrote that their ideological concoctions were not only removed from reality but suited the sensationalism of Shanghai publishing:

> If you live in this world, how can you get away from it? This is as much of a fraud as claiming that you can hoist yourself off this earth by pulling on your ear. If society remains static, literature cannot fly ahead on its own. If it flourishes in such a static society, this means it is tolerated by that society and has distanced itself from revolution, the only result being a slightly larger magazine circulation or the chance for publication in the journals put out by big commercial firms.[92]

Among his most memorable remarks of this kind were those he made in 1929 about a poem by Wang Duqing. Wang, a Creation Society cofounder and an influential poet of the time, had published a long symbolist poem in 1928, inspired by the failed Communist uprising in Guangzhou of December 1927. The poem's title, which appeared in English as "II DEC," announced its avant-garde tenor. The uprising itself was a tragic failure, and the brutal Nationalist retaliation that followed resulted in the wholesale slaughter of that city's besieged Communists. A contemporaneous news report noted of the aftermath that there was a growing stench of blood as "every street everywhere" became strewn with "the corpses of massacred men and women."[93]

In Wang's now largely forgotten poem, eulogizing the uprising took precedence over mourning the dead, a priority that provoked the withering comment from Lu Xun that although the poem was banned "here, there and everywhere," it was nonetheless "written in the International Settlement in Shanghai," with the poet "looking from afar at the uprising in Guangzhou." Having dismissed Wang as a shameless poseur, Lu Xun noted acerbically of the poem's onomatopoeia of cannon fire: "His use of 'PONG, PONG, PONG' in increasing font size merely tells us he is excited by Shanghai film posters and advertisements for soy sauce. He is imitating *The Twelve* by Blok but without Blok's force and talent."[94] These remarks, which remain widely quoted, have become a lasting indictment not only of Wang but of the Creation Society's revolutionary literature as a whole.

But although Lu Xun was scathing about the Creation Society's celebration of armed conflict, he said nothing about the aggressive policies pursued by the underground Communist leadership. These policies, articulated in a violent rhetoric in the late 1920s, reflected the underground Party's vain hopes of overturning Nationalist rule. Translated into commands, these were policies that cost thousands of lives through failed uprisings. The first Communist leader to pursue this reckless course after April 1927 was Qu Qiubai, who grew close to Lu Xun in 1932. Insofar as Lu Xun frequently accused the Creationists of being blind to the human costs of violence, his silence on Communist calls for actual violence is noteworthy. Moreover, he must have known of the Communist Party's growing insistence on obedience that led to Jiang Guangci's denunciation and expulsion in October 1930. But Lu Xun chose not to leave a record of his thoughts about these matters.

Dangerous Living

What is certain is that like others on the left, Lu Xun was keen to lend his support to the underground Communist Party. The writer Xu Jie (1901–1993), already a Communist living in Shanghai in 1927, wrote in his memoirs of the special importance that the underground Party leadership placed on cultivating Lu Xun. He recalled that shortly after Lu Xun's arrival in Shanghai in October 1927, the leading Party member in the French Concession, Wang Bi (using the alias Wang Wangping), approached Lu Xun for assistance with setting up a journal. The innocuous title *Mutual Aid (Hu ji)* was chosen to avoid arousing suspicion, and Xu noted that Wang invited both Lu Xun and Yu Dafu to dinner to discuss this project. He observed that whereas Yu Dafu displayed a casual attitude and remarked laconically they should "just set it up," Lu Xun took pains to outline the range of problems associated with running a journal, urging them to heed "the need to be bold as well as consistent." However, with tightened censorship and increased policing in 1928, the journal was never established.[95]

An even larger cross-section of socially concerned intellectuals was moved to assist their Communist peers because of the sheer brutality of Chiang Kai-shek's "Party purification" campaign. As a fledgling Communist organization in 1928, the Sun Society benefited in particular from this type of support. For instance, Yu Dafu gave the society's Chunye Press an anthology of his writings to publish; not only did his celebrity status help to boost the publishing house's reputation, but the fact that he sacrificed his manuscript fee also financially assisted the Sun Society.[96] Yu's generosity, given his personal dislike of the society's vanguard pretensions, was a mark of his fondness for Jiang Guangci. Personal support of this kind was often a reflection of the depth of friendship between benefactor and recipient, artistic and political differences notwithstanding.

Broader forms of support included career and financial assistance offered by senior members of Shanghai's publishing world. In his memoirs, Qian Xingcun expressed gratitude to Zheng Zhenduo (1898–1958) and Ye Shengtao for his literary success. Both these men rose to fame in Beijing as part of the New Culture movement and as founding members of the Chinese Literary Association, a highly successful *baihua* organization. By the mid-1920s both were successful authors and influential Commercial Press editors in Shanghai. Qian stated that as an unknown young writer in 1927, Zheng's and Ye's "warm-hearted assistance" gave him a head start by publishing his work in the prestigious *Short Story Monthly.*[97]

Zheng Zhenduo was absent from China between May 1927 and October 1928, as he had placed himself at political risk for organizing an open letter condemning the Nationalists of unprecedented violence. His father-in-law, Commercial Press director Gao Mengdan (1870–1936), arranged for him to take a seventeen-month tour of the libraries of Paris and London.[98] During Zheng's absence, Ye Shengtao served as *Short Story Monthly*'s editor-in-chief. Qian recalled that on learning of his financial difficulties, Ye broke the company's rule and paid him his manuscript fee in advance.[99]

Zheng Zhenduo's family connections at Commercial Press made him a sought-after individual among the besieged left in Shanghai. Despite the fact that Zheng enjoyed a close friendship with the Crescent Moon Society's leading figure Hu Shi, in late 1928 he was one of several people whom the Creation Society and Sun Society approached for assistance with organizing a formal coalition of socially concerned writers and critics.[100] Help was also solicited from several other influential figures in Shanghai publishing, including Geng Jizhi (1898–1947) and the Sun brothers, Fuyuan and Fuxi (1898–1962), all of whom had earlier played a leading role in promoting New Culture in Beijing.[101] The Sun brothers, in addition to their Chinese Literary Association links, were key members of *Threads of Talk*. These were the very people whom the Creation Society had first denounced in the early 1920s as elite monopolists of *baihua* and then as "petty bourgeois laggards" from the mid-1920s onward (joined by the Sun Society in this heckling in early 1928).

The coalition the leftist radicals envisaged was an enlarged version of the aborted collaborative venture that Guo Moruo had proposed to Lu Xun a year earlier. This newer proposal did not include Lu Xun, for the Creation and Sun Societies had effectively alienated him with their vitriolic attacks of early to mid-1928. In his memoirs, Qian Xingcun recalled that despite the even more straitened circumstances of the left in late 1928, the didacticism of some continued to hinder productive collaboration with sympathetic fellow travelers. Initial discussions were held, but the coalition never got off the ground. As Qian recalled, the more extreme advocates of class struggle "expressed fierce opinions that undoubtedly caused a number of our associates to feel apprehensive about becoming embroiled in yet another round of debates. As a result, not long after the association was formed, several of the initiators became lukewarm about participating in its programs."[102] In any case, by mid-1929 discussions about the formation of the League of Left-Wing Chinese Writers were under way, and the process of reconciliation between Lu Xun and his Marxist detractors had begun.

The numerous rapid reversals of this kind in late 1920s Shanghai were a direct consequence of both the sheer belligerence of the self-styled vanguard and the dangers confronting the left as a whole. The belligerence was partly an affectation: with "revolutionary literature" rising in Shanghai publishing after 1927, the Creation and Sun radicals were eager to capitalize on their popularity as pioneers of the genre. Yet to be fashionably lauded as a Marxist prophet was also to attract the unwanted attention of the anti-Communist state. The result, according to Lu Xun, was an adrenaline-charged anxiety that dogged the publications of both organizations. In March 1928 he wrote that even though these self-styled radicals evidently feared persecution, they were keen to inform their readers of their intentions, whether of "going abroad," "shutting themselves up in their studies," or "winning over the masses." Referring to the hectoring tone of his accusers, he added sarcastically, "People who are farsighted, cautious, who hate getting into trouble and are opportunistic had better offer [this vanguard] a 'revolutionary salute' right here and now, for it may be 'too late for regrets' once the future arrives."[103]

In 1928 there were four educational institutions in Shanghai that served as key bases for the underground Communist movement: the Chinese University of the Arts (Zhonghua yishu daxue); the Shanghai University of the Arts (Shanghai yishu daxue), Pujiang Middle School, and Quanzhang Middle School. Of these, the Shanghai University of the Arts was the most prominent. Located in the French concession, it provided vital shelter for the members of the Creation and Sun Societies in the late 1920s. In 1928 and 1929 leading members from both organizations, including Feng Naichao, Jiang Guangci, Li Chuli, Li Yimang, Peng Kang, and Qian Xingcun, were star attractions at the Shanghai University of the Arts, whose lectures on revolutionary literature drew large crowds. Nonetheless, the university (with an alleyway house as its "campus") also attracted suspicion, and at the behest of the Nationalist government the French concession authorities placed it under increased surveillance. In 1930 it was shut down permanently.[104]

To the extent that the Creation and Sun were organizations that were proud of their success in the marketplace, Lu Xun's disparagement of their market instincts did not injure them. It was his ridicule of their intellectual and literary capabilities that gave offense. Conversely, they saw their commercial success as a sign of revolutionary progress. Hence, in boasting that the Creation Society had single-handedly effected a turn "from literary revolution to revolutionary literature," Cheng Fangwu pointed to popular demand for the society's publications as evidence of its unrivaled stewardship of *baihua*. He claimed that the Creationists "possessed a spirit of resistance" and "a fresh perspective" that not only had "fostered an innovative spirit in Chinese literature within just four or five years" but had become "a source of inspiration to Chinese youth at large."[105]

In the mid- to late 1920s, the Creation Society's journals were undeniably in huge demand among students. According to one contemporary observer, copies of new issues were often sold out within the first three days of their appearance in bookstores across China.[106] Meanwhile, despite its recent arrival, in 1928, the Sun Society also basked in the reflected limelight of Jiang Guangci's extraordinary best-selling success. When Jiang's novels of "revolution plus romantic love" reached their height of popularity in mid-1928, his friend and fellow Sun Society founder Qian Xingcun announced a new phase in the Sun Society's revolutionary progress. Qian wrote in the 1 July 1928 issue of *Sun Monthly*: "In the preceding period of the Sun [Society], revolutionary literature was our slogan, and we did no more than orient ourselves toward it. From now on, our work must change ... in this second phase in the work of the Sun, we will concentrate on gaining mastery over proletarian consciousness and refining our literary skills."[107]

But by then state censorship had begun to stymie this nervous pursuit of profit and publicity. Qian's announcement of a new phase for the Sun Society was published in the final issue of *Sun Monthly*, which, together with the Creation Society's *Cultural Critique*, became the first casualties of the Nationalist government's tightened censorship.[108] With state censors now vigilantly inspecting publications for Communist content, the left faced enormous pressures, and their journals were forced underground. In this regard, they benefited from the network of covert outlets the underground Communist Party in Shanghai had developed for the sale and distribution of its propaganda. This network extended out of Shanghai into Nanchang, Ningbo, and Guangzhou, as well as several cities in the Yangtze region.[109] In Shanghai itself, the Communist network also proved relatively successful in sheltering its members.

Meanwhile state censorship, which was formalized with the issuance on 15 April 1929 of the Nationalist government's first comprehensive blacklist, spread quickly to include not only leftist publications but a wide variety of nonpartisan journals featuring dissenting views.[110] Even the avowedly anti-Communist *Crescent Moon Monthly* encountered difficulties when it criticized the Nationalist regime of abusing human rights and civil liberties. The entrepreneurial Li Xiaofeng also fell foul of these new restrictions; Beixin Publishing House was forced to shut down briefly in 1931. The further tightening of censorship resulted in an explicit ban in 1932 on writings bearing Lu Xun's name. From then onward Lu Xun was forced to use pseudonyms and increasingly to publish underground. Because of these increased political pressures, the last of his books that Beixin published was a collection of essays titled *Essays on False Freedom (Wei ziyou shu)* in October 1933.[111]

The Lu Xun scholar Lin Xianzhi observes of the some 140 pseudonyms Lu Xun invented in his lifetime that more than 80 appeared between 1932 and 1936. Of Lu Xun's later pseudonymous publications, Lin writes that they exemplify the author's erudite approach to veiled criticism. Lin observes that in these later publications, Lu Xun skillfully evaded the undiscerning censor by ostensibly discussing topics about "history, culture, literary allusions, and foreigners." Yet to the informed reader, he conveyed clear dismay about the reality at hand.[112] In 1934 Lu Xun himself lamented of this necessary recourse to covert writing that it proved he was "no match for those fake heroes stepping out bravely under the commander's sword."[113] (He was alluding to Hu Shi, among others).

"The commander's sword" became one of Lu Xun's favorite expressions for Chiang Kai-shek's government, together with "party elders" *(dang laoye)*, "literary giants" *(wenhao)*, and producers of "helpful literature" *(bangmang wenxue)* to designate those whom he saw as Chiang's willing allies and servants. These sardonic references enabled him to express muted outrage against repression and censorship. They appear in his personal correspondence as well. One memorable instance is the brief note he wrote in March 1936 to the young woodcut artist Cao Bai (pen name of Liu Pingruo, 1914–2007), then newly released from jail. Thanking Cao for the gift of a print, Lu Xun remarked frankly of the work (a portrait of Lu Xun displayed in a woodcut exhibition shut down the previous year) that it "lacked maturity" but promptly assured Cao of its value to him: "first, it is the work of a young person who has undergone an ordeal; second, it bears the party elders' hoof-marks; and third, it commemorates, for the first two reasons, something of the present darkness and struggle."[114]

The "party elders' hoof-marks" evokes a sense of the galloping pace at which censorship and surveillance were being systematized in the 1930s. The Nationalist government's determination to eradicate the Communists was part of its broader ambition to bring Shanghai's thriving economy ever more fully under its control. In Meng Yue's study of the city, she describes this process as one of urban renewal, guided by the adoption of a Haussmann-like "class strategy," aimed at maximizing the city's economic potential and achieved largely through intimidation. Comparing post-1927 Shanghai to the remaking of Paris under George Haussmann into a city of "high capitalism under strict political control," Meng writes that China's largest treaty port was remodeled to a plan aimed at preventing street protests and facilitating police surveillance:

> The nationalist government, for example, rebuilt Zhongshan Road, making it Shanghai's widest north–south arterial route. The government also registered and restructured the street numbers of the entire city's residences. The sports field, large memorial square, and public parks constructed in the years following the coup [of 12 April 1927] were all designed, in one way or another, to remove the spatial facilitation of continued strikes and resultant chaos.[115]

Ordinary activists without a public profile faced the greatest risk because their arrests and executions failed to attract widespread attention. Reduced to a makeshift existence, they operated out of multipurpose rooms in alleyway houses in Shanghai's foreign concessions, from which they conducted their domestic lives, held meetings, organized underground activities, and ran and printed their journals. It was in these alleyway houses that they also ran their underground schools and universities. The dangers they faced were compounded by financial hardship, as their employment opportunities were severely limited by their need to remain hidden.[116]

Prominent intellectuals, by contrast, enjoyed varying degrees of protection and were able to establish more permanent homes. In this regard, Lu Xun's international renown afforded him an uncommon degree of protection. The eminent writer Cao Juren (1900–1972), who as a young man in the 1930s became a friend of Lu Xun's, opined that although there were numerous occasions when "the Nationalist authorities persecuted Lu Xun and spread scary rumors about him," they were, on the whole, unable to cause him serious harm. Lu Xun's fame and influential connections meant that he was "not only actively shielded by the Communist Party's organizational powers but that Nationalist agents also feared the repercussions that might follow if they were to arrest him."[117] According to Cao, the fear that Lu Xun experienced was thus always tempered by the considerable advantage of his intellectual stature.

Cao also claimed that the Nationalist government fought a losing propaganda war against the left because it proved "simply no match for organized Communist intellectuals." He added that the left also benefited from the distinct "air of European superiority" with which the authorities of Shanghai's foreign concessions enforced their extraterritorial rules and privileges.[118] Qian Xingcun made a similar point in his memoirs. He recalled an occasion in 1929 when he and his Communist colleagues were arrested by the International Settlement's patrol police for distributing political pamphlets on the street. The Nationalist government demanded their extradition, claiming that Communists must be dealt with under Chinese law. The Settlement's Municipal Court refused to comply, and the presiding judge chose instead to sentence the offenders to jail for just over a month. Qian credited "that little bit of so-called democracy" for saving him and his fellow activists from certain death at the hands of the Nationalists.[119]

Others were far less fortunate. Lu Xun's protégé Rou Shi was arrested together with more than thirty other Communists on the evening of 17 January 1931, when the British police raided their meeting at the Eastern Hotel in the International Settlement.[120] These Communists were promptly handed over to the Nationalist government, and on 7 February twenty-three were secretly executed in Shanghai's Longhua district. Chinese leftists were prevented from voicing their condemnation, but the executions attracted international attention. In fact the Nationalists' recourse to secret executions was a reaction to bad press, following their initial widely publicized massacre of Communists during "Party purification" in 1927. Nonetheless the news did filter out of China, and several letters and editorials were promptly published in influential overseas newspapers and journals attacking the actions of both the British police and the Nationalist government. Among others, Malcolm Cowley (1898–1989), editor of the *New Republic,* wrote an impassioned commentary in the magazine's 8 July 1931 issue, warning that "the campaign of extermination against Chinese writers still continues. A vigorous and hopeful generation is being butchered off."[121]

In any case, from late 1928 onwards the number of suspected Communists arrested and executed was sharply reduced as "Party purification" gave way to postrevolutionary "Partification" *(danghua)*. This new campaign was zealously pursued after Chiang Kai-shek's inauguration as president on 6 October 1928. In June 1929 the Nationalist government in Nanjing announced that the "Programme of Political Tutelage" it had inaugurated in October 1928 would continue for six years, to be concluded in 1935.[122] An integral part of this state tutelage was the establishment of Nationalist Party cells and departments of political education on the campuses of colleges and universities. In essence, this "Partification of education" represented a further expansion and consolidation of the Leninist model first implemented in 1920s Guangzhou: it was a practice that the Communists would continue and improve on themselves when they assumed power in 1949.[123]

In his essays from the late 1920s onward, Lu Xun generally avoided directly attacking pro-Nationalist publications; in this regard his manifest prudence bears little resemblance to the fearless accuser of Nationalist misrule portrayed in Maoist and post-Maoist hagiographies of Lu Xun. He expressed his revulsion toward the Nationalist government in cryptic and erudite ways. As Jon Kowallis points out, at times Lu Xun positively "relished the idea of turning a traditional literary form against the 'third-rate' men of letters he believed were staffing the [Nationalist] censorate."[124]

His criticisms of the left, like his relationships with individual Communists, were much more variegated. From 1930 to 1933, Lu Xun played an active part in the Left-Wing League's activities because of his closeness to Feng Xuefeng and Qu Qiubai, two leading members of the League's core group of Party theorists who carried out the instructions of the central Cultural Committee. By late 1933, however, both Feng and Qu had been transferred out of Shanghai to the new Party base in Ruijin, Jiangxi Province.[125] Thereafter relations grew tense between Lu Xun and the Party group under the new leadership of Zhou Yang (born Zhou Yunyi; 1908–1989), the Party's rising cultural tsar. At this time his private correspondence began to show a real bitterness about political intrigues within the League. As a non-Party member, Lu Xun's leadership was nominal, and he became increasingly alienated from the new doctrinalism that prevailed in the League from 1934 to 1936 under Zhou. He was barely consulted when Zhou dissolved the League in March 1936, under orders from Wang Ming (born Chen Shaoyu; 1904-1974), the underground Party's general secretary, who was then in Moscow.

In 1936 the League's founding mission of producing literature for the masses was sidelined when the Communist leadership once again promoted a "united front" with the Nationalists in the looming war effort against Japan. In the Party's crude uses of revolutionary rhetoric to justify this shift of direction, Lu Xun discerned distinct echoes of the first "united front," which had resulted in the butchery of Communists in April 1927. He criticized Zhou's call for a "national defense literature" as a betrayal of leftist principles and insisted on a continued defense of "mass literature" (an issue examined more fully in Chapter 4).

According to Feng Xuefeng, as Lu Xun approached death in mid- to late 1936, he often expressed regret about the League's abrupt end and once exclaimed in a reproachful tone, "How could they dissolve it just like that! They don't care in the least that it stood for a battle line."[126] Lu Xun complained bitterly about the selective amnesia of the left and scorned the alacrity with which his fellow leftists "wiped all memories of oppression in an instant." He also told Feng he was "incapable of changing so quickly" and that "If it's wrong to hold onto thoughts of revenge when thinking of the enemy, then I'd rather be wrong . . . letting bygones be bygones, what utter rubbish!"[127]

Fearful Speed

Unlike the majority of his contemporaries, who praised the speed of revolutionary change, Lu Xun sought instead to create an impression of speed by exploring people's reactions to violence. He paid particular attention to the emotion of contagious fear, presenting vivid images of a fierce velocity in two essays of May 1919 on the theme "It's here" (laile). In the first essay, he observed that the prospect of Bolshevism appeared to be rapidly spreading panic among the rich and powerful in China. He argued that this fear, though palpable, was unwarranted because the inequalities of Chinese society were so thoroughly institutionalized as to prove highly resistant to change. He then described genuine fear as a universal emotion induced by the unexpected nature of violent death: "If it's an ism that has come, it can disappear as quickly as it arrived. But when confronted with 'It's here,' all one knows is that 'it' is always on the way, there's no end to its coming, and the shape of what eventually arrives can never be known beforehand."[128]

In these words and throughout the essay, Lu Xun suggested that because the impression of accelerating toward death is intensified in an age of violence, fear had become the ruling emotion in Chinese society. The second essay offered a poetic crystallization of this thought: "All in all, there's nothing in Chinese history resembling an idea or principle. There are only two material properties [wuzhi]: fire and the blade. 'It's here' is their common name."[129]

This affective figuration of Chinese history as a continual series of fearful episodes of violence is characteristic of Lu Xun's critical art. From the late 1910s onward, as the *baihua* writings of his peers teemed with tropes of surging waters, hurricanes, tides, and storms to celebrate the destructive powers of "the new," Lu Xun remained deeply ambivalent about the praise of such violence. He first articulated his misgivings as a student in Japan, in critical writings that he produced in archaic *guwen* prose. In his lengthy reflective essay of 1908, "Toward a Refutation of Malevolent Voices," he wrote of "animalistic forms of patriotism" that were then gaining ground in China. He condemned such praise of revolution as a malevolence that could only further erode the peace-loving qualities of the Chinese to encourage an inhuman brutality in its place. His remarks in this early essay about the usefulness of weapons are worth quoting at length, for they shed light on his resolute opposition to "revolutionary literature" and its weapon-laden rhetoric two decades later.

In 1908, at the age of twenty-seven, Lu Xun observed that war appeared to be integral to human existence insofar as humans were territorial creatures. He followed with these remarks:

> Weapons were invented for self-defense, to deliver us from tigers and wolves, they were not intended to be used as claws and teeth with which to maim and devour the weak and vulnerable of the earth. Weapons should be used for humanity's welfare; not as the means to enslave us. Only when people have understood this can they be considered responsible enough to discourse upon military affairs and to refrain from unleashing new horrors upon the world. Be that as it may, in the case of China, I find the theories which are current to be of a completely different order. Although there are those who mouth patriotism and those who champion the cult of the warrior, their motivations are particularly savage. In the name of culture, they roar like carnivores about to sweep down upon their prey; were they equipped with talons and fangs, they would lay waste to vast tracts.[130]

Twenty years later he found the violent rhetoric of his leftist peers equally repellent but nonetheless defended a Marxist view of social revolution. His Marxist turn was, in this regard, more a radicalization of his humanistic disposition than a conversion to Marxist theory. In July 1928, while engrossed in reading and translating Lunacharsky and Plekhanov, he wrote to his protégé Wei Suyuan recommending "books using historical materialism" as "straight and to the point" and capable of "elucidating a number of unclear and difficult-to-explain problems."[131]

Lu Xun's replies to his critics that year and ever after evince a clear indifference to Marxism as a system or a science. He saw historical materialism as intellectual reinforcement for his own literary goals of encouraging empathy and cultivating a sense of common belonging with the downtrodden. When he invoked "the proletariat" in the 1930s, he did so in the general sense of an inclusive society in which the rights of all would be respected. He advocated neither "class struggle" nor the "dictatorship of the proletariat." Moreover, he never bothered to distinguish between philosophical Marxism (what later became known as Western Marxism) and the then evolving Leninist orthodoxy of the Soviet Union.

Despite his general indifference, he was keen to champion a literature of the masses by citing Soviet writings and Russian revolutionary paragons. Lu Xun's knowledge of Marxism came mainly from Japanese translations of Soviet works. By 1930 he had produced three volumes of his own translations: two featuring the selected writings of Lunacharsky and one consisting of Plekhanov's essays and letters.[132] But he remained unconvinced about using Marxist theory as a method. As he wrote in a letter to his young disciple Yao Ke in November 1933: "What do I know of these things called economics or propaganda literature? I've never even touched a copy of Capital, let alone read it." He continued, with a characteristic emphasis on empirical observation: "Rather, it is facts that inspire me, and I'm not referring to the realities abroad but to those of China's non-'bandit areas' [places under Nationalist rule]."[133]

In 1933 Lu Xun contrasted warlord rule under Duan Qirui with Nationalist rule under Chiang Kai-shek to suggest that despite Chiang's revolutionary credentials, he proved a far greater hindrance to social progress than Duan. He wrote that Beijing under Duan in the 1920s was a violent place where the rifles of the warlord's soldiers "spat bullets at students who were trying to deliver a petition." Nonetheless people were allowed to mourn the dead students publicly, including shouts of

"Down with Duan Qirui!" as they marched past Government House. "In those days Beijing still masqueraded as a republic"; thus even Duan's chaotic regime afforded freedoms that Chiang Kai-shek's disciplined dictatorship denied.[134] In the latter's witch hunt for Communists in the name of revolution, those who served Chiang left no stone unturned: "They give explicit orders and use military weapons; they resort to the printed word and the forging of facts as well as to arrests and torture." He noted that the Draconian rule of the Nationalist state proved so effective that when a group of students were murdered for petitioning in 1932, no one dared utter a word of mourning in public.[135]

Lu Xun's comparison of Duan and Chiang should not be read as suggesting a favorable reappraisal of the former. His condemnation of Duan's brutality was unequivocal. Rather, in this instance he used Duan to highlight the intensification of state violence under Chiang. Duan ruled Beijing in a time of acute political instability. He was the capital's longest-serving premier over four periods between 1916 and 1924 (alternating with other premiers who served for periods ranging from one to six months) before he styled himself Regent of Beijing, a position he held from November 1924 to April 1926. Thereafter he was defeated by Zhang Zuolin, who occupied Beijing until his own defeat by Chiang Kai-shek in June 1928. What Lu Xun sought to highlight was the further deterioration of political freedom under Chiang's Leninist-inspired regime, replete with its own national ideology.

For Lu Xun, a highly disciplined party machine was a thing to be feared, and as the Lu Xun scholar Sun Yu points out, 1927 proved "a most awkward year" for him in this regard.[136] By virtue of being in the Northern Expedition's headquarters, Lu Xun lent his services to an organized politics whose repressive tendencies dismayed him greatly. In April 1927 he made the sardonic quip that in China the spread of revolution resembled the growth of Mahayana Buddhism in premodern times. The similarities between revolutionary and religious tutelage, he implied, were the result of teachings that grew rigid and hollow with the expansion of hierarchical institutional power.

He elaborated on this analogy in the essay "In the Belfry," published in December 1927, concerning his life at Sun Yat-sen University. As Sun notes, Lu Xun's ambivalence is particularly telling in this essay. Among other things, Lu Xun observed that Buddhism's rise in China, accompanied as it was by countless lay persons declaring themselves as true believers, eroded its spiritual significance and the rigors of self-discipline that its proper practice entailed. He then noted that the growing authority of the idea of revolution, with increasing numbers of people swearing allegiance to "the Nationalist flag with its blue sky and white sun," marked a similar erosion of what revolution means. Alluding to the triumph of power over principle (or fear-driven belief over a genuine quest), he remarked elliptically that when a political or religious movement gains strength and becomes increasingly organized, "one does not know whether to read this as success or failure."[137] In the same essay he also wrote:

> To be honest, I am quite delighted to learn of revolutions in distant lands involving people not known to me; but alas, the truth is that if revolution happens around me, or people well known to me have gone to join the revolution, then I am not so pleased. If people tell me that I must throw myself into the revolutionary cause, naturally I would not dare to do otherwise. But my gratitude would be all the greater if they had asked me to sit down and rest and poured me a glass of reconstituted evaporated milk.[138]

By 1928, the metamorphosis of Guangzhou's revolutionary propaganda into the commercial success of "revolutionary literature" in Shanghai led Lu Xun to focus his criticism on a different type of aggression: the economics of speed in a highly competitive industry with constant demands for ever more novel versions of "the new." In a 1930 essay he wrote that in Shanghai "revolutionary literature," despite having been all the rage in the late 1920s, had clearly been toppled by a new publishing trend in the "social sciences."[139] He likened the preponderance of slogans in revolutionary literature to Daoist incantations (fuzhou), thereby reprising his earlier remarks about the similarities between organized politics and religion. He stated that the effects of revolutionary slogans proved just as ineffectual as the incantations. The novelty of revolutionary literature lasted only as long as young readers could be inveigled into believing that its "advertisement-style criticisms" might actually "save them and rescue society."[140]

In the essay, Lu Xun wrote that he welcomed the recent trend for translated works in the social sciences but warned that it was just as susceptible as revolutionary literature to profit-driven publishing. He noted that publishing houses were already rushing to cash in on this new market demand, and against the growing proliferation of social sciences titles, he advised: "What we need at this juncture are a few reliable and clear-headed critics who really understand the social sciences and theories of the arts." Their role, he explained, would be to help readers identify books that were worth reading before "fake critics" (alluding to pro-Nationalist reviewers) jumped up once more to dismiss their rivals' work as that of "cats and curs" (a quote from one such reviewer). He concluded with the warning that without true critics in the marketplace, the rise of the social sciences, despite promising wholesome and "down to earth" fare for the arts and other fields, was ever at risk of being hijacked by commerce and greed.[141]

On this topic, the editor Hu Qiuyuan (1910–2004) noted in 1929 that of the 140 or so translated books on social sciences published that year, "nine-tenths were of a Marxist, socialist, or Communist nature." He added that if each of these titles had sold 3,000 copies, there would have been some 400,000 copies in circulation, and "their influence on the contemporary youth must have been tremendous." The historian and editor Tao Xisheng (1899–1988, who served as Chiang Kai-shek's secretary in the 1940s) wrote in his widely read 1931 work *Gleanings of Chinese Social Phenomena* that "the leftist tendency of the publishing business" should not be attributed to canny left-wing publishers. Rather, he claimed it was the enormous demand for leftist works among educated youth that led Shanghai's publishing companies to produce them in vast quantities.[142]

In 1932 Hu Qiuyuan observed that novels of the "revolution plus romantic love" genre that had catapulted Jiang Guangci to literary stardom in 1928 were well and truly a thing of the past. In fact Jiang was already largely forgotten. By the first anniversary of his death in June 1932, his books were already obsolete. Hu concluded wistfully: "An age [*shidai*] that gives us the greatest stimulation also delivers the greatest disillusionment. Rose-tinted dreams have evaporated from our world. . . .

In such an age, even those who dream of revolution are forced to retreat, to become history."[143]

Lu Xun's experience of the quickened pace of life in Shanghai took a direct personal shape with his open cohabitation with Xu Guangping in October 1927 and with the birth of his son, Zhou Haiying, on 27 September 1929 (d. 2011). According to Xu, the first-time father, aged forty-eight, was a doting parent who happily shared the daily chores of changing diapers.[144] While visiting his mother in Beiping to deliver the news of Xu Guangping's pregnancy in May 1929, Lu Xun fulfilled several speaking engagements at Yenching University and Peking University. At that time his friends and acquaintances had pleaded with him to return to the north, and he gave the idea some consideration. Following Beijing's demotion to Beiping in 1928, leading universities in the former capital were anxious to attract prominent academics and offered generous salaries of up to 1,500 dollars per month.[145]

The numerous letters Lu Xun and Xu Guangping exchanged while he was in Beiping reflect their profound affection for each other. He signed himself variously as "L," *xun,* "EL," and "ELEF" (the last two being short for "elephant," the nickname that Xu gave him, based on Lin Yutang's archly ambiguous praise of Lu Xun as a rare cultural asset, a "white elephant").[146] He missed her deeply and counted the days before he could see her again. He left Beiping by train on 3 June 1929 and arrived back in Shanghai two days later.[147] In a letter to Guangping on 23 May 1929, Lu Xun wrote:

> Beiping's a fine place if one's planning on a carefree life of leisure. It's now so utterly different from the south that I feel as if I've landed in some other-worldly "Land of Peach Blossoms." In the ten days I've been here, I've not been stimulated in the slightest. Here, there's no fear whatsoever of "falling behind in the race" if I'm not careful. Shanghai annoys me, but all the same it has its own unique vitality.[148]

Lu Xun also had other personal reasons for favoring Shanghai over Beiping. By 1926 a large number of his friends and protégés had traveled south to Shanghai. The notable exception was his brother Zhou

Zuoren, with whom, in any case, he was no longer on speaking terms. Moreover, in Shanghai he and Guangping did not have to endure the same degree of rumor and gossip to which they would have been subjected in Beiping. Also in Shanghai, Lu Xun was able to avoid the social awkwardness that proximity to his first wife, Zhu An, would have presented.

In another letter to Guangping, he revealed his attachment to fast-paced Shanghai. Despite his dislike of Shanghai's fluctuating literary fashions, he told her he had grown "too rash and impulsive" to return to the newly pacified north.[149] Zhang Zuolin was gone, and Beiping was a good safe distance from Chiang Kai-shek's headquarters in Nanjing, but the former capital was bereft of the intellectual excitement it possessed in its New Culture heyday.

The 1930s began with a series of incursions by Japan and renewed conflict between Chiang Kai-shek and his erstwhile warlord allies. As military violence grew and the threat of full-scale war with Japan loomed, Lu Xun reflected on the dangers of encouraging a foolhardy patriotism. In his 1933 essay "On 'Going into Battle' and 'Running Away,'" he observed that unbridled revolutionary rhetoric was on the rise once more. Lu Xun wrote that calls for national resistance, which began with Japan's occupation of Manchuria in 1931, had grown so febrile that "heroic full-blooded poems . . . on stopping the mouths of enemy guns with corpses or bogging down the Japanese bayonets with hot blood" had become quite ordinary fare. He noted the futility of such egregious clichés in the face of a superior enemy capable of killing people "like ants." The young should be told the importance of heeding their fight-or-flight response, for "the tiresome thing is that these foreign aggressors are too quick and too many for us."[150] Accordingly, it was vital not to mislead naïve young minds into believing they should "go into battle" when "running away" was their only practical option.

These were ambiguous statements, for it was Lu Xun's intention neither to encourage fear nor to negate the heroism of those prepared to fight. Rather, he sought to imply that a murderous dictatorship was no different from a foreign invading force and thereby to highlight the volatile unpredictability of life under Nationalist rule. In writing that a quick-minded preparedness to flee was essential for one's survival,

Lu Xun was also mourning the deaths of young activists: commending their courage while lamenting their recklessness.

Less than three weeks after completing "On 'Going into Battle' and 'Running Away,'" Lu Xun wrote the remarkable essay "Remembering in Order to Forget," dating it "7–8 February 1933" in commemoration of Rou Shi and four other leftist writers who had been shot dead two years earlier. The five were collectively mourned as the "five martyrs" of the League of Left-Wing Chinese Writers. Lu Xun's essay was mostly a belated eulogy to Rou Shi, although he also briefly discussed the other four writers. He had written a brief biographical account in 1931 commemorating Rou Shi upon his death, and he had mentioned Rou Shi's name in several other essays, but it was only in this essay that he wrote with profound emotion about their relationship.

He remarked that, unlike the aspiring writers who sought his support and were invariably "hypersensitive and full of themselves," Rou Shi stood out as the one young person with whom he had felt completely at ease.[151] He recalled that Rou Shi, upon joining the Communist Party in 1930, announced that he "felt obliged to write works with a different content and form in the future." Lu Xun had asked him: "How is it possible for someone who has always used a knife to suddenly become expert with a stick?" He lamented the young man's eagerness to prove his revolutionary mettle but noted admiringly that Rou Shi's reply, "I can always learn!" [zhiyao xueqilai], proved no empty boast.[152]

Lu Xun's eulogy included a self-criticism of his attitude toward Feng Keng (1907–1931), a female Communist writer posthumously lauded as one of the "five martyrs." He confessed he blamed the "frail and decidedly plain-looking" girl as a bad influence on Rou Shi and that, in his first brief exchange with Feng, he felt "a great barrier" between them and suspected her at once of being "a romantic of sorts, impatient for quick success." In hindsight, however, he wondered if under cover of blaming her for undermining Rou Shi's nascent literary talents, he was actually envious of his beloved protégé's newfound sense of purpose as a Communist novice. He confessed that his resentment of Feng Keng's influence over Rou Shi was unfounded and showed him to be no better than the hypersensitive and self-important writers he disdained.[153]

When in 1929 Lu Xun told Xu Guangping he had grown too "rash and impulsive" to live in Beiping, he implied that the enthusiasm of young leftists like Rou Shi had changed him. In the essay, he wrote of Rou Shi's uprightness and kindness, his faith in the goodness of human nature, and recalled the unfailing solicitude his protégé showed toward him. He noted that in a letter Rou Shi had written from jail, he had asked the recipient to tell "Mr. Zhou" (Lu Xun) not to worry about him and to alert him to repeated demands from the interrogators for information of Lu Xun's whereabouts.

Lu Xun ended his eulogy for Rou Shi with self-conscious remarks about his own good fortune in a brutal age. He wrote that when the five leftist writers were executed in 1931, he was forced to lie low in a hotel; a year later he was fleeing for the International Settlement through gunfire, and on the second anniversary of their death he was at home once again, peacefully ruminating while his wife and son slept. He noted that he was reliably informed that Rou Shi had died with ten bullets in his body but that the burial site of the five executed writers remained unknown.

The essay's title recalls a passage in the *Zhuangzi* about the mutual love and compassion that suffering can inspire. Lu Xun was silently invoking the following Daoist sentiment: "When the springs dry up and the fish are left stranded on the ground, they spew each other with moisture and wet each other down with spit—but it would be much better if they could forget each other in the rivers and lakes."[154] In calling forth this scene of dying fish caring for one another as they draw their last breath, Lu Xun projects a spiritual image of suffocation quite different from the political sense of suffocation in his 1922 "iron house" trope. That famous earlier evocation of suffocation had been intended to inspire a quickened commitment to destroy the iron house of "old" China. In this 1933 eulogy, a palpable suffocation is used instead to affirm selfless love, born in extremis, as the highest form of humanism.

In commemorating Rou Shi's loving concern toward him, Lu Xun transforms his grief into a celebration of human belonging and intimacy. He calls attention to the interdependence of remembering and forgetting as two sides of the same coin. In this process, he turns the sympathetic image of the dying fish in the *Zhuangzi* into the scene of a tragically belated insight. He implies that a proper appreciation of those whom one loves comes only through experiencing death's fearful speed; that while loved ones still live and breathe, the ordinariness of their presence precludes the intensity of yearning that their death occasions. The essay concludes with these lines:

> It is no longer the young who write in remembrance of old people. Over the last thirty years, I have witnessed the spilt blood of so many young people that its ever-rising quantity now submerges me to the point of suffocation. All I can do is to make use of this ink to write a few lines of prose. It is no different from making a little hole when buried in mud so that one may draw a few more wretched breaths. How is such a world possible? The night is so long, the road stretches on, it is perhaps best to forget and say nothing at all. But I know that even if I don't write, there will be others who, in times to come, will remember them [the "five martyrs"] and speak of their times...."[155]

Lu Xun presents his grief as a never-ending nocturnal passage—"the night is so long, the road stretches on." Yet the essay's title also suggests a modicum of social hope: that his belated insight, born of a violent age and achieved at the cost of another's sacrifice, may one day cease to matter. Thus his words can also be read as implying that he is indeed remembering for the sake of a future idyll of blissful forgetfulness, so that a fortunate posterity may one day marvel that the old once lived to mourn the young dead; that an ordinary peace (beyond his ken) will make alien the sense of writing as if one were buried in mud, in a state of near suffocation and attempting to "draw a few more wretched breaths." In the final sentence, Lu Xun suggests that, unlike future impersonal commemorations of the five murdered writers, his is a deeply personal act of remembrance, however fleeting and imperfect. The ellipsis points that conclude this still frequently quoted essay were intended to project an uncertainty about the future. In hindsight, they remind us of the political appropriation of Lu Xun that turned his mourning of a beloved friend into a celebration of Communist sacrifice.

4

Debating Lu Xun

In 1926 Lu Xun wrote that the idea of his writings' being turned into "a kind of respectable monument" filled him with dread. By then his writings had attracted countless commentaries that ranged from the laudatory to the condemnatory, the serious to the frivolous. Nine years later, having produced an impressive range of polemical writings in response to his critics, he published seven short essays under the common title "Mutual Contempt among the Lettered." In this series his preoccupation with self-vindication and his fear of being misread are perhaps most evident. He reiterated in a variety of tones the importance of not "putting up with all sorts of young dandies posing as fine writers, hooligans pretending to be cultured, or pimps hawking pornography," as if to persuade the reader that even at his most polemical, he was never merely curmudgeonly and quarrelsome.[1]

In the final essay of the series, Lu Xun asserted that intellectual judgment was essential in order to "fight the 'preachers of death.'" His invocation of this Nietzschean phrase bespeaks an anxiety to establish a solid moral integrity for his perennial criticism of his contemporaries. The essay concludes with the tellingly defensive statement: "Only those able to hate are able to love, and only those able to give life and love can write."[2] Written a year before his death, this declaration became Lu Xun's timely plea to posterity to heed his quickness to anger as an indispensable moral emotion.

This chapter explores those issues that clearly separated Lu Xun from his critics, the ambivalence that accompanied his leftist turn, his troubled relationship with the League of Chinese Left-Wing Writers in the mid-1930s, Lu Xun's posthumous metamorphosis into the Party's own revolutionary saint, and the consequent misfortunes that befell his former critics because of his canonization. Indeed in the 1950s and 1960s most of them were retrospectively charged with the crime of attacking Mao's chosen revolutionary hero.

The years 1927–1930 were a frenetic period during which Lu Xun locked horns with both the Marxist Creation and Sun Societies and the anti-Communist Liang Shiqiu (1903–1987) of the Crescent Moon Society. These vigorous polemics preceded the founding of the Left-Wing League, and their liveliness stands in stark contrast to the narrow, wooden roles to which Lu Xun and his critics were consigned under Mao twenty years later. Indeed, the significance of these quarrels is that they occurred before the Chinese Communist Party had settled on its own monological version of history and revolutionary becoming; the Party as yet had no policy on literature, let alone an entire orthodoxy.

In 1928 and 1929, despite Chiang Kai-shek's anti-Communist campaign, it was as dangerous as it was fashionable to be perceived as a revolutionary. The resulting intellectual volatility was thus a reflection of rival arguments and trends circulating in Shanghai's cosmopolitan marketplace. In this turbulent environment, Lu Xun's fame, coupled with the pointed accusations he repeatedly leveled at others for encouraging an unholy alliance of politics and commerce, elevated him into a singularly controversial and preeminent figure around whom a divisive clamor took root and flourished. As Lu Xun frequently noted in his ripostes, his Marxist accusers reveled in being *outré* at his expense. A 2003 survey of some 270 polemical writings on revolutionary literature published in 1928 and 1929 notes that more than 100 featured Lu Xun. (These include the dozen or so essays and letters that he contributed to the debate.)[3]

Struggling against Lu Xun

In his March 1928 essay "The Haze of 'Drunken Eyes,'" Lu Xun mused about what the Creation Society radicals would do if they had the power to affect his life:

> If by then they stop saying "Those who are not revolutionary must be counterrevolutionary" or that *Threads of Talk* has delayed the revolution, it might still be possible for us to earn half a loaf of bread for sweeping floors. Then in my leisure after an eight-hour workday, I shall sit in a dark room and go on copying out *The Lore of Chinese Fiction* and discussing the literature of other countries because I enjoy doing this. I am only afraid that Cheng Fangwu and his cronies may actually become so many Vladimir Illyiches and "win over the masses." In that case they will probably soar even higher, and I will accordingly be "promoted" to that class of nobles and emperors who deserve, at the very least, to be banished to the North Pole. It goes without saying that all my writings and translations will be banned.[4]

Parodic quotation was the favored device of both Lu Xun and his Marxist detractors in their disagreements of the late 1920s. In the preceding passage he quotes liberally from Cheng Fangwu's position piece, "From Literary Revolution to Revolutionary Literature," using burlesque mimicry to disparage Cheng's essay as a pointless diatribe. To highlight Cheng's hyperbole, Lu Xun presents himself as a humble sweeper toiling for a mere pittance. The comical incongruity between this teasing self-diminution and Lu Xun's public stature was doubtless a source of considerable amusement to his fans.

His reference to his *Lore of Chinese Fiction* (published in August 1926) was a delayed riposte to a taunt of Cheng's. In a February 1927 essay, "Complete Our Literary Revolution," Cheng had lampooned the title of Lu Xun's then latest anthology of essays, *Huagai ji*, published by Beixin in June 1926. The term *huagai* has two meanings: as a proper noun, it is the name of an inauspicious star; as a common noun, it refers to a royal canopy. Lu Xun deployed the term and the oddness of its dual connotation to suggest that in turbulent times, when the privileged continue to prosper, sheltered under their "royal canopy," the ordinary must simply endure whatever the "unlucky star" brings. Cheng, writing mockingly of Beijing's pioneers of *baihua,* was expounding that their elite tastes *(quwei)* had hastened the demise of China's "literary revolution." In this context he remarked: "There sits our Mr. Lu Xun under his *huagai,* copying his lore of Chinese fiction," implying that it was a royal canopy that gave Lu Xun shelter.[5]

Lu Xun neither forgot nor forgave Cheng's slur on his scholarship on premodern fiction. At the time he published his essay on Shanghai's intellectual haze in March 1928, Beixin Publishing House had just released Lu Xun's *Strange Tales from the Tang and Song Epochs.* This two-volume anthology of premodern fiction, a sequel to his *Lore of Chinese Fiction,* would have been fresh in readers' minds (the first volume appeared in December 1927 and the second in February 1928). Against this evident fame and authority, his description of his own scholarship as being confined to "a dark room" was as incredible as his self-relegation to a humble sweeper. Lu Xun also punned on the notion of the royal canopy with the quip about being promoted to "the class of nobles and emperors."

This thrust-and-parry, volley-for-volley style of retaliation, which frequently included clever mimicry of his critics' taunts, was typical of Lu Xun's polemical writings of the late 1920s. His critics replied in kind, but he also played up his intellectual stature because his critics insinuated that fame had made him unbearably self-important. A particularly striking instance of this tactic appears in his mischievously titled essay of May 1928, "My Attitude, Tolerance, and Age," in which he stated in his own defense:

> All that I have discussed are my own concerns, not those of the "greatly impoverished"[6] ... but even though I speak only of my personal concerns, and some no doubt see only the individual, others will always insist on a background or context. Take the book *Lu Xun in Guangdong,* for instance. This year, quite out of the blue, these warriors accused the editor and the edited of seeking immortality and expressed their "irritation" with the book, disparaging it as "dense and dull." I fear they are being much too idealistic, because immortality is hardly the issue here. Besides, as modern folk ought to know,

immortality doesn't amount to much these days. Such a book exists simply because someone has produced pages of printed text, bound the pages together, and turned the object into merchandise. Thus, this thing called "Lu Xun," however concocted, is mostly fodder, mere grist for the mill. This approach is one that the Creation Society, "whose path cannot be considered incorrect,"[7] can hardly avoid themselves.[8]

In October 1927 Lu Xun had publicly chided Li Xiaofeng for falsely advertising *Lu Xun in Guangdong*. Reprising this matter six months later, he claimed that the Marxist attacks on his reputation were essentially no different from Li's publicity stunt. The same zeal for turning a profit, he implied, inspired the Creationists and Li alike to concoct products by using (or misusing) his name. The only difference was that they assigned opposite values to "Lu Xun."

Yet, insofar as the Creation Society's onslaught on Lu Xun formed an integral part of its desire for a unified Marxist orthodoxy, its members were not as cynical or opportunistic as he claimed. While the name "Lu Xun" was a handy foil to attract publicity, Cheng Fangwu, like Guo Moruo, commanded enormous influence among young leftists in his own right. Moreover, the Creation Society enjoyed an enviable reputation, and the Marxist discourse it championed was clearly in the ascendant. Indeed, when Cheng's essay "From Literary Revolution to Revolutionary Literature" appeared in the 1 February 1928 issue of *Creation Monthly* (the oldest and most prestigious of the Creation Society's numerous journals), it immediately became a slogan among the devotees of revolutionary literature. Cheng explained that the title conveyed the "dialectics of history" at work in Chinese literary discourse. An effective slogan in its day, the phrase remains frequently used in present-day Chinese scholarship to describe and represent *baihua*'s development from the late 1910s to the late 1920s. Cheng's essay appeared at a time when it had become intellectually fashionable to speak of the modern Chinese vernacular as transiting from the "third" to the "fourth" stage of an international class struggle.

As noted in Chapter 1, Guo had popularized these gradational concepts in 1926 with his model of a universal process of dialectical change.

With regard to "the evolution of revolutionary literature," he claimed that whereas the displacement of the (bourgeois) "third class" by the (proletarian) "fourth class" in Europe had been a gradual process occurring over a century or more, in China the same process had taken less than ten years. This accelerated velocity of change, he explained, was the effect of societal unrest brought on by global capitalism's rapid exacerbation of socioeconomic inequalities. He claimed in this connection that revolutionary literature was acting as a superaccelerant for China's ideological transformation.[9]

Cheng's February 1928 essay reiterated this simple idea. Like Guo, he wrote of revolutionary literature as the premier vehicle of Marxist "revolutionary consciousness." Cheng claimed that within the space of a decade, *baihua* had gone from being the short-lived triumph of a bourgeois "literary revolution" against feudal *wenyan* to a potent vehicle of socialist becoming via the rise of a truly proletarian "revolutionary literature." In claiming that the Creation Society was chiefly responsible for rescuing *baihua* from bourgeois decadence, Cheng added that *baihua* remained yet still under their threat and that the safe passage "from literary revolution to revolutionary literature" was not yet fully secured.[10]

To rescue *baihua*, he declared, it was essential to identify recalcitrant petty-bourgeois intellectuals and denounce them as enemies of revolutionary progress. The essay's hectoring style doubtless added to its sensationalist appeal. Among other things, Cheng accused Beijing's *baihua* pioneers of capitulating to feudalism. He wrote that they betrayed the "literary revolution" when they retreated "into their lair," having grown "exhausted and hoarse after calling out a few times." Their inability "to negate old ideas" led them ultimately "to suck desperately on a broken old wine bottle in the vain hope of rejuvenation, with a motley group of urchins trailing after them making a din."[11]

Basing this high dudgeon on Fukumoto Kazuo's famous slogan "separation before unification" *(fenli jiehe)*, Cheng argued that the time for total dedication to the true revolution had come: "No one is allowed to stand in the middle: you're either over there with them or here with us."[12] The irony here is that in 1928, when the Creation Society styled itself as a vanguard in emulation of Fukumoto, the latter was already a spent force in Japan. He had come under criticism from the Comintern in mid-1927 for his "sectarianism." Twelve months later his troubles were compounded when, during the Japanese government's anti-Communist drive, he was arrested and sentenced to a fourteen-year prison term, which he began serving in June 1928.[13] Nonetheless, the Creationists, evidently undeterred by Fukumoto's personal misfortunes, continued to espouse his ideas in Shanghai's leftist discourse of 1928 and 1929.

At the peak of his influence in 1926 and early 1927, Fukumoto accused fellow travelers and social democrats of being enemies of Marxism. The Creationists followed suit, condemning their contemporaries as petty-bourgeois pessimists and blamed them for hindering the momentum of revolution. Before Fukumoto's political fall in mid-1927, he had been the Japanese left's leading exponent of Marxist theory. He delighted in engendering controversy and accorded a special importance to the power of theoretical struggles in hastening the revolution.[14] In this regard, Lu Xun's reference to the Creationists as budding "Vladimir Illyiches" was a satirical allusion to Fukumoto's lionization in Japanese Marxist circles as "a second Lenin."

Before his "Fukumotoist" phase, Cheng in early 1927 had already denounced Lu Xun and several other Beijing luminaries as self-appointed arbiters of taste and sensibility. In particular, he derided Zhou Zuoren (then editor of *Threads of Talk*) and the Beixin Publishing House (the journal's publisher). He claimed that these pioneers of *baihua* had degraded literature into a mere petty-bourgeois frivolity. Hence, in his February 1927 essay "Complete our Literary Revolution," Cheng wrote: "Perhaps that type of art is inevitable because their lives accord with that kind of *Rhythm*. Their lives should not overly concern us here, but we must note that because we don't have 'taste' and are not so privileged as to breathe that type of air in Beijing, we have no choice but to examine ourselves."[15]

At the time that Cheng wrote these sentiments, he was still working as a "united front" propagandist for the Northern Expedition. Removed from power after April 1927, he stepped up his assault on all actual and perceived critics of the Creation Society's vanguard role. Newly inspired by Fukumoto, Cheng Fangwu's pugnacious writings became even more rancorous. In "From Literary Revolution to Revolutionary Literature" he no longer merely accused "Zhou Zuoren and his ilk at *Threads of Talk*" for allowing China's literary revolution to stagnate but called for heavy artillery to destroy "their motto of 'taste.'" As he put it: "Previously, I noted that what they defend is 'leisure, leisure, and, a third time, leisure.' They represent the leisured bourgeoisie and cocooned petty-bourgeoisie. They live as if they transcend and float above their times and have done so for many years. If we don't use 100,000 ounces of TNT to destroy this putrid fog in Beijing, they will go on living like this forever."[16]

This passage made a particular impression on Lu Xun, for he was clearly indicted as one of Zhou's "ilk at *Threads of Talk*." In April 1928 he wrote that Cheng was mistaken about his circumstances when he had lived in Beijing, noting that in 1926 his problems with the warlord regime were serious enough to cause him to leave: he did not have to "wait to be blown up" by Cheng's TNT.[17] In 1930 he named an anthology of his essays *Three Leisures* in satirical commemoration of Cheng's bombast.

In his March 1928 essay on Shanghai's intellectual haze, Lu Xun quoted the passage about TNT in full to make the quip that since his "class status has been decided by Cheng Fangwu," he should "feel alarmed about being forced into the 'capitalist class' (for 'leisured' means 'moneyed')." Segueing from Cheng to Li Chuli (who lauded revolutionary literature as an actual weapon of war), Lu Xun joked that, faced with the threat of being obliterated by Cheng's TNT, he was relieved to discover that Li was far more generous. Lu Xun then quoted a passage from Li Chuli's essay "How to Construct Revolutionary Literature," which featured the exuberant statement that anyone could "join the proletarian literary movement" whether their class was "first, second... hundredth, or thousandth," so long as their motives were pure.[18] Lu Xun mused comically that if he were poor, his membership of "the fourth class" would have been automatic, but unfortunately his motives, when examined, would clearly exclude him from participation in the "proletarian literary movement" under way.[19]

Lu Xun's essay "The Haze of 'Drunken Eyes'" was a study in polemical verve that wove together an artful parody of elements drawn from three key articles by Creation Society members (Cheng Fangwu, Feng Naichao, and Li Chuli), all of which had been published only weeks earlier, in January and February 1928. Although Lu Xun focused his criticism on Cheng's "From Literary Revolution to Revolutionary Literature," he had not been mentioned by name in that essay (it was Zhou Zuoren whom Cheng singled out). In Feng's and Li's articles, he was discussed in the company of several other intellectual luminaries who stood equally accused of self-perpetuating petty-bourgeois pessimism and decadence. But while others ignored these taunts, Lu Xun was determined to retaliate. No doubt he felt an obligation to do so in defense of *Threads of Talk,* as he had then recently assumed the journal's editorship in Shanghai.

The Creation Society journal *Cultural Critique,* newly established in January 1928, was inspired by Fukumoto's notion of "a totalizing critique" *(quanbu pipan).* It was promoted as an authoritative source of Marxist theory but attracted considerable notoriety, since a large part of the "theory" featured in *Cultural Critique* took the form of vicious attacks on prominent writers and academics.[20] In his celebratory piece for the monthly's inaugural issue, Cheng sought to sanctify these attacks as a necessary part of the "comprehensive revolutionary theory" *(quanbude gemingde lilun)* needed for revolutionary action. He described *Cultural Critique* as a publication aimed at providing the reading public with "well-reasoned critiques of capitalist society, depictions of the extravagances of recent imperialism, and a response to the question of 'what is to be done' that will set us on the correct path."[21] Lu Xun had poked fun at *Cultural Critique* for featuring a preponderance of Marxist terms in awkward transliteration: "As for the Creationists' transliteration of *Aufheben [aofuhebian],* which means 'to eliminate,' I can't understand why they've chosen to translate it in such a way as to make it even more difficult for the fourth class to learn than the original term."[22] Such remarks provoked his critics into dedicating the whole fourth issue of *Cultural Critique* to denouncing Lu Xun.

Accordingly, the fourth issue of *Cultural Critique* on 15 April 1928 was intended to expose to all Lu Xun's ideological flaws and pernicious influence. The journal's contributors sought to present themselves as defenders of Marxism's moral and scientific integrity. Rhetorically at least, they claimed they were waging a courageous war against a famous (hence formidable) enemy, prompting Lu Xun to deride them as "warriors" and "heroes." More practically, however, the point of targeting Lu Xun was to undermine his considerable reputation. But although the discursive tactics of Lu Xun's detractors resemble those that were utilized some fourteen years later at the Communist Party's wartime base in Yan'an, there were some important differences between them.

During the Party's first Rectification Campaign of 1942–1944, "struggle sessions" were established as part of everyday revolutionary practice. By then it was standard practice to ostracize outspoken Party members by highlighting the dangers that their "incorrect" ideas posed to collective well-being. This "totalizing critique" of the 1940s, based on Mao's speeches and writings, was a far cry from the rhetorical freedom, and frisson, of its late-1920s predecessor. In Yan'an, as Mao Zedong Thought was in the process of being systematically instituted, struggle sessions provided a form of "exegetical bonding," as David Apter and Tony Saich aptly put it. This austere practice combined "articulated principle and ruthless struggle" with the aim of inducting participants into a discourse of revolution resolutely intolerant of any alternative view. The discourse inexorably condensed into a tool of power: "separating the enlightened from the unenlightened and segregating a good communist from the backsliders and dissidents."[23] The brutal punishments meted out to the targets of "struggle" also served to coerce the spectators' obedience.

In stark contrast, in 1928 the Creation Society and Sun Society lacked the minimal political and logistical support required for creating such exegetical bonding. Its "theoretical struggle" was by and large contingent on market demand. Nonetheless Lu Xun observed of the Creation Society that its members were just as keen to impose their will on others. The problem, as he explained in March 1928, was that neither they nor anyone else could "guarantee the final victory." He wrote that despite Cheng Fangwu's confident predictions in "From Literary Revolution to Revolutionary Literature," the future simply could not be determined in advance. He cautioned the Creation Society that no amount of incendiary prose could alter the plain fact that people desired self-preservation as much as they desired justice and that revolutionary success was equally dependent on both.[24] Hence, in response to the Creation Society's frequent tropes of "gunning down" and "shelling the enemy," he remarked: "Exposé and resistance are a case of 'chewing and gnawing on words' [*yaowen jiaozi*] rather than 'direct action.' I have no wish for people who write essays to take direct action. I know that people who write essays are mostly capable only of writing essays."[25]

The phrase "chewing and gnawing on words" was one that Lu Xun had first used in 1925 when disparaging Chinese discussions of modernization as a hollow exercise. In an essay bearing this title, he had written that the popular practice of domesticating European names into Chinese-sounding ones was an apt reflection of China's essentially ineffectual modernization. He added that the related trend of modernizing street names using similar-sounding but different characters was equally pathetic. As he put it, in domesticating Gogol into a "Mr. Guo" and Oscar Wilde into "Mr. Wang," or in renaming Dog-Tail Alley *(gou weiba hutong)* "Noble Uncle Alley" *(gaoyi bo hutong)* and Scorpion Alley *(xiezi hutong)* "Joint Capital Alley" *(xiezi hutong)*, "the wording has been changed but the meaning remains the same." He concluded that the Chinese term for "slave" *(nuli)* should accordingly be retranscribed as "crossbow logic" or "conscientious ritual observance," as these two terms were also pronounced *nuli*. He quipped that this might prove an effective way of freeing the Chinese from their perennial anxieties about being "enslaved" (a frequently used word in the nationalistic lexicon of early Republican China).[26]

In 1925, "Chewing and Gnawing on Words" provoked a sharp reaction from readers who evidently felt personally accused by Lu Xun. In 1928 the insult was just as clear to the Creation Society's members. In *Cultural Critique*'s April 1928 special issue on Lu Xun, at least three of the articles mentioned the phrase "chewing and gnawing on words" and quoted the offending passage from Lu Xun's essay, "The Haze of 'Drunken Eyes.'"[27] Lu Xun's critics angrily retorted that his language was not only hollow but also confused. Playing on the term "hazy," Feng Naichao wrote that Lu Xun's attack on the Creation Society showed "the theoretical confusion of an idealist who sees the phenomenon but cannot grasp its essence. This is someone who evidently cannot see the wood for trees. It is no surprise then that he is incapable of understanding our mission. Instead, he uses such remarks as 'Those who want to show their true colors cannot avoid being a bit hazy" to deny the achievements of revolutionary theory."[28] Reprising the idea of "chewing and gnawing on words," Feng added:

> Lu Xun's holier-than-thou demeanor is merely a thin disguise that does not free him from the social connections that bind him. In fact he is a sick man who obsesses about "flattery" and "fear," which is why he grinds his teeth and rails at others, accusing them of "fear" and "flattery." Ah Lu Xun, why burden yourself with these self-inflicted fixations? You know you'll only end up seeking solace from a Shaoxing wine jar and continue "talking about taste as of old."[29]

Similarly, Li Chuli queried: "Are you criticizing people for 'haziness' in attitude or in their use of theory? Or could it be that when you see the variety in other people's use of language, you must insist that 'a bit of haziness comes across as well.' Certainly 'haziness' in attitude and theory should not be tolerated, but flexibility in language is a strategy the revolutionary writer should nonetheless possess."[30] Likening Lu Xun to Don Quixote, Li sneered: "On seeing the phrase 'xyz is a form of art' in some journal or other, our Don Lu Xun begins to wrestle with it as if it were some giant and not a mere windmill. It is as if the phrase had willy-nilly struck a nerve in this Don Quixote's memory with the impact of an axe's blow, and thus 'the art of weapons' became the enemy of Don Lu Xun in his drunken haze."[31]

When Feng Naichao first called Lu Xun an old drunk in his essay of January 1928, he added the barb that the advocates of humanism who praised Tolstoy's "three kinds of love" (love of beauty, self-denying love, and active love of the other) were just so many Don Quixotes tilting at windmills. He also castigated Christianity and anarchism as varieties of petty-bourgeois humanism and accused their Chinese defenders of prolonging "China's eighty-year-old opium addiction."[32]

Li Chuli drew upon Feng's remarks when he titled his rebuttal of Lu Xun "Look at the Wild Dance of Our Chinese Don Quixote." He also parodied the titles of Lu Xun's prose fiction and referred to his criticism of the Creation Society as the "'call to arms' [nahan] of a mentally disturbed person."[33] As these examples indicate, the Creation Society's "theoretical struggle" against Lu Xun was an attempt to discredit his views by besting him in rhetorical play.

The Creationists were particularly aggrieved by Lu Xun's ridicule of their theoretical propositions, which they frequently presented in the form of slogans like "No revolutionary action without revolutionary theory; no revolutionary theory without revolutionary action."[34] The idea inherent in this slogan was the basis on which Li compared revolutionary literature ("the weapons of art") to the power of guns ("the art of weapons"). In one instance when defending himself against Lu Xun's ridicule, Li quoted Marx. He wrote that the attitude that Marx recommended in the essay "Toward a Critique of Hegel's Philosophy of Law" demonstrated the indispensability of philosophy to the proletariat's transformation. He claimed that it was because the Creation Society was dedicated to such a philosophical mission that its publications should be considered a veritable "art of weapons" that was actively hastening the *"Aufheben" (aofuhebian)* necessary for the rise of China's fourth class.[35]

Lu Xun's polemical mistranslation of *Aufheben* (a term in which he had no personal investment) as "elimination" led Peng Kang, another Creation Society theorist, to pen the riposte, "Let's 'Eliminate' Lu Xun's 'Eliminate'!" Taking Lu Xun to task for his apparent ignorance, Peng wrote:

> We transliterated *Aufheben* because we could not find an equivalent term in Chinese to express the meaning of *Aufheben* in its entirety. We felt that such alternatives as "to curb and to raise up" [*yiyang*], "to discard and to raise up" [*qiyang*], "to halt and to raise up" [*zhiyang*] were not reliable. Similarly, Mr. Mai Ke'ang's [Guo Moruo's] translation, "a qualitative transformation," does not fully convey the positive connotations of the term. Hence we opted for the transliteration *aofuhebian*. This is a common enough occurrence; there's nothing here that people "can't understand."[36]

Echoing Feng Naichao's and Li Chuli's jeering comments, Peng proceeded to deride Lu Xun's humanism as similarly misguided and confused. He wrote that Lu Xun should stop worrying about the learning difficulties of the fourth class, for he was putting them at considerably greater risk with his incorrect translation of *Aufheben*. Peng concluded: "In this matter, we ought to thank him on behalf of the fourth class for his wifely 'humanistic' concern. . . . But grateful thanks aside, we must 'eliminate' his 'eliminate'!"[37]

It was in response to this collective assault that Lu Xun wrote "My Attitude, Tolerance, and Age." The essay was completed five days after the April 1928 publication of *Cultural Critique*'s special issue devoted to denouncing Lu Xun. Its title was a quotation from an article published in *Battlefront*, a Creation Society-affiliated journal.[38] Lu Xun began: "There is now a profusion of heroic publications, and 'the literary field' has certainly been enlivened by their appearance." "The literary field" *(wenyide fenye)* was a term frequently used in the Creation Society's publications. Lu Xun sought to draw attention to the organization's pursuit of institutional power. Cheng Fangwu, among others, had declared the need for a "full assessment" of "the literary field" so as to eradicate "the opioids numbing our social consciousness and the paeans being sung to our enemies."[39]

Playing on precisely this combative rhetoric, Lu Xun remarked that a Creationist writing under the name Ruo Shui (a pseudonym of Pan Zinian's) had "lobbed a hand grenade" at him by explaining Lu Xun's errors as the result of his "attitude, tolerance, and age." Quoting a lengthy passage from Ruo Shui, Lu Xun noted that it exemplified the criticisms of the Creation Society as a whole but noted wryly that the author had added a touch of sophistication by posing as an impartial observer.[40]

Ruo Shui had written that whereas Lu Xun's criticisms of Chen Yuan and Gao Changhong (resulting in a spate of angry exchanges in 1925 and 1926) had been "honest and fair-minded," his criticisms of the Creation Society were ill conceived and wrongheaded. In response, Lu Xun remarked that the better part of Ruo Shui's text was aimed at indicting him as a quarrelsome old man, whose "mean and tart" treatment of the Creation Society was symptomatic of his inability to accept his obsolescence. He noted that Ruo Shui had even compared him to Lin Qinnan (also known as Lin Shu, the eminent translator and modern pioneer of the 1890s and 1900s who later became an object of ridicule during the "literary revolution" of the late 1910s). Lu Xun wrote that in making these insults, Ruo Shui revealed himself to be wise to the ways of "old fogeys dead two thousand years," since he was using a ploy first recommended by Lao Zi (sixth century B.C.E.), namely, "To conquer your enemy, you must first appear to be with him." Lu Xun continued: "The supposed fair-mindedness of this tactic does not fool me. Chen Xiying [Chen Yuan] also knew this style of attack. He praised my fiction in order to condemn my critical essays as if to demonstrate his impartiality."[41]

Lu Xun's intellectual authority became a matter of public debate in 1928 when his Marxist detractors pronounced his writings irrelevant and obsolete. By then it had become a well-established tactic among Lu Xun's critics (whether Marxist or otherwise) to disparage his polemical skills by recourse to inventive name-calling. The first of such attacks on Lu Xun's prestige came not from a Marxist but from the "gentlemanly" Chen Yuan of the Crescent Moon Society, following Lu Xun's public excoriations of Chen. In 1926 Chen famously mocked Lu Xun as having the temperament of a "Shaoxing legal clerk" *(Shaoxing xingming shiye)*. This regional slur, well known to the educated elite, was used to suggest that Shaoxing (Lu Xun's hometown) was famous for producing men of modest talent who, in dynastic times, ran errands for the local magistrates. The insinuation was that, over time, Shaoxing bred a type of person who was cunning, pernickety, and punitive.[42] In several of his essays thereafter, Lu Xun made a point of reminding his readers that Chen had abused him in this fashion.

In 1928 Lu Xun attracted even more derogatory epithets from the Creation Society and Sun Society. Li Chuli had attacked him not only as a celebrity spoiled by fame but as "the most loathsome agitator against the proletariat."[43] When recalling these insults in 1932, Lu Xun wrote: "I found myself encircled by literary giants all aiming their pens at me, with the Creation Society, Sun Society, and the 'virtuous gentlemen' of the Crescent Moon Society all saying that I was bad." He remarked that this onslaught had the effect of turning him into fair game, such that "even those who at the time could not flaunt an affiliation with one or another faction, but who have now risen to become writers and professors, often directed a few veiled taunts my way to show how wise they are." He noted with bitter humor that the accusations grew harsher as time passed: "At first, I was no more than 'rich and idle,' 'a dreg of feudalism,' and 'part of a moribund breed.' Later I was pronounced a fascist who called for the murder of young people."[44]

This last reference to Lu Xun as a murderous fascist, arguably the nastiest insult he received, appeared in an August 1928 article published in *Creation Monthly*. The writer used the pseudonym Du Quan. Most people, including Lu Xun, were unaware that Du Quan was Guo Moruo, as Guo never revealed his use of this name.[45] Decades later, in 1977, when Feng Naichao asked Guo whether he was Du Quan, the octogenarian Guo coyly replied he could not remember.[46] Clearly, he did not want to be remembered for having used the most vicious invective against Lu Xun.

From Lu Xun's private correspondence and the memoirs of his confidants, it is clear that these attacks on his character and reputation preyed on his mind and wounded him deeply. Nonetheless, in his public replies he presented himself as unperturbed and characteristically retaliated with succinct and mordant wit. This studied equanimity enhanced the acerbic effect of his remarks, a fine example of which appears in his published exchange in April 1928 with someone calling himself "Y, a young man poisoned by you." This anonymous correspondent had written an irreverent response to Lu Xun's famous letter to Shi Youheng, published in October 1927, which included an impassioned self-criticism. In this letter Lu Xun accused himself of having inspired Chinese youth to rebel, only to watch them perish in anguish at the hands of their enemies.

Recalling Lu Xun's trope of cannibalism, "Y" wrote that reading Lu Xun had turned him from a sheltered "petty-bourgeois hothouse plant" into a live ingredient for the gruesome dish, "shrimps steeped in wine," to be served up to the enemies of Chinese youth. He ended his letter with the facetious plea: "Last of all, I urge you, sir, to let well alone. Don't round up any more tasty morsels for the warlords, but spare other young men like me. If forced to write for a living, write more polemics. With your literary reputation, you may be sure of winning rank and riches. 'Commissionerships' and 'chairmanships' are yours for the taking."[47]

In his reply, Lu Xun told his correspondent either to be grateful that he was still alive or to congratulate himself for having the cunning and ingenuity to survive a dangerous age. He added that if canny survivors like his correspondent were to "glance in the mirror," they would "surely receive the reflection of their heroic mien."[48] Lu Xun also opined that since he and his writings were being roundly attacked for having delayed and obstructed the revolution, he could hardly be guilty of having inspired the young to rebel. Toward the letter's end, Lu Xun advised:

> So long as you write a few revolutionary articles urging revolutionary youths not to talk of love, you will be all right. Only if some powerful man or enemy puts you on trial may this be counted as one of your crimes, in which case you may regret having taken my advice. So first I must make this clear: once they put you on trial, even if you are innocent in this respect, they will pin something on you. The way of the world is to make a man stand trial first, and collect evidence of his crimes—usually ten of them—afterward.[49]

Lu Xun added that the attacks on him were merely "empty talk," noting there was "no need for all this excitement" just because "alas, in a careless moment, one has smudged the noses of the new heroes."[50]

It is useful to compare once more the voluntary revolutionary discourse of 1928 with the mandated revolutionary discourse of 1940s Yan'an. As David Apter and Tony Saich write, the orthodoxy of Yan'an involved "the turning over of the meaning of words and phrases and the learning of certain stock ways of saying things" with the aim of converting "the larger discourse of Marxism and the dialectic to a specific Chinese language of the text." This was a language of revolution now fused with the authority of Mao's words: "an interior language that was originally shared by those in Yan'an and would become the meta-language for the instruction of others."[51] As such, it was a language that had deadly serious consequences for those who wrote critically of it, as became evident in the case of Wang Shiwei (1906–1947), an intellectual in Yan'an who spoke against the Party's increasingly oppressive rule in the early 1940s.

Lu Xun's 1928 remarks about a person's being made to "stand trial first" with evidence of crimes collected afterward proved sadly prophetic in Wang's case. During the 1940s Rectification Campaign in Yan'an, he was jailed in April 1943 as an "internal traitor" together with some 200 others, and put to death in 1947. He was attacked for being "antiparty" and a "Trotskyist." In addition, Wang was accused of "slandering party leaders by calling them corrupt, of disrupting party unity, and of using the term 'hardbone' (brave) in reference to his friends and 'softbone' (coward) for other comrades. Finally, it was said that by describing himself as a modern Lu Xun, he was calling on the youth of Yan'an to embrace him."[52]

This misuse of Lu Xun by a dictatorial revolutionary power that meted out the death penalty to its critics stands in monstrous contrast to his dismissive remarks about the "theoretical struggles" of 1928 as merely a "chewing and gnawing on words." At the time he regarded his critics as merchants of a new verbose language of "class struggle" succeeding in Shanghai's marketplace while still failing the very masses they claimed to be serving. Hence in his reply to "Y" Lu Xun wrote that those of his detractors who "felt compelled to harp on about the final victory" were motivated less by the utopian visions they espoused than by calculations of gains and losses. Highlighting a common propensity between political and commercial interests, he remarked:

> Those revolutionary writers were so terrified by my descriptions of darkness and so fearful there was no way out that they felt compelled to harp on about the final victory—your profit depends on your investment, just as in an insurance company. . . . You have lost your property through revolution, but some acquire property through it. Others lose even their lives while yet others get salaries and fees for writing, but lose the title of revolutionary.[53]

Humanness versus Class Traits

When Lu Xun attacked the unscrupulous merging of the political and the commercial, which he did frequently after 1927, he generally confined himself to pithy and even cryptic remarks, without elaborating on what he meant. But in "The Divergence between the Arts and Politics," a lecture presented at Shanghai's Jinan University on 21 December 1927, he spoke at some length about the moral ambiguity of revolutionary discourse. This text immediately predates the collective assault on Lu Xun in 1928 and highlights his unequivocal opposition to the subjugation of "the arts" to "politics." In the lecture, Lu Xun presented these terms as moral antagonists. He claimed that revolution inspired one of two attitudes in people: some were prepared to risk their lives in aid of a better society while others remained preoccupied with their own advancement. He spoke of the former attitude as befitting and benefiting "the arts" and the latter as a disposition that flourished in "politics," most especially in an age of violence.

Having opposed "the arts" to "politics" in this manner, Lu Xun observed that whereas politics invariably served the powerful, the arts encouraged dissent, thereby exceeding the calculations of power. Politicians, he added, "loathe the opponents of their views" and actively sought their suppression. Lu Xun then offered a similar contrast, this time between "the arts" and "revolution." He observed that although both terms conveyed a sense of "restlessness about the status quo," they also carried quite opposite expectations. He explained that whereas artistic restlessness sought no greater reward than the achievement of true art, an ambition to rule was inherent in a restless revolutionary who sought to overthrow the present order. He spoke of the ruthless pragmatism of revolutionaries who, on their way to power, applauded the discontent of writers because it helped their cause. Once they attained power, they became politicians who "use the same old methods as their former enemies to oust and even to behead those writers who cannot help remaining dissatisfied."[54]

In idealizing "the arts" as fidelity to truth unencumbered by power, Lu Xun revealed his profound ambivalence about writing in aid of revolution. On the one hand, he highlighted the uselessness of mere rhetoric against actual weapons of war. On the other, he praised socially engaged literature for "causing us to feel that we ourselves are being roasted" such that "we will be so deeply moved we want to be involved in society!"[55] Lu Xun's fluctuating comments about the purpose of art furnished his critics with convenient evidence of his "petty-bourgeois indecisiveness." Using parodic quotation, the Creationist Peng Kang wrote that Lu Xun's preference for "sitting in a dark room" had blinded him, such that he mistook his "collisions with the walls" of his self-imposed prison for "a form of humanistic resistance."[56]

Lu Xun, however, saw his ambivalence as inherently human. In the same December 1927 lecture, he presented the will to revolution as an act of conscious altruism, describing it as the humanism inherent in overcoming selfish interest to yearn for "an ideal world." He stated that such yearning was typically expressed in literature as sympathy for the poor. Opposing humanism to individualism, he characterized the latter as signifying extreme selfishness and even a "cruel indifference" toward others. He illustrated this difference with the example of a self-made success raised from rags to riches. He proposed that such a person could choose to imagine "an ideal world" and resolve to work toward its achievement. Hence this person "seeks to help others who now face the same hardships he once endured and thereby attains his humanism." Conversely, he could opt to feel that "he has fought hard to get to where he is, to conclude from his previous suffering that life is meant to be hard and cruel, and drift toward individualism." Lu Xun then surmised: "In this China of ours, individualists are probably in the majority," noting that this suited politicians, who, being individualists themselves, had no genuine desire "to help the poor" or "change the status quo."[57] In this context, Lu Xun commended Leo Tolstoy (1828–1910) as a humanist who opposed war because "despite being an aristocrat, he had experienced life on the battlefield and felt the true pain and agony of war."[58]

If Lu Xun's comparison of humanism and individualism appears overly simplistic, we must remind ourselves that he discussed these terms not as *concepts* but as *attitudes*. His focus on temperament and life experience makes plain that it was moral conduct (not theoretical disquisition) that held his interest. Unlike his contemporaries who held forth on issues of secular enlightenment, inalienable human rights, or class struggle, Lu Xun chose to frame his defense of humanism around the cultivation of empathy as a vital moral emotion.

In discussing Lu Xun's humanism, the eminent Lu Xun scholar Wang Furen reminds us to heed the Confucian moral burden implicit in the premodern Chinese sense of *ren* (the human as benevolent) as something quite distinct from modern Western humanism. Wang follows Lu Xun in defining humanism *(rendaozhuyi)* as love and concern for one's fellow humans. He notes, however, that whereas the modern

Western idea of "loving others" is mostly discussed as a "psychological attitude" or "internal emotional experience," the Confucian notion of "loving other humans" *(ai ren)*, as enshrined in *The Analects*, revolves around the externalization (and active realization) of this emotional experience in pragmatic action. In Wang's view, Lu Xun retained the benevolence implicit in Confucian humanism but disavowed its hierarchical and inherently stagnant bifurcation into the "compassionate love" *(ci ai)* of a benevolent superior for his inferior and the "respectful love" *(jing ai)* this inspires in the inferior for his superior.[59]

Indeed, the Confucian morality implicit in Lu Xun's understanding of humanism is evident in his description of humanists as people who seek "to help the poor and change the status quo." As such, he evinces the benevolence that Wang describes as "loving compassion." "Human" and "benevolence" are not only cognate Confucian ideas but closely intertwined by their common pronunciation as *ren*, rendering them indistinguishable in speech. The locus classicus for their interdependence is a passage in *The Analects* where Confucius has the following exchange with his disciple Fan Chi: *Fan Chi wen ren, zi yue ai ren* (Fan Chi asked "What is benevolence?" and Confucius replied, "Loving other humans"). What this implies is that only a benevolent person—someone already fully human—is capable of loving other humans.[60]

In the Confucian orthodoxy of dynastic China, benevolence became exalted as an exacting virtue: a preparedness to sacrifice one's life in defense of the true path. In Lu Xun's praise for the suicides of Esenin and Sobol as virtuous acts motivated by integrity, we find a tacit affirmation of this moral presumption. .

In a lecture in October 1927, Lu Xun endorsed Confucian benevolence quite explicitly. He noted that true virtue resides in persons who not only "embrace perpetual suffering as the legacy of the old society" but "anticipate self-sacrifice" as the outcome of their labors. He added:

> The true intellectual does not weigh risks and gains: if he does, he is an impostor, passing himself off as an intellectual. Nonetheless, such impostors get to live longer. An example of an impostor would be someone who promotes something today but holds a different opinion tomorrow and thus appears to be progressing daily in his

thinking. In reality it is impossible for a true intellectual to progress at such speed.[61]

Lu Xun's praise of moral constancy, as exemplified in these remarks, came under attack as "petty-bourgeois" pessimism. But although the most vitriolic denunciations came from the Creation Society's members, it was Qian Xingcun of the Sun Society who wrote the most comprehensive negation of Lu Xun's "class" attitude.

Qian shot to notoriety with his essay "The Dead Era of Ah Q," published in *Sun Monthly* in March 1928. The essay opened with the strident declaration: "No matter how prolific Lu Xun is, no matter the extent to which some readers worship him, no matter how witty and venomous the prose in *The True Story of Ah Q*, the fact is Lu Xun simply cannot speak for the present age. The ideas contained in his works are equally incapable of representing the flow of ideas in the Chinese arts over the last decade!"[62]

The use of repetitive negation for emphatic effect (with the phrase "no matter" appearing three times in the first sentence alone) was a popular device in the "revolutionary literature" of the late 1920s. It remained a staple of leftist polemic thereafter and became a standard feature in the Communist Party's denunciatory language. In 1928, however, Qian's words were merely sensationalist and lacked the draconian power of later decades.

In essence, Qian Xingcun accused Lu Xun of encouraging an unhealthy and nihilistic outlook. He wrote that Lu Xun was morbidly preoccupied with the past and with recounting human pain. He illustrated this claim with several examples taken from Lu Xun's best-known prose works, notably *A Call to Arms, Wandering,* and *Wild Grass,* to conclude:

> Even when a shining path—a way out [*hen guangmingde chulu*]—is right there in front of him, he continues to "dislike" it and refuses "to go there." He is dissatisfied with reality yet bereft of hope. Thus he can only pace up and down along the wrong path and wander in nothingness! This is the psychological reason for Lu Xun's failure to offer a solution. His petty-bourgeois temperament has damaged him! ... Furthermore, Lu Xun is trapped in this state of mind because he has been damaged by so-called liberal ideas, for these lead

inevitably to contradiction and indecision. In this world, so-called liberalism is a deceptive term, and Lu Xun is among those who have been deceived by it.[63]

These criticisms were interwoven into Qian's synoptic account of China's historic progress toward a proletarian victory. He wrote that, following the protests and strikes of 30 May 1925, "China's class situation" underwent a dramatic and irreversible sharpening of class antagonisms. Carefully avoiding any mention of the 1927 massacre of Communists, Qian referred only to an "intense bloody struggle" between the oppressed poor and "their bourgeois oppressors." He commended the "surging growth of literature of the fourth class" as the requisite knowledge that would empower workers and peasants and praised China's revolutionary youth for accelerating its dissemination. These were visible signs of class struggle that "exceed the confines of the nation-state," thus enabling China to join cause with "the united front of all the oppressed classes in the world."[64]

According to Qian, the obsolescence of Lu Xun's writings derived from his manifest inability to reflect these revolutionary changes. It was no accident that Qian singled out *The True Story of Ah Q* as key evidence of Lu Xun's irrelevance. It was a brazen attempt to attack Lu Xun's best-known work of fiction: in 1928 *Ah Q* not only showed no sign of fading into obscurity but was well on its way to becoming an enduring classic. First published in 1921, the novella soon attracted an enormous body of commentary within China and, by the mid-1920s, had achieved international acclaim. A Russian translation was under way in 1925, and a French translation was produced in 1926 through the recommendation of Romain Rolland, who, having read a draft translation, described Ah Q as memorably "both tragic and comic" such that "you can't bear to part with him."[65]

In late 1921 and early 1922, Lu Xun first brought the roguish yet hapless Ah Q to life in nine serial installments in Beijing's *Morning Post* supplement, which was then edited by his protégé Sun Fuyuan. Lu Xun published the work under the pseudonym Ba Ren, and, as he recalled in 1926, the fact that the author's identity was unknown intrigued readers, causing them to speculate whether the story was a *roman à clef.* He

also learned from an article by the writer Gao Yihan (1884–1968) that
there were people who felt personally accused by the story. One man
even suspected the author of being a malicious personal acquaintance
who, being privy to the details of his private life, was attacking him by
innuendo. Lu Xun noted: "when he finally learned the author's name
and realized that he had never met him, a great load was lifted from
his mind and he went about telling everyone that the story was not an
attack on him after all."[66]

The controversy surrounding this work continued even after Lu
Xun was revealed as the author. Reprinted in 1923 in the anthology *A
Call to Arms, Ah Q* continued to attract commentary and debate. By
then the novella was widely known throughout China, with Sun Fuyuan
noting of an informal survey he conducted in 1924 that nine out of ten
readers voted it the best story in *A Call to Arms*.[67] Of the many questions that readers posed about the story of Ah Q, one in particular led
Lu Xun to write a formal response. This was the question of whether
Lu Xun ought to have turned Ah Q into a revolutionary, and it was the
influential editor Zheng Zhenduo who posed it in his November 1926
review of *A Call to Arms*.

Zheng praised *Ah Q* as "the most outstanding" story in Lu Xun's anthology while expressing dissatisfaction with its ending. He remarked
that it was hardly convincing for a venal character like Ah Q to become
a revolutionary and then meet a tragic end on the execution ground and
concluded that Lu Xun must have written the latter half of the story in
haste. Zheng argued that the author's sympathetic portrayal of Ah Q's
revolutionary turn and subsequent death gave the character something
of a split personality. In response to Zheng's review, Lu Xun wrote that
he had not "casually" ended Ah Q's life on the execution ground. Rather,
he had agonized "week after week" as to whether Ah Q would indeed
become a revolutionary. "To my mind, Ah Q would not become a revolutionary as long as there was no revolution in China; but once there
was one, he would. This was the only fate possible for my Ah Q, and I
would not say that he has a split personality. The inaugural year of the
Republic is long past, never to return; but the next time there are reforms, I believe there will still be revolutionaries like Ah Q."[68] Lu Xun
thus defended his story as a critical portrait of human foibles in a time

of violence. In 1934 he elaborated on his reasons for doing so in an open letter. Commenting on the importance of fostering empathy through literature, Lu Xun wrote that the point of *Ah Q* was "to make the reader unable to distinguish this character from himself" and hence to provide "a path to self-interrogation."[69]

This authorial intention is incommensurable with Qian Xingcun's stark treatment of *Ah Q* as documentary evidence of a long since superseded stage of class struggle. In 1928 Qian described Lu Xun as having evoked "a dead era" and accused him of misleading readers about the Chinese masses. According to Qian, the "aberrant national character" that Lu Xun presented in the story was an insult to the Chinese masses:

> Over the last decade, Chinese peasants have ceased to be as naïve as the peasants of Ah Q's era. If we consider the changes that have occurred in literary thought, we can see that Ah Q belongs neither to the May Fourth period [1919] nor to the May Thirtieth period [1925], let alone the present era of the great revolution [since 1927]. First, Chinese peasants today ... mostly belong to tightly knit organizations and are quite knowledgeable about politics. Second, the revolutionary nature of Chinese peasants has already been fully expressed. They have rebelled against landlords and joined the revolution. Recently they even expressed a primitive form of *Baudon* when they carried out a revolution of their own, without the slightest trace of an Ah Q spirit of bowing to the gentry. . . . Their struggle is political: it is significant and purposeful and not just an outpouring of anger. . . . Led by their interest, the peasants today have progressed from individual to political concerns along the path of revolution.[70]

Qian claimed that Lu Xun's story gave the false impression that the Chinese poor still "lived and died in ignorance" trapped in "an attitude of passive fatalism" that made them victims of the powerful. Qian's declaration of *Ah Q*'s obsolescence incurred the ire of Lu Xun's admirers. Among them, Liu Dajie (1904–1977) retorted:

> Lu Xun is the most successful among realist writers in China. He is truly rich in life experience and wields a pen among the sharpest and most sarcastic I have encountered. Practically every work in *A*

Call to Arms and *Wandering* is based in what he has personally experienced or witnessed. These are vivid and highly moving portrayals of life. Now we have a group of literary youth lacking in life experience who create literature based solely on their ideals. This makes their literature lacking in reality. Their experience amounts to no more than what they experienced in their student days combined with a few brief episodes of romantic love. This is why the works of our new writers today are full of love affairs.[71]

This passage is typical of the many commentaries published in defense of Lu Xun's oeuvre in 1928. Similarly, in response to the charge that Lu Xun's "petty-bourgeois" literature was hindering China's revolutionary progress, his supporters ridiculed his accusers in turn. Among them, Gan Ren remarked drolly that their vindictive slapdash approach to promoting "proletarian consciousness" was akin to an attempt "to govern the empire with half a chapter of *The Analects*."[72] But it was also evident that accusations of "petty-bourgeois laggardness" carried a moral valence that worried Lu Xun and his supporters. Accordingly, Gan Ren, a staunch defender of Lu Xun, was at pains to explain:

The arts do not depend on material provisions. . . . There's nothing the fetishists of materialism can do about this. . . . Unlike the material aspect of human existence, spiritual life is not subject to [material] constraints. Thus, even though someone may belong to a particular social class, this does not confine him to being a writer of that class. This has always been the case, and one can't break the rule just to accommodate those who are in such a hurry to create revolutionary writers that they recruit members of the first and second classes and squeeze them into the theory of dialectical materialism to remake them into members of the third and fourth classes.[73]

Here Gan Ren was referring to the growing popularity of the Marxist metanarrative that Qian Xingcun invoked to judge *Ah Q* as obsolete. According to Qian, the portrayal of Ah Q was proof that Lu Xun lacked revolutionary enthusiasm. Describing the revolutionary writer as someone not content merely to write about social problems but who sought to advance the masses, Qian stated that it was crucial for such a writer to reflect in his work "a trace of the spirit that yearns to transcend the age." He added that this eagerness to leap ahead was the defining quality of a revolutionary writer.[74]

And indeed, Lu Xun had once commended the revolutionary writer as someone who "speaks a little too soon."[75] But what Lu Xun sought to valorize was simply the writer's heightened sensitivity to the injustices of his day, not fidelity to a given political system. Hence, whereas Lu Xun drew attention to the revolutionary writer as a harbinger of upsetting news, always at risk of inspiring public hatred, Qian imagined instead a vanguard seer to whom the masses would obediently look for instruction on class struggle.

Given this incommensurability, it is not surprising to find Qian accusing Lu Xun of an utter failure to "catch up with the times" or "be fully engaged with the age." Of Lu Xun's oeuvre as a whole, Qian wrote: "Literature produced out of this ideology can neither achieve greatness nor become eternal. Instead, it degenerates into trash; into useless and meaningless diversions for the capitalist class."[76] The kind of moral empathy Lu Xun valorized as humanism had no place in the "stages of class struggle" that young critics like Qian were advancing as a true science.

In 1928 Qian highlighted three landmark moments of revolutionary struggle in his story of China's progress toward Communism: 4 May 1919 and 30 May 1925—two dates that, in leftist discourse, were already frequently marked as milestones in the masses' forward march—and a third milestone capaciously named as "the present era of the great revolution." Qian's conspicuous avoidance of any mention of the Northern Expedition offers a poignant reminder of how disastrously this Soviet-aided revolution—the otherwise anticipated third milestone—had turned out for the Communists.

In 1927 Lu Xun had described the revolutionary slogans of Guangzhou as self-deluding intoxicants. He reprised the idea in 1928 to ridicule the prescriptive historicism of his Marxist accusers. In "Ditties on Universal Peace," a short essay he published in *Threads of Talk* in April 1928, a month after Qian Xingcun declared "Ah Q's era" dead, Lu Xun wrote about three local ditties mocking the construction of the Sun Yat-sen Mausoleum in Nanjing then under way.[77] He lauded these ditties as reflecting the wit of ordinary people in expressing disaffection with the Nationalist state. He noted that such simple and vivid utterances as "You summon but no one heeds you, so on your own head must the tombstone be borne" conveyed a depth of feeling that "writers skilled at exposing the darkness in society" seemed incapable of achieving.[78]

He then turned to mock the ready claims of a "shining path" on the left: "Of late, revolutionary writers seem especially fearful of the dark and seek to conceal it, but the townsfolk have not bothered to be discreet in the least and have gone and made it known anyway." He described his critics as purveyors of false prognostications who "turn into anxious old women because they lack the courage to see what is happening in society. They welcome the auspicious magpie but loathe and fear the owl's hoot and become so intoxicated with a selected good omen or two as to convince themselves they have transcended the age."[79]

The humanism that Lu Xun privileged was inspired by Confucian benevolence (as "compassionate love"), transposed into a modern critical register of self-making. In the importance he placed on adhering to a moral decision at personal cost, we can discern a resemblance to the Kantian idea of the categorical imperative. Lu Xun's valorization of humanism was never of a received paradigm. Rather, he gestured to an internalized constant law or principle, achieved through intuitive, self-reflective inquiry and capable of fostering an ever-evolving humanness of feeling. In praising writers who committed suicide as an ultimate form of moral protest, ranging from the ancient Chinese poet Qu Yuan (c. 340–278 B.C.E.) to the modern Russian writers Esenin and Sobol, he offered them as paragons of this proclivity.

In this connection, Lu Xun frequently emphasized the importance of artistic skill and technique in portraying the human condition and declared the writings of his Marxist detractors as inferior to news reports. In reaction, the journals of the Creation and Sun Societies frequently featured such snide comments as "bourgeois literary critics treat literature as if technique alone should decide a work's value, as though literature had its own purpose regardless of content."[80] Hence Qian Xingcun was at pains to point out that he was attacking not only Lu Xun's ideas but his literary style and approach:

It is not only the era of Ah Q that is dead; the artistry of *The True Story of Ah Q* is also dead! If we were to appraise the work using petty-bourgeois literary rules, its merits are naturally quite considerable and worthy of praise. But it is well and truly dead and gone! The present era exceeds the grasp of the writer skilled in insidious and venomous expression. The present age cannot be represented by someone who relies on artful wit. The present age cannot be portrayed by a writer who lacks a political mind! . . . This era of hurricanes and storms can be expressed only by a writer imbued with the revolutionary spirit of hurricanes and storms, whose entire body burns with feelings of faith and sincerity, who has firsthand knowledge of politics, and who stands on the revolutionary front line! The artistry of *The True Story of Ah Q* simply lacks this power! The era of Ah Q is long dead and gone! Let's not be smitten with this skeleton; let's bury Ah Q body and soul, let's bury Ah Q body and soul![81]

The fact that Lu Xun was prepared to reconcile with his accusers by early 1929, despite the frenetic diatribes leveled against him in 1928, indicates the importance he accorded to promoting the work of the left.

In August 1928 Lu Xun articulated the relation between "humanism" and "class struggle" as the asymmetry of human emotion and abstract ideal. In his reading of Soviet works in Japanese translation during this time, he found arguments that supported his view of socially committed writing as motivated in the first instance by a spontaneous and powerful empathy for one's fellow humans and not by political ideals per se. In this regard, he wrote approvingly of Trotsky:

Trotsky once used "the fear of death," common to everyone down the ages, to show that literature contains elements that are not of a class character. This way of stating the problem is quite sufficient. For my part, I believe that if we subscribe to the theory that our personality, emotions, and so forth are "controlled by economics," it follows that all these must bear a class character. But note that they only "bear" and do not "consist solely of." Thus, while on the one hand I do not believe there are literary giants whose writings transcend their class character and are as eternal as the sun and the moon, on the other hand I am equally skeptical of revolutionary writers who live in Western-style homes and drink coffee but exclaim, "I am the true proletariat because I alone have mastered proletarian consciousness."[82]

Two years later he provided an elaboration of these remarks in the lengthy essay "'Hard Translation' and the 'Class Character of Literature,'"[83] published in March 1930 to coincide with the founding of the League of Chinese Left-Wing Writers. In this later essay, Lu Xun accused the left and the right alike of corroding the integrity of *baihua* each with its own special agenda. The essay's title is a reference to criticisms issued by Liang Shiqiu, the Crescent Moon Society's leading literary critic.

Liang, the sole Crescentist to exchange words with both Lu Xun and Lu Xun's Marxist accusers, published several essays in 1928 and 1929 in which he ridiculed the idea that literature had a "class character." He also mocked the notion of "hard translation" that Lu Xun had coined to describe his translations, from Japanese to Chinese, of Soviet literary criticism.[84] In stating that Lu Xun's translations were barely intelligible, Liang made the cutting remark that so-called hard translation required such extreme fidelity to the original that it might as well be called "dead translation" (that is, literal translation). Liang added that a smooth mistranslation was infinitely preferable to Lu Xun's "hard translation" because, notwithstanding its fatal errors, an eloquent mistranslation would at least "give the reader a sense of pleasure."[85]

In his response, Lu Xun pointed out he did use "hard translation" to suggest a faithful translation but more importantly to highlight the limitations of Chinese as a language "awaiting new constructions."[86] He wrote that "new constructions" were necessary because "Chinese grammar is even less adequate than classical Japanese." This state of affairs was reflected in the pitifully small number of innovations in Chinese grammar, syntax, and vocabulary across the centuries, from "Sima Qian's [c. 145–86 B.C.E.] *Records of the Historian* and *The Book of Han*" through the Tang (618–907) and Yuan (1260–1368) eras and down to his time, with each rare innovation requiring a protracted period of assimilation.

In proposing "hard translation" as a remedy for these grammatical deficiencies, Lu Xun offered the following guidelines: first, the act of translation must avoid "dismembering the original syntax" so as to prevent "the loss of the original tone"; and second, it must prise open the Chinese language to accommodate new ways of sense-making. In using the attribute "hard" *(ying)* to highlight the difficulties a conscientious translator must overcome, Lu Xun also implied an unyielding diligence on the part of the intended reader. As he put it, "hard translation" was meant for those who "work hard at reading," not people who merely sought pleasure: "I don't translate to enhance the reader's 'pleasure.' Instead, I seek to make the reader uncomfortable, even frustrated, irate, or just plain furious."[87] To the extent that Lu Xun's "hard translation" proved a strain to read and was at times barely intelligible, these remarks that bespeak a spirit of radical inventiveness point to the scale of linguistic innovation he sought but failed to produce.

Regarding Liang's argument that literature transcended class because it expressed "human nature at its most basic," Lu Xun expressed only scorn. He accused Liang of promoting a spurious universalism. Liang had argued that capitalist and worker alike shared the same human capacity for joy and anger. Lu Xun contended that this notion was "contradictory and meaningless," because "just as the poor are not troubled by the prospect of stock market losses, the coal tycoon cannot understand the bitter toil of the old woman in Beijing who collects scraps of coal from the cinders."[88]

He wrote derisively that since Liang favored a class-free human nature, he ought to champion "literature describing the basic animal functions—eating, breathing, movement, and procreation—or, better still, let's ditch 'movement' and retain only biological nature, which ought to be ranked in top place." Accusing Liang of a cavalier indifference to the gulf between the rich and the poor, Lu Xun proceeded to defend the social importance of literature as a necessary mirror of social inequality and injustice. In this context, he described Liang's defense of literary genius as a sordid attempt to sanctify the educational and cultural privileges of the wealthy by presenting them as the natural advantage of "the gifted few."[89]

Lu Xun was equally dismissive of Liang's proposal to create wholesome popular operas, movies, and crime stories to cater to the working poor. He noted that such condescension amounted to denying the poor any access to good literature. Lu Xun concluded that although Liang sought ostensibly "to eradicate class character from literature," he was actually attempting to preserve the unequal status quo so as to keep literature in the hands of the powerful (rather than "gifted") few.[90]

Having condemned Liang as an elitist, Lu Xun turned to accuse Qian Xingcun of displaying an alternate arrogance toward the masses. He wrote that the popularity among Chinese leftists of invoking Upton Sinclair's maxim, "All literature is propaganda," was of a piece with the unhealthy proliferation of "poems and stories interwoven with slogans, passed off as proletarian literature." He wrote that Qian's fondness for the Stalinist dictum that literature must "bring out the right slogan at the right moment so that the masses echo the slogan and the slogan finds expression in reality" was a complete distortion of Lunacharsky's argument.[91] "When Lunacharsky spoke of writing that the masses could understand, he had in mind the sort of pamphlets Tolstoy printed and distributed to his peasants, using songs and jokes in language that workers and peasants could easily comprehend. We see this too from the fact that Demyan Bedny [1883–1945], who received the Red Flag badge for his poetry, has no slogans in his poems."[92]

Lu Xun commented that unlike the situation in Russia, where revolutionary slogans might have served a genuine purpose, Shanghai's revolutionary literature was replete with slogans "precisely because the works themselves have nothing proletarian in form and content." He added that "slogans thus become the sole means for flaunting the 'brand-newness'" of the literature in question. Lu Xun thus accused Qian of the elitist presumption that people with little or no formal education were fit only to receive slogans.[93]

Lu Xun then cited several passages from the essays of Liang Shiqiu and Qian Xingcun to illustrate the similarities he perceived in their reasoning. He concluded that, despite their manifest opposition as respective spokespersons for the right and the left, they shared a predilection for lofty abstractions. In describing Liang's valorization of "human nature" and Qian's endorsement of "worthy slogans" as sharing the same magisterial conceit, Lu Xun offered the witticism: "If we were to place two plush tiger-skin armchairs side by side, majestically facing south in the 'humanistic Palace of Art' (I'm borrowing this phrase from

Mr. Cheng Fangwu), we could certainly invite Messrs. Liang Shiqiu and Qian Xingcun to sit on them, with the former holding a copy of *Crescent Moon* in his right hand and the latter displaying *The Sun* in his left hand. Now that would make a pretty picture of 'labor and capital' indeed."[94]

This evocative caricature of the right and the left as rival elites plying their competing brands of didacticism in the marketplace aptly captures Lu Xun's disaffection with his intellectual peers. From 1930 onward, when he actively promoted "mass literature," he was keen to distinguish his proposal as one of a *personal* commitment to the cause of mass literacy, not as a *political* vision of class struggle. He was at pains to highlight this distinction when he contrasted a true resolve with mere ideological rectitude in his inaugural speech to the Left-Wing League on 2 March 1930:

> First, in the struggle against the old society and old forces, we must be resolute and maintain a constant stance. Above all, we must know our actual strength. The roots of the old society go deep, and we are unable to dislodge them unless our new movement gains greater strength. Moreover, the old society has effective ways of compromising the force of the new while itself remaining impervious to compromise. To date, there have been numerous new movements in China, but each has succumbed to the old, mainly for want of broad and resolute objectives but also because these movements make modest demands that are easily satisfied. For instance, the *baihua* movement met initially with the old society's formidable opposition but was soon tolerated and given a pitifully small space in which to exist. *Baihua* accordingly became visible in the marginal columns of newspapers. From the old society's perspective, this new thing turned out to be nothing and certainly not anything to be feared. Thus . . . those on the side of the new were also satisfied that *baihua* had attained the right to exist. Something similar has happened to the movement for proletarian literature over the last couple of years. Because proletarian literature turned out to be harmless, the old society has also become tolerant of it, and some of its members have even dabbled in writing proletarian literature. They treat it as an ornament, as if they were placing a coarse workman's bowl among

the fine porcelain and antiques in the parlor to create an unconventional effect. As for the proletarian writers, once they were given their own little corner and their manuscripts became saleable, they no longer had any need to struggle. Critics also sang paeans to "the victories of proletarian literature"! But apart from the victories of certain individuals, what gains have there been for proletarian literature? If proletarian literature is a wing of the proletarian struggle for liberation, it must grow together with the forces of a proletarian society. The fact that proletarian literature is being celebrated in the literary scene while the social status of the proletariat is so low proves only that the writers of proletarian literature have become divorced from the proletariat and have returned to the old society.[95]

The sentiments expressed in this passage, so revealing of Lu Xun's ambivalence toward leftist politics, are repeated in several of his essays during this period. He frequently highlighted the difference between helping the working class find their own voice and speaking on their behalf. In this regard, he warned against the delusion of imagining that intellectuals who proclaimed themselves as a revolutionary vanguard would be revered by the working class. In his address to the League, he observed satirically: "It goes without saying that the intellectual class has important work to do that should not be trivialized, but the working class is clearly under no obligation to offer special privileges to poets and writers."[96]

Lu Xun's remark needs to be understood in the context of rapid developments in the discourse of the left from 1928 to 1930. By late 1928, the Creation Society's and Sun Society's raucous diatribes against "petty-bourgeois" intellectuals earlier that year had been replaced by more sober disquisitions on the flaws of "petty-bourgeois" literature. Accordingly, the pitch and volume of their published attacks on Lu Xun was reduced, alongside a shift in focus to more formal literary concerns. Theoretical issues, such as the relative importance of form and content and the relation of objectivity to subjectivity, became the new themes of contention.

The Creation and Sun theorists frequently used the terms "consciousness" and "ideology" to accentuate the importance of inculcating proletarian values among intellectuals, workers, and peasants alike. They endorsed "subjectivity" in opposition to the "objectivity" that Lu Xun's admirers attributed to his writings, and dismissed objectivity as a petty-bourgeois ruse.[97] They also privileged "content" over "form" in tacit rejection of the many essays and commentaries that volubly praised Lu Xun's technical achievements. The Marxist radicals argued instead that whereas literary form was merely an indication of technical achievement, literary content fully reflected the author's class values. In elevating content over form, they sought also to vindicate their own vanguard status. Frequently ridiculed as lacking artistry and technique, Lu Xun's Marxist accusers now expressly defended their own writings as the ideological blueprint needed for "going over to the proletariat."

Li Chuli played a key role in the theoretical defense of the revolutionary vanguard. In a widely read essay of September 1928, he wrote that the vanguard alone was fully equipped with "a consciousness of political struggle" and a "militant materialist view." As such its members were instrumental in the work of "instructing the working class on how to acquire true proletarian consciousness." Without this tutelage, the lives of the struggling masses would remain confined to "material production alone," leading them to "put greater value on small change than the whole of socialism and politics." Consequently, "they would be capable only of struggling for themselves and their children but not for entire future generations."[98] In March 1930, it was in explicit opposition to this vanguard aspiration and presumption that Lu Xun told the League's aspiring writers to expect the unexpected. Implying that a triumphant working class would make demands that no vanguard could possibly anticipate, he conjectured that this vocal newly risen proletariat would "want the whole place and not just one corner."[99]

Defending and Disparaging the Left

In three consecutive publications of March–April 1930, Lu Xun repeated the complaint that the left was characterized by a debilitating disunity resulting from factional and selfish interest. In " 'Hard Translation' and the 'Class Character of Literature,' " he wrote that his Marxist detractors had subjected him to "an excess of nonsense where scalpels fail to pierce the flesh and bullets could not inflict a mortal wound."[100] In his inaugural address to the League's members, he took evident pleasure in mocking the Creation Society and Sun Society, noting that their attacks had proved "so paltry a force that even I became bored and lost interest in rebutting them." He continued:

> This is because I discovered that my foes were just putting up a brave front [kong cheng ji]. At the time, they were preoccupied with making a din, not with recruiting and training their troops. Although there were plenty of articles attacking me, you could tell at once that the authors used pseudonyms, and the accusations boiled down to the same few things repeated *ad nauseam*. At the time, I was looking forward to being hit by a crack shot in the art of Marxist critique, but no such person appeared.[101]

On a more conciliatory note, he urged the audience, which included the majority of his erstwhile accusers: "We ought to be cultivating new warriors, a whole troop of them, because we are very shorthanded at present. . . . If there is no specialist among us, and we're all just dabbling in this and that, whether translating, fiction writing, reviewing, poetry writing, how would we do well at anything?"[102]

He elaborated on this warrior trope in the essay "We Need Critics," published in the same issue of *Sprout* (1 April 1930) that carried the transcript of his League address. In this essay, Lu Xun made a point of criticizing his former detractors for aiding the enemy by targeting their own side. He wrote of the intellectual left in Shanghai:

> All of these groups state their commitment to reform and declare war on the fortress of the old, but on the way, at the foot of this fortress, they start wrestling each other. This fighting goes on until everyone is utterly exhausted. But since they are just "wrestling," no one's seriously wounded [da chuang]: they are merely out of breath. And each as he gasps for air imagines himself triumphant and starts singing of victory. Thus the fortress of the old has no need for sentries, for its inhabitants need do nothing but simply watch with folded arms the comedy being sung by their new foes down below. They make no sound, but they have triumphed.[103]

Although Lu Xun's Marxist accusers were no longer hurling insults at him in 1930, they were by no means converted to his way of seeing and continued tacitly to adopt a superior tone toward him. A good example of this appears in Qian Xingcun's 1930 review essay, simply titled "Lu Xun," published mere weeks before the founding of the Left-Wing League. Whereas in 1928 Qian had vigorously denounced Lu Xun and pronounced both the author and his oeuvre dead, in 1930 he commended Lu Xun's stories for their "antifeudal" spirit but did so with a telling qualification. Qian wrote that Lu Xun showed an unfortunate sentimentalism about the past. Nonetheless, he was keen to hail Lu Xun as a fellow leftist and urged his incoming League leader to embrace "the passions that inflame the present stage of the revolutionary struggle like fire; like flowers in bloom." He ended with the patronizing remark: "We look forward to seeing Lu Xun adopt the position of the proletariat to create a new kind of antifeudal literature."[104] This qualified welcome was nothing like the simple exuberance that Lu Xun had encountered three years earlier in Guangzhou, when young Communists like Bi Lei had praised him as a revolutionary mentor.

Lu Xun felt no camaraderie with the majority of his fellow League members. His contempt is plain in the letter of 27 March 1930 he wrote to his trusted disciple Zhang Tingqian, recounting the League's inaugural meeting. Lu Xun told Zhang that because "in truth, apart from me, there are only a handful of people in China capable of being a ladder," he frequently found himself surrounded by "future gentlemen . . . who spare no thought for me as they step on my shoulders" in pursuit of their own advancement. He wrote that as he surveyed "Shanghai's revolutionary writers" assembled at the League's inauguration, he suspected he faced "a thoroughly useless lot [qie hua se]." He complained that he was "at risk once more of becoming a ladder," but, even worse, he feared that this self-styled vanguard "might not even have the skill needed to climb the ladder, alas!"[105]

In his reading of this letter, David Pollard observes that Lu Xun's extreme scorn might have been brought on by the miserable mood he was in, as his chronic dental problems had resulted, three days earlier, in the extraction of all of his remaining lower teeth.[106] Pollard rightly notes that Lu Xun's indictment of Shanghai's revolutionary writers was at odds with the situation in which he found himself in 1930, with his former detractors "honoring him purely on the orders of their political leadership." Pollard also observes: "Lu Xun was extremely generous of his time and money in assisting young writers and translators when they deferred to him as pupils to master, and submitted their work to him for correction, but felt betrayed when they went their own way. Though he would have been horrified at the thought, this was one element of 'feudalism' that he hadn't shaken off."[107] In one sense, and notwithstanding Lu Xun's customary disavowal of the guiding role that others foisted on him, his throng of eager fans and followers would have made it very difficult for him not to grow accustomed to being treated as a mentor.

The founding of the League itself was a signal event for the party's intellectuals. It represented a consolidation of purpose among Party members and "fellow travelers" and was modeled largely on the "proletarianization" of literature then under way in the Soviet Union.[108] For the more radical members of the League, the Russian Association of Proletarian Writers (RAPP), with its dictatorial insistence on ideological rectitude, was something of an exemplar organization. As Katerina Clark observes of the rapid destruction of what little intellectual pluralism remained in the Soviet Union from 1927 to 1932: "The literary battles became progressively dirtier and more dire in their consequences for the losers. And RAPP (the most powerful and militant group in this 'proletarian' literature) became a sort of monster that seemed to be swallowing the small independent writers' organizations, one by one."[109]

RAPP was an organization founded in 1925 that absorbed in 1928 the militant group that had previously called itself VAPP—the All-Union Association of Proletarian Writers, founded in 1920. Under the aegis of the expanded RAPP from 1928 onward, class warfare was actively pursued, thereby aiding Stalin's implementation of "proletarianization" as official Soviet cultural policy. These developments helped to further consolidate Stalin's autocracy following Trotsky's expulsion in late 1927.[110]

Soviet literary debates of the more open and politically diverse mid-1920s were known in Chinese intellectual circles. Between June 1928 and April 1929, Lu Xun translated and serialized a Japanese anthology of

Soviet theoretical writings of this earlier period in *Torrents,* the journal he cofounded with Yu Dafu. In the notes accompanying his translation, Lu Xun observed with interest the diversity of views in Soviet intellectual circles in 1924 and 1925, stating that the fundamental conflict appeared to be between those who were interested only in class warfare (as represented by the VAPP journal *Na Postu* [*On Guard*]) and others who accorded equal importance to political and artistic goals (such as Trotsky, Nikolai Bukharin [1888–1938], Lunacharsky, and Alexander Voronsky [1884–1937]).

In 1928 Lu Xun confined himself to making neutral statements, merely observing that the intellectual climate in Soviet Russia was no longer the same as in 1925 and that Trotsky and Voronsky had been politically eclipsed.[111] Given his fondness for Esenin, Lu Xun was probably aware that Voronsky was a vocal champion of Esenin and that Esenin's poetry had appeared in *Red Virgin Soil,* the experimental and politically inclusive journal that Voronsky edited. Lu Xun's insistence on artistic integrity makes it clear that his sympathies were with Trotsky, Voronsky, and others who had argued the same. He made a point of noting that in 1925 Voronsky, as editor of *Red Virgin Soil,* became the principal target of the group behind *Na Postu.* Nonetheless, Lu Xun scrupulously avoided any comparisons with the polemics over revolutionary literature in which he was then embroiled. Instead he merely observed that the Soviet debates showed that "Russian literary theory and practice" constituted "the command center of working-class literature." He added the elliptical comment: "China at present, I fear, is unable to benefit from this example," but without explaining what he meant.[112]

Two years later, in 1930, Lu Xun reprinted his translation in book form under the title *A Policy on the Arts,* explaining he had done so because no newer translation of recent Soviet theoretical writings had appeared. He wrote that his anthology was an attempt to extend the shelf life of these Soviet works because of their importance to literary developments in China.[113] Liang Shiqiu published a short polemic under the title "About the So-Called 'Policy on the Arts,'" specifically mentioning this publication and reprising his criticism of Lu Xun's "hard translation." Liang noted that although Lu Xun had revised his translation (Lu Xun's afterword included an acknowledgment of Feng Xuefeng's editorial assistance in preparing the anthology), it remained as unintelligible as the earlier version published in *Torrents,* and provided several examples from the work as evidence.

Liang then pointedly noted that Lu Xun had not revealed his own attitude to this "policy on the arts" and mockingly remarked: "The very idea of 'the arts' having a 'policy' is itself a contradiction in terms." In this manner, Liang returned Lu Xun's barb about the Crescent Moon Society as "pugs" of warlord power intent on turning *baihua* into the property of an elite minority. In calling Soviet cultural policy "the malaise of monomania" (with "monomania" appearing in English), Liang insinuated that Lu Xun was in abject servitude to a political organization hostile to the arts.[114]

In the 1930s Lu Xun and Liang continued sporadically to exchange insults, but the exclusivism of the Crescent Moon Society that incurred Lu Xun's wrath in the mid- to late 1920s no longer occupied his attention. He was far more concerned about being undermined by his fellow League members. Although the League operated covertly under constant threat from the anti-Communist Nationalist government, it was nonetheless a Communist-led organization that demanded obedience from the Party rank and file. As Wang-Chi Wong states in his comprehensive study of the League, "Lu Xun's position in the League was peculiar."[115] He commanded respect as the organization's nominal leader but was largely absent from its activities. Feng Xuefeng and Qu Qiubai, as confidants of Lu Xun who were also members of the League's Party group, ensured that harmony prevailed between Lu Xun and other League members from 1930 to 1933. Lu Xun's apprehension about defending an organization in which a leftist orthodoxy was gathering pace is evident in his October 1932 essay, "On the 'Third Type.'" This was his response to an essay by a disgruntled fellow League member, Su Wen (pen name of Dai Kechong, 1907–1964), who had intimated that the League had degenerated into a mere tool of the Communist Party.

On this occasion Lu Xun wrote in the League's defense but acknowledged its manifest flaws. He commented that whenever there was political danger, opportunistic members were quick to abandon the League, noting that some had become "foot-soldiers of 'Nationalist literature'" (then rumored to be subsidized by the Nationalist government in Nanjing) or even "enemy spies" while others had retreated from the fray to become "bookstore owners." He then argued that despite the many and varied problems of "the leftist literary scene" (*zuoyi wentan*), people should redouble their efforts to promote the League's goals, because leftist writers were being "actively persecuted, imprisoned, and slaughtered" and the left as a whole was "too crushed to publish critical commentaries."[116] In response to Su Wen's remark that the League had turned into an aggressive organization that attacked nonpartisan writers as "capitalist running dogs,"[117] Lu Xun wrote with uneasy equivocation:

> If the leftist literary scene should one day enjoy freedom of expression, would the "third type of person" [a phrase used by Su Wen to designate independent intellectuals] be denounced, at the slightest provocation, as a "capitalist running dog"? If leftist critics have not given their word that they would not do so, and, moreover, if they choose to view things solely from a negative angle, it is entirely possible that this may happen. Besides, one can imagine much worse scenarios. But I think such predictions are as pointless as contemplating suicide on the grounds that the Earth might fall apart one day.[118]

This last remark about the absurdity of killing oneself because the world might end was Lu Xun's way of belittling Su Wen's prediction that Communist success would usher in a repressive regime. Despite his own vociferous opposition to doctrinalism, in the early 1930s Lu Xun was quick to publicly defend his fellow League members as people who would not waste their time "writing about things that belong to the future," as if to imply that there were far more pressing matters at hand . Citing Tolstoy and Gustave Flaubert (1821–1880) as exemplars, Lu Xun observed that "they wrote for their age," adding reflectively, "the future is the future of the present; hence only what has meaning today will acquire a significance in the future."[119]

From 1934 to 1936, when his relationship with the League's Party group under Zhou Yang rapidly deteriorated, Lu Xun privately denounced his fellow League members while publicly endorsing the

League and praising the Soviet Union and the Chinese Communists. For instance, in a May 1934 interview, he stated that "the existence and success of the Soviet Union have convinced me that a classless society will certainly come into being: not only have my doubts been swept away but my courage has greatly increased." But he was careful to qualify his own position as that of a writer who was "out of the revolutionary vortex," unable to travel and hence limited to the role of "exposing the evils of the old society."[120]

Lu Xun's correspondence with those whom he liked and trusted, such as his letter of 12 September 1935 to writer and fellow League member Hu Feng (pen name of Zhang Guangren, 1902–1985) affords a glimpse of his emotional turmoil. Lamenting his figurehead role in the Communist-led League, he wrote:

> I feel it would be better to have a few new writers appear among the people who do not belong [to the League]; they may show something fresh. Once a man has joined he is forever involved in petty squabbles and cannot make his voice heard. Take me as an example. I always feel that I am bound in an iron chain while a foreman is whipping me on the back. No matter how hard I work, the whip will fall. When I turn my head and ask what my faults really are, the man will clasp his hands and politely shake them and say that I am doing an extremely fine job; that he and I are surely the best of friends; and what a fine day ha, ha ha. . . . That so often disconcerts me. I dare not speak to the outsiders about ourselves; to the foreigners, I simply avoid the subject. If I have to speak, I only lie. You see what a predicament I am in.[121]

Lu Xun's deepening unhappiness about the League's Party leadership from 1934 to 1936 was accompanied by a growing schism on the left during this period. By 1936, two distinct factions had crystallized in the Chinese Communist Party. On the one side was Mao Zedong, who in 1936 became the chairman of the Politburo at the Party's remote hinterland base in Shaanxi. On the other side was Wang Ming, China's Soviet-trained Party representative at the Comintern, who enjoyed far greater influence than Mao outside China. In 1936, with the rising threat of a full-scale Japanese invasion, the Maoists and the Bolsheviks (under Mao and Wang respectively) set aside their differences in response to the exigencies of fighting a war of resistance. Nonetheless, intraparty tensions continued to fester and were further complicated by the pragmatic reconciliation the Communists sought to forge with the Nationalists in 1936, in aid of a second "united front"—this time against the Japanese.[122]

These realpolitik maneuvers caused a major rift within the Left-Wing League in Shanghai. Feng Xuefeng's recollections of these events suggest that Lu Xun agreed to the dissolution of the League in early 1936 because Zhou Yang, under orders from Wang Ming, had presented him with a virtual fait accompli. Numerous studies point to the significance of the rivalry between Zhou Yang (who answered to Wang Ming) and Feng (who was an envoy from Mao's hinterland base).[123]

In June 1936, three months after the League's dissolution, Zhou Yang established the Association of Literature and Art with the aim of promoting "national defense literature" in preparation for the Party's envisaged "united front" with the Nationalists. Lu Xun, who had never liked Zhou Yang, was unimpressed.[124] Feng Xuefeng recalled Lu Xun expressing extreme displeasure with Zhou Yang's new organization, dismissing it as "not meant for battle and not a patch on the 'Left-Wing League.'"[125]

Lu Xun's refusal to join Zhou Yang's association soon led to verbal confrontations between those who supported Zhou's advocacy of "national defense literature" and those who defended Lu Xun's alternative slogan of "mass literature of the national revolutionary movement." The word "mass" was the crux that divided the opposing parties in what became known as "the debate of the two slogans." Essentially, whereas Zhou's group elided the issue of class in advocating "national defense literature," Lu Xun and his supporters insisted on an abiding commitment to the proletariat. As T. A. Hsia observes, Lu Xun's discussions with Feng Xuefeng reveal not only his deep hatred for Chiang Kai-shek's Nationalist regime but extreme dislike of Zhou Yang. Lu Xun perceived Zhou as shamelessly welcoming the left's persecutors with open arms.[126] Hence, it was in explicit opposition to Zhou's avowal of "national defense literature" that Lu Xun and his supporters proposed the title "mass literature" in defense of the left's guiding mission.[127]

Feng Xuefeng, Hu Feng, and Mao Dun were among the better-known Communist intellectuals who stood with Lu Xun in opposing Zhou Yang. For them, this literary conflict also reflected an intensification of the developing rivalry between Mao Zedong and Wang Ming. In this regard, modern telecommunications made it far easier for the orders of distant Moscow to reach Shanghai than for those issuing from Mao's hinterland base to be relayed.[128] Unlike Zhou Yang, who was in regular communication with Wang Ming in Moscow, Feng Xuefeng traveled to Shanghai from Wayabao to ensure that the urban underground Communists remained in touch with Mao's Soviet government in Shaanxi.[129]

Lu Xun stated his own independent position in the controversial open letter that he published in August 1936, laboriously titled "A Reply to Xu Maoyong and Remarks on the Issue of a United Front in Resistance to Japan." Xu, former secretary of the League and a keen supporter of Zhou Yang, had written to Lu Xun urging him to reconsider his opposition to Zhou's new organization. Prior to this letter, Xu had enjoyed cordial relations with Lu Xun. The mixed tone of Xu's letter, fluctuating between studied respect for Lu Xun's intellectual authority and blunt criticism of his poor judgment, exemplifies the complex predicament over which Lu Xun frequently agonized in his private correspondence. On the one hand, he knew the Party leadership prized him as a unique asset. On the other, he was keenly aware that his distaste for orthodoxy was fast turning him into a burden and an irritation to the leadership.

Xu Maoyong (1911–1977) had obliquely chastised Lu Xun for wrongly favoring such perpetrators of "sectarianism" as Ba Jin, Hu Feng, and Huang Yuan (1906–2003), young writers who opposed Zhou Yang. Xu accused Hu and Huang of creating disunity among the left and insinuated that by acting as their "shield," Lu Xun had inadvertently advanced their selfish interests.[130] Infuriated, Lu Xun replied:

One day last year, a famous person invited me over for a chat. When I got there, a car drove up, and out jumped a posse: Tian Han, Zhou

Qiying [Zhou Yang], and two others. They looked so important, all dressed up in their Western suits. They said they had come over especially to inform me that Hu Feng was a traitor sent by the [Nationalist] government. When I asked for proof, they told me they had heard this from Mu Mutian [1900–1971]. I was totally speechless that members of the League would treat as gospel the words of a turncoat.[131] After they answered several more of my questions, I told them their evidence was far too flimsy for me to believe! Of course we parted on bad terms, but it put an end to rumors that Hu Feng was a "traitor."[132]

Earlier in the same letter, Lu Xun wrote that his "suspicions of self-declared 'instructors' and young people of Xu Maoyong's ilk" would prevent him from ever joining Zhou Yang's Association of Writers and Artists. He continued:

Experience has taught me that that people who adopt the mien of a "revolutionary," who are capable of casually slandering others as "turncoats," "counterrevolutionaries," "Trotskyists," and even "national traitors," are mostly people who walk a crooked path. I say this because their present disregard for the interests of the masses shows that they mean to cut down the nation's revolutionary forces on the sly. They use the revolution as an excuse to advance their own interests. In honesty, I've even wondered whether they were sent by the enemy.[133]

"A Reply to Xu Maoyong" was Lu Xun's final polemical essay; he died two months after dictating it to Feng Xuefeng from his sickbed in August 1936. It was both a furious rebuttal of Xu's accusations and a definitive exposition on the difference between "patriotic" and "mass" literature. In his study of Lu Xun's troubled relationship with the League, T. A. Hsia observes that the composition of the text and "the passion that went into it must have been quite an ordeal," as Lu Xun had been "snatched back only a month before from the brink of death." Hsia also notes that around the time that Lu Xun dictated this reply to Xu's letter, his weight, as recorded in his diary, was a mere 38.7 kilograms (85.8 pounds).[134]

Lu Xun was clearly also appalled by Zhou Yang's supporters. In his sickbed reply to Xu Maoyong, he noted that He Jiahuai (another of Zhou Yang's supporters) had had the temerity to misquote remarks Lu Xun had made six years earlier (during his inaugural League address in 1930) about the need for inclusiveness. Lu Xun was outraged that his words were being used to promote Zhou's "national defense literature" and that He was describing Zhou's opponents as people who supported a "literature of national traitors." As Zhou Yang and his supporters appeared so keen to provide "instructions on how to write," it was farcical for them to claim they were endorsing the broadest coalition in the name of patriotism.[135]

It was one thing to be patriotic, Lu Xun argued, noting that "purveyors of new-style 'brother-sister' romances in *baihuawen,* thee-thou archaists, and 'Mandarin Duck and Butterfly' authors" were as capable as anyone else of patriotic conduct. But it was quite another, he continued, to abandon the leftist commitment to a people's literature in favor of an ill-defined "national defense literature." Lu Xun even commended his former adversary, Guo Moruo, for having at least the good sense to highlight the difference between patriotic "national defense" and socially engaged art for the masses.[136]

A good part of Lu Xun's letter was devoted to a vigorous defense of Hu Feng against Xu's accusations. He insisted that Hu Feng was merely carrying out his instructions and that the slogan "mass literature of the national revolutionary movement" had been arrived at after extensive discussion with numerous writers. Most importantly, Lu Xun wrote, the point of the slogan was to preserve the erstwhile League's raison d'être of defending the common people's interests.[137]

As a polemic, "A Reply to Xu Maoyong" is without the sardonic wit that characterized Lu Xun's ripostes to the Creation and Sun Societies in 1928. As he approached death in 1936, Lu Xun no longer bothered with humorous caricatures of his opponents. Instead he denounced Zhou Yang and his men as "slave foremen" *(nuli zongguan),* reprising the language he had used at the start of his *baihua* career in the late 1910s to scorn the Chinese "national character" as a blend of fawning obsequiousness and slavish submission to power. Further, Lu Xun accused Zhou Yang of encouraging a different type of slavery. He wrote that Zhou's pursuit of orthodoxy produced a cowed obedience that damaged relationships among the left and stripped intellectual life in Shanghai of its few remaining "traces of human decency."[138]

The sheer length and wrathfulness of a frail Lu Xun's dying reply to Xu Maoyong led Guo Moruo to dub it "that 10,000-word missive" (in irreverent memory of the Creation Society's own verbal wars with Lu Xun eight years earlier).[139] Given Lu Xun's former disdain for slogans, his vigorous defense of the slogan "mass literature of the national revolutionary movement" is a poignant index of his despair about the future of Chinese letters. The publication of Lu Xun's reply quickly elicited a barely conciliatory response from Xu Maoyong, and an end to the dispute was brokered. The war machines were reverberating once more, and leftist discourse was again subordinated to realpolitik. Shortly before Lu Xun's death, the common decision of the Maoist and Bolshevik factions to pursue a second "united front" with the Nationalist government ensured that "national defense literature" prevailed over the idea of "mass literature."

In his elegant summation of the losing side's predicament, Theodore Huters writes: "It is easy to see how writers who had submerged a certain number of private scruples about submitting to Party dictation in the interests of creating a new world view would be most disturbed when they saw the new world view being de-emphasized and only the dictation remaining."[140] Lu Xun did not live to see this further withering of critical independence on the left.

Historicizing "Revolutionary Literature"

Throughout the 1930s, the unbridled polemics of 1928 continued to accrue historical authority as a watershed event in the development of modern Chinese thought. It was Lu Xun's enterprising protégé Li Xiaofeng who had helped to market the assault on his mentor that year as "*the* debate over revolutionary literature." Quick to capitalize on the heated exchanges between Lu Xun, his supporters, and his critics, by mid-1929 Li's Beixin Publishing House had published the anthology *A Debate over Chinese Literature,* thereby placing Beixin at the forefront of the latest leftist trends in Shanghai publishing.

The editor of the volume was Li Helin, a young Communist based in Beijing who in 1928 had been involved with the Beijing-based literary organization the Yet to Be Named Society, run by several of Lu Xun's former students.[141] Despite Li's proximity to close associates of Lu Xun, the maestro played no part in the anthology's publication. Indeed, it was not Lu Xun but Cheng Fangwu whom Li echoed in his editorial preface when he wrote that the anthology's purpose was to show that in China, a crucial transition had occurred from "literary revolution" to "revolutionary literature."

Li presented the Shanghai polemics of 1928 as a battle between "revolutionary" and "counterrevolutionary" forces and described it as a five-way debate *(lunzhan)* involving the following literary organizations: the Creation Society, *Threads of Talk*, the Chinese Literary Association (and its flagship journal, *Short Story Monthly*), the Crescent Moon Society, and *Contemporary Culture* (a journal operated by a group of self-styled anarchists). He named "argument" *(lun)* and "contention" *(zhan)* as the criteria he used for the anthology's selections, noting that he had chosen only essays representative of a broader social attitude, rejecting those that merely expressed personal opinion.[142]

The anthology has several interesting anomalies. Given the notoriety that Qian Xingcun attracted through his attacks on Lu Xun, Li's omission of Qian's essays is striking. In fact he excluded the Sun Society altogether and chose instead to highlight the roles of the Chinese Literary Association, the Crescent Moon Society, and the group that produced *Contemporary Culture*, even though these three organizations had seldom contributed articles to the 1928 polemics. Moreover, despite Li's declared intention of rejecting personal opinion, much of the anthology revolves around Lu Xun, who repeatedly described his essays as personal opinion.

Li's selections reflect a preoccupation with the prominence of organizations and authors as opposed to their level of participation. He was keen to elevate the polemics to an epochal class struggle, echoing the views of the Creation Society and Sun Society in this regard but without their febrile zeal. Writing in even-tempered prose, Li noted that the struggle for cultural progress in China lagged far behind the Soviet Union's. He urged his readers to heed the effectiveness of Soviet debates over the arts, explaining that these debates benefited from the highly structured environment of a postrevolutionary national conference, organized by no less than "the Party's highest organs."[143]

By the early 1920s, modern anthologies of "discursive wars" (*lunzhan* or *lunzheng*) were fast becoming a publishing genre in their own right because of the market demand for such compilations among urban educated Chinese. Moreover, as warring intellectuals were keen to have their words preserved for posterity (beyond the shelf life of the periodicals in which their essays first appeared), book-length anthologies dignified their quarrels as pathbreaking debates of historic consequence. As part of this anthologizing trend, Li Helin's 1929 anthology, sponsored by Beixin Publishing House, helped to promote a Marxist understanding of *baihua* polemics as evidence not only of modern progress but of class struggle.[144]

Indeed, in his editorial preface Li encouraged his readers to discriminate between "revolutionary" and "counterrevolutionary" elements in the selected essays. To guide the reader's judgment, he commended the view proposed by Feng Xuefeng in "Revolution and the Intellectual Class," an essay published in late September 1928. Li reproduced Feng's essay, placing it at the start of his anthology, and praised its "evenhanded and impartial" account of the polemics and "just assessment" of the contending positions.[145]

Feng's essay, written under the pseudonym Hua Shi, had first appeared in September 1928 in the short-lived *Trackless Train (Wugui lieche)*, a fashionable avant-garde journal that he cofounded. In it, Feng provided a sympathetic account of "fellow travelers" that stood in contrast to the denunciatory attitude of the Creation and Sun radicals. He identified three types of intellectuals on the side of revolution.[146] He described the first type as committed revolutionaries who had "abandoned their individualistic stance to embrace socialism" and now sought "boldly to destroy the old culture and the society that sustains it." He stated that the second type consisted of intellectuals "who support the cause of revolution and yearn for its arrival but who also turn around to gaze upon the old and regret its passing." Identifying Lu Xun as this second type, Feng claimed that such intellectuals, despite being mired in doubt and filled with regret and uncertainty, were useful to the revolution. He then proceeded to describe the third type as "opportunistic intellectuals" who evinced "an enthusiasm for self-advancement greatly outweighing their enthusiasm for revolution."[147]

Feng accused the Creation Society radicals of a "narrow exclusionary spirit" that discouraged wider support for the leftist cause, hence implying that they were members of this "opportunistic" third type. Of their journal *Cultural Critique* he wrote that "more than half of the essays are attacks on Lu Xun, together with frequent mentions of the 'Creation Society,' writ large." He chided them for failing to acknowledge Lu Xun's prowess in "attacking the national character and society's 'darker aspects.'" Writing in Lu Xun's defense, Feng remarked, "Turning around to gaze upon humanism is not a bad thing," but concluded elliptically that "as an ideal, revolution cannot wholly part with humanism even though, for strategic purposes, revolution must abandon humanism."[148]

In his memoirs, Feng noted that when he published this essay, he had not yet met Lu Xun. He learned from Rou Shi that Lu Xun was angered by Feng's description of him as a well-meaning idealist and pessimist. Rou Shi also informed Feng that despite his criticisms of the Creation Society, Lu Xun suspected him of being a dissembler in the "Creation Society's camp."[149] Three months after Lu Xun first fumed about Feng's essay, Rou Shi successfully interceded on Feng's behalf to arrange their first meeting. According to Feng, this meeting in December 1928 led him promptly to revere Lu Xun's "practical combative ideas" and his "unflinching capacity for facing darkness."[150] Following Rou Shi's death in 1931, he became Lu Xun's leading disciple.

The intellectual typology that Feng produced in 1928 attracted public notice through Li's recommendation in 1929 and was further elevated to an authoritative view in Li's influential 1938 survey work, *Trends in Chinese Literature of the Last Twenty Years*. In this later work, published two years after Lu Xun's death, Li repeated his endorsement of Feng's 1928 criticism of the Creation Society's attacks on Lu Xun. This time he did not omit the Sun Society from his account of "revolutionary literature": instead he accused both the Creation Society and Sun Society of ideological extremism that alienated Lu Xun and other "fellow travelers." The result, he claimed, was that the "struggle with the true enemy"—which he identified as the Crescent Moon Society—was delayed.[151]

Utilizing a simple narrative of dialectical development illustrated with lengthy excerpts from selected key texts, Li's 1938 work presents twentieth-century Chinese literary thought as the story of the proletariat's progressive awakening to their "historical mission as the leaders and the mainstay of the national movement for revolution."[152] As one of the earliest attempts to map literary events as revolutionary milestones, Li's historical survey was regarded as a pioneering work of Marxist scholarship and enjoyed considerable influence in subsequent decades. It portrayed Lu Xun as *the* guiding intelligence of China's proletarian literature and accorded special importance to Qu Qiubai as a theoretical pioneer.[153] This was a perspective in happy agreement with Mao Zedong's view.

Although Li made no mention in his 1938 work of factional differences on the left, he quoted substantially from Lu Xun's "Reply to Xu Maoyong," featuring key passages in which Lu Xun denounced Zhou Yang, as if to demonstrate the maestro's advocacy of "mass literature" as far superior to Zhou's "national defense literature."[154] Li's tacit indictment of Zhou Yang is indicative of continued tensions on the left concerning the 1936 "battle of the two slogans," but in any case Lu Xun had also been rendered inviolate as a revolutionary exemplar. It had become de rigueur to exalt the posthumous author. At the then newly established Party base in Yan'an in 1938, three institutions were established bearing his name: the Lu Xun Library, the Lu Xun Teachers' College, and the Lu Xun Academy of Art and Literature.

By 1940 Mao was hailing Lu Xun as "the chief commander of China's cultural revolution" to augment his own views as indigenous Marxist orthodoxy. When Mao formalized his doctrine on "revolutionary literature" at his renowned 1942 Yan'an talks on art and literature, it was Lu Xun whom he invoked as his moral guide. Meanwhile his rival Wang Ming extolled Lu Xun "as the Chinese Gorky and the friend of the Soviet Union."[155] Of these two approaches, David Holm observes that Lu Xun was more central to Mao's, as Mao "was much more interested in social construction and base-building, and hence in the conscious development of a revolutionary vanguard to carry out these tasks. His remarks on Lu Xun were intended to outline the essential characteristics of the true revolutionary *character* and had immediate, active and prescriptive implications."[156] Holm notes that following Mao's triumph over Wang Ming in the "Rectification" purges conducted between 1942 and 1944, "a synthesis was produced and elements of both viewpoints became part of the Party's repertoire of Lu Xun propaganda."[157]

Throughout the 1940s, Lu Xun's criticisms of his contemporaries were turned into the defining feature of his revolutionary legacy. Holm writes that in 1941, as part of the fifth-anniversary commemorations of Lu Xun's death, a pocket-size booklet of *Quotations from Mr. Lu Xun* was issued of which "the vast majority expressed Lu Xun's merciless attitude to his enemies and his uncompromising 'spirit of struggle.'"[158] By the 1950s, Maoist functionaries were regularly using Lu Xun's writings in aid of their own attacks on individuals whom Lu Xun had once criticized. For instance, in 1957, when Xu Maoyong was purged as a "rightist," the fateful letter he wrote that incurred Lu Xun's wrath in 1936 now furnished Xu's accusers with ready evidence of his evil intention "to disrupt the relations between Lu Xun and the Party."[159]

At Lu Xun's funeral in October 1936, Xu mourned him with regret, lamenting: "Was I your enemy or your friend? I ask myself this question. Did you understand me or go on blaming me? Sir, you no longer speak."[160] In Lu Xun's private correspondence with Yang Jiyun of 28 August 1936, he expressed only contempt for Xu. In response to Yang's concern for his health, Lu Xun explained that despite his illness, he felt compelled not only to expose Xu but to respond at length because he wanted to "shed light" on "the ugly faces of all the goblins" that Xu's letter carried. Lu Xun wrote that when read closely, Xu's letter revealed an ambitious emissary of power, holding a handful of nails, eagerly poised to hammer them into someone else's coffin. Thus, "the letter represents a group even though it is signed by one man."[161]

In death, Lu Xun could not prevent his detractors from contributing to the making of his revolutionary legend. In the late 1930s, Xu Maoyong became a teacher at the Lu Xun Academy of Art and Literature in Yan'an, and Zhou Yang, whom Lu Xun had despised even more, was appointed as the academy's dean and director of education.[162] Zhou's political influence grew throughout the 1940s, and with the founding of the People's Republic in 1949 he became China's deputy minister of culture. He also held concurrent senior positions in the Propaganda Department and Art Bureau. The didactic Zhou proved adept at using Lu Xun, whom he now extolled as "a warrior in the realm of the spirit," to lend moral authority to the Party's directives. In 1942, to consolidate the Party's literary orthodoxy, Zhou edited the anthology *Marxism and Literature,* in which he featured Lu Xun "alongside Marx, Engels, Lenin, Stalin, and Mao as an important thinker in the realm of Marxist literary theory."[163]

As a powerful bureaucrat, Zhou Yang ensured that anthologies of Lu Xun published in the 1950s lacked the numerous angry missives and commentaries that Lu Xun had written against him. Zhou also played an active role in purging his former critics, Hu Feng and Feng Xuefeng, in the antirightist campaigns of that decade. As Merle Goldman has pointed out, although it was Mao who "set the general direction of the campaigns," it was "Zhou and his cohorts [who] chose their particular emphases." Moreover, in accusing Feng of "dividing the Leftist cultural movement in the 1930s," Zhou implicitly attacked the people whom Lu Xun had liked.[164] But Zhou Yang's triumph was short-lived. By 1966, as the campaign for Cultural Revolution gained momentum, it was his turn to be accused of having seditiously attacked Lu Xun in the 1930s. Jiang Qing, Mao's wife, who had newly risen to power to control the national media, now reprinted Lu Xun's criticisms of Zhou that Zhou had so carefully obscured from public view in the 1950s.[165]

At the height of Mao's personal power, from 1966 to the early 1970s, anyone with a published record of quarreling with Lu Xun became fair game. The members of the long-dissolved Creation and Sun Societies, who had risen to positions of power in the Party bureaucracy, were no exception. Peng Kang fared worse than most. In 1928, as a fashionable twenty-seven-year-old and a minor celebrity among his student fans, he had attracted notoriety by ridiculing Lu Xun's confusion of *Aufheben* with "elimination." In early 1968, at the age of sixty-seven, a different generation of young radicals subjected Peng to ferocious public humiliation. Then the president of Jiaotong University in Xi'an, he was forced to wear the infamous dunce's cap, paraded in the streets, and physically abused. An account widely circulated on the Internet indicates that on 28 March 1968, Peng's Red Guard persecutors forced him to run continually around a sports field from 6:00 A.M. to 9:00 A.M., cracking a whip to urge him on, until he collapsed. Peng never regained consciousness.[166]

In 1928, when Lu Xun asked Cheng Fangwu, "If you cannot 'guarantee the final victory,' would you still go over?" Cheng had countered with: "If you cannot 'guarantee the final victory,' can you afford not to go over?"[167] In July 1931, Lu Xun noted that the Creation Society possessed the three requisite qualities for succeeding in Shanghai's competitive environment: they were "quick to show intensity, quick to calm down, and quick to grow decadent."[168] Despite Lu Xun's frequent assertions about the narcissism of the Creation and Sun members, they placed themselves at the Communist Party's service. Cheng was no exception. He became an active Communist operative in the 1930s. In 1933 he sought and received Lu Xun's assistance when he returned to Shanghai after working for the Party in the hinterland. After 1949, when Cheng's extensive record of published quarrels with Lu Xun made him especially vulnerable to the charge of being "anti-Lu Xun," he frequently referred to this 1933 instance of Lu Xun's goodwill toward him. It proved insufficient to save him from persecution. Cheng's attacks on Lun Xun in the late 1920s became one of the three "serious political mistakes" of which he was accused during the Cultural Revolution.[169]

Feng Naichao, Li Chuli, and Qian Xingcun suffered similar fates: their homes were ransacked, and they were subjected to repeated verbal abuse, periods of incarceration, and public humiliation. Guo Moruo, of whom Mao said on 30 March 1966 that "his merits outweigh his flaws," publicly declared on 14 April 1966 that "by today's standards, everything I have written up to now should be burned, as it is utterly worthless."[170] While he survived the Cultural Revolution relatively unscathed, two of his sons died (allegedly by suicide) after being persecuted by Red Guards. Lu Xun's former adversaries in the Crescent Moon Society, Chen Yuan, Hu Shi, and Liang Shiqiu, were denounced in absentia. Having left China during the 1940s, they continued to enjoy the social rewards of their "gentlemanly" status that had so riled Lu Xun, and lived comfortably into old age.[171]

A special kind of torment awaited Xu Guangping. As the years passed, the reflected glory of being Lu Xun's widow became ever more fraught. In the 1950s and 1960s, before her own death in 1968, she was compelled time and again to distort her husband's legacy to express such absurd anachronisms as "Mao Zedong's invincible thought was the supreme guide for Lu Xun."[172] She was also turned into a weapon against Lu Xun's former critics. Cheng Fangwu was among those whom she allegedly denounced. An article published at the height of the Cultural Revolution in the Party-state's premier newspaper, *People's Daily*, reported that she had accused Cheng of being "anti-Lu Xun" throughout the 1950s. Following his political rehabilitation in the 1970s, Cheng commented that he found this hard to believe, as they had become good friends and she knew of his gratitude to Lu Xun.[173]

In death, Lu Xun was also turned into the preeminent exemplar of Cheng Fangwu's slogan "from literary revolution to revolutionary literature." When Lu Xun parodied this and other slogans in 1928, he was opposing the reduction of human complexity to a bare doctrine of class struggle. The tragic irony is that, in the Maoist years, Lu Xun's caustic wit was turned into the very thing he hated: a servant to orthodoxy. In 1928 he had surmised that if the Creation Society rose to power with its "totalizing critique," he would be banished to "the class of nobles and emperors," and his entire oeuvre would be banned. He did not anticipate that he would be propelled into the Maoist stratosphere of "the bravest and most correct, the firmest, the most loyal, and the most ardent national hero,"[174] or that former adversaries like Qian Xingcun (who, having declared *Ah Q* and its author dead four decades earlier) would be labeled "traitors" and "cow demons and snake monsters" in the late 1960s.[175]

That Lu Xun's writings were enlisted to endorse Mao Zedong Thought was a fate more grotesque than the one he had imagined under the Creation Society's aspiring "Lenins." The Party-state's posthumous manipulations of Lu Xun do not merely contradict the facts of his life and deform his critical legacy. They also violate the humanistic faith at the core of his polemical *baihua*. Maoist justifications of violence using

Lu Xun's phrase "to beat a drowning dog" are a particular case in point. In 1937, on the first anniversary of Lu Xun's death, Mao praised Lu Xun for showing an uncompromising attitude toward his enemies. He encouraged the youth of China to imbibe Lu Xun's revolutionary spirit of "beating a drowning dog."[176]

In so doing, Mao turned Lu Xun's name-calling into something much more sinister. Lu Xun had first berated Chen Yuan as a "pug" in 1925 for supporting Zhang Shizhao's decision to close the Peking Women's Normal College. It was his way of denigrating Chen as a puppet of power. The phrase "to beat a drowning dog" *(da luoshui gou)* was part of an exchange between Lu Xun and Lin Yutang after Lin published an article in *Threads of Talk* in December 1925 calling for tolerance among intellectuals. In the same month, a public outcry over the proposed closure of the Women's College prompted Zhang's resignation as minister of education. To encourage an end to hostilities between the warring parties, Lin quoted Zhou Zuoren's transliteration of the English term "fair play," *fei'e bolai*, featuring it in several places in his essay. With pointed reference to Zhang's downfall, Lin wrote that a triumphant polemicist should grant his defeated adversary some latitude of tolerance. In this implicit address to Lu Xun, Lin added that "don't beat a drowning dog" was a good way of understanding what "fair play" meant.[177]

Lu Xun retorted that because "pugs" were so smug they behaved more like cats than dogs, it was necessary to push them into the water and also give them a sound beating. In calling Chen Yuan a "pug" that deserved to be beaten even if drowning, Lu Xun's words did no more than hurt Chen's pride. Chen, then an influential Peking University academic with powerful friends in Duan Qirui's warlord regime, had suffered no damage from his altercations with Lu Xun. In fact it was Lu Xun who incurred a loss of income when he was peremptorily sacked in August 1925 for his defense of the students. At the time he wrote his riposte in January 1926, he had just been reinstated to his position in the Ministry of Education.[178]

Thus, in calling Chen a "drowning dog" that deserved beating, Lu Xun was merely exercising poetic license in further belittling his rival. This strategy was distorted by Mao into a license for actual violence.

Given the vital role that Mao came to play in shaping Lu Xun's after-life, it remains one of history's ironies that the two men never met. Most of what Lu Xun knew of Mao came from Feng Xuefeng, who knew Mao personally and had witnessed his rise during the Long March of the mid-1930s. The sole brief mention of Mao in Lu Xun's writings appears in an open letter, published in July 1936, declaring unequivocal support for "the proposal of Mr. Mao Zedong and others to unite against Japan." In the post-Maoist 1980s, it became clear that the letter was in fact the work of Feng Xuefeng and the result of sectarian Party politics. Nonetheless in 1936 a gravely ill Lu Xun assented to Feng's letter's being published under his name.[179]

Precisely because the Maoist state turned the polemics between Lu Xun and his critics into tools of persecution, it is all the more important to recall the thriving and open marketplace in which they were conducted. Audacious transliterations like *fei'e bolai* (fair play); the sesquipedalian coinages of Lu Xun's Marxist accusers like *aofuhebian (Aufheben), yintieligenzhuiya* (intelligentsia), *buerqiaoyayi* (bourgeoisie), and *puluolietaliya* (proletariat), as well as Lu Xun's own "hard translation," all exude a zest for literary invention and novelty that Shanghai's marketplace accommodated and encouraged. In the 1920s and 1930s, despite increasing censorship, literary production remained largely shaped by consumer demand. Thus, when in 1929 Liang Shiqiu declared that "on no account must the fashion for literal translation be encouraged," Lu Xun retorted that he had "the capitalist system" to thank for allowing readers who liked his endeavors to "keep 'hard translation' alive."[180] He similarly commented in 1934 that a published work was a commodity, and "whoever buys it has the right to praise or condemn it." He went on: "Criticism is necessary to literature. If a criticism is incorrect, we must oppose it with criticism. This is the only way to help literature and criticism advance. If we hold our tongues and assume that all is well in the world of letters, the result will be the reverse."[181]

In August 1936, around the time that he rebuked Xu Maoyong in print, Lu Xun wrote a short piece in which he recalled the statement from the Daoist classic *Zhuang zi,* that "a corpse can be placed anywhere, since it is destined 'to feed the birds above and the ants under-

ground.'" Fond of figuring his textual corpus as flesh, Lu Xun remarked that he was not quite so generous. He clearly had some of his
adversaries in mind when he wrote: "If I had to feed my flesh to animals, I'd give it to the lions, tigers, and eagles. I wouldn't leave a morsel
for the mangy dogs."[182] Lu Xun's frequent derogatory references to
"dogs" make it plain that he was no dog lover. Nonetheless he distinguished between different breeds of canine loathsomeness: by "mangy
dogs" *(laipigou)*, he meant feral creatures on the left quite unlike the
pampered "pugs" on the right that he normally railed against.

Lu Xun evinced an anxiety about his posthumous fate in the remainder of this piece which, in extending the Daoist metaphor of a
food chain, enjoined the reader to aspire to a nobility of character.
Given his decades-long servitude to Mao Zedong Thought, it seems
only appropriate to end with Lu Xun's own parting injunction to the
reader to consume his corpus with due care and consideration:

> Well-fed lions, tigers, and eagles, as they move across deserts and
> jungles, or soar in the skies and around the cliffs, offer a wondrous
> and majestic spectacle. After they are captured and placed in zoos,
> and even after they are killed and turned into stuffed specimens,
> they continue still to hold us in thrall, dispelling meanness from
> our hearts and minds.
>
> Conversely, a pack of well-fed mangy dogs will only run around
> and bark like mad. They are truly despicable![183]

5

Lu Xun's Revolutionary Literature

Although Lu Xun never described his own writings as "revolutionary literature," he did remark, no doubt in characteristic dry self-parody: "As soon as a writer turns left, all his past works are immediately ennobled too, so that even his childhood blubberings join the ranks of revolutionary literature."[1] This was in 1932, a time when he was increasingly self-conscious and clearly ambivalent about his propaganda value for the League of Left-Wing Chinese Writers. Lu Xun's death in 1936 at least spared him the fate of his former leftist contemporaries who were forced to pay abject homage to Mao Zedong Thought from the 1940s onward. Despite the egregious uses of his language from the 1940s into the 1970s, his disdain for Party doctrine remained safely preserved in his corpus postmortem. This preservation smoothed the progress of his post-Maoist redemption as a critical exemplar and humanist, concomitant with the erasure of his Mao-endorsed "revolutionary spirit."

Yet Lu Xun's writings were revolutionary inasmuch as they stretched the expressive limits of the Chinese language of his day into hitherto uncharted expressive terrain. This achievement is nowhere more evident than in his 1927 collection of experimental prose compositions titled *Wild Grass,* whose individual pieces were first published in 1924–1926.

The post-Mao era saw an enormous resurgence of interest in this the smallest of his books, which, although it remained in print throughout the Maoist decades, had been subjected to outlandish misreading or else simply neglected.

In the 1980s *Wild Grass,* with its sixty-odd pages of mostly enigmatic language, facilitated the recovery of Lu Xun from Maoist exploitation. As a work that actively invites interpretation, *Wild Grass* was reinterpreted in the post-Maoist years as offering a "philosophy of life" *(shengming zhexue),* in repudiation of the eclectic uses previously made of it to exemplify Mao's "philosophy of struggle" *(douzheng zhexue).* Pioneers of this post-Maoist approach to *Wild Grass* such as Sun Yushi and Qian Liqun read the work primarily as Lu Xun's exploration of his own complex response to both the social ills of his day and the revolutionary movement they fueled. They argue that *Wild Grass* offers a poetic defense of individual morality in a time of violence, reflecting Lu Xun's resolute opposition to tyranny in all forms and his pessimism about the prospect of true justice.[2] Summing up Lu Xun's "philosophy of life" in 2001, Qian remarked that *Wild Grass* was its very embodiment, reflecting the writer's determination to "'journey on' without end, in response to an absolute command, but without calculating the consequences or anticipating success." Indeed, it brought Lu Xun into communion with "an always open living force."[3]

After *Wild Grass,* Lu Xun never again experimented as boldly in *baihua.* From the memoirs of his Communist protégé Feng Xuefeng, it is evident that Lu Xun anticipated the criticisms that *Wild Grass* would receive. Negative assessments first proliferated in early 1928 (some six months after its publication) at the hands of Lu Xun's Marxist accusers and became an important reason for his polemical wars with them. Feng recalled that he likewise found the work "too obscure" and noted that it remained among his least favorite of Lu Xun's writings; that it was mostly "an expression of Mr. Lu Xun's inner conflict and his cry of anguish," reflecting little of his fighting spirit.[4]

Feng recalled that he first informed Lu Xun of his negative response to *Wild Grass* when he grew close to the maestro in 1929. Lu Xun responded by acknowledging that his outlook in the work was "indeed rather dark," adding somewhat defensively: "I'm by no means suggesting that my view is absolutely correct." Feng also reported that Lu Xun often mentioned *Wild Grass* and his second anthology of short stories, *Wandering (Panghuang)*, and evinced particular pride in these works as literary achievements.[5]

The revolutionary poetics of *Wild Grass* contributed significantly to the labeling of Lu Xun as "petty bourgeois" in 1928. Whereas revolution for leftists of a prescriptive bent was contingent upon an unquestioned faith in Marxist doctrine, Lu Xun's faith was of an entirely different dimension. *Wild Grass* presents his poetic expressions of faith in the emancipatory potential of *baihua,* envisaged and defended as an egalitarian pan-Chinese language in the making. Because Lu Xun often reemployed the unsettling tropes of *Wild Grass* in his subsequent essays, the work also has a special significance in his oeuvre as a whole.

Traversing *Baihua* and *Wenyan*

Lu Xun often encouraged literary experimentation and urged his contemporaries to nurture the evolution of *baihua* into future alien forms presently beyond their imagination. Reflecting on his own literary journey in November 1926, he wrote: "Ultimately, everyone's an intermediate entity [*zhongjianwu*] in the evolutionary chain."[6] Consequently, "it is only natural to find a handful of writers producing aberrant texts at a time when writing undergoes an initial stage of reform." In this context, the writer who is "awakened and alert" (*jingjue*) is duty bound "to make a new kind of noise."[7] These words appear in the famous epilogue he wrote for his 1927 anthology, *The Grave*, which consists of a selection of essays first published between 1907 and 1925, with the earliest written in ancient *guwen* and premodern *wenyan* and the later ones in modern *baihua*.[8] He described this mix of *guwen, wenyan,* and *baihua* prose in *The Grave* as a "small burial mound in which lies entombed the carapace of what was once a living thing."[9]

For all Lu Xun's denunciations of *wenyan* as a tool of dynastic power, he remained deeply attached to this classical literary language over which he possessed a formidable mastery. As a young man studying in Japan during the 1900s, it was in both *wenyan* and *guwen,* the archaic language of the pre-Qin classics (out of which *wenyan* sprang and evolved), that he first articulated his resolve to embark on a literary career dedicated to transforming Chinese hearts and minds through language. And it was in a Buddhist-inflected blend of *guwen* and *wenyan* that he wrote his famous essay "On the Power of Mara Poetry" in 1908, in which he extolled the poetry of Byron, Pushkin, and Shelley, among others, as exemplifying the seductive powers of the demon Mara, the Buddha's final temptress and archenemy. In so doing, he invoked Mara, claiming that only a destructive force of satanic proportions could stir whole nations to action.[10]

Following the publication in 1918 of his first work of *baihua* fiction, "The Diary of a Madman," Lu Xun frequently described *wenyan* as a "dead language" yet one still jealously possessed by an elite minority. He wrote that the difficulty of *wenyan* made it inherently elitist: hence it was a language that could only ever be wielded against the masses, as it denied them literacy. Against *wenyan*, he contrasted the fundamentally egalitarian qualities of *baihua* as a "living vernacular" open and accessible to one and all. In 1927 he quoted Sun Yat-sen's phrase "a dish of loose sand" to characterize China's widespread and crippling illiteracy: "Because we use the language of the ancients, which the people cannot understand and do not hear, we are like a dish of loose sand—oblivious to each other's sufferings. The first necessity, if we do want to come to life, is for our young people to stop speaking the language of Confucius and Mencius [third century B.C.E.], Han Yu [768–824], and Liu Zongyuan [773–819]."[11]

In *baihua*, Lu Xun imagined a written and spoken vernacular that would one day become a national mother-tongue accessible to all. He yearned for the arrival of a Chinese language that would finally enable people to give "clear expression to their thoughts and feelings" and thus open the way to their emancipation by their own hands.[12] He offered a striking account of this literary mission when he wrote in May 1935:

A writer should not be accommodating: indeed he does not know how to accommodate others. Only those who are always seeking to avoid conflict know how to be accommodating. To choose not to be accommodating is the exact opposite of avoiding problems by only praising positive things or extolling the things you love, as if the things you find disagreeable or hate don't matter at all. Instead, a writer must attack what strikes him as false with the same intensity as he promotes what he holds to be true. Even more fervently than he embraces what he loves he should embrace what he hates, just as Hercules held the giant Antaeus in a tight embrace in order to break his ribs.[13]

The precipitate turn of this passage from a general proposition about criticism to a vivid image of the critical act as a lethal embrace is characteristic of Lu Xun's language. The figure of Hercules, so clearly suggestive of his *baihua* vocation, evokes *wenyan* as an indomitable foe in the opposite figure of Antaeus. As it was *wenyan* in which he felt personally most at home and at his expressive best, Lu Xun's figuration of his *baihua* experimentations as close quarter hand-to-hand combat with *wenyan* also implies that writing in the nascent modern Chinese vernacular came at a great personal cost, for it wounded and crippled his own remarkable powers of expression in *wenyan*. Insofar as he used the figures of Hercules and Antaeus to present the act of writing as involving an elemental agon, the passage above also highlights his sensibility to literature as a transformative, and hence spiritual, ordeal.

Michel Foucault offers a useful definition of "spirituality" when he calls it the set of "researches, practices and experiences, which may be purifications, ascetic exercises, renunciations, conversions of looking, modifications of existence, etc." undertaken "not for knowledge" per se but "for the subject's very being, the price to be paid for access to the truth." Hence, in a spiritual pursuit "there can be no truth without a conversion or a transformation of the subject."[14] There was a clear divergence between Lu Xun's solitary pursuit and the path of orthodoxy pursued by those of his contemporaries who proclaimed their conversion to Marxism and their faith in the Communist Party or, alternatively, swore allegiance to Sun Yat-sen's "Three Principles of the People." Although these disparate pursuits all presumed a rite of passage and an act of conversion or transformation, Lu Xun's fidelity was never to a received set of ideas or utopian vision. Instead it was authenticity in speech and conduct that he invoked and defended, pure and simple, as a general moral principle. This valorization of honest communication, which led him to disavow prescience in favor of an affective self-knowledge, imparted a particular emotional intensity to his *baihua*.

Read in this light, his allegories, confessions, and parodies resemble practices or exercises in the art of provoking moral disquiet. In Lu Xun's frequent literary excursions into negative emotional intensities, he dwelt in particular on revenge as a marker of authentic human experience. Revenge mattered to him first and foremost as the attitude necessary to redeem Chinese culture. It also gave him a way of dignifying his polemical writings as righteous outrage against those whom he perceived as enemies of *baihua*, including producers of *baihua* on both the right and the left, whom he accused of attempting to turn the language again into the proprietary skill of the privileged few.

If he disavowed *wenyan* as utterly corrupted by the hierarchism of dynastic culture, he was even more averse to the idea of *baihua*'s being put in the service of what he regarded as empty universalisms. As *baihua* became progressively institutionalized as the written standard, Lu Xun grew more insistent about using the language for moral self-improvement. This is particularly evident in his lectures of the late 1920s and early 1930s, in which he frequently reiterated the importance of nurturing an active empathy for the poor and the dispossessed.

In this context, Lu Xun's frequent figurations of *baihua* as a path or road were both a play on Confucian-Daoist-Buddhist conceptions of the Way *(dao)* and a literalization of the Chinese term he used for humanism, *rendao* (literally, the human path). Although he never offered a theory of humanism as such, he was perennially preoccupied with the question of what it meant to be human. This led him to use terms like "human" and "humanism" in an open-ended fashion, to gesture to a self-aware, other-oriented altruism as the most fitting attitude to possess and navigate along the road of life. Like many of his *wenyan*-schooled contemporaries, Lu Xun attached great importance to the active cultivation of moral (or righteous) emotions for guidance in life, but his aversion to doctrine and ideology led him characteristically to commend a given emotion without prescribing any particular course of action.

His 1919 essay "Dissatisfaction" is a case in point. To commend dissatisfaction *(buman)* as a properly moral emotion, Lu Xun wrote: "Dissatisfaction is a vehicle of ascendance. Only humans capable of bearing dissatisfaction can progress toward humanism."[15] To alert readers to the interpretability of humanism, he remarked that even though the English word "humanism" had been translated into Chinese as *rendao*, the two words were clearly not equivalent. He criticized his contemporaries for bandying the word about in hollow mimicry of European commentators mourning the loss of life in the Great War and opined that the Chinese language had yet to acquire its own modern senses of the human. As a Chinese word, humanism should (for the time being at least) be kept within the ellipsis points ". . . "[16] This punctuational symbolism corresponds with Lu Xun's own literary mission of attempting to fill in the gap opened up by this visual ellipsis. In his words:

> Humanism clearly cannot lodge itself in the minds of people whose sole response to humanism is ". . . ."
>
> This is because humanism becomes established, nourished, and protected through the unceasing struggle of each and every person. We don't receive it as an act of charity from others or in the form of a donation.[17]

Over time, Lu Xun elaborated on this intertwining of "dissatisfaction" and "humanism" through his many sharply observed accounts of injustice and violence inflicted on the poor. By the 1930s these vignettes of human suffering had acquired a Marxist cadence through his ironic use of such terms as "high-class Chinese" *(gaodeng Huaren)* and "low-class Chinese" *(xiadeng Huaren)* to castigate the former's indifference to the latter. However, Marxist class struggle for Lu Xun was neither a philosophical truth nor a political blueprint. It mattered to him primarily as a means of highlighting and sensitizing people to the harsh realities of existing social inequities.

This is evident in such essays as "Pushed." Written on 8 June 1933, this essay begins with Lu Xun's recounting of a contemporary news report about the death of a newspaper boy. The boy was killed when he fell under a moving tram, after being roughly pushed by an irate passenger whose gown the boy had accidentally stepped on. Lu Xun noted of the unidentified passenger, who fled from the scene, that his long gown indicated he was of "upper-class standing." He proceeded to distinguish between the gait of "foreign masters" and "high-class Chinese" on a crowded Shanghai street, noting that whereas the former "do not use their hands but stride forward on long legs," expecting people to make way for them, the latter "bend their arms and hold their palms upturned like the pincers of a scorpion as they push forward, not caring whether the people they have pushed out of their way have fallen into a pool of mud or a fiery pit."[18] Four days later, in the essay "Experience," he commented that "whether the so-called fruits of experience are good or bad, they demand the same enormous sacrifice: even the smallest incident exacts a shocking price." He explained that a person's most valuable experiences are mostly gained at someone else's expense, for it is the sacrifice and death of the other that offers a lesson for the one who survives. In sum, "experience in its entirety belongs only to the living."[19]

Hence, in stark contrast to the theoretical diction of his leftist peers who extolled an ideality of Communist perfection, Lu Xun wrote plainly about an ethics of experience and urged his readers to redouble their efforts to deepen their empathy for their fellow humans. It was thus an acute fellow-feeling that guided his literary enterprise. Although he never idealized the poor, Lu Xun perceived them as possessing a greater potential for empathy because of their kinship with and through suffering. Consequently, the lives of working-class Chinese were an abiding theme in his fiction which marked *baihua* as a language they did not yet possess.

The Art of the Critical Blade

Throughout the 1920s Lu Xun frequently figured the act of criticism as a dagger or a javelin. In 1933 he figured these weapons specifically as the short, personal essay *(xiaopinwen)* he favored as a mode of composition. Stating that this literary genre was in crisis, he explained he was using "crisis" in the clinical sense of a critical juncture when a person hovers between life and death. He accused his contemporaries of promoting an amnesic anesthesia in their essays and warned against the

ensuing soporific drift of Chinese intellectual discourse it would induce. In calling for "essays that affirm our survival," Lu Xun wrote that
these were "necessary daggers [*bishou*] and javelins [*touqiang*]." He continued: "They must engage the reader in the struggle to clear a path vital to
our survival. Naturally, they can also bring happiness and respite.
These are no mere 'knickknacks'; still less do they bring comfort or induce numbness. Rather, the happiness and respite they offer is a form
of convalescence: a stage of preparation between toil and combat."[20]

The dagger and the javelin complement Lu Xun's other recurring
figuration of literary reform as involving a close personal combat with
the forces of what he once described as "dark China" *(hei'an Zhongguo)*
and stand at opposite poles to the tropes of heavy theoretical artillery
his Marxist critics favored.[21] In this regard, Lu Xun's weapons of choice
find an echo in George Orwell's remark of 1945 that "[a] complex
weapon makes the strong stronger while a simple weapon so long as
there is no answer to it gives claws to the weak."[22] In 1928 Lu Xun delighted in parodying the ear-shattering tropes that his Marxist critics
used when exalting revolutionary literature as "a ton of TNT," "machine guns and trench mortars," or through onomatopoeic coinages
like "gonnon" that evoked cannon fire.[23] He was evidently appalled yet
bemused by the gulf between their rhetorical preferences and his.

After April 1927, the slaughter of Communists had so disheartened
Lu Xun that he likened his writings to "the futility of an arrow aimed at
the sea."[24] But by the same token, he could not bear being demeaned as
a wavering, ineffective pessimist by the left and hence was determined
both to defend himself and to justify his counterassault on his critics.
This mix of apprehension and disdain is evident in an open letter he
published in April 1928, when the Creation and Sun polemics against
him were reaching a peak:

> Of course I hold out some hope that reform will come to China; that
> things will change for the better. Some people have accused me of
> offering no way out. Ha ha! Does a way out mean something like
> coming first in the former imperial civil service examinations? I've
> also been called a "poison pen," but I'm convinced that I haven't
> obliterated all hope. I've always believed the lower classes to be better

than the upper classes and young people better than old fogeys, and so I chose not to spatter them with the blood from the nib of my pen. Nonetheless, I also know that when their own interests are affected, young people will often behave in ways not unlike upper-class old fogeys. But this is simply the way of things in a society organized like ours. Since there are so many detractors of the lower classes and the young, there's clearly no need for me to cast stones at them as well. Thus, I used to expose the darkness from only one side, but it was never my intention to deceive my young readers.[25]

In March 1930, on the eve of assuming nominal leadership of the League of Left-Wing Chinese Writers, Lu Xun reprised the figure of the critical blade to mock his erstwhile critics. In an essay he quipped that since their aim was "to dissect and devour the enemy," they could have benefited from consulting "books on anatomy and cookery" in order "to produce something tastier." With this sardonic counsel, he then compared himself to a latter-day Prometheus, stating: "I stole fire from abroad to cook my own flesh in the hope that if the taste proved agreeable, those who tasted it would benefit more, and my sacrifice would not prove in vain." He noted that true revolutionaries were "often compared to the legendary Prometheus because in spite of the torture to which Zeus exposed him he had so much love and fortitude that he never regretted stealing fire for mankind." In the next sentence, he mocked his own Promethean pretension and wrote in mimicry of his former accusers that his writings were "wholly motivated by individualism and bear the taint of petty-bourgeois affectation." He added that he found it irresistible to "reach for my scalpel to plunge it into the hearts of my dissectors, out of sheer 'vengefulness,'" He then ameliorated these remarks to note that he was not entirely self-absorbed, since he was also motivated by a sincere desire "to be of some use to society," such that "when all's said and done, the onlookers may see some fire and light."[26]

In these twists and turns, Lu Xun played up the ambivalence of his writing as "mixed impressions" while also reiterating his poetic valorization of revenge as a true emotion. Six years earlier, in 1924, Lu Xun had made revenge his signature emotion when he published two literary compositions titled simply "Revenge" and "Revenge II" (both were later included in his 1927 anthology *Wild Grass*).[27] For Lu Xun, revenge possessed the virtue of endurance that he saw as essential for conducting a protracted war against the enemies of honest communication. To the extent that Mao Zedong invoked Lu Xun to affirm revenge as a virtue, it is important to remember that, unlike Mao, Lu Xun neither encouraged nor endorsed physical violence. Rather, his conception of revenge was distinctly literary: an empowering emotion inhabiting his language through which he sought to destroy the malevolent forces he saw corrupting Chinese habits of speaking and writing.

The first of Lu Xun's two "Revenge" compositions in 1924 indicates what he found life-affirming about this both punitive and passionate emotion. Lu Xun began by likening revenge to "the desperation to caress, kiss, and embrace: to experience life as intoxication and ecstasy." With this fusion of love and hate into a mutual emotional intensity, Lu Xun described an eternal face-off in which two people "stand naked, wielding sharp knives as they confront each other in a vast wilderness, poised to embrace; to annihilate one another." This image presents the antagonists as sharing a fatal attraction: their bond of hate is unique to them alone and opaque to mere observers. He wrote of crowds that gather around the antagonists, hoping "to enjoy the spectacle of their deadly embrace" with a vicarious lust for "the taste of sweat and blood, anticipated on the tongue." The crowds, however, are thwarted because the antagonists "face off into eternity," and as the spectators' disappointment turns into boredom, they disperse. Lu Xun ended the poem by returning to the antagonists themselves.[28] Facing one another in a vast and barren wilderness, the two lone figures remain forever poised in "atrophied confrontation," unified by a mutual hatred that "suffuses them with the soaring and sublime passion of being truly alive."[29]

If extolling revenge as life-affirming instead of destructive seems counterintuitive, we must recall Lu Xun's acute ambivalence toward *wenyan*. He often drew attention to a process of self-destruction under way in his abandoning *wenyan* as if to highlight the vital importance of *wenyan* to his personal *cogito* and sense of identity. More importantly, however, he implied that being driven to write in *baihua* nonetheless brought new life to his language. Hence the pure intensity of revenge, as his composition suggests, nourished his desire to cut himself loose from *wenyan.*

In this regard, the image of revenge as a timeless facing-off between two antagonists is highly suggestive of Lu Xun's own language in which *baihua* and *wenyan* belong together yet are held apart, tensely poised in a symbiotic poetics such that the destruction of either would result in the extinction of both. As he wrote in 1926: "My torture is that I have to carry on my shoulders a collection of extremely ancient phantoms; it is a load I cannot shed and I constantly feel that I am being choked under its crushing weight."[30] His antipathy to *wenyan* was thus quite unlike the simpler advocacy of *baihua* that was prevalent among those of his contemporaries who hailed the modern vernacular as if it were wholly independent of its classical antecedent.

Lu Xun also frequently explored the symbiosis of *baihua* and *wenyan* through the use of botanical tropes. A striking example appears in his 1927 preface to *Wild Grass,* where he extols *baihua* as "wild grass" thriving parasitically on the "decayed ground" of *wenyan:* "Wild grass has shallow roots; it boasts no beautiful flowers and foliage yet imbibes dew, water, and the flesh and blood of rotting corpses. It survives despite all attempts to deprive it of life. It lives only to be trampled on and cut down, until it finally dies and decays."[31] In this poetic privileging of *baihua's* unkempt nature, flourishing untended in an endless cycle of living and dying, Lu Xun nonetheless highlights *baihua's* rootedness in *wenyan.* Exuberantly reiterating the symbiosis of *baihua* and *wenyan,* he writes: "I love my wild grass [*baihua*], but I loathe the ground [*wenyan*] that decks itself with wild grass."[32] This statement is of a piece with a remark about *baihua* that Lu Xun made three years earlier, in 1924, when he commented that "good soil" was essential for "fine trees and lovely flowers" to take root and grow.[33]

In these botanical tropes, Lu Xun bespeaks a yearning for organic wholeness that resonates with the question Martin Heidegger (1889–1976) posed in his "Memorial Address" of 1955: "Even if the old rootedness is being lost in this age, may not a new ground and foundation be granted again to man . . . out of which man's nature and all his works can flourish in a new way even in the atomic age?" Heidegger answered the question in the lecture's conclusion with a quotation from German poet Johann Peter Hebel (1760-1826): "We are plants which—whether we like to admit it to ourselves or not—must with our roots rise out of the earth in order to bloom in the ether and to bear fruit."[34]

A similar idea is at work in Lu Xun's letter of 9 April 1934 to the young artist Wei Mengke (1911-1984). Urging Wei to heed the reliance of the new on the old, Lu Xun wrote: "No new art sprouts forth without root or stem. It does not suddenly appear but is invariably an inheritance of what precedes it. Some young people think that making use of something is tantamount to capitulation, and that's because they have confused 'making use of' [caiyong] with 'imitation' [mofang]."[35]

Read in this light, Lu Xun's denunciations of wenyan's decrepitude also carried a utilitarian hope of rejuvenating its rhetorical force through the untamed and as-yet-untried powers of baihua. Hence it is significant that he freely acknowledged his indebtedness to the language of two ancient exemplars in particular, Qu Yuan and Zhuangzi (fourth century B.C.E.). He also wrote moving portraits of Laozi and Confucius and expressed admiration for the famous recluses of China's dynastic past.[36] Among Lu Xun's many scholarly publications on different aspects of wenyan and traditional Chinese aesthetics, he devoted considerable energies to compiling the extant works of Xi Kang, one among the seven famed recluses of the Wei-Jin era collectively known as the "Seven Worthies of the Bamboo Grove." As John Wang observes, Lu Xun's edition of The Works of Xi Kang represented "the highlight of his life as a scholar. He certainly spent more time and care on it than on almost any other work: he started the project no later than 1913 and kept at it until 1931."[37]

Moreover, as Simon Leys observed, Lu Xun clearly enjoyed writing classical poetry, which, like his scholarly studies of "ancient works" (guji), allowed him to roam free in China's literary past. Of Lu Xun's erudite poetics, Leys noted:

His classical poems, where his genius for language is displayed in all its abundance, are hard to read. Without removing anything from their beauty, it must be admitted that their poetry is of a learned, not to say pedantic kind. Crammed with elliptical, abstruse historical and literary allusions—an average of one or two concealed in every line—they present innumerable pitfalls for translators.[38]

In this context, in his Promethean trope of 1930, the sense of sacrifice implicit in his remark about having "[stolen] fire from abroad to cook my own flesh" is greatly heightened. Indeed, this abiding sense of having forfeited something of great personal value led Lu Xun frequently to assess his fellow producers of *baihua* in terms of their preparedness to sacrifice their own interests. In fact three years before he locked horns with his Marxist critics in the 1928 polemics over revolutionary literature, Lu Xu had accused the Crescent Moon Society in very similar language. In June 1925 he wrote a short essay directed against Chen Yuan and his Crescent Moon confreres in which he listed three basic obstacles to social justice in China: a predilection among his contemporaries for "superficial propaganda," their readiness to label people with dissenting views as "traitors or slaves of foreign masters," and a preponderance of people acting in their own self-interest.[39] In December 1925 he gave full rein to his antipathy toward the Crescent Moon "gentlemen" in the composition "Such a Warrior" (later collected in *Wild Grass*).

To ensure that readers knew he was attacking the Crescent Moon Society, Lu Xun made a point of noting that the piece was inspired by his loathing for "littérateurs and scholars who aided the warlords" (a sentiment repeatedly expressed in his polemical writings against Chen throughout 1925).[40] In this text, Lu Xun extols the javelin as his weapon of choice. The central figure is an anonymous warrior who, like the locked couple in "Revenge," is a bare sketch, distinguished only by the intensity of his desire to slay the enemy.

Lu Xun begins by praising this lone javelin-wielding warrior as someone on a mission who "relies solely on himself," equipped only with "the weapon of the savage." To highlight the warrior's primal independence, he describes him as "neither ignorant like African natives toting well-polished Mausers nor listless like the incompetent Chinese troops of the former Qing army who carried automatic pistols." He writes of the warrior "entering the ranks of the incorporeal" (here figuring the discursive and textual as the incorporeal) to hunt down the ones whose heads are "festooned with such honorable titles as philanthropist, scholar, writer, elder, youth, dilettante, and gentleman." These titles, he continues, are complemented by "fine cloaks brightly adorned with the names of scholarship, morality, national essence, public opinion, logic, justice, and Eastern civilization." He notes that these are his enemies, for they kill without bloodshed by merely nodding their heads.[41]

Doing battle in "the ranks of the incorporeal," Lu Xun's warrior serves as an allegory for effective criticism. As he puts it, the warrior's mission is to "pierce the heart" of the opponent with a single thrust of the javelin. But he hastens to add in the next sentence that the warrior's triumph is ephemeral, for then "everything collapses and falls to the ground, leaving only a cloak of the incorporeal. The essence of the incorporeal has escaped, and victory belongs to it, for now the warrior stands accused of murdering the philanthropist and the rest." Here Lu Xun alludes to the duplicities of language that allow the dishonest to pervert the words of the honest critic. "But he raises his javelin" appears five times in "Such a Warrior." The reiteration suggests that criticism requires dedication and persistence precisely because the enemy is legion. Toward the poem's end, Lu Xun ponders the limitations of criticism: "The warrior grows frail and dies of old age amidst the ranks of the incorporeal. In the end he is no warrior, and it is the essence of the incorporeal that is the true victor."[42]

In this figure of the aging warrior, Lu Xun reminds us that the mortal critic cannot secure a permanent meaning for his words. In the end, it is language that triumphs as an incorporeal medium, hospitable as much to falsehood as to truth. This notion of criticism as perishable and vulnerable to distortion is a recurring motif throughout *Wild Grass*. Its most vivid presentation appears in his 1924 prose poem "The Shadow's Farewell," where the shadow (as a ventriloquist for the words on the page) announces the "emptiness" of its own words to evoke a sense of textuality as the opaque "darkness" of pitch-black ink traces.[43]

By 1926, Lu Xun had largely shifted from fiction to short personal essays, calling them *zawen* ("miscellaneous jottings") and *zagan* ("mixed impressions") to accentuate their hybrid form and ambivalent content. These essays became the "new kind of noise" that dominated the last phase of his literary career from 1926 to 1936. They fill fifteen anthologies. The first, *Re Feng* (Hot wind), appeared in November 1925, followed by *Huagai ji* (Inauspicious star) in June 1926. Two more followed in 1927: *Fen* (The grave) in March, and *Huagai xubian* (Inauspicious star: A second volume) in May. *Eryi ji* (And that's that) was published in October 1928, *San xian ji* (Three leisures) in September 1932, *Erxin ji* (In two minds) in October 1932, *Wei ziyou shu* (Essays on false freedom) in October 1933, *Nanqiang beidiao ji* (A collection of confused accents) in March 1934, *Zhun feng yue tan* (A pseudo-romantic discourse) in December 1934, *Jiwai ji* (Addenda collection) in May 1935, and *Huabian ji* (Fringed literature) in June 1936. Three volumes of Lu Xun's final essays were edited and released posthumously, all in July 1937: *Qiejie ting zawen* (Essays from the semi-concession pavilion), *Qiejie ting zawen er ji* (A second volume of essays from the semi-concession pavilion), and *Qiejie ting zawen mobian* (A final volume of essays from the semi-concession pavilion). Dozens of essays not included in these anthologies have been published in *Lu Xun quanji* (The complete works of Lu Xun), of which there are five editions in mainland China (1938, 1958, 1973, 1981, and 2005). The majority of essays he wrote during this last phase were rebuttals or commentaries on topical issues; as Leo Ou-fan Lee observes, Lu Xun's friend Qu Qiubai named them *feuilletons* to highlight their "combative and polemical" quality.[44]

In his 1926 epilogue to *The Grave*, Lu Xun remarked that contrary to the view of some that he "dashed off essays at will," writing for him was an excruciating process of self-examination burdened with "so very many misgivings and memories." In contrast to the destructive will he espoused in "Such a Warrior" in 1925, here he declared: "I have long known that I am not cut out to be a warrior, nor could I pass for some vanguard figure."[45] He wrote of the need for writers to exercise constant vigilance against the danger of misleading their readers. Accordingly, he expressed misgivings about exposing young impressionable minds to his own unripened ideas with the caution that "those who have grown fond of the fruits of my garden may be poisoned by those that are still green."[46]

Nonetheless, in his polemical attacks on his contemporaries, he clearly implied that readers would be better off consuming his words, however unripe, than the writings of those he despised. For instance, he wrote in February 1926, arrogating to himself the authority of an honest judge:

> I am well aware that in China, my writings are more caustic than most and, at times, show no mercy whatsoever. This is because I know only too well how some people use the fine names of universal law and justice to pass themselves off as cultivated men of virtue or pretend to be kindhearted and sincere. Rumor and public opinion are their weapons. Their circuitous mumblings are so self-interested that they leave those who are defenseless, who have neither sword nor pen, simply unable to breathe.[47]

In presenting his *baihua* as a "weapon" for cutting down elitist sophistry, Lu Xun was effectively counterposing honesty in negative relief, to suggest that unlike the "circuitous mumblings" of his rivals (in the mid-1920s, Chen Yuan was his chief target), his statements were frankness itself. As to what he meant by honest communication, a telling clue is offered in the eight lines he composed in October 1926 to mark the completion of the anthology *Unlucky Star: A Second Volume*. Eschewing "fine names," he wrote with affective force of the inchoate feelings that the violence of the age induced in him, thereby explaining the origin of "mixed impressions" as his own personal genre:

> I've seen yet more bloodshed and tearfulness these last six months
> But I'm left with mixed impressions, and that's that.
> The tears have dried, and the blood has vanished,
> The butchers roam fancy free as they've always done,
> Some wielding swords of steel while others carry softer knives,[48]
> Still I'm left with "mixed impressions," and that's that.
> But when my "mixed impressions" are "put where they ought to belong,"
> Then all I'm left with is "that's that," and that's that.[49]

"Put where they ought to belong" was a quotation from Chen Yuan's famous open letter to Xu Zhimo of January 1926, in which Chen remarked that Lu Xun ought to be directing his accusations at himself. Lu Xun was evidently fond of these eight lines, since he reproduced them in the preface to his 1928 anthology of essays *And That's That*.[50]

At this juncture it is useful to consider the hybrid fusion of the poetic and the prosaic in Lu Xun's *zagan*. When reflecting on our received sense of "what is and is not possible in discursive prose," J. M. Coetzee has written that "a strange logic prevails" whereby "when a real passion of feeling is let loose in discursive prose, you feel that you are reading the utterances of a madman."[51] Lu Xun presented *baihua* in his first short story, quite literally, as madness. But whereas fictional prose gave him license to celebrate *baihua* as a necessary derangement, the essay form that he utilized for social criticism imposed stricter conventions of reasoned discourse on his *baihua*. Hence, to infect his "mixed impressions" with a real passion of feeling, Lu Xun resorted time and again to recalling the javelin-hurling warrior and other figures of revenge that populate his prose poems in *Wild Grass*. The result is a tension of undecidability enabling the *baihua* of his essays to traverse a fine line between tempered rationality and unbridled passion.

A good example of this fusion of the poetic and prosaic appears in Lu Xun's 1926 epilogue to *The Grave*. He writes practically, in one sentence, of seeking to "cause discomfort to cultivated men of virtue and their ilk," adding the realistic qualification "at least for a few days." In the next sentence he departs entirely from the prosaic to echo the poetic sentiments of "Such a Warrior," declaring: "I have taken the trouble of strapping a few sheets of armor on my body so that I may confront them and bring a few defects into their world, and the armor will stay on until exhaustion forces me to remove it."[52]

In 1933 Lu Xun summoned the same warrior specter to express opposition to "anesthesia." It was imperative, he wrote, to ensure that the short personal essay remained "fully reliant on struggle and combat for its very existence."[53] In this instance he was indirectly attacking Lin Yutang, whose friendship with Lu Xun had rapidly deteriorated that year. Lin's journal, *The Analects,* which was centered on personal musings and witty prose, was the implied object of Lu Xun's criticism.[54] In calling for vigilance against anesthetizing tendencies that would turn the personal essay into a mere "knickknack" and result in the genre's demise, Lu Xun was undoubtedly also signaling disapproval of his estranged brother Zhou Zuoren.

Zhou's 1929 essay "In Praise of Anesthesia," was republished in his acclaimed 1932 anthology, *Cloud Gazing.* It was a droll exposition on the merits of anesthesia for coping with life in a violent society. According to Zhou, anesthesia came in different varieties—as opium, wine, romantic love, "belief in a religion or ideology," or "the ability to dream"—but its singular purpose was to provide an antidote to human pain and suffering. He remarked: "I suppose there's nothing better than to live in intoxication and to die while dreaming, but some would disagree with this."[55]

He noted that those who disavow anesthesia belonged to a rare minority, for they must be persons gifted with superhuman qualities to withstand the painful trials of leading an authentic life. Among them he cited Guan Yu, whom legend credits with the ability to calmly play a game of chess while being cut open without anesthetic for poison to be scraped off his bone; the Stoics, with their uncommon courage; and "Cossack heroes . . . who savor life's tribulations without the slightest hesitation as if draining every last drop of a bitter wine." Zhou concluded that "ordinary folk like us" must be content with "living in intoxication and dying while dreaming" but added the twist: "The sad truth is I don't have the stomach for heavy drinking and don't know how to numb myself. So I see and hear everything clearly but lack the energy to cry out loud. I guess I'll just have to put up with this sorry plight of being plain ordinary."[56]

It is highly plausible that Zhou's statement about lacking the energy to cry out loud was a gibe at Lu Xun's *A Call to Arms,* for Zhou's message of quiescent acceptance was nothing if not squarely opposed to Lu Xun's insistence on "struggle and combat." In the 1930s Lu Xun was particularly angered by what he perceived as the complacent indifference of those who produced belles-lettres (for which his brother Zuoren enjoyed a wide reputation). He noted acerbically that at a time "when a sandstorm's in our eyes and wolf packs and tigers are on the prowl," what people needed were "daggers and javelins, sharp of blade and highly practical. Elegance is of no use whatsoever." Accordingly, he pointed an accusing finger at writers who were encouraging their disciples "to massage" their prose in order to "turn what is rough and ready [*cubao*] into something sophisticated and elegant [*fengya*]."[57] He defended the opposite: turning the sophisticated and elegant into the rough-and-ready.

On the Way to *Baihua*

Wild Grass presents Lu Xun at his most inventive in the attempt to produce a *baihua* poetics of the rough-and-ready, transmuted out of the elegant sophistication that was and remains *wenyan*. When he first began composing the individual pieces of this anthology in 1924, he was deeply impressed by the writings of the Japanese critic Kuriyagawa Hakuson, whose Freudian-inspired work, *Symbols of Mental Anguish (Kumende xiangzheng),* he had translated that year. Leo Ou-fan Lee's discussion of Kuriyagawa's influence on Lu Xun is especially helpful in this regard. Lee writes that Lu Xun's language reached an experimental peak in the two years following his completion of this translation (1924–1926), and observes of *Wild Grass* and its "array of tormented figures roaming a dream-like landscape" that it appears to be Lu Xun's own attempt at creating his own figures of mental anguish.[58] Indeed, the importance Lu Xun accorded to symbolism is tellingly indicated in the following passage from his translation of Kuriyagawa: "The most essential ingredient of art is its symbolic nature. Only when the contents of thinking are expressed through such lively things as concrete characters, plots, and scenes, or, in other words, when they appear in the same way as the latent contents of a dream appear in a redressed form, do they become art."[59]

Kuriyagawa commended the personal essay as a superior genre for exploring dream images, arguing that it highlighted the author's "coloring" (or aura) while facilitating a symbolic synthesis of prose and poetry through its fluidness of form. In *Wild Grass*, Lu Xun appears to have taken Kuriyagawa's counsel to heart. The personal essay form dominates this anthology together with a preponderance of dream imagery. The timelessness of dream narratives allowed Lu Xun to dispense with the physical, temporal, and spatial properties of real life in order to heighten the symbolic significance of the persons and events narrated. While Lu Xun utilized dream images in *Wild Grass* to flesh out emotional intensities, their affective aura, in turn, was the result

of a radical defamiliarization (or anomie) of traditional Chinese poetics, specifically of what Lee calls "the typical *qing-jing* (feeling and scene)
ideal" of classical poetry.[60]

In stark contrast to the traditional melding of affections *(qing)* and
natural scenes *(jing)* to produce a happy concordance, Lu Xun projected alien and surreal images of a primal anguish. In place of vistas
of pastoral serenity and cosmic harmony, he substituted dark barren
wastelands against which to enact an entirely different kind of spiritual
communion with nature: one that, in displacing the mannerly *wenyan*
of Confucian cultivation with untamed *baihua,* celebrated acute animal
senses as integral to human experience.[61] In Lu Xun's 1935 remark about
a Herculean embrace that breaks the ribs of the hated Antaeus, we catch
a glimpse of the intensity with which he conducted these literary ex-
periments as deliberate transgressions of China's classical poetics.

Wild Grass was composed at a time when Lu Xun was increasingly
critical of his contemporaries' attempts to establish institutional standards for writing in *baihua.* In 1925, while working on this anthology,
he wrote an essay urging the young to resist the blandishments of self-
styled teachers and mentors "displaying their gilded placards."[62] When
asked the same year to recommend a list of "compulsory readings" in
aid of modernization, he stated he found the idea totally alien and
consequently had nothing to suggest. He wrote that, in his experience,
reading Chinese books took him away from social reality while non-
Chinese works spurred him to action. Accordingly, his only advice to
the young was that they should read more of the latter. He concluded
that the only drawback with reading fewer Chinese books was that
one's writing skills would suffer: "But what is most urgent for Chinese
youth at present is 'action' not 'words.' What matters is that you know
how to be fully alive: not being good at writing is hardly important."[63]

Meanwhile, as his literary reputation continued to soar, Lu Xun
grew increasingly conscious of and ambivalent toward the public interest that he attracted. He wrote to Li Xiaofeng in January 1927 expressing serious misgivings about the impending publication of *Wild
Grass.* Two months earlier, his erstwhile fractious protégé Gao Changhong had published a review of Lu Xun's "Autumn Night" (the first
piece in *Wild Grass* and initially published in *Threads of Talk* in December

1924).[64] To boost his literary standing, Gao intimated that he knew Lu Xun so well as to be privy to his "innermost thoughts." The review so irritated Lu Xun that he told Li he felt the publication of *Wild Grass* was premature, noting that the individual pieces had all appeared fairly recently in *Threads of Talk* (mostly in 1925 and 1926). Lu Xun wrote that what he feared most was the likelihood that *Wild Grass* would inspire a flurry of comments from those who were already "passing themselves off as my soul mates" and who appeared only too eager to profess knowledge of even more of "my innermost thoughts."[65] At any rate, the first edition of *Wild Grass* was released in July 1927.

It was around this time that Lu Xun felt he had reached a crossroads in his career. On 1 November 1926 he wrote (from Xiamen) to Xu Guangping (then already in Guangzhou) that he was "highly uncertain as to how to proceed from this point on." He felt torn between writing (in *baihua*) and teaching (Chinese literary history: the legacy of *wenyan* and the premodern vernacular) and explained that "these two things are irreconcilable" because "whereas writing demands passion, teaching requires detachment." Exploring his options, he continued:

> To pursue them together without putting in a serious effort would lead only to glib and facile results in both. Conversely, to make a real fist of doing both would mean that you're letting your blood boil in one instant and then forcing yourself to be calm and pleasant in the next. This would leave me utterly sapped, and I wouldn't do justice to either task. Outside China, there are very few writers who are also academics, and this has always been the case. As I see it, my scribblings are not without some good for China, and it would be a pity to give them up. By the same token, if I were to study some aspect of Chinese literature, I could come up with something new that people hadn't yet encountered, and thus it would equally be a pity to abandon this work. And so I think it might be best for me to write a few meaningful essays while turning my scholarship into something to be pursued in my spare time. Clearly, this plan wouldn't work if there were too many social engagements.[66]

Lu Xun appears to have adopted this general approach after 1926, though he clearly did not anticipate that by 1928 many of his *baihua* "scribblings" would take the form of rebuttals to the onslaught of criticism from his Marxist detractors. In the 1930s he repeatedly emphasized the need to keep *baihua* plain and simple to facilitate its development as the people's language, using terms like *putong* (common) and *dazhong* (the masses) to accentuate *baihua*'s communal properties. In this connection, he frequently warned his fellow leftists not to ostracize the masses with their newfangled terminology. For instance, he reprised his 1928 criticisms of the Creation Society when he wrote in 1934: "Intellectuals often despise others, thinking that they can understand new and difficult terms whereas the masses cannot, and therefore, for the sake of the masses, we must get rid of those new and difficult terms: the simpler our speech and writing, the better. If they carry this further, they will unconsciously become the new classicists."[67] But as many scholars have noted, *baihua* in its formative years from the 1910s to the 1930s was a language largely confined to China's urban intellectual elite and inaccessible to the masses. Indeed, it was from the very outset filled with "new and difficult terms."

Wang Hui puts it succinctly when he writes that the hybridity and cosmopolitanism of *baihua* was, in effect, a sign of its estrangement from the society of the masses for which the language was intended. In this context, Wang writes of Lu Xun that while on the one hand he offered a sustained critique of China's entrenched hierarchism, on the other his own *baihua* was also replete with glib references to Western thinkers and writers, such that he had no qualms about featuring "Stirner, Nietzsche, Tolstoy, and Rousseau" on the one page. For Wang, this Europeanized aspect of *baihua* was indicative of its exclusivity as the lingua franca of an elite minority and a vehicle for their interests, tastes, and preferences.[68] There is thus both an irony and sleight of hand in Lu Xun's use of a privileged language to disavow the elitist tendencies of his peers.

For all his insistence on fostering simple communication in *baihua*, Lu Xun's language was by no means common fare. His essays feature a plenitude of allusions drawn from *guwen* and *wenyan* and literary puns opaque to the untutored reader. In particular, the experimentalism of *Wild Grass* demands a connoisseurship quite at odds with his desire to create an egalitarian language. Yet the writings that make up this anthology also demonstrate Lu Xun at his most passionate in his willful embrace of *baihua* as a language in the making. When advocating *baihua* in 1926, he had noted self-referentially that a person steeped in the classics was the best equipped to denounce them effectively. He called this a case of "using one's own spear to pierce one's own shield," invoking an ancient fable attributed to the Legalist thinker Han Feizi (d. 233 B.C.E.) about a salesman who claimed that his spears and shields were equally invincible.[69]

While Lu Xun never commented on the constitutive elitism of his own *baihua*, there is nonetheless a tacit acknowledgment of "self-defeat" in his use of this ancient fabled boast. Indeed, despite his tirades against those of his contemporaries who continued to write in *wenyan*, Lu Xun's own lectures and essays on the classical literary corpus, which he so loved as a scholar, were widely read in his day. Of Lu Xun's *baihua*, Leys writes evocatively:

> One often has the impression that he is handling a foreign language (and it *was* foreign for him, as it was for most intellectuals of his generation) or a language still in a stumbling and uncertain stage of transition (and it is true that *baihua* only approached maturity with the writers of the succeeding generation): there is anyway something moving about seeing this eagle, who might have soared high and free in the classical tongue, voluntarily clipping his own wings to hobble among the crowd in the vernacular.[70]

Leys's "hobbling" reference is quite deliberate, for Lu Xun frequently resorted to tropes of stumbling, limping, and crawling to highlight his frustrations with writing in *baihua*. He first evoked the image of a crippled language in the short story "Kong Yiji" (first published in April 1919).[71] In his portrait of Kong Yiji as a hapless impoverished scholar unable to transcend Confucian archaisms to become a modern person, Lu Xun offers a concrete metaphor of *wenyan* as a language on its last legs, and further accentuates its bleak prospects by ending the story with the physical crippling of the protagonist. The final image of Kong Yiji is of a broken alcoholic whose hands are covered in mud as he crawls away from the tavern to an unknown fate.

This evocation of a crippled *wenyan* is complemented by Lu Xun's numerous references to *baihua* as a language in its infancy, stumbling and tottering toward eventual maturity. There is a memorable passage in his February 1927 lecture in Hong Kong, in which he urged his audience to persist with using *baihua* because it was no different from a child falling down "while learning to walk." He noted that *baihua*'s advent had met with strong opposition from the aficionados of *wenyan* who not only called it "vulgar and worthless" but ridiculed "the writings of the young as childish." In response to such criticisms, Lu Xun countered:

> But how many in China can write the classical language [*wenyan*]? The rest can only use the vernacular [*baihua*]. Do you mean to say that all these Chinese are vulgar and worthless? As for childishness, that is nothing to be ashamed of, any more than children need be ashamed of comparison with grown-ups. The childish can grow and mature; as long as they do not become decrepit and corrupt, all will be well. As for waiting till you are mature before making a move, not even a country woman would be so foolish. If her child falls down while learning to walk, she does not order him to stay in bed until he has mastered the art of walking.[72]

A related trope of unsteady ambulatory learning serves as the guiding motif of his 1925 composition "The Wayfarer," the longest piece in *Wild Grass*. "The Wayfarer," often praised as a defining moment in modern Chinese literature, is now mostly read as an allegory of Lu Xun's literary mission.[73] Written as a play script, it features three characters: the shabbily dressed wayfarer aged "between thirty and forty" and two people living in a mud hut whom he meets along the way: an old man in his seventies and a girl of ten. All three are presented as nameless age-based archetypes, with the old man serving as the wayfarer's chief interlocutor. The wayfarer displays a dogged determination to keep on traveling. He tells the old man he has spurned "the society of celebrities and landlords" and turned his back on a world of "expulsions and cages," "sham smiles and fake tears." Despite the old man's entreaties that compassionate humans also inhabit the world, the wayfarer vows never to return. He tells the old man he has rejected compassion and declares: "there is a voice up ahead often urging and summoning me to keep on going." The wayfarer remarks that though his feet are bloodied and blistered, he feels compelled to obey.[74]

On 11 April 1925, shortly after "The Wayfarer" first appeared in *Threads of Talk,* Lu Xun wrote to his student Zhao Qiwen (1903-1980), explaining that he conceived of the anonymous wayfarer as a person who "insists on traveling despite knowing full well that only the grave lies ahead." He noted that the wayfarer had chosen to "defy despair," and urged Zhao to heed the enormous difficulty of this kind of revolt, calling it "much more heroic and soul stirring than waging a battle in hope." He then remarked: "But it can easily be tripped up by 'love'—not to mention gratitude as well—which is why the wayfarer was almost unable to proceed when the little girl gave him a cloth bandage for his feet."[75]

Lu Xun's letter to Zhao Qiwen confirms that he intended "The Wayfarer" as an allegory of unwavering dedication to *baihua.* He endowed the wayfarer with a praiseworthy bearing through the stage directions he included in the play script: for instance, noting the injured man as "struggling to his feet" in one instance, "raising his head" and "moving resolutely toward the west" in another, and closing with the image of the wayfarer "limping toward the wilderness ahead" at twilight.[76]

By drawing attention to the wayfarer's exhaustion, Lu Xun accentuates the strength of will required to continue the journey, despite the uncertainties ahead. In this connection, we must also note the solitariness of the wayfarer's journey. It is no accident that Lu Xun's favorite ambient word *jimo* (desolate solitude) makes a frequent appearance in his writings to suggest the loneliness of his literary pursuit. The common ambiance of the wayfarer's journey and Lu Xun's stated mission allows us to read the wayfarer as a poetic anthropomorphism of Lu Xun's *baihua.* In the wayfarer's statement that he finds himself compelled to journey on in response to a disembodied voice, we find an echo of Lu Xun's description of his *baihua* prose, in his 1922 preface to *A Call to Arms,* as an undertaking in response to "my general's orders."[77]

In "The Wayfarer," the protagonist replies to the old man's question about his origins: "I don't know. As far back as I can recall I've been traveling like this, always toward some destination ahead of me. All I know is that I've walked a very long way to get here. After this, I must continue (pointing west) and go that way!"[78] It is no accident that the wayfarer is described as heading west, for Lu Xun himself sought through *baihua* to travel further and further away from *wenyan*'s dynastic and

Sinocentric origins. By 1934, together with Qu Qiubai and other proponents of a "Latinized" *(ladinghua)* mass language *(dazhongyu)*, he was calling for the eventual abolition of the Chinese character script and its replacement with Romanized Chinese.[79]

This image of a wayfaring *baihua* on a redemptive journey of self-discovery is the antithesis of *wenyan* embodied in the earlier tragic figure of Kong Yiji. Whereas the wayfarer steps into the unknown, guided by the call of a higher purpose, Kong Yiji's final exit from the tavern he frequents is a humiliating withdrawal into the night, with the derisive laughter of the other customers still ringing in his ears. In his analysis of "The Wayfarer," Tang Tao, the eminent scholar and former Lu Xun protégé, wrote that the disembodied voice urging the protagonist onward is best understood as "the voice of life itself."[80]

In commending the wayfarer as a heroic figure who "goes on" (or battles on) without anticipation of success, Lu Xun was, first and foremost, presenting an ideal attitude for writing in *baihua*. The use of prosopopoeia to evoke the presence of a personal moral conscience was clearly a favorite device, for he employed it in several of his stories and essays; but it was in "The Wayfarer" alone that Lu Xun presented this conscience as a voice that could just as easily be disregarded as heeded. Hence, Lu Xun tells us it was not only the wayfarer who heard the voice; the old man confesses that he too had heard the same voice years earlier but had chosen to ignore it. The old man adds: "It stopped calling, and I no longer remember it clearly," to which the wayfarer responds: "Oh how could you have ignored it . . . (While deep in contemplation, he is suddenly startled and listens intently) No! It's best that I go. I can't rest. How I wish my feet weren't so blistered."[81] The stage direction inserted midsentence alerts us to the fact that the voice had summoned the wayfarer once more.

Lu Xun's valorization of the wayfarer's struggle shares much with the premodern Chinese conception of learning as involving an ordeal of self-examination. This attitude of interrogating one's own flaws and limitations in the bid to discover one's true purpose first flourished in the discourse of Ming-era literati. It became, by the fifteenth century, a trend toward the unification of the "Three Teachings" (Buddhism, Confucianism, and Daoism). Hence it is not surprising that when in 1933 Lu Xun declared the *xiaopinwen* (short personal essays) to be in crisis and urgent need of defense, he made a point of commending socially engaged essays of the Ming era.[82]

The rhetoric of longing for self-transcendence that Lu Xun and his peers inherited and reinvented has continued to evolve in Chinese intellectual culture. To this day, figurations of learning as spiritual nourishment remain prevalent. Hence, in present-day Chinese scholarship, such phrases from "The Wayfarer" as "traveling without speaking of tiredness" and "bearing up without expressing hunger" remain in frequent use, both to eulogize Lu Xun and to prescribe an ideal attitude to learning.[83]

In the purported autobiographical text "My Father's Illness," completed in October 1926, Lu Xun turned the device of the summoning voice into a source of self-accusation. Here the narrator recalls how, as a child, he was urged by Mrs. Yan, "a woman thoroughly knowledgeable about ritual protocols," to call his dying father repeatedly in a loud voice. Summoning his father's spirit, as protocol demanded, disturbed his father: his face, which "had been composed, grew suddenly tense again; and he raised his eyelids slightly, as if in pain." In response to this incessant shouting, the narrator's father was forced to ask: "What is it? . . . Don't shout! . . . Don't . . ." Yet at Mrs. Yan's behest, the commotion continued. Lu Xun concludes the story with the narrator's expression of abiding remorse for preventing his father from departing the world in peace: "I went on calling until he breathed his last. I can still hear my voice as it sounded then. And each time I hear those cries, I feel this was the greatest wrong I ever did my father."[84]

This confession complicates the disembodied voices of conscience that Lu Xun presents with elegant simplicity in "The Wayfarer" and *A Call to Arms*. Here, he suggests that the grief-stricken voice of the child does not so much command as haunt and sadden the attentive listener. In this context, his description of Mrs. Yan's unfeeling adherence to ritual serves to accentuate the emotional pain he ascribes to the child's ritual cries. In so doing, he turns an integral part of Chinese folk tradition into a figure of tragic miscommunication, whose tragic element is further heightened by the fact of the narrator's childish ignorance and later regret. More fundamentally, the moral lesson that Lu Xun implies in "My Father's Illness" and in numerous essays that dwell on death is that because humans are distinguished from other animals by awareness of their finitude, they must learn to articulate their shared mortality in ways that nurture a mutual empathy.

The same theme of miscommunication is differently explored in his 1925 *Wild Grass* composition "The Tremor of Debased Lines," in which the figure of a voice is used to present true suffering as audible and palpable but inarticulate. The text consists of two dream scenarios, both of which take the form of "a dream within a dream," with the second serving as a continuation of the first. The first dreamscape is set late at night, in the interior of "a tightly sealed cottage" with dense stonecrop on the roof reflecting its state of disrepair. The dream opens with a scene, lit by the glow of a kerosene lamp, of two bodies pressed together: "a hairy well-built stranger lies on top of a slight and delicate body that trembles with hunger, pain, shock, humiliation, and pleasure." The suggestion of a woman forced to prostitute herself is deepened through the subsequent introduction of a hungry two-year-old girl, whom the trembling woman seeks to comfort with promises of sesame cakes upon the pieman's arrival as she clutches a hard-earned silver coin in her hand.[85]

The second dreamscape is presented as the continuation many years later of the first. The woman, described in the first dream as young but haggard, with a complexion glowing "like lead painted with liquid rouge," has now grown old. A young couple and their offspring accuse her of wrecking their lives, with the youngest child brandishing a dry reed as a make-believe sword as he shouts, "Kill!" The narrative continues with the old woman calmly leaving the cottage to walk out into the night. She keeps walking until she reaches "the boundless wasteland," and there, surrounded by a barren landscape, she stands "stark naked like a stone statue."[86] She recalls her entire life, trembling and convulsing at memories of "loving attachment and total estrangement, adoration and revenge, nurture and annihilation, blessings and curses," and proceeds "with every ounce of her energy to raise both hands toward the sky as a language falls from her lips, both human and animal but unlike any existing human language: wordless."[87]

In this figure of an alien tongue yet to find the words to fully express human pain, Lu Xun offers a powerful allegory of the egalitarian ideal he envisaged for *baihua*. In their translation of this story, Yang

Xianyi and Gladys Yang gave it the English title "Tremors of Degradation," thereby reducing Lu Xun's phrase *tuibai xiande zhandou* (the tremor of debased or degraded lines) to just *tuibai de zhandou* (tremors of degradation).[88] Their omission of *xian* (lines) from the translated title makes a crucial difference to how we read the text. In effect, the omission reduces the text to a surreal narrative depicting human suffering: a modernist tale of the oppressed. Yet once we take into account Lu Xun's deliberate reference to "debased *lines*," the prospect of writing (as language), wounded and driven into as yet inchoate expression, assumes a pivotal importance.

In this regard, Lu Xun instructs us to read the anonymous woman not only as giving voice to her suffering but as finding the capacity to do so *only after* leaving home to walk into the wilderness. Once the woman gave utterance to the emotions that consumed her as she stood alone in the wasteland,

> her wasted and decaying yet statuesque frame began to tremble. This tremble was like a myriad of quivering fish-scales. As each scale rose and fell like water boiling away over a hot flame, the air at once grew turbulent and became like violent storm waves crashing in a remote ocean. She then raised her eyes to the sky. Her wordless utterances ceased, and silence ensued. There was only the trembling, radiating like sunlight and causing the heaving air to whirl like a cyclone, sweeping its way across the boundless wasteland.[89]

In this passage language is celebrated, first and foremost, as a vehicle of emotional expression. If we read the woman's speech as a glyph for *baihua*, what Lu Xun implies here is that inarticulateness presents no obstacle to the communication of suffering. Indeed, we are instructed to read the woman's unintelligible speech as nonetheless producing a tremor of such magnitude as to convulse the entire wasteland. The wasteland, suggestive of *wenyan*'s decrepitude but also of what lies outside society—the as yet unknown reaches of language—allows Lu Xun to imply that people who are blind to the ravaged state of Chinese culture are equally deaf to the urgent necessity of *baihua*. In other words, the revolutionary force of the woman's alien tongue, sweeping across the wasteland, had yet to be felt in society.

This liberated voice of the passionate human-animal is unique in Lu Xun's oeuvre. He is better known for depicting the wholly intelligible voices of the socially oppressed, whether the familiar ritual cries of the child in "My Father's Illness" or the utterances of the working poor. The story "My Old Home," written in 1921, highlights in one particularly poignant scene the abject language in which the poor are imprisoned. The narrator, a scholar, returns home after an absence of more than twenty years to find his childhood friend Runtu, the son of a poor peasant who is now a poor peasant himself, addressing him as "Master." The narrator experiences paralysis in the face of this institutionalized inequality: "I felt a shiver run through me; for I knew then what a lamentably thick wall had grown between us. Yet I could not say anything."[90]

This shiver, the shock of alienation from a childhood friend because of entrenched class inequalities, complements the "trembling, radiating" power Lu Xun imparts to the woman's inchoate utterances. Images of shivering and trembling are cognates of the stony hardness favored by Lu Xun in depicting intense emotions of grief and hate. Whereas the former highlights what human animals experience in common as a biological response to extreme stimuli, the latter draws attention to the rigid tautness into which negative and violent feelings throw our human bodies. The positive valence of these sensuous physiological tropes in Lu Xun's writings complements his privileging of a profoundly affective humanism over a merely reasoned one. It also exemplifies his poetics of "the rough-and-ready."

In figuring his own *baihua* as "wild grass," Lu Xun sought to capture a sense of the transient and makeshift nature of human expression. His image of language as "wild grass" finds a distinct echo in J. M. Coetzee's phrase "an imperfect medium born of an imperfect world." In this connection the distinction Coetzee makes between "human language" born of an imperfect world and "the language of the ideal order" offers a useful analogous elaboration of Lu Xun's sensibility to *baihua*:

Unfortunately for utopians, the language that people, real people, stubbornly desire to speak and hear is not perfect and other-worldly: it remains the imperfect this-worldly language of the flesh. The only expedient through which the language of the flesh can be redeemed for the ideal is by interpreting it, abstracting it. As this process is performed, as the flesh is flayed off it, the skeleton of the ideal, it is hoped, will begin to gleam through.[91]

Coetzee's remarks chime with Lu Xun's frequent injunctions against the mere invocation of lofty ideals, whether of democracy, humanism, revolution, or the proletariat. Indeed, it was in explicit opposition to skeletal ideals stripped of human feeling that Lu Xun counterposed the figure of "wild grass" (and the prose of *Wild Grass*) as emblematic of *baihua*'s imperfect but plain speaking and immediate humanness. Above all, as the botanical image of "wild grass" suggests, he regarded humanness as bound up with the will to survive and, by extension, as involving that defining human capacity to forever inventively draw sustenance from whatever happens to be within reach.

As Lu Xun put it in his preface to *Wild Grass*, the marvel of an ugly weed is that, despite its "shallow roots," it "imbibes dew, water, and the flesh and blood of rotting corpses. It survives despite all attempts to deprive it of life. It lives only to be trampled on and cut down, until it finally dies and decays."[92] The preface concludes with an almost incantatory dedication:

> Between light and darkness, life and death, past and future, I dedicate this tussock of wild grass as my pledge to friend and foe, man and beast, those whom I love and those whom I do not love. For my own sake and for the sake of friend and foe, man and beast, those whom I love and those whom I do not love, I hope for the swift death and decay of this wild grass. Otherwise it means I have not lived, and this would be truly more lamentable than death and decay. Go, then, wild grass, together with my preface![93]

The impermanence that Lu Xun celebrates in this passage permeates the language of *Wild Grass*, finding expression in decidedly organic images that range from a swarm of insects "hurtling recklessly" toward death in a flame (in "Autumn Night"); through symbols of expired life (in "Amid Pale Bloodstains"); to language *speaking* its desire for release from an icy prison to set itself aflame once more (in "Dead Fire"). In exalting these elemental qualities, the *baihua* in *Wild Grass* presents itself as unconfined by the abstract ideals and "fine names" that crowded the elite *baihua* discourse of the day.

Lu Xun's affirmation of linguistic impermanence (and of the "swift death and decay" of his *Wild Grass*) bears a striking resemblance to Heidegger's notion of language as a journey without end: as something always already "on the way"—in perpetual transit. Yet language is also the house and only house of being, indeed the enabling ground of being, not a mere instrument of expression. In particular, Lu Xun's meditations on *baihua* resonate with Heidegger's observation in *On the Way to Language:* "Mortals are they who can experience death as death. Animals cannot do so. But animals cannot speak either. The essential relation between death and language flashes up before us, but remains still unthought."[94]

For this reason, even though the two men did not know of each other, Heidegger's reflections on "the essence of language" capture something of the asymmetry that Lu Xun established between the impermanence of his "wild grass" and the realm of language in which it thrives and dies. As Heidegger put it:

> We human beings, in order to be who we are, remain within the essence of language to which we have been granted entry. We can therefore never step outside it in order to look it over circumspectly from some alternative position. Because of this, we catch a glimpse of the essence of language only to the extent that we ourselves are envisaged by it, remanded to it. That we cannot know the essence of language—according to the traditional concept of knowledge, defined in terms of cognition as representation—is certainly not a defect; it is rather the advantage by which we advance to an exceptional realm, the realm in which we dwell as the mortals, those who are needed and used for the speaking of language."[95]

Lu Xun appealed to a kindred essence of language when dedicating *Wild Grass* to an indefinite realm "between light and darkness, life and death, past and future." In doing so, he highlighted the unearthliness of language as a realm beyond the physics of time. This idea is expressly articulated in "The Shadow's Farewell" (discussed in Chapter 1) through the shadow's declared preference for "wandering in a *non-place*" *(wu di panghuang).*[96] The shadow, as a surreal agent of the words on the page, allows us to catch a glimpse of ourselves being spoken to and envisaged by language. The shadow's gifts of darkness and emptiness require the surrender of our time-bound truths. Thus Lu Xun offers an insight akin to Heidegger's notion of advancing by means of the insight that we can never *know* the essence of language.

Despite the kinship of Lu Xun's and Heidegger's meditations on language, they pursued divergent goals. Whereas Heidegger sought to undo the metaphysics of Western philosophy, Lu Xun's *Wild Grass* was a poetic celebration of *baihua,* aimed at nurturing a language of common belonging into being. Nonetheless, both were profoundly ambitious projects, and it is perhaps no accident that just as Heidegger produced a unique discourse of such theoretical density that his oeuvre is largely inaccessible without expert scholarly guidance, Lu Xun's *Wild Grass* demands similarly erudite counsel for a productive reading. Of Lu Xun's experimental language in *Wild Grass,* the eminent scholar T. A. Hsia writes evocatively that it is "genuine poetry in embryo images ... flowing and stopping in darkly glowing and oddly shaped lines, like molten metal failing to find a mold."[97] But despite this radical undecidability, *Wild Grass* was crafted using plain words, and as such bears testament to Lu Xun's literary prowess in creating a turbulent aesthetics out of the elements of a fledgling *baihua.*

Feng Xuefeng recalled Lu Xun stating on several occasions that he would "never again write anything like [*Wild* Grass]," and that there was invariably a tinge of regret in his voice.[98] In Feng's stilted criticism of *Wild Grass* as "intellectually and emotionally individualistic," as evidence of a "dark, nihilistic, pessimistic, and hopeless" outlook, and as lacking "any real importance" in Lu Xun's oeuvre of "fervent social struggle," we get a sense of the trivialization of Lu Xun's artistry even among his close associates. This lends an even greater melancholy to his depictions of *baihua* as a language forged in solitariness upon a wasteland.[99] This wasteland image, in turn, points to the Daoist inspiration for Lu Xun's figuration of language as a weed. In the preface he wrote for *Wild Grass* in April 1927, he implied that it was only through ongoing spontaneous evolution that a common language could ultimately emerge to triumph, as it were, over any would-be Confucian gardener who sought to keep it in check.

The same idea is differently expressed in his Hong Kong lecture of February 1927 two months earlier. On that occasion, he focused on the scale of difficulty involved in fostering linguistic and literary invention. Gesturing to written Chinese as a language so long confined by the orthodoxies of dynastic culture as to become a stranger to spontaneous expression, he remarked: "To restore speech to this China which has been silent for centuries . . . is like ordering a dead man to live again. Though I know nothing of religion, I fancy this approximates to what believers call a 'miracle.' "[100]

Five years later, in 1932, when pressed by the leftist journal *The Dipper (Beidou)* for tips on writing, he complained there was already a surfeit of foreign and Chinese literary manuals. He wrote that all he was prepared to offer were a few personal insights:

1. Make careful notes of what you see, observe closely and don't start writing when you've barely had a glimpse;
2. Don't force yourself to write when you feel you can't;
3. Don't base a character on a specific person; you should adapt something from the many people you encounter;
4. Read over what you've written at least twice and make every effort to take out words and phrases that are superfluous. Don't regret the loss. . . . ;
5. Read foreign stories, by which I mean the literature of eastern and northern Europe as well as Japanese works;
6. Don't invent adjectives and words that, with the exception of yourself, no one can understand;
7. Don't believe any talk about "the rules of fiction writing";
8. Don't believe the words of China's so-called critics and their ilk. Read instead the reviews of reliable foreign critics.[101]

These eight points, addressed to the younger members of the Left-Wing League, also convey Lu Xun's unease with the progressive institutionalization of socialist realism in the 1930s. A corollary to this advice appears in a telling passage in his 1933 essay "In Perfect Awareness of Being Worldly Wise." Here, Lu Xun invites us to read him intuitively, not analytically. Having warned his readers of the many dangerous traps that lay in wait for writers living in a "dark" society, he concludes with a lighthearted piece of Buddhist- and Daoist-inspired advice:

> To discuss a thing is to lose some of its essence: just as you forget the trap once you've caught your fish, the words slip away from you when you get hold of an idea. When this occurs, the state of perfect awareness [sanmei; Samadhi in Sanskrit] has eluded you yet again. Thus, to discuss what it means to be "in perfect awareness of being worldly wise" will only serve to confirm that the phrase is not what it purports. The true essence of perfect awareness is to be found in actions not words. But in saying "actions not words," I've lost the true essence of perfect awareness and find myself some distance away from it. True knowledge is only ever understood intuitively. Aum![102]

One of the most touching remarks he made about his relationship to baihua appears in the 1933 preface he wrote (at Edgar Snow's request) for an anthology of his short stories in English translation. In this text Lu Xun recalled a story from the Zhuangzi to describe his predicament of being "unable to write the new and unwilling to write the old." He compared his baihua to the folly of young folk from the ancient town of Shouling, who, according to the Zhuangzi, dreamed of walking like the stylish sophisticates in the capital Handan. Their desire took them to Handan. Later they discovered that not only had they failed to master the metropolitan stride but they had forgotten how to walk altogether. Thus they were forced to crawl home to Shouling. Lu Xun ended the preface with the declaration: "I'm still crawling, but I'm willing to keep on learning so that I may eventually stand upright."[103]

In using this Daoist allegory to illustrate his linguistic predicament, Lu Xun implied that, like the self-disabled youth of Shouling, his ambition to write baihua turned out to be self-crippling. Nonetheless he changed the tone of the original story from one of *crawling back in defeat* to one of *progressing forward in hope.* In so doing, he also altered the valence of the familiar in "home" to instead commend an unknown future: thus unlike the youth who returned to Shouling, Lu Xun looked toward a home he had yet to experience, one that he would reach only after he has learned to "stand upright" in *baihua.*

In using ambulatory tropes to anthropomorphize language, Lu Xun not only put flesh and bones on *baihua* but transfigured the act of writing into an agon of self-reflection on the road to attaining humanness. Although his vocabulary had acquired an occasional Marxist inflection after 1930, he remained committed to the mission he set himself back in the 1910s, the mission of forging a human path *(rendao).*

As Lu Xun journeyed in *baihua* against a rapidly changing historical landscape of endemic violence from the 1910s into the 1930s, with warlord regimes giving way to Chiang Kai-shek's Nationalist government and its anti-Communist purges only to be followed by the growing threat of Japan's military incursions, he also became more circumspect about "the old," "the new," and "the foreign." He began his June 1933 essay "Experience" with the statement: "Some of the experience handed down to us by the ancients is exceedingly precious, having cost many lives, and remains of great value to posterity."[104] In June 1934 he coined the term "appropriatism" *(nalaizhuyi)* to encourage a judicious approach to the reception of foreign works.

Writing pensively of Chinese history after the Opium Wars, he began the essay "Appropriatism" with the observation that ever since "cannon fire tore down the gates," China's inveterate "closed-door approach" had given way to "an indiscriminate 'give-away-ism.'" He observed that a steady stream of unwanted "gifts" from abroad accompanied this involuntary generosity. To commend the merits of "appropriatism" at a time of rising nationalistic feeling and a widening boycott of Japanese goods, he wrote:

> We've been scared stiff by the things we've been "given"; first came England's opium, then Germany's discarded cannons, followed by French cosmetics, American movies, and Japanese bric-a-brac stamped "Made in China" [*wanquan guo huo*]. Hence clearheaded young people now recoil from foreign goods, the reason being that these things

were "given" to us; they weren't things we sought to "appropriate."
Thus we must use our brains, extend our gaze, and take what we
want![105]

Such formulations exemplify the plain or sparse style *(pingdan)* that
Lu Xun favored—a style that despite its evident modernity was inspired by the ancient literary exemplars whom he held dear.[106] When
describing these influences ambivalently as "extremely ancient phantoms" that threatened to choke him, he mused: "Is there any place in
my thinking that isn't somewhat infected by the poison of Zhuangzi
and Han Feizi of oscillating between an easy manner and quickness to
anger [*shi'er suibian shi'er junji*]?" He added that "though the works of
Confucius and Mencius were the first books I read and the ones I knew
best, they never seemed to have anything to do with me."[107]

In his July 1927 lectures on "The Style and Prose of the Wei-Jin Epoch
and Their Connection with Wine and Drugs," he drew particular attention to *tongtuo* ("unconfined spontaneity") as a highly commendable trait in the writings of Cao Cao.[108] Moreover, although Lu Xun
never mentioned Xi Kang as an influence on his prose, his student
Tang Tao offered the helpful observation that his teacher's decades-
long devotion to editing the writings of this ancient martyr bears testimony to his deep affinity with Xi Kang's "raging against the world"
(fenshi).[109] Lu Xun also viewed irony and satire as indispensable tools for
expressing acute disaffection. As he wrote in May 1935, the artistic use of
"concise or even rather exaggerated language" allowed the truth "about
certain aspects of some group of people" to be vividly presented.[110]

In December 1935, ten months before his death, Lu Xun completed
the story "Exit from the Pass," in which he paid tribute to the Daoist
sensibilities that inform his poetics as a whole. He did this through
reinventing the traditional fable of how Laozi came to write *The Classic
of the Way and Virtue (Daode jing)*.[111] In this story, Lu Xun presents the
Daoist invocation of unboundedness as an enduring hope of discursive openness. Using the founding figures of Confucianism and Daoism as symbols of two contrasting attitudes, Lu Xun casts Laozi as an
astute mentor to an ambitious Confucius. He writes of how Laozi departed for the unknown as soon as he recognized that Confucius,

having learned all he could from Laozi, now perceived his mentor as a threat.

Thus, Lu Xun's Laozi explains in a plainspoken *baihua* to his disconsolate disciple Kengsang Chu: "Confucius has grasped my ideas and must feel ill at ease, as he knows that I alone see right through him. If I don't go, things will get difficult." Lu Xun then allows Laozi the privilege of encapsulating the difference between his own unfettered approach and Confucius's rule-bound enterprise. In response to Kengsang Chu's question "Aren't you both pursuing the same path [*dao*]?" Laozi answers: "No, our paths are different. We may wear the same kind of sandals, but mine are for traveling the deserts while his take him to the imperial court."[112]

In figuring the Chinese language as the "sandals" of Laozi and Confucius, Lu Xun presents the vivid image of a common vehicle that has long served the opposite goals of spiritual fulfillment and dynastic rule. Moreover, in opposing the unknown reaches of "the deserts" to the policed confines of the "imperial courts," Lu Xun recalls the numerous wastelands and desolate scenes that populate his prose as figurations of spiritual renewal. We can only speculate as to whether his portrayal of Laozi and Confucius was also an allusion to his disappointment with his many ambitious protégés. But what the story does amply demonstrate is Lu Xun's preference for solitary encounters with the infinitude of language—in the sense that "only language knows no conceptual, no projective finality," as George Steiner has put it.[113] This spiritual aspect of Lu Xun's *baihua* was incommensurable with the narrowing discourse of his leftist contemporaries and the tightening grip of their ideological certitude.

A Humanistic Appetite

Lu Xun's essays display a singular flair for focusing on the deficiencies of the here and now. Although he did so without utilizing the vast theoretical armature of Marxism, the dissatisfaction he sought to induce remained consonant with the concepts of class struggle, dialectical materialism, and classless social perfection that prevailed in the leftist writings of his day. However, in contrast to this Marxist lexicon,

Lu Xun dwelt on empathy and honesty as the indispensable virtues for promoting an egalitarian humanism in China.

The immanence of Lu Xun's social criticism is most striking in his inventive reworkings of the Chinese aesthetic of *quwei* (literally, zest and flavor). *Quwei,* as the much-prized sensibility of taste in the premodern writings of China's scholar-literati, evolved into a modern twentieth-century aesthetic as part of the New Culture movement. Among its foremost proponents were Zhou Zuoren and Lin Yutang. As noted earlier, they were the implicit targets of Lu Xun's attack in 1933 on dilettante connoisseurs: namely, those who would turn the "rough-and-ready into something sophisticated and elegant."[114] Although Lu Xun's own powers of ironic humor and satire made him an acknowledged master of *quwei* (and in 1928 his Marxist critics were quick to disparage him along with Zhou as a key representative of this "petty-bourgeois" trait), his interest was not to rejuvenate *quwei* as a modern elite sensibility but rather to sharpen the effectiveness of his social criticism using rhetorical devices associated with *quwei.*

In particular, his gastronomic tropes, which effect a literalization of *quwei,* present an image of learning as a somatic experience: truth is akin to knowing what is good and fit to eat. In this regard, Lu Xun has something in common with Epicurus's philosophy of *physiologia,* and it is appropriate to describe his critical purpose in terms of an attempt to nurture a healthy appetite for humanism. As Foucault observed, Epicurus (341–270 B.C.E.) commended *physiologia* as the rigor of a thoroughgoing self-examination in opposition to "a culture of boasters . . . concocters of words whose only aim is to be admired by the masses."[115] Similarly, in likening words to food, Lu Xun highlighted a physiological dimension to inquiry. This is especially evident in his use of the phrase "chewing and gnawing on words" (discussed in Chapter 4) against his Marxist accusers in 1928. Lu Xun implied that because their publications were unaccompanied by any useful nutrition, they posed a threat to the future well-being of the modern Chinese vernacular.

He reprised this sentiment in a 1930 essay to deride the writings of his former adversaries turned fellow League members as spoiled food. Lu Xun wrote that the unwitting consumers of "revolutionary literature" when it was all the rage in late 1920s Shanghai lost their appetite upon discovering that they were consuming huge quantities of "old vinegary wine in new bottles and rotten meat freshly packed in red paper." He claimed that this was the probable cause of the rapid shift to a new trend for publications in social science. He quipped that the taste of so-called revolutionary fare would have proven "so nauseating that they must have felt like vomiting."[116] To accuse the left and the right alike, in another essay of 1930 Lu Xun referred to "poisonous official books that make you want to vomit" to express revulsion toward Chiang Kai-shek's brand of revolutionary tutelage.[117]

In using tropes of the unwholesome, rottenness, and nausea Lu Xun clearly sought to invoke a synesthesia of language and taste or odor (wei) and, in so doing, to shape the resulting sense of disgust into an instructive emotion. Of these, cannibalism remains his best-remembered trope. Lu Xun used it in "The Diary of a Madman" to condemn the intricate hierarchism of Chinese kinship and society. To highlight the magnitude of change that China needed, he wrote as the penultimate entry of the protagonist's diary: "Here I am, the product of cannibalistic predecessors stretching back four thousand years. Although I was unaware at first, I now know the truth. How hard it would be for me to find a real human!"[118]

Lu Xun's metaphor of cannibalism works at two levels. Symbolically, it produces a visceral indictment of "the old society's" anthropophagic appetite, the depth of which is progressively revealed to the protagonist. Grammatically, the metaphor presents premodern wenyan as a logophagy: a language of naturalized inequalities and honorific norms that continues "eating away" at the independence of all those who inhabit the language.

A year later Lu Xun transmuted the madman's revulsion into empathy for those who were trapped within "cannibalism." In his 1919 story "Medicine" he dwelled on the desperation that led the superstitious parents of a consumptive child to feed him bread soaked in the blood of an executed revolutionary in a futile attempt to cure his illness.[119] Such figurations share an analogous logic with Brillat-Savarin's (1755–1826) maxim, "Tell me what you eat, and I will tell you who you are."[120] It is perhaps significant that at the height of Chiang Kai-shek's "Party purification" campaign in 1927, Lu Xun complicated this idea when he accused himself of having helped to turn young readers into "live shrimps steeped in wine" ready for delectable consumption by their enemies.

These potently negative figurations of the aesthetic of *wei* (flavor) are complemented by a range of relatively lighthearted criticisms of a growing elitist taste in *baihua*. From 1925 on, as Lu Xun's antagonism toward the Crescent Moon Society deepened, he compared his own critical pursuit to the feeding habits of fleas and flies. In an essay that year he wrote that although fleas were unpleasant insects that sucked the blood of humans, they were nonetheless "straightforward and frank" in biting people without a word. Flies, he continued, "alight after much preliminary buzzing and fuss" to feed on boils and sores as well as "to leave some filth on anything good, beautiful, and clean." Nonetheless, they too were to be admired, for "they do not gloat over what they have done and turn to laugh at the filth of what they have defiled. At least they have that much decency." In contrast to these two commendable insects, he continued, the mosquito was most disagreeable, with its whining "long harangue" about "feeding on human blood." Lu Xun wrote that he was glad he did not know its language.[121]

In comparing himself to an insect, Lu Xun drew an extravagant contrast between his literary pursuit and those of the Crescent Moon Society's leading members. He presented himself as feeding on their "fine" blood so as to cast them as enemies who were turning common *baihua* into gourmet fare fit only for elite consumption. This high-low binary appears in another of his 1925 essays, in which he accused the Crescentists of enjoying the high life, in unconscionable obliviousness of the sufferings of the poor. He then described himself as "a wasp with wet wings crawling around in the mud who is clearly no match for the erudite folk living in Western mansions; a wasp filled with sorrow and indignation beyond the ken of the erudite folk living in Western mansions."[122] In his 1926 preface to *The Grave*, he extemporized further on the figure of the fly, noting that whereas the actual insect was unaware of how much people hated its buzzing, he on the contrary sought "to buzz as often as he could" so as "to cause some small discomfort" to those who "devote their lives to building a comfortable world for themselves." To ensure that readers appreciated the depth of his loathing, he added with vengeful humor: "if I hope to prolong my life by abstaining from alcohol and taking cod-liver oil, it is not solely for the sake of my loved ones. Rather it would mostly be because of my enemies . . . so that I may leave a few flaws in their otherwise beautiful world."[123]

In his December 1927 essay, "Rousseau and Appetite," Lu Xun summed up his dislike of the Crescent Moon Society more straightforwardly. This was an essay directed against Liang Shiqiu in particular. Lu Xun wrote that although Liang normally echoed his mentor Irving Babbitt in denouncing Rousseau, in one unexpected instance in a recent essay he had enlisted Rousseau to defend the conservative view that women should be given "a proper education" to nurture their feminine qualities. Quoting Liang's remark that people tend "to accept and promote ideas that suit their appetite," Lu Xun concluded that he and Liang were bound to clash, because they had entirely opposite kinds of appetite. He wrote that, unlike Liang, he disagreed with Rousseau specifically on the issue of women's education but shared Upton Sinclair's broader appetite for "the torrent of new ideas and new feelings that Rousseau let loose upon the world."[124]

These various statements from Lu Xun all indicate the importance he assigned to critical inquiry as a somatic experience. Of this privileging of the fleshly in acts of thinking, he provided a metacritical conception in his *Wild Grass* composition "The Epitaph." In this enigmatic text completed on 18 June 1925, Lu Xun presented a dreamscape where the narrator stands before a crumbling tomb tablet on which two fragments of an inscription remain. The first commemorates the dead person as follows: ". . . caught a chill while reveling in song; saw an abyss in heaven. In all eyes saw only nothing; in hopelessness found salvation . . ."[125] The second equally mystifying fragment reads: "There is a roaming spirit that turns itself into a very long snake with poisonous fangs. It does not bite humans but eats itself and so ultimately perishes . . . Go away!"[126]

It is tempting to read these barely intelligible, hence highly interpretable, epitaph fragments as a self-reflexive allegory of Lu Xun's own literary adventures in *baihua*. The first fragment reprises his theme of linguistic infinitude in "The Shadow's Farewell" to suggest that the utopian "heaven" of revolutionary rhetoric is no more than a ruse, promising a reality it cannot actually deliver.[127] As the fragment implies, language is quite literally an abyss insofar as it is an endless signifying chain that ultimately turns every promise of insight into an airy nothingness. Yet the counterpoint idea of finding salvation in an abysmal state indicates optimism about the prospect of meaningful communication across time, through the past, present, and future permutations of discourse.

This idea of keeping faith with the future, in and as language, is elaborated and crystallized in the second fragment as the unmistakable image of the self-consuming Ouroboros. It seems likely that, at the very least, Lu Xun was aware of the Ouroboros as an ancient symbol, but he did not indicate whether he knew that it stood for immortality and self-generation in early Western alchemy. His contemporary Carl Jung (1875–1961) wrote of the Ouroboros that the idea of "devouring oneself and turning oneself into a circulatory process" suggested wholeness and infinity through "the integration and assimilation of the opposition." In Jung's psychological scheme, this is the opposition between the self and the shadow; the agon between the conscious and unconscious aspects of mortal existence.[128] Of the Ouroboros, Jung explains: it is "the dragon that devours, fertilizes, begets, slays, and brings to life again. Being hermaphroditic, it is compounded of opposites and is at the same time their unifying symbol: at once deadly poison, basilisk, scorpion, panacea, and savior."[129] Although Lu Xun may not have read Carl Jung, he clearly shared Jung's interests in Freudian analysis, symbolic language, and alchemy.

Moreover, Lu Xun had an avid scholarly interest in the alchemical pursuits of emperors and recluses in dynastic China. In particular, it was the Wei-Jin epoch from the third to the fifth centuries C.E. for which he had a particular fascination, an epoch during which the quest for the elixir of immortality flourished. But whereas Jung read the Ouroboros as signifying psychic integration through the resolution of contradictory tendencies, Lu Xun used the same symbolism to stage a "self-consuming" encounter with language. "The Epitaph," in this regard, presents a ghoulish tribute to the vast repositories of funereal texts in *wenyan,* of which the autobiographical obituary was an important subgenre. It was the customary practice among premodern scholar-literati to prepare an autobiographical obituary against the possibility of future biographical distortions. That Lu Xun was gesturing toward this form of self-written epitaph is clear from the link he establishes between the Ouroboros image of the second fragment and the corpse he proceeds to describe as lurking behind the crumbling tomb tablet.

Of the corpse, he wrote that its "chest and stomach are torn open and absent of heart and liver; its face reflects not the slightest joy or sorrow but conveys the haze of a trail of smoke."[130] Lu Xun then revealed a fragment on the tomb tablet's obverse side: "I tore out my heart to eat it, wanting to know its true taste. But the pain was so agonizing, how could I tell its taste? . . . When the pain subsided, I bit into it gingerly. By then the heart had grown stale, so how am I to know its original taste? . . . Answer me or go away!" As the narrator made haste to leave, the corpse sat up and said "without moving its lips": "When I have turned into dust, you will see my smile!"[131]

Here the extension of the Ouroboric metaphor draws attention to the yearning for linguistic transparency as both compulsive and impossible. The corpse, as symbolic of the once-living author, highlights the impulse to communicate one's true intent as an impulse that proves ultimately futile. The desire for purity of expression, likened to the pain of tearing out and eating one's own heart, conveys a desire for an ideal linguistic vehicle capable of transporting and preserving the author's intended meaning fully intact. But as Lu Xun implies, the pain of tearing out one's own heart—of laying bare the author's entire rhetorical armature in an attempt to distill an "original taste"—cannot be achieved without recourse to yet further words. Interpretation, in piling words upon words, would inevitably turn the original meaning "stale."

In putting the anthropophagic device to this self-reflexive end, Lu Xun suggests via the speaking corpse that no path exists in language to take us back to the authorial intention. Rather, the Ouroboric pursuit, as the impossibility of knowing the true taste of one's own heart, is a path that opens only to the infinitude of language in which the authorial self must "perish" as his words are progressively overtaken by the words of others. In this regard, the corpse's parting remark, "When I have turned into dust, you will see my smile!" evokes the Nietz-schean sense of the abyss staring back if one gazes into it, since it is not the author's voice that ultimately speaks but the incorporeal force of language itself.

In this regard, Lu Xun's prose shares a cadence with Jean-Paul Sar-tre's (1905–1980) remarks about "Writing for One's Age." Whereas Lu Xun presented a speaking corpse, Sartre offered the equally supernat-ural courier of Marathon, who, having "died an hour before reaching Athens," announced the victory of the Greeks "running dead." As Sar-tre put it: "This is a fine myth; it shows that the dead still act for a little while as if they were living. . . . This is the measure we propose to the writer: as long as his books arouse anger, discomfort, shame, hatred, even if he is no more than a shadow, he will live. Afterwards, the del-uge. We stand for an ethics and art of the finite."[132]

Sartre also pondered the true taste of literature when he reflected, less morbidly than Lu Xun, on the difference between dead and living fruit. He wrote that dates and bananas were dead fruit of which he had been told: "In order to know what they are, you have to eat them on the spot, when they've just been picked." Noting that the "real live taste" of bananas had always escaped him, Sartre offered this analogy: "Books that are handed down from age to age are dead fruit" that "in another time" had "another taste, tart and tangy," noting in this re-gard that *Emile* or *The Persian Letters* should have been read when they were freshly picked."[133]

In reading this passage, Jacques Derrida drew attention to Sartre's desire for true taste as an acknowledgment that the ambition to "write for one's age" is bedeviled by an irresolvable contradiction. He quoted from Sartre: "To write for one's age is not to reflect it passively; it is to want to maintain it or change it, thus to go beyond it towards the fu-ture, and it is this effort to change it that places us most deeply in it." Moreover, the desire to write for one's age is bound up with a certain attitude of turning one's back on it, to recognize that one's words are already "dead fruit" offered up to a future age that one cannot foresee. Thus, any invocation of the future in a given present must recognize its own finitude: to quote Sartre, the future as imagined "never became a present."[134] Yet it is this very insight of being a "dead man running" that compels the writer forward.

Similarly, Lu Xun implies that it is the knowledge that feelings turn "stale" as soon as we seek to express them in language that goads the writer to aspire all the more to an impossible purity of language. The broader idea here is of the asymmetry of life and art—between mortal humans and immortal art. This has long been an object of contemplation in Western and Chinese aesthetics. In the Western tradition, the Hippocratic maxim "Life is short, art is long" has attracted diverse interpretations that range from Hippocrates's original and practical comparison of one physician's knowledge with the cumulative art of an entire medical community; through Seneca's (d. 65 C.E.) moral injunction that because life is short, one must know how to live; to J. W. von Goethe's (1749–1872) Faustian notion of transcending the brevity of life in an eternal moment. This Faustian disposition encouraged the romantic valorization of artistic genius as surpassing time itself, such that the very idea of genius became associated with a short life and tragic death. In Harald Weinrich's elegant summation: "Art 'consumes' and so no energy remains to carry on a long life 'on a low flame.' "[135]

Although the "Literary Revolution" of the 1910s nurtured among Chinese writers a European-derived sensitivity to tragic genius (complementing preexisting views of tragic genius in premodern Chinese literature), the asymmetry of life and art was discussed in a mostly agnostic diction. The dominant Confucian tradition did not include a theologically mandated war between God and the devil; hence, even though Faust was well received in Chinese translation during the Republican era, the cost of genius, understood as a Faustian wager with the devil, never became a serious object of contemplation.

The Confucian classics provided a simpler and highly durable idea of immortality *(buxiu)* that influenced Chinese writing in the twentieth century and to this day. This is an idea about leaving one's mark on the world, typically presented as the transmission of moral excellence, and thus the Way, through the production of an exemplary corpus. Hence it is stated in *The Analects:* "The Master said, 'The gentleman worries lest he might disappear from this world without having made a name for himself.' "[136] The properness of this anxiety to leave a lasting legacy was rendered paradigmatic as the axiom *li de, li gong, li yan,* which conveys the sense that immortality consists in establishing virtue, establishing deeds, and establishing words.[137]

This Confucian aspiration to textual immortality gave impetus to the autobiographical obituaries of premodern elite culture that Lu Xun subjected to a radical reinterpretation in "The Epitaph." But as opposed to commemorating a respectable monument, Lu Xun enjoins us to heed the spirit of the ravaged corpse (a figure suggestive of his writerly self), to savor its craving for the true taste of human emotion as a dissatisfaction that can never be relieved. As he suggests, it is this craving that animates literature, enabling it to keep alive and transmit something of the author's lived experience.

He presents a related idea in the preface to *Dawn Blossoms Plucked at Dusk,* his 1927 anthology of autobiographical stories to which he had earlier given the more prosaic working title *Recollections of the Past.* The preface was completed on 1 May 1927 as Lu Xun witnessed the ferocity of Chiang Kai-shek's "Party purification" in Guangzhou and learned of students' and suspected Communists' being rounded up and executed. He begins by noting that "when a person reaches the stage where memories are all that he has left, his career has probably become pointless, but there are also situations in which people find themselves utterly bereft of memories." To explain the change of title, Lu Xun wrote that he wanted to convey something of the elusiveness of lived experience and memory:

Of course plucked flowers with the dew still on them are far brighter and more fragrant, but these are not available to me. And so it is with the alien and confused feelings that entangle me at this time. I am not yet able to magically transmute these feelings into a literary composition. Perhaps, one day when I'm looking at the drifting clouds above, I may get a glimmer of how it can be done.

For a time I kept recalling the vegetables and fruits I ate as a child in my old home: caltrops, broad beans, bamboo shoots, muskmelons. So succulent, so delicious were they all, they beguiled me into longing for my old home. Later, tasting these things again after a protracted absence, I found them nothing special. It was only in my memory that they retained their old flavor. They may keep on deceiving me my whole life long, making my thoughts turn constantly to the past.[138]

In this passage Lu Xun extends the idea of literature as a craving for "original taste" to suggest that an intense memory can so transform an otherwise ordinary flavor that one becomes captive to a taste "so succulent, so delicious" even as one knows it to be a fiction. Moreover, by setting these lines in juxtaposition to the "alien and confused feelings" aroused in him by the brutal slaughter then under way, he implies that the act of bearing witness to mass murder follows a similar logic but in grotesque opposition to happy childhood recollections. In these two adjacent paragraphs—the first a tacit commemoration of lives brutally cut short and the second a remembrance of favorite childhood foods—Lu Xun stages an unsettling proximity of the barbarous to the civilized. Both, he implies, have their own unique texture. In counterposing the inarticulate horror of witnessing inhuman acts to the sheer delight of recalling childish pleasures, he implies that an ethics of memory requires these discordant intensities to be recorded together as integral aspects of his lived experience.

On 23 August 1936, a by then terminally ill Lu Xun completed the essay "This Too Is Life," in which he reflected wistfully on the thinking behind traditional Chinese gastronomy. Of the "ancient Chinese predilection for possessing 'the whole' of something," he wrote: "And so, those 'black chicken pills' in aid of women's health are made up of all parts of the chicken, including the feathers and blood. Although this method is patently ridiculous, the idea behind it is not without merit." The merit, as he goes on to discuss, inheres in the preservation of a sense of organic unity. In the next sentence he compares this idea of holistic nutrition to a botanical image of natural literary development, warning: "Those who eradicate the branches and leaves will most definitely not obtain flowers and fruit."[139]

These remarks reflect a distinct amelioration of the hatred Lu Xun professed early in his career for the "cannibalism" of the "old society." In his later life, as this and several other essays of the 1930s indicate, he emphasized the need to bind the old and the new in a holistic approach to inquiry. In "This Too Is Life," he proceeds from his initial remarks about partaking of "the whole" to comment critically on a short essay promoting patriotic feeling that had just appeared in the *Spring and Autumn Annals* supplement of the newspaper *Shen bao* (in which he also regularly published). The piece, published in the "Tidbits" *(diandi)* column of 12 August 1936, featured the statement: "When a very round watermelon is being carved up, I am immediately struck by how similar it is to the future carving up of the world into ever more colonies." Lu Xun's response illustrates his meticulous use of gastronomic tropes:

> We are asked to think as we eat the watermelon that our territory is being carved up just like the watermelon. Naturally, it goes without saying that we must be patriotic at all times, no matter where we are or what we are doing. But if you want me to think like this while I'm eating the watermelon, I'm afraid I wouldn't be able to swallow. Even if I were to force myself to swallow the watermelon, I wouldn't be able to digest it properly, and it would rumble away in my stomach for the better part of the day. This may have nothing to do with the fact that my illness has left me with a bad case of nerves. I suspect that a person who uses the watermelon as an analogy when holding forth on national humiliation to then promptly eat a watermelon with gusto for his own physical nourishment is somewhat numb to emotions. No amount of lecturing will have any effect on such a person.
>
> . . . I ask myself: If a warrior were to eat a watermelon, would he partake of this ritual of thinking as he eats? I suspect this has never happened. Most likely, he would eat the watermelon to quench his thirst and because it tastes good. I'm sure he wouldn't be thinking about some or other fine-sounding grand truth. Eating the watermelon lifts his spirits and allows him to fight differently from when his throat is parched. So there's clearly a connection between eating the watermelon and resisting the enemy, but this has nothing to do with the strategies worked out in Shanghai on how we should think. If throughout the day we eat and drink teary-faced, it won't be long before we lose our appetite altogether. What use then will we be in resisting the enemy?[140]

In this passage Lu Xun not only calls for an ethics of literary representation. He also implies that such an ethics must be cultivated from within, so that a writer's sensitivity to the affective powers of language becomes a reflection of his moral character. Accordingly, a person who blithely mixes metaphors of humiliation and nutrition is impervious to the instructive power of disgust as a moral emotion. The Russian poet Osip Mandelstam (1891–1938) made a similar point when he indicted the grotesque brutality of Stalin's regime in the concluding line of his "Stalin Ode": "Whenever he's got a victim, he glows like a broadchested Georgian munching a raspberry."[141]

In contrasting an irresponsible use of the watermelon trope with the nutrition of the actual fruit, Lu Xun was also making a final appeal. Close to death, he invoked the figure of the warrior one last time, urging his readers to acquire a discerning appetite for revolutionary fare: to eat well in order to live and fight another day. In this context, it is worth noting that in present-day Sinophone discourse, a phrase Lu Xun once used as a somatic figuration of human life, "fleshly vessel holding human juices" *(renrou jianggang)*, is frequently confused with the idea of "a soy sauce vat" (the conventional meaning of *jianggang*), used derogatorily to suggest that Chinese culture overwhelms everything it encounters with the one homogenizing and overpowering flavor.

The confusion began with an article written by the Taiwan-based writer Bo Yang (pen name of Guo Dingsheng, 1920–2008) in 1967, in which he described the worst aspects of Chinese culture as a "soy sauce vat" containing the combined powers of "the forces of erosion and the forces of stagnation," mixed with "a politics of enslavement" and "a malformed morality." This "soy sauce vat," Bo Yang wrote, brought about "a confused society in which the intelligence peculiar to man is put out of action or made to vanish without a trace."[142] Bo Yang's trope was inspired by a 1919 essay of Lu Xun's, in which Lu Xun had remarked: "it is a great pity that upon entering China, all foreign things seem to fall into a vat of black dye [*heise rangang*] robbing them of their color." In mimicking Lu Xun's proposition but replacing a "vat of black dye" with a "soy sauce vat," Bo Yang committed the type of category mistake of which Lu Xun disapproved: that of confusing the edible with the execrable. Nonetheless, the enormous popularity of Bo Yang's musings on China's "soy sauce vat," an idea reprised and extended in his famous 1980 speech "Chinese People and the Soy Sauce Vat," has obscured Lu Xun's original metaphor of a "vat of black dye." More crucially, Bo Yang's "soy sauce vat" (*jianggang*) has also indelibly corrupted Lu Xun's gently enigmatic notion of a "fleshly vessel holding human juices" *(renrou jianggang),* a phrase that appears in his elegiac essay of June 1934, "In Praise of Night."[143]

In this essay, Lu Xun begins with the observation that "people speak and behave differently by day and by night; in sunshine and under lamplight." He then eulogizes night as "a heavenly garment, dark and sublime, woven by Providence to envelop the whole of humanity in such warmth and serenity as to cause people unconsciously to shed their artificial masks and clothing bit by bit until, totally naked, they wrap themselves inside this limitless fabric that resembles dark cotton." At the essay's end, he likens the hustle and bustle of daylight to "ornamentation for the night, the gilded lid on the fleshly vessel holding human juices, Hazeline Snow on the face of a devil" to declare "the night alone is honest" and to confess: "I love the night, hence I write 'In Praise of Night' in the middle of night."[144]

The Ouroboric insight of "The Epitaph" allows us to see the displacement of Lu Xun's figuration of a mortal vessel of sublime experience by Bo Yang's derogatory image of a "soy sauce vat" as a case of the latter's "consuming" the former over time, in a signifying chain of language beyond either writer's control. This transmutation also alerts us to discursive potentiality as an "abyss" that accommodates "friend and foe, man and beast" alike (to recall the preface to *Wild Grass*). For this reason, it is important to commemorate the clarity and precision of Lu Xun's humanistic appetite.

The ethical rigor with which he employed gastronomic tropes is amply demonstrated in the 1934 essay "Forgetting the Taste of Meat and Not Knowing the Taste of Water."[145] This was a critical commentary he wrote about the festivities held in honor of Confucius on 27 August 1934. He quoted a news report about the celebrations in Shanghai as having attracted "more than 1,000 representatives of the Nationalist

Party" and featuring no less than forty Chinese musical instruments, ancient and modern, that were used to recreate the ancient *shao* music that Confucius allegedly loved. This musical venture was staged to honor a statement in *The Analects:* "When the Master heard *shao* music in the state of Qi, he forgot the taste of meat for three months."[146] Lu Xun remarked that since the performance in question was a modern interpretation of Confucian worship, forty instruments were probably necessary to transport Confucius into a state of forgetfulness of such contemporary culinary delights as shark's fin and bird's nest (as latter-day equivalents of "meat" in *The Analects*).

He noted that on the day of these celebrations in Shanghai, a tragic incident occurred in the drought-stricken rural city of Yuyao in Ningbo, when two men fought so fiercely over drawing water from the same well that one battered the other to death and was forced to flee. Lu Xun used these two synchronous events reported in Shanghai's newspapers to highlight "the gulf between superior and inferior persons." Criticizing the Confucian moral vocabulary of *junzi* (superior person or gentleman) and *xiaoren* (inferior person), he observed: "*Shao* music belongs to one world, thirst to another. Meat-eaters who forget the taste of meat belong to one world, thirst and fights for water to another." He then remarked mordantly that since Mencius reminds us of the interdependence and mutual responsibility of superior and inferior persons, such that "without their inferiors, superior persons would not be fed," inferior lives should thus be considered as valuable too. Consequently, they must "not be allowed to bash each other to death or die of thirst."[147]

The essay concludes with the biting quip: "And so, in addition to *shao* music that makes meat-eaters forget [*buzhi*] the taste of meat, we need another kind of '*shao* music' to make those who do not know [*buzhi*] the taste of water forget that they are thirsty."[148] Here Lu Xun plays on the dual senses of *buzhi,* substituting the literal *baihua* sense of "not knowing" for the archaic connotation of "forgetting" in *The Analects.* In so doing, he demonstrates the sardonic irony with which he embraced what he hated.

In the present-day People's Republic, the birth of Confucius is now annually commemorated with official pomp and ceremony. As official corruption under one-Party rule remains rife and fuels popular anger in tandem with rural hardships caused by prolonged drought, a bitter aftertaste of Lu Xun's call for quenching the thirst of the masses (as opposed to subjecting them to yet another kind of "*shao* music") continues to linger.[149]

6

Raising Revolutionary Specters

M ore often than not, people hate Buddhist monks and nuns. They also hate Muslims and Christians, but they don't hate Daoist priests. The one who understands the logic behind this understands the better part of China."[1]

This enigmatic text was one of the twenty-one "fleeting mixed impressions" Lu Xun wrote in September 1927. He gave fullest elaboration to the logic behind these lines in his 1934 essay "Discussing Writing from the Outside," in which he compared Chinese writing to a Daoist talisman:

> Because the written script was the property of the privileged class, it acquired a dignity not to mention a mystical nature. To this day, Chinese characters remain dignified, and we often see baskets hanging on walls carrying the injunction: "Every piece of paper featuring written characters must be respected and cherished." And so it is with Daoist talismans, which rely on their mystical nature to ward off evil and cure the sick. The thing about the dignity of Chinese characters is that dignity, in turn, is bestowed on the literate, such that the rise of an endless stream of new dignitaries could only pose a

threat to the stature of the old dignitaries. Moreover, with a growing number of literate people, the mystical nature of Chinese characters would be undermined. The power of Daoist talismans seems to reside in the fact that these objects have characters written on them. Since no one except Daoist priests knows how to read them, the priests most certainly want to ensure their monopoly of the written word.[2]

In accusing Chinese intellectuals and Daoist priests alike of exploiting their ill-gotten authority, it was Lu Xun's polemical intention to present Chinese writing as a foundational injustice, designed for the sole purpose of enslaving an illiterate majority to the whims and fancies of the lettered few. He argued that China's character script was difficult to learn and required such an enormous expenditure of time and effort that it excluded all but a privileged minority from becoming literate. Hence, he declared the time had come for its demise.

In its place, he proposed a new "Latinized" *(ladinghua)* script that he believed would be easy to master and that would both descralize the idea of writing and accelerate the spread of mass literacy in China. We should note that his proposal was partially realized more than two decades later, in 1958, when *pinyin* became the official Romanization system of the People's Republic. Although *pinyin* did not replace Chinese characters, its adoption by the International Organization for Standardization in 1982 and its current global status as the Chinese Internet's "input language" would have elicited an approving smile from Lu Xun's ghost.

Writing as Alchemy

Lu Xun saw China's character script as a "document of barbarism" masquerading as a "document of culture," to recall Walter Benjamin's famous statement.[3] He argued that centuries of dynastic rule had turned countless generations of ordinary Chinese into the witless victims of tyrants and their scholar-literati minions. He wrote that the character script became sacralized because it evolved in conjunction with dynastic rule and, as a tool of power, encouraged a fetish for abstruse formulations among China's cultural elite. Lu Xun concluded that, as the exclusive property of the literate few, the script and the discourses it engendered not only kept the Chinese masses illiterate but obscured their humanity.

The esoteric characters (fuwen) on Daoist talismans gave Lu Xun an effective analogy of dynastic power. Apart from signifying the authority of an initiated priesthood, these characters were surrounded by liturgical adjurations (mostly of exorcism) that mimicked the diction of imperial decrees. Similarly, Daoist priesthood became Lu Xun's favorite metaphor for intellectual elitism because it combined the roles of faith healer, medium, and soothsayer to evince a more flamboyant shamanism than the functions of Buddhist, Christian, and Muslim clergy. After settling in Shanghai in 1927, he frequently portrayed his contemporaries on both the right and the left as self-appointed shamans, contending with one another in the temple of commerce as they sought to woo converts to their particular "scripture."

He observed that his fellow leftists appeared particularly vulnerable to the seductions of their own incantations. For instance, in March 1930 he wrote that the phrase "a change of direction" (fangxiang zhuanhuan) had suddenly become de rigueur in the discourse of Shanghai's stylish literary left. The ensuing "hubbub" did not augur any actual change of direction but revealed instead a slavish imitation of leftist Japanese magazines, where the phrase had first appeared. Alluding to the kinship between revolutionary slogans and Daoist chants, he wrote that this was simply "the same old malaise of being dazzled by names without any interest in thinking things through."[4]

Yet despite Lu Xun's blanket condemnations of Daoist priesthood, the idea of alchemy central to Daoist magic—and the special expertise of the Daoist priest—was a source of inspiration for his own writing. Two forms of alchemy developed out of Daoism's preoccupation with immortality: outer alchemy (waidan), which involved the concoction and ingestion of elixirs of immortality; and inner alchemy (neidan), which turned on meditative techniques and the manipulation of qi to achieve self-transcendence.

Lu Xun regarded the former as reflecting a base desire for longevity among members of the rich and powerful, seeking to prolong their enjoyment of worldly pleasures. Upon realizing the futility of their quest, such people "build sepulchers to preserve their corpses, wanting to occupy one piece of land forever." And because this was among "China's highest ideals, when everything else has failed," "modern people are still in thrall" to this vainglorious alchemy.[5] Inner alchemy, conversely, finds an indirect echo in Lu Xun's representation of *baihua* as an ordeal of self-destruction undertaken in hopes of self-regeneration.

Lu Xun expressed this spiritual aspect of his literary praxis in a variety of ways, most notably in "The Epitaph." His remarks in a 1935 essay about the regenerative power of passion offer an insight into his perception of aesthetic experience as an act of active imagination: one that involves the alchemy of recovering from an ancient object its once living sense.[6] This was an essay he wrote in critical response to the literary scholar Zhu Guangqian (1897-1986), who had praised Tao Yuanming's (365-427) poetry for its sublime serenity. Zhu had likened the aesthetic effect of Tao's poems to the eternal beatitude of Greek sculptures and, in this context, declared that Tao surpassed "Qu Yuan, Ruan Ji, Li Bai [701-762], and Du Fu [712-770]," whose poems he accordingly dismissed as flawed by passion.[7]

In his response, Lu Xun wrote that Zhu's valorization of serenity was tantamount to setting "an abstract standard of ultimate perfection" such that "in art men fall under the spell of patina on bronze, in literature they are forced to lift lines out of context." He claimed that this disposition was fatal for the arts and could lead only to "a dead end." To illustrate his contrary preference for passion, he recounted an anecdote about a rich man he knew in Beijing who acquired an ancient *ding* cauldron "with an exquisite patina and an air of great antiquity." Unwise to the reverence for patina in elite circles, this man hired a coppersmith to strip the object of all traces of patina so that it gleamed brightly in his living room. Lu Xun wrote that while at first he laughed along with others at this unwitting display of ignorance, he soon realized that the rich man's action had taught him a valuable lesson:

> The insight I had carries no "philosophical connotation": I simply felt I was finally seeing something close to the real Zhou-era *ding* cauldrons. In Zhou times, the *ding* cauldrons were like our modern bowls, and, just as we would not leave our bowls unwashed for a

whole year, in their day the *ding* cauldrons would have been washed and cleaned until the metal shone and glistened. To put this in technical terms, they were by no means "serene" [*jingmu*]; rather they conveyed a clear "passion" [*relie*]. The fact that this kind of vulgarity endures to this day has changed the way I see and appraise ancient art. As for Greek sculptures, I've always thought that, in their present state, all that remains for us to see is "a mere plainness," one reason being that as they were buried in the earth or exposed to the elements across centuries, these sculptures have lost their former sharpness of form and radiance. When they were first finished, they must have appeared strikingly new, white as snow and sparkling. Thus, because the Grecian beauty we behold in our times is most likely not what the ancient Greeks regarded as beautiful, we should exercise our imagination to see it as something new.[8]

In commending an active imagining of ancient art in its original newness, Lu Xun valorized a communion with the human emotions embodied in art as opposed to objectifying art through detached aesthetic judgment. The Daoist undertow of Lu Xun's remarks is evident in his articulation of aesthetic experience as akin to seeing the dead as once robustly alive.

Some thirty years after Lu Xun, Umberto Eco made a similar comment about the Greek statues on display at the Getty Museum in Los Angeles. In noting that the Greek statues were actually good Roman copies, Eco wrote that the Getty's archaeologists had nonetheless taken great pains to ensure that the exhibits were housed in a structure emulating the ambiance of a Roman temple in all its "freshness," with an "air of being just completed."[9] For Eco, this discordance was an apt reminder of the contrast between the original polychrome appearance of the statues and their erosion into the classical whiteness of modern fascination. In this connection, Eco's remark "in the eyes, now blank, there was a painted pupil" offers, by analogy, an insight into Lu Xun's insistence on "seeing with eyes wide open."[10] Lu Xun would probably have been thrilled to discover that the statues did not begin their lives in unadorned white, as this fact would have enhanced the critical second sight he sought to promote.

In his essays of the mid-1920s and thereafter, when Lu Xun enjoined his readers to see clearly, he meant that they should discern in themselves and the world around them patterns of inequality and injustice normalized and internalized as accepted social conduct. Apparitions of the ancient and more recent Chinese past were often present in the examples he used to illustrate this sensory perspicacity. Thus, when mocking Zhu Guangqian's praise of serenity, Lu Xun remarked that Daoist priests across the centuries had similarly worshipped "things they could not see, that must therefore exist in some distant place." He insinuated that Zhu's effusive praise of Tao Yuanming resembled the Daoist chant "With absolute devotion to the Way, we worship the Great Jade Emperor of Heaven!" In the extravagance of their declared faith, such believers betrayed an anxiety brought on by the worship of abstract things; an anxiety they sought to drown out with loud chanting.[11]

To affirm instead an exemplary perspicacity of the past, in November 1934 Lu Xun cited the (1669) essay "Journey from North Shanxi to the Capital" by the late Ming-early Qing era writer Qu Dajun (1630–1696). He praised Qu as a true witness of his time who wrote with such plain precision as to also bring into sharper focus the destitution of the present day. Quoting a passage from Qu on the hardships endured by Mongolian and Han nomads on the road during the turbulent early years of the Qing, Lu Xun wrote that the seventeenth-century conditions Qu described—such as the unbearable stench of cramped quarters and the depiction of Han women carrying on their heads "willow crates filled with horse dung or charcoal," walking barefooted but wearing fur capes, "their hair coiled round their heads" and their faces unwashed—remained as lucid three centuries later. With a gesture to the modern poverty he had witnessed, Lu Xun added that the affective force of Qu's words might have even deepened over time.[12]

Lu Xun accorded immortal status to Qu Dajun's plain and sparse (pingdan) prose when he praised its enduring haunting power. If we read this alongside his 1927 statement that baihua's mission of restoring speech to a silent China was nothing less than the miracle of "ordering a dead man to live again," we see the outlines of an inquiry that takes language in deadly earnest as the prima materia for a regeneration of the senses. It was a sensory experience (as opposed to a dispassionate understanding) that Lu Xun sought to crystallize in his writings: a sense of language in creative action, connecting souls across time and place. He explored this idea in his commemorations of historical persons and events as specters haunting the world of the living. In relation to this aspect of Lu Xun's literary craft, Zhou Zuoren's remarks about the Daoist priest's talent for spotting ghosts are especially apposite.

Despite their political differences, Zhou shared not only his brother's commitment to humanism but his fascination with ghosts. In a 1928 essay comparing official and unofficial histories, Zhou likened the former to "shrine portraits of ancestors, which paint them all solemn and severe" while commending the latter for evocative accounts that "at times . . . make the observer let out a cheer." Like Lu Xun, Zhou sought an affective experience of history that would turn the reader into an active spectator capable of seeing ghosts and "marveling at the miracle of heredity." He saw history as a drama in which "ancestral repulsive features and shifty looks reappear after ten generations," in which "historical personages pop up again on the contemporary stage, as if they are spirits possessing a new body and keep you riveted." Zhou continued: "This terrifying pleasure is debarred to those who don't know their history. Someone well versed in history is in the position of the Daoist Supreme Genie, who could see through demons in disguise: no matter what a person calls himself, you can tell whose incarnation he is, and can find his prototype in ancient times, and trace his line in every period from the year dot."[13]

Zhou's remarks in this passage enrich our sense of what Lu Xun meant when he wrote that he carried on his shoulders "a collection of extremely ancient phantoms" and felt choked under its "crushing weight." This remark from Lu Xun's epilogue to *The Grave* is a corollary to a statement he made in a 1919 essay, "How Should We Be as Fathers Today?," included in this 1926 anthology. The statement (widely quoted to this day) was one that Lu Xun evidently liked, for it appears both toward the start and at the end of the essay: "Despite carrying an enormous burden of old customs and traditions, a person can nonetheless hold up the gate of darkness, bearing its weight on his shoulders, to let the children out so that they may enter the vast and bright world beyond and lead happy lives thereafter as decent and reasonable human beings."[14]

One particular phantom looms large here. T. A. Hsia (1916–1965) was among the first to highlight the striking resemblance between Lu Xun's image of a superhuman figure holding up the gate of darkness and the Herculean figure of Xiong Kuohai, who first appeared in the popular seventh-century work of fiction *Life Stories of the Tang Dynasty (Shuo Tang quanzhuan).*[15] The legend of Xiong Kuohai, widely known to this day among aficionados of Chinese chivalric tales and martial-arts romances, features a heroic outlaw of towering physique who fought against the soldiers of the tyrannical Sui Yang emperor (569–617). In Yangzhou, when he and his band of rebels were trapped by the imperial troops, an already weakened Xiong propped up the "thousand-pound" city gate on his shoulders so that his fellow rebels could escape. Having saved the lives of others, this physical giant died, crushed by the gate's ultimately unbearable weight.

Lu Xun invoked this much-loved legendary figure tacitly, without mentioning his name, so as to focus attention more fully on his self-sacrificial act. In doing so, he endowed cultural reform with a somatic dimension, likening the "darkness" of elitist *wenyan* to the "thousand-pound" gate that killed Xiong Kuohai. As he put it more plainly in 1930, "An ounce of reform attracts ten pounds of reaction."[16] Similarly, it was to highlight a sense of the dead and the living as inhabiting the realm of language in common that Lu Xun referred to Daoist magic as a malevolent ancient presence, haunting and distorting the psychic energies of *baihua* and "revolutionary literature."

A poignant example of other apparitions more affectionately recalled appears in his 1933 eulogy to Rou Shi. Lu Xun wrote that his late protégé's brusque manner and uncompromising disposition reminded him of Fang Xiaoru (1357–1402), the eminent Ming-era Confucian scholar from Rou Shi's hometown of Ninghai in Zhejiang Province, whose loyalty to the Jianwen emperor proved so unwavering that the usurper to the throne, the Yongle emperor, executed not only him but also 873 of his relatives, friends, and followers.[17] In summoning Fang Xiaoru to commemorate Rou Shi, Lu Xun drew on both the historical renown of Fang's steely resolve and the vivid knowledge of his gruesome end (Fang survived another seven days in jail after his mouth was slit open from ear to ear, during which time he continued to mock the new emperor in writing). In binding these two individuals across a temporal gulf, Lu Xun immortalized them as incarnations of the same psychic personality and, in this archetypal conception of history, turned them into tutelary spirits for the living.

Jacques Derrida's observation of a nuanced but vital distinction between (abstract) "spirit" and (fleshly) "specter" provides a useful insight into this type of literary conjuration. Derrida wrote, in the course of engaging with Marx's use of rhetoric: "The production of the ghost, the constitution of the ghost effect, is not simply a spiritualization or even an autonomization of spirit, idea, or thought, as happens par excellence in Hegelian idealism." Rather the ghost, as sensory affect, involves a "becoming-specter of the spirit" that requires "at least an appearance of flesh."[18] For Marx, according to Derrida, sovereign power induced "a surplus of hallucinations," subjecting a person to the "phantomatic appearance of the bodies—of the Emperor, the State, the Fatherland." In order to see clearly, this person must "get to the bottom of a purely imaginary or spectral flesh" in order to discern "the 'practical structures' of the world: work, production, actualization, techniques."[19]

It was a kindred interest in seeing the phantomlike appearance of power that inspired Lu Xun's conjuration of Fang Xiaoru as a specter of fearless courage in the face of a ferocious imperial wrath. But whereas Marx sought philosophical clarity on the practical structures of political oppression and social inequality, Lu Xun set his sights on their literary enactment. In his fiction and essays, he brought into view the varied dispositions, habits, and conditionings that traversed Chinese society as so many historical "presences," shaping people's lives for good and for ill. In this process, his attempts at retranscribing the ordinary Chinese appetite for the supernatural into an active imagining of justice are remarkable.

A Specter of Justice

In 1926 Lu Xun wrote the essay "Wu Chang: Life-Is-Transient" to commemorate one of Shaoxing's guardian spirits of the underworld as a particularly fond childhood memory. In recalling Wu Chang as an integral part of the street operas and temple fairs he attended as a young boy in Shaoxing, Lu Xun explained that the very name Wu Chang—meaning "impermanence" or "transience"—exemplified the creative powers of the so-called lower classes *(xiadeng ren)* in conjuring up a powerful image of mortal finitude. More importantly, he wrote, in Wu Chang's literal embodiment of the idea that "life-is-transient," the masses afforded themselves a consoling prospect of the afterlife as the realm of true justice, insofar as this summoner of the newly dead did not discriminate between rich and poor. In this context, Lu Xun quoted mockingly from his adversary Chen Yuan to highlight a contrast between ordinary and elite sensibilities:

The "lower classes" are simply incapable of producing a febrile witticism such as this: "At present, it is a narrow and perilous track that we travel. To our left there's a barren and boundless marshland; to our right there's an equally barren and boundless desert, while far ahead, shrouded in distant and infinite mists, lies our destination."[20] Nonetheless they have an intuitive and clear understanding of the road that takes us to our destination "far ahead, shrouded in distant and infinite mists": namely, seeking marriage, getting married, raising children, and dying.... Most of them—and I'm referring here to the "lower classes" of my unworthy county—have lived and suffered; they have been slandered and falsely accused. Over time, the accumulation of these experiences has given them the knowledge that, in the world of the living, the means for upholding "universal law" is left up to a single assembly of people, and, as they see it, that assembly is inaccessibly "distant and infinite." This is why they can't help feeling pulled toward the apparitions of the nether world. Most people consider themselves to have suffered some form or other of injustice. As for the "cultivated men of virtue" who live among us, they can hoodwink only the most gullible. If you ask the ignorant masses, they will tell you without any pretense to cogitation: True justice is delivered only in the nether world!

When you think of life's happier aspects, you clearly feel you want to go on living, but when you contemplate the bitter side of life, Wu

Chang's visit may not be so unwelcome and fearsome. Whether high or low, rich or poor, we invariably appear "empty-handed" before Yama, King of the Underworld. Those who were wronged will be rewarded and those who wronged others will be punished.... Wu Chang holds a huge abacus in his hand, and you can strike any number of venal poses but to no avail.[21]

Lu Xun completed "Wu Chang: Life-Is-Transient" on 23 June 1926, six months before his arrival in revolutionary Guangzhou and ten months before Chiang Kai-shek's purge of the Communists brought the "united front" to an abrupt end. This was a time of heightened enthusiasm for mass politics among intellectuals. Unwilling to hail revolution as the panacea to social ills, Lu Xun instead privileged the ordinary person's sensibility to justice.

Toward the end of "Wu Chang," he described the ritual enactments of this summoner of souls as projecting a personality that was "ghostly yet human; principled but not without feeling; scary yet lovable." He noted that whereas the Wu Chang of the opera stage spoke scripted lines, the Wu Chang impersonator of the temple fair was silent. His role was to trail behind a jester who carried a plate of food, the implication being that although Wu Chang wanted to eat, the jester denied him the food. Of this ritual scene of "Farewelling Wu Chang" during the temple fair, Lu Xun wrote that it conveyed the ludic nature of local funerals: that the requirement to prepare a feast for Wu Chang affirmed a common humanity: "Everyone likes teasing Wu Chang because he is so straightforward, likes a good debate, and has human feelings."[22]

Eight years later, in his 1934 essay "Discussing Writing from the Outside," Lu Xun summoned Wu Chang once more. In 1926 he had quoted the following lines, assigned to Wu Chang on the street-opera stage, as emblematic of the impartial justice delivered by the summoner of souls:

Never again will anyone be let off the hook!
Don't think you can shield yourself behind a wall of bronze or iron!
Don't think that being related to the emperor protects you![23]

In both 1926 and 1934, Lu Xun pointed out that Wu Chang of the opera stage uttered these lines in response to the punishment he received from Yama. This was a popular scene in the epic of the Buddhist saint Maudgalyāyana's descent into the underworld to rescue his mother.[24] Out of pity for his young nephew's grieving mother, Wu Chang had allowed the boy, newly dead from an incurable illness, to live on for "a brief moment." For this dereliction of his duties, and suspecting Wu Chang of having accepted a bribe, Yama ordered the summoner of souls to be tied up and given forty lashes. In 1926 Lu Xun wrote that Wu Chang's declared resolve never again to show leniency reminded him of the self-assuaging remark from the *Zhuangzi:* "Despite a troubled heart, one does not blame the whims of Fate."[25]

In 1934 he repeated the same lines from "Wu Chang" to exclaim: "Can our writers produce literature so human, so conscience-stricken, so law-abiding, and so resolute?"[26] This evocation of humanism as empathy, forbearance, and justice held together in delicate balance underlines the importance Lu Xun placed on self-accountability in advocating *baihua.* As the title, "Discussing Writing from the Outside," makes plain, he was an "insider" willfully positioning himself on "the outside" to announce the obsolescence of elite *wenyan,* the written language that constituted his very being. In reading Wu Chang as the property of illiterate "outsiders," he imparted to their spoken language an authenticity and dignity he saw as lacking among the elite initiates of written Chinese.

Humanizing Language

To heighten the plight of the illiterate and barely literate in this 1934 essay, Lu Xun reprised the image of the "iron house." He lamented that the popular primer, *One Thousand Characters for Common Instruction,* turned the working poor into the inmates of "a prison, which, to be sure, gives people a piece of land but imposes such restrictions as to fully confine their movements to the allotted space. There is absolutely no way for them to slip through the iron bars and run outside."[27] On one level, Lu Xun employed this analogy to highlight the limited uses to which 1,000 characters could be put: "barely enough for writing a ledger or a letter" and thoroughly inadequate for "expressing the things in one's heart." On another, he used it as a vividly negative counterpoint to the "Latinization" he proposed. Specifically, he figured the Chinese "square-shaped character" *(fangkuaizi)* as "a piece of land" and transposed the rigor of stroke-order and direction into an image of "iron bars." He implied that in contrast the linear progression of alphabetic writing offered a prospect of true freedom.

According to Lu Xun, "Latinization" (as the phonetic representation of spoken Chinese) had already shown some success in overseas Chinese communities and was a plausible alternative to the character script. He argued that as there were only twenty-eight letters used in a variety of permutations, the masses would learn to write in no time.[28] Lu Xun's vision was of a written modern vernacular that would evolve spontaneously yet remain sufficiently standardized to be used nationwide. Hence Latinized *baihua* would most likely evolve to reflect the predominance of the northern dialect, spoken by a majority of Chinese. In the initial dissemination of this Latinized written script, the question would naturally arise as to whether it should conform to a national standard of pronunciation or be adapted to reflect the various Chinese dialects. His preference was for the latter:

> Each district should represent its own local dialect in writing, without heeding whether it would be understood in other places. As the illiterate among us never used Chinese characters to express themselves, when they learn how to write using the Latinized script, there would be no risk of introducing a new evil. On the contrary, people who speak the same local language would enjoy the benefits of exchanging their views in writing and absorbing new wisdom. Naturally, we will also need some people to write useful books.[29]

It would be wrong to conclude from this passage that Lu Xun held a naïve view of Latinization, for he was at pains to reiterate that he was ultimately promoting a language whose future was necessarily opaque to him. It is much more plausible to read the simplicity of his remarks here as an intended literary effect. What he sought to convey was his intense yearning for a motility of linguistic form capable of accommodating diverse tongues and interests across the widest possible spectrum. Hence he proceeded from proposing Latinization to emphasizing the importance of adaptability in keeping a language alive. In this context, he warned against the dangers of a preoccupation with precision *(jingmi)*, noting that precision inevitably entailed the construction of complex codes that would once again direct the written script down an exclusionary path.[30] Although language must rely on some degree of specialization *(zhuanhua)* to facilitate the development of new syntax and vocabulary, overspecialization would prove fatal for linguistic evolution. Hedging his bets between methodical development and organic evolution, he remarked: "While the proposals discussed among a handful of scholars in their reading rooms tend to fail in actual implementation, it would be equally foolish to just let things take their own course."[31]

Lu Xun's endorsement of Latinization conveys a certain equivocation about the spontaneity of linguistic form as remaining inexorably contingent on the institutional nature of writing. Nonetheless, he was unequivocal in opposing any assumption of cultural or vanguard authority on the part of the educated elite. What he affirmed was "human language," a notion that he explored in 1933 in an essay of that title.

The essay begins with a scene from the children's story "Little Johannes" (by the Dutch writer Frederik van Eeden [1860–1932], which Lu Xun had translated in 1927), in which Johannes encounters a pair of quarreling mushrooms. In the mushrooms' alarmed response to the child's interjection that they were merely two different poisonous species ("Are you human? This is what a human would say!") Lu Xun gave a new twist to the adage "One man's meat is another man's poison," using it to highlight the contingency of language on the speaker's position and the power he commands. He noted that the mushrooms were smart enough to recognize that "poison" was meaningful only in the vocabulary of mushroom-eaters.[32]

In this manner, he set the scene for the argument he proceeded to present: namely, the "human" is fragile, open to interpretation and habitually under the sway of power. Lu Xun began by noting that in the language of science, "the human" typically acquired meaning in opposition to the nonhuman. He wrote that the distinction was by no means straightforward, because humans were prone to turn a natural phenomenon into a source of moral instruction and that even J. H. Fabre's (1823–1915) *Souvenirs entomologiques* was not free of this flaw. Lu Xun then quoted from a Chinese article that he had recently read on the bird-dung spider and the mantis: "In the animal kingdom, there are many creatures that feed savagely on their own husbands but the aforementioned spider and mantis we are about to discuss are the most famous among them." He remarked that writers often commit the fatal error of condemning the creatures of the natural world when the habits of these creatures offend human sensibilities. He surmised that this unfortunate moralizing tendency was inherent in "human language."[33]

Lu Xun then drew attention to the heterogeneous nature of "human language," noting such varieties as "English human language," "Chinese human language," "upper-class Chinese human language," and "lower-class Chinese human language." The true object of Lu Xun's criticism occupies the final two paragraphs of the essay, in which he retold a popular joke circulating in elite circles about a peasant woman who, as she toiled under a fierce midday sun, wishfully exclaimed, "The empress doesn't know what a merry life she leads. If she's not still in bed at this time, she must be calling out, 'Eunuch, bring me a dried persimmon!'"[34]

Lu Xun observed that the joke (centered on the woman's oblivion to the end of dynastic China) reflected a typical disrespect for the masses in the language of China's "upper class." He continued: "It is likely that no 'lower-class Chinese' said anything like this, but even if they had, it would not have been said as a joke." Noting that he had nothing more to add, for fear of "all the bother about class and literature," he observed that people who write books as if they were instructing the young must naturally think that they are producing "human language." He ended with a series of ironic interrogations: "But I wonder what kind of 'human language' they are using. Why don't they write for people who are more advanced in years? Do they think older people are not worth teaching? Or is it simply that the young are just more pure and honest and hence easier to hoodwink?"[35]

In "Human Language," Lu Xun juxtaposed the verdicts delivered on mushrooms and insects with the judgments made of the "lower class" by the "upper class." He did so to draw attention to the paternalism of the educated Chinese person's habits of language. He suggested that Chinese intellectual discourse was captive to a tutelary impulse, such that the lettered found themselves predisposed to writing in an instructive mode, as if they were only ever addressing "the young."

Given Lu Xun's own references to writing in aid of "saving the children" or clarifying young minds, and (even more explicitly) of "clearing the minds and intensifying the feelings of honest and innocent young people,"[36] it makes sense to read in his closing remarks a self-reflective criticism of the inherited paternalism in his own discourse. This was a paternalism he consciously avoided in his conjurations of such plebeian specters as Wu Chang. In these instances, he positioned himself as an adult seeking instruction from his childhood memories, dwelling at length on how the culture of the poor captivated him as a young boy in Shaoxing.

He reserved an instructive tone specifically for criticizing elite culture, which he customarily presented as contrived and hypocritical. In compositions like "Wu Chang," he attributed an honest creativity to the discourse of the poor. He also sometimes sought to impart an acoustic experience of "the masses," to accentuate the absence of this *vox populi* from Chinese intellectual discourse. Most of his examples of common speech were chosen to highlight the educated elite's ingrained disregard for those less educated and powerless.

Hence, in repeating the joke about the peasant woman, Lu Xun's intention was to present a divided experience of her wishful lament. We first encounter the words as hers but are subsequently instructed to read them as an "upper-class" invention. In staging this ambiguity, Lu Xun suggested that the provenance was less important than the empathy required to hear the words as carrying two very different sets of connotations: namely, even if she had actually uttered them, it would not have been a joke but a genuine lament.

In his 1930 attack on Liang Shiqiu's valorization of "human nature" as the essence of literature, Lu Xun elaborated on the importance of heeding the experiences of the poor. As noted in Chapter 4, when accusing Liang of offering an insidious "upper-class" sentiment in the name of "human nature," Lu Xun wrote that the task of literature was clearly not to celebrate some abstract universal but to explore concrete inequalities that divided the life experiences of the poor from those of the better-off.

In this context, he likened human experience to matter, and writing to scientific experimentation: "Chemistry presents the nature of elements and compounds in their reactive capacity; physics reveals the nature of things in terms of degrees of hardness. To express the reactivity or hardness of a thing, you would need to compare it with something else. There is no magical method that would allow you to define reactivity or hardness 'as such.'"[37] The analogy offers an insight into his sense of literature as the work of discerning and expressing complex shades across the broadest spectrum of lived experience.

Years earlier, in his 1919 essay "The Road of Life," Lu Xun had provided an ethical defense of this literary orientation. The essay was written in praise of life as an indomitable force that "laughs and leaps about in the face of death, stepping over the bodies of those who have perished as it forges ahead." He ended the essay with a meditation on the enchantments of such lyrical pronouncements. Staged as a dialogue between the authorial "I" and "L" (a cipher for Lu Xun), the text literalizes the idea of self-examination. The authorial voice muses: "A person's death is a tragic event for him and his family, but it means little for the people of his village or town. The same logic holds when we consider the village or town in relation to a province, the province in relation to the nation, or even an entire race in relation to . . ." His inward interlocutor "L" intercedes at this point, stating: "This is the language of nature, not the language of mortals. You should watch what you say." The essay ends with the authorial self's acknowledgment of his interlocutor's wisdom.[38]

The ethical disposition demonstrated through this self-encounter draws implicitly on the Daoist insight into the "insentient" or "inhuman" *(buren)* nature of heaven and earth. The *Laozi* states: "Heaven and earth are *buren* and treat the myriad creatures as straw dogs. The sage is also *buren* and treats the people as straw dogs."[39] These dual connotations of the insentient and inhuman are recalled in Lu Xun's caution about "the language of nature." What he leaves unstated but clearly alludes to is the corollary statement in the *Laozi* about the sage who, in emulation of "heaven and earth," treats people like straw dogs. There are two ways of reading this statement. The more obvious (Confucian) reading is of a moral injunction against adopting an inhuman (literally, "unbenevolent") attitude to one's fellow humans. The less evident (Daoist) reading is of the sage as someone who is "impartial" rather than "inhuman": who recognizes that "straw dogs" (chugou), as traditional sacrificial objects of worship that are destroyed after the ceremony, evoke the finitude of human life as part of nature. This more nuanced reading of "the sage is also buren" provides a Daoist critique of Confucian hierarchism. Unlike his Confucian counterpart, the Daoist sage disavows all forms of human exceptionalism and accords respect instead to the finite lives of humans and nonhumans alike.

When Lu Xun cautioned against straying from "the language of mortals" in 1919, it was the negative (Confucian) reading of buren that he echoed. But the positive (Daoist) reading is a far stronger presence in his various acts of summoning specters. Here it is worth recalling that Lu Xun affirmed a "rough-and-ready" humanism in opposition to the mannerly discourse of his Crescent Moon rivals like Chen Yuan and Liang Shiqiu, whom he regularly derided as Confucian "gentlemen." He loathed their version of humanism and disparaged it as a spurious universalism. In this regard, Lu Xun's praise for Wu Chang registers a desire to pit against an abstract ideal the ghostly flesh of a fallible personality that is "straightforward, likes a good debate," has a conscience, and strives to be law-abiding and resolute.

Thus Lu Xun's essay "Wu Chang" directs the reader's attention away from mere cognition to a somatic experience of the human. After all, the word wu chang signifies nothing other than the common insight that "life-is-transient." In this act of incorporating the summoner of souls into his authorial self-projection, Lu Xun also enjoins the reader to partake of his language as an act of self-reckoning: to commune with Wu Chang as a specter that haunts every journey on the same mortal road unto death.

He wrote in his 1926 epilogue to The Grave that in the language of the supernatural he found an effective medium of critical introspection. Thus, to express frustration with his contemporaries for misunderstanding his baihua experimentations, Lu Xun wrote that he felt like "driving everyone away so that the few who do not spurn me are my friends: even if they are owls and snakes, ghosts and monsters, they alone are truly my friends. But if I lack even these friends, then I must travel alone."[40] He evidently liked this line, for he repeated a version of it two months later; in a letter to Xu Guangping on 21 January 1927 he told her that "reputation and position" meant nothing to him: he was happy to be in the company of "owls and snakes, ghosts and monsters," whom he considered his true friends.[41] Here Lu Xun implied that Xu (who called herself Lu Xun's "little devil") was an esteemed member of his select grotesquerie.

Of Revenge and Forgiveness

On 20 September 1936, one month before his death on 19 October, Lu Xun completed "The Hanged Woman," pointing out that he intended the essay as a complement to "Wu Chang," written ten years earlier. He stated that these two ghosts appeared to be unique to his hometown of Shaoxing and commented that whereas Wu Chang "simply put up with death without making a fuss," the Hanged Woman embraced death with a vengeance. Whereas Wu Chang reminded Lu Xun of death as the great leveler, the Hanged Woman enjoined him to heed the call of justice.[42]

He described her as a specter radiant with unbridled hate for those who had wronged her in life; who had chosen an unnatural death to end her suffering. She powdered her face chalk-white and dressed in bright red before hanging herself, thereby clearly signaling an intent to metamorphose into an avenging ghost. Lu Xun explained that her choice of color was "understandable" because "red possessed a positive energy [yang qi] that made it easier for her to approach the living," noting that this was essential for a ghost bent on haunting her persecutors and instilling fear in others. He observed that the Hanged Woman had such force of presence in local Shaoxing culture that women intent on ending their lives of misery often copied both her mode of suicide and her dress.[43]

He devoted most of the essay to recounting his childhood memories of the Hanged Woman, highlighting the special place she occupied as a key event on the street-opera stage, her entrance announced by the blare of mournful trumpets. He wrote that he had long forgotten the lines she sang, noting that even the one line he cited in the essay, "I was a daughter of the Yang family, ah me, unhappy me!," was a contribution from his younger brother, Jianren. For Lu Xun, what was memorable about the Hanged Woman was her appearance: her red jacket, black coat, disheveled hair, pitch-black eyebrows, and crimson lips rendered all the more prominent against the whiteness of her powdered face. She was, for him, the specter of the oppressed calling out for justice. He stressed that the female gender of this archetypal vengeful ghost was no accident: even though there was also the specter of the Hanged Man, his female counterpart commanded greater potency in the afterlife.[44]

Lu Xun nonetheless indicated that the Hanged Woman was subordinated to patriarchal power by describing a scene from the street opera in which she wrestled the Hanged Man for the soul of a new ghost to take her place, only to be defeated. He wrote that she was thus forced to rely on the pity of the Daoist Heavenly Guardian Wangling guan, who killed her rival so that she could "do as she pleased." Lu Xun remarked ironically that this ghostly official was, after all, "a fierce champion of women's rights." Here he also suggested that it was because the oppressed yearned so acutely for just redress that Chinese stories about the "lives" of ghosts were highly versatile, such that even the dead could be repeatedly "killed" in order that wrongs might be righted. Lu Xun observed that "the one bad habit" of Chinese ghosts was their preoccupation with finding a "substitute" to bear their burdens. He concluded:

This makes their quest based entirely on self-profit. Otherwise we would be able to coexist with them in perfect ease. Since this is the custom, even the Hanged Woman is no exception. Sometimes she is so fixed on "seeking a substitute" that she forgets to take revenge. In Shaoxing, most people cook rice in an iron pot over coal or straw. Once the soot accumulates, the pot loses its receptivity to heat. Hence we often find soot scrapings on the ground. The soot is always scattered, because no village woman would dare take the more convenient path of simply turning the pot upside down on the ground to scrape off the soot, for this would form a black circle. The reason for this is to prevent the spirits of the hanged from turning the soot circle into a noose to lure and trap the living. Scattering the soot is a form of passive resistance, but the aim is merely to guard against being turned into a "substitute" and not out of fear that she seeks revenge. Insofar as the oppressed do not set out to take revenge, they are not burdened with the fear of being the target of revenge: this fear belongs to murderers and their lackeys who surreptitiously feed on the flesh and blood of others. Hence the latter are wont to offer such advice as "Don't repay evil for evil" or "Let bygones be bygones." This year I have seen more clearly into the mysteries of these creatures with human faces.[45]

In summoning the Hanged Woman so close to his own death, Lu Xun clearly intended to turn her into a parting image of his critical inquiry. The idea of conjoining revenge and death also framed the essay titled "Death," which he wrote a fortnight before "The Hanged Woman." In "Death," Lu Xun sought to put his worldly affairs in order (he knew his tuberculosis was incurable and the end was imminent): in it he published his instructions so that his family, friends, and protégés were left in no doubt about his wishes, and he also dwelt on his own fascination with the intricacies of Chinese ghost stories.

Reprising the theme of the afterlife as the sole prospect of justice for the oppressed, he wrote that whereas the Buddhist idea of transmigration inspired the poor to yearn for rebirth into a better life, its impact on those who were comfortably off (xiaokangzhe) was entirely different. The comfortably off were complacent and sought nothing more than to maintain the status quo: hence "they would see an advantage in remaining as ghosts" so long as there were no disruptions to their way of life. For his own part, he belonged to the category of persons who would go "without making a fuss" (suisuibianbian); who "would not think too much upon it even when the end is near."[46] Two weeks later he used "without making a fuss" in "The Hanged Woman" to describe Wu Chang, to evoke an equanimity about passing on, in emulation of his favorite childhood ghost.[47]

But Lu Xun made clear that his wish to go quietly was entirely separate from what he wanted for his textual afterlife. Accordingly, having dedicated most of "Death" to discussing his practical thoughts and wishes, he devoted the last two paragraphs to a consideration of his critical legacy. He wrote that a bout of delirium had caused him to think about the European tradition of a dying person's begging forgiveness from the people he had wronged and forgiving those who had wronged him. As he lay feverishly ill, he wondered what reply he would give to someone who asked his view on this. He considered the many enemies he had made and then answered his hypothetical interviewer: "Let them continue hating me; I shall not forgive any one of them." He noted that as he pondered this scenario in the midst of his fever, he was struck by the painlessness of his condition, and thought that if this was what dying felt like, it wasn't too bad. He ended with these words: "But then there was a change, and my condition improved. Hence, I now think that the state I was in and the thoughts I had might not be true of a person actually facing death. As to what one ultimately encounters, I have no idea."[48]

While these final quotidian remarks belong to the mortal author, the declared intent never to forgive any of his enemies (so as to fan their continued hatred) bespeaks an aspiration to immortality. Two weeks later he provided an allegorical elaboration of this intent in "The Hanged Woman." We must also read "The Hanged Woman" against Lu Xun's remark in "Death" that his rapidly deteriorating condition lent urgency to his considerations as to what he should write or translate in the amount of time remaining to him. He clearly entrusted this apparition with an intensity of will, calling her a "creation" of the "ordinary people of Shaoxing" with "a vengeful nature; even more beautiful and far stronger than all the other ghosts."[49]

In brief, Lu Xun turned the Hanged Woman into a sensory figure of hope. He invested her with a spark of revolutionary desire, so that she might haunt the living with the rage of the oppressed dead. What he intended was a literary experience of horripilation, a hair-raising visualization of dissatisfaction, writ large in the redness of the Hanged Woman's garb, her white complexion, and, last but not least, the outline of her noose that prudent village women knew to avoid. In expressing regret for the selfish preoccupation of Chinese ghosts with finding "substitutes," he cautioned against conflating the Hanged Woman with justice. He wanted readers to empathize with this ghost but also to remind themselves that she remained a captive of the very same system that denied her justice.

In this final conjuration of his favorite emotion, Lu Xun suggests that while revenge offers inspiration, it does not deliver justice. He also implies that justice will come only when revenge and forgiveness become equally unnecessary, because "murderers and their lackeys" will have ceased to exist. In this regard, the Hanged Woman recalls the punitive intensity that Lu Xun described as "intoxication and ecstasy" in the first of his "Revenge" prose poems in *Wild Grass*. The second of these poems presents the critical impetus behind Lu Xun's notion of revenge.

In "Revenge II," Lu Xun offers his interpretation of the scene of Christ's crucifixion. He begins by recounting the bare facts of the accusation and subsequent torture of Jesus for "thinking himself the Son of God." He avoids mentioning the name of Jesus, referring to the crucified person throughout only as "he." In so doing, he generalizes the crucifixion as a scene of execution, focuses attention on Jesus as a man in agony, and proceeds to imagine his thoughts as he suffered on the cross. He [Jesus] refused the wine mixed with myrrh in order to "savor with absolute clarity how the Israelites were treating the Son of God"; he did this "to prolong the pity he had for their future even as he hated their present." As [Jesus] looked upon "these accursed men" who were "crucifying their very own Son of God," he found "comfort in pain." Lu Xun reinforces this emotional paradigm of pity mixed with hate through a series of alternative formulations and then quotes in transliteration the cry: "Eli, Eli, lama sabachthani?" He ends with the assessment:

> God indeed has forsaken him and so ultimately he is the "Son of Man," but even as the "Son of Man," the Israelites have crucified him all the same.
>
> Upon those who crucify the "Son of Man," the stain and stench of blood is far greater than upon those who crucify the "Son of God."[50]

"Revenge II" presents an entirely different emotional configuration from the first "Revenge" poem. Whereas the first poem centers upon the bond of hate that forever feeds the unique relationship between two sworn enemies, the second suggests that revenge requires an acknowledgment of the enemy as a fellow human; that those who fail to do so can only grow more barbarous with "the stain and stench of blood" and become inhuman in the process. What is tellingly absent from the second poem is the Christian message of forgiveness central to the crucifixion. Lu Xun's deliberate omission of Jesus crying out "Father, forgive them, for they know not what they do" reflects his disbelief that the crucified Christ performed this redemptive act.

In his secular yet distinctly spiritual reading of the crucifixion, Lu Xun presents Jesus agnostically as the Son of Man but nonetheless respects the Christian claim that he is the Son of God. It is the despairing cry "My God, my God, why have you forsaken me?" that Lu Xun finds moving, for it allows him to commemorate Jesus as a visionary who (as the self-declared Son of God) remained true to his belief and hence, even as he was dying on the cross, was capable of both pitying and hating his persecutors *as humans.*

Another text in *Wild Grass,* "The Kite," written as an autobiographical confession, offers further insight into Lu Xun's unease with forgiveness. The narrator recounts a childhood injustice committed against his younger brother and recounts how, some twenty years later, the memory of his thoroughly malicious destruction of his brother's beloved kite came back to haunt him. Seeking relief from the guilt of having "willfully wounded another's spirit," he begs his brother's forgiveness.[51]

The narrator states he had imagined redemption in the form of his brother's saying, "I don't blame you at all," and was taken aback when his brother smiled instead with puzzlement and asked, "Did that really happen?" This response leads the narrator to ponder whether forgiveness is possible if the injured person does not even remember the crime: "To forgive without having felt hatred is tantamount to telling a lie."[52] Undoubtedly what troubled him about the passion of Christ was that if the redeemer bore no hatred toward his crucifiers, and if they in turn felt no guilt, what purpose did his forgiveness serve?

Lu Xun found himself on surer ground in relation to the sufferings of the common man. The final paragraphs of his novella *The True Story of Ah Q* offer an alternative scene of execution: one in which, unlike

Christ, the illiterate victim is a thoroughly flawed character who lacks the purpose and vision necessary for a true passion. In this text, via the device of "seeing" with Ah Q's eyes, Lu Xun offers an insight into the assembled crowd as a collective predator. As Ah Q faced the spectators on the execution ground, he

> suddenly became ashamed of his lack of spirit because he had not sung any lines from an opera. Ideas turned in his mind like a whirlwind: *The Young Widow at Her Husband's Grave* isn't grand enough; "I regret having killed . . ." in *The Battle of Dragon and Tiger* lacks impact; so that leaves "Steel mace in hand, I shall trounce you." But when he wanted to raise his hand, he remembered that they were bound together and so did not sing "Steel mace in hand" either.
>
> "In twenty years I shall be another . . ." In a state of panic Ah Q uttered half a saying he had never used before, as if he somehow knew it even though no one had taught it to him [*wushi zitong*]. The crowd's roar, "Good!," sounded like the growl of a wolf. . . .
>
> So Ah Q took another look at the shouting crowd. . . .
>
> Now he saw eyes more terrible even than the wolf's, dull yet penetrating eyes that, having devoured his words, still seemed eager to devour something beyond his flesh and blood. And these eyes kept following him at a set distance.[53]

Here Lu Xun presents the macabre theater of a condemned man anxious to heighten the audience's enjoyment of his own execution with a timely crowd-pleaser from the local operatic repertoire. Like the "madman" who launched Lu Xun's literary career, Ah Q realizes too late, in the final anguished moments of his life, the magnitude of the predatory force he confronts in the eyes of the crowd, whose eyes are "more terrible even than the wolf's."

More crucially, in drawing attention to Ah Q's newly acquired sense of being "devoured" by tradition, Lu Xun bestows upon him a leap of self-awareness. It is no revolutionary leap, but Ah Q nonetheless attains for the first time a critical distance from the crowd to feel the burden of the customary role expected of the condemned man. His performance anxiety offers him the insight that he is capable of uttering half a saying he has never been taught—"as if he somehow knew it." The clarity of this momentary insight sits in stark contrast to Ah Q's narcissistic delusions of "victory" that are presented in painful detail through most of the story.

Lu Xun sought also to highlight the absence of an afterlife for Ah Q. "Everything turned black" before Ah Q's eyes as he died, "as if his whole body were being scattered like so much light dust." Lu Xun accentuates this desolate effect by highlighting the spectators' utter indifference to the destruction of a human life. He suggests that it was Ah Q's belated insight into the crowd's predatory violence that deprived him of the will to sing a rousing aria. Hence, even in death he attracted the contempt of his spectators, who, as they dispersed in disappointment, dismissed him as "a wretch of a condemned man" and grumbled that they had followed him "over such a long stretch of road" for nothing.[54]

In reality, Lu Xun's unforgiving portrayal of this abysmal scene made Ah Q immortal. Moreover, when citing news reports of actual executions in subsequent essays, he focused on the gruesome appetite of the crowd, as if to reprise over and over the scene of Ah Q's execution. What he sought to highlight was the fetishizing of power he perceived in Chinese habits of speech and mind. In the spectators' demand for a display of bravado from the condemned, he saw an enduring "cannibalism" to which even the victims themselves remained enthralled. To these grisly depictions, Lu Xun posed the critical corollary in his 1923 essay "What Happens after Nora Leaves Home?" inspired by Henrik Ibsen's (1828–1906) play *A Doll's House,* in which he wrote:

> The masses—especially those in China—are always spectators at a drama. If the victim on the stage acts heroically, they are watching a tragedy; if he shivers and shakes, they are watching a comedy. Before the mutton shops of Beijing a few people often gather to gape, with evident enjoyment, at the skinning of the sheep. And this is all they get out of it if a man lays down his life. Moreover, after walking a few steps away from the scene they forget even this modicum of enjoyment. There is nothing you can do with this type of crowd; the only way to save them is to give them no drama to watch. The same goes for those who hanker after some earth-shattering sacrifice: there's simply no need; far better to wage a deep and tenacious war.[55]

In his twilight essay "Death," Lu Xun expressly used the line "In twenty years I shall be another good fellow," describing it as the signature tune of the illiterate condemned man whose craving for a better rebirth proves so intense as to render him fearless before death.[56] The parade of the condemned and the crowd's expectation of a few heroic stanzas evidently haunted Lu Xun as he approached death himself. Earlier that year, in an April 1936 essay, "Written in Deep Night," Lu Xun remarked that one of his contemporaries had, incredibly, attempted to dignify the brutality of Chinese executions by describing the crowd's reception of the condemned man's song as akin to "worshipping a defeated hero." Lu Xun wrote that he found the contrary to be true: what the crowd witnessed was "the favor of 'a successful ruler' who, by daring to let the condemned person speak, offers proof that he is fully confident in his power."[57]

He then compared the ghoulishness of murder-as-entertainment with "murdering people in secret" to conclude that, for the victims at least, the latter fate was far more cruel and tragic. In implicit commemoration of Rou Shi, whom the Nationalist government had executed in secret (earlier in the essay he noted that it was the fifth anniversary of his protégé's murder), Lu Xun likened being murdered in secret to the agonies that Dante depicted in *The Inferno*, with the added twist: "Given what I have read and experienced [since I first read Dante], I now see his portrayal as kind and honest. It was not yet possible for him to imagine the type of hell we have now, so cruel and tragic yet so ordinary that no one sees it."[58]

Language as Experience

Lu Xun wrote for a cosmopolitan Chinese elite (sufficiently well-read to appreciate his remarks on *The Inferno*) but with the intent of haunting them with a multiplicity of images and voices "from the outside." His conception of "the outside" was both political and spiritual: on the one hand, a valorization of the oppressed as bearers of human possibility and imagination; on the other, a commitment to celebrating the sensory powers of language as the very stuff of being human. Accordingly it makes sense to see his critical practice as wedded to the idea of a spiritual or psychic aura (*shenyun,* a literary term from premodern *wenyan*).

Lu Xun explored the relevance and import of "aura" as *shenyun* in his 1934 essay "Snow Everywhere, Swirling in Profusion." The essay's title, "Da xue fen fei," captures the economy of *wenyan*. In Lu Xun's day the expression was part of the educated elite's vocabulary and was commonly used to add a literary flair to the description of heavy snow. In 1934 the scholar Li Yansheng (1897–1973), an advocate of *wenyan* who attacked the kinds of linguistic reform that Lu Xun proposed, quoted this phrase in an article. Li was endorsing the view put forward in a recently published article in which the writer had claimed that the *wenyan* expression *da xue fen fei* was far superior to its *baihua* equivalent, *da xue yipian yipian fenfende xiazhe* ("snow everywhere, falling profusely, sheet after sheet"). Specifically, Li echoed the writer's praise of the *wenyan* expression for its "conciseness" and for being "possessed of an aura [*shenyun*]."[59]

In his riposte, Lu Xun wrote that the "language of the masses" he had in mind was versatile and open-ended and that, according to need, the language could borrow freely from *wenyan*, from *baihua*, and even from foreign expressions. He remarked that this was happening to the Chinese language in any case. Of *da xue fen fei*'s being used as an example of *wenyan*'s superior properties, he wrote that "there is something very fishy about the defense mounted." Noting that the *baihua* equivalent Li presented bore little resemblance to the image suggested by *da xue fen fei* (the original phrase "certainly does not carry 'sheet by sheet' as part of its meaning"), Lu Xun remarked that the result was a spurious comparison, "no more than a showy trick [*qianghua*] aimed at concocting an effect of cumbersomeness to discredit the language of the masses."[60]

He then explained his own understanding of *shenyun*, noting that in matters pertaining to the aura of language, it was especially important to heed the fact that "just as *baihua* has no direct translation into *wenyan*, similarly, the language of the masses cannot be directly translated into either *wenyan* or *baihua*." As for the expression *da xue fen fei*, in the language of ordinary people it would "most likely be captured in such words as 'fierce' [*xiong*], 'violent' [*meng*], or 'punishing' [*lihai*]." He implied that in the image's translation from the perspective of the rich to that of the poor, its aura would be transposed from a serene contemplation of heavy snow to a somatic experience of its impact. In this connection, he quoted a sentence from *The Water Margin* (the Ming-era classic written in the premodern vernacular), "It snowed so hard" *(na xue zhengxiade jin),* as "an expression far closer to the language of the masses today."[61]

In this 1934 essay, when Lu Xun criticized the proponents of *wenyan,* he used the term *qianghua,* whose connotation of "showy tricks" derives from the lexicon of Chinese martial arts. The combination of the two characters *qiang* (the modern word for "gun" but which once meant "spear") and *hua* (flowers) conjures up an image of someone brandishing a weapon, attempting to dazzle his opponent with a rapid flurry of movements. This is an evocative clue as to why he took such delight in mocking his leftist detractors for failing "to inflict a mortal wound" despite the literary guns, grenades, and cannons they used against him.

Throughout this book, we have seen how Lu Xun loathed and combatted the vanguard pretensions among his leftist contemporaries while maintaining his political commitment to the left. The tragedy was that for all his critical acuity and literary verve, Lu Xun could not prevent the rise of a Communist orthodoxy, though he was spared having to witness its more egregious forms under Party-state rule. In this context, it is worth recalling that in Chinese, "aura" can also be translated as *feng* (literally "wind," with the extended connotations of "manner," "style," and "trend"). The "Lu Xun aura" *(Lu Xun feng)* introduced upon the author's death was a lesser travesty than Mao's subsequent appropriation and subversion of Lu Xun, but it was a travesty nonetheless and one that was actively promoted by his widow Xu Guangping, among others.

Against Lu Xun's Ouroboric notion of writing as a compulsion to "consume" language that leads inevitably to self-dissolution in the boundless realm of language, the promoters of the "Lu Xun aura" sought instead to erect an altar to his polemical spirit. In 1939 Xu Guangping wrote a mission statement for the short-lived Shanghai-based magazine *Lu Xun feng (The Lu Xun Aura)* in which she encouraged readers to emulate his example. As David Pollard observed, she noted that "the intention was not to idolize the dead but to try to improve existing conditions, as he had done." Nevertheless her essay was, in many ways, a paean to her dead husband. In essence, she praised him for "being so protean," for having "led the way in so many directions that to be courageous, forward-looking, and self-exacting was tribute enough." Accordingly she averred that "the best prescription for dealing with the Japanese invaders, whose conduct was worse than bestial, was Lu Xun's forcefulness and steadfastness; he tore the masks off hypocrites, locked firmly onto targets and took setbacks in his stride."[62]

Xu's 1939 essay, however unwittingly, gave force to the sanctification of Lu Xun then under way, since, as his widow, her words served as a distinctive imprimatur. Her essay also reflects something of the "official history" genre that Zhou Zuoren mocked as "shrine portraits of ancestors, which paint them all solemn and severe." In 1959, under the sway of Party diction, she declared: "It was fortunate for Lu Xun that even though he was hoodwinked [by Hu Feng], he was consistently and thoroughly loyal and obedient to the policies of the Party leadership. Under the Party's leadership, he willingly served as a footsoldier."[63]

In "This, Too, Is Life," written in August 1936, Lu Xun recounted a brief exchange between himself and Xu Guangping when he was still bedridden but on the mend from one of the many bouts of fever and fatigue brought on by his worsening condition. He had awakened in the middle of the night and asked Guangping to bring him a glass of water. He also wanted her to turn on the light so that he could have a good look around him. He speculated that the alarm in her voice when she asked him "Why?" was "probably because she thought I was still delirious." He replied: "Because I want to experience life [guo huo]; do you understand? This, too, is life, and I want to take a really good look around me." After a tentative "Oh . . ." in response, she brought him some tea, "showed some hesitation, and then quietly lay down again without turning on the light." He concluded the vignette with the statement: "I know that she did not understand my words."[64]

We can only speculate why Lu Xun chose to write this statement into his textual legacy. He loved Xu Guangping dearly, as is evident from the 1933 publication of *Letters between Two Places,* an anthology of their correspondence from 1925 to 1932. Nonetheless, in 1936, as he felt the end approaching, he sought to record a gap of understanding between them on this particular occasion. In fact, several paragraphs later in "This, Too, Is Life," he reminded the reader of his unhappiness with Guangping for not turning on the light, noting that he brought the matter up with the people who visited him the following day.

Immediately after stating that Xu Guangping "did not understand" his words, Lu Xun described what he did see in the dark:

> The light of the streetlamp streaming in through the window gave the room a hint of brightness, and I was able to make out the familiar walls, the lines where the walls meet, the familiar pile of books, and, next to it, the loose drawings to be bound into a volume. The night outside making its progress; the infinite distance of remote places; a countless multitude of people—these are all connected with me in some way. I exist, I live, I will go on living, I begin to feel myself getting stronger, I now bear some hope that I might move again—it wasn't long before I fell into a slumber once more.[65]

With these lines, Lu Xun bound the experience of language to the experience of night while also recalling the sense of night as enveloping "the whole of humanity" (as he wrote in his 1933 essay "In Praise of Night"). When he woke the next day he "looked around in sunlight, and, sure enough, there were the familiar walls and the familiar pile of books . . ."[66] Here the device of suspension, which highlights the incompleteness of the sentence, suggests a profound absence: the nocturnal insights that daylight cannot inspire.

Lu Xun wrote these lines only twenty days after completing his stinging attack on Xu Maoyong (discussed in Chapter 4), in which he accused Xu of being Zhou Yang's lackey and of belonging to the category of people who "walk a crooked path"; who adopted the mien of a "revolutionary" to slander others as "turncoats," "counterrevolutionaries," "Trotskyists," and even "national traitors" but who themselves "use the revolution as an excuse to advance their own interests."[67] Thus, it is all the more important to note the sharp turn that Lu Xun took in "This, Too, Is Life" when he proceeded from contrasting nocturnal and sunlit observations to considering the plight of the famous at the hands of their biographers.

Having suggested that the familiar objects of a person's habitat appear much plainer by day, Lu Xun wrote that he frequently contemplated these objects "as a form of relaxation," noting that "we tend to trivialize and treat them as part of life's scenery, ranking them below the activities of tea-drinking and scratching an itch or simply not giving them a thought."[68] There is an evident affinity between these remarks and Jorge Luis Borges's (1899–1986) observation that we grow blind to the familiar objects in our midst because they "serve us like silent slaves."[69] Having recast the undistinguished nature of familiar objects as tangible proof of a human existence, Lu Xun likened them to the everyday events of a person's life that are mostly neglected in biographical accounts because they are hidden in plain sight:

> Just as our attention is drawn to the glorious fruit, never to the branches and leaves, those who write accounts of famous people tend to lavish attention on their peculiarities: such as how Li Bo wrote his poetry; how drunk he got; how Napoleon waged war; and how he was an insomniac. Nothing is said about how they did not get drunk and how they managed to fall asleep. In fact, a life devoted solely to getting drunk and not sleeping is bound to be cut short. The reason we can speak of a person's getting drunk or being an insomniac is because this happens only some of the time: at other times, he stays sober and goes to sleep. Unfortunately, people regard such mundane realities as the dregs of life and do not spare them a glance.[70]

Undoubtedly, this was Lu Xun's appeal to readers of the future not to turn him into a caricature.

Notwithstanding the decades-long abuse of his oeuvre in the service of state and institutional power, Lu Xun's vitality and the fleshly textures of his language continue to haunt his readers. But as he wrote in his 1933 essay "In Praise of Night," to see the legion shades that haunt the Chinese language, one must learn to read by a nocturnal light:

> Although we speak of night, it has its own properties of brightness and darkness. There is the hint of brightness, there is twilight darkness, there is the kind of darkness that prevents you from seeing your outstretched hand, and there is also the pitch-black darkness

of hopeless ignorance. Lovers of night must have ears to hear the night and eyes to see it. They must survey the whole of darkness even while standing in its midst. When a cultivated gentleman leaves a lit room and enters a dark chamber, he permits himself a leisurely stretch. When a courting couple steps out of the moonlight to stand in darkness under a tree, the way they look at each other quickly changes. When night descends, it blots out the transcendent, inchoate, terse, and agitated essays that the lettered and the scholarly compose on dazzling white paper in broad daylight. The night air reveals instead a pitiful plea, a bid to curry favor, a flagrant lie, an attempt to deceive others, an empty boast, and pure mischief at work—turning these qualities into a resplendent golden orb that forms itself around the heads of the uncommonly learned, just like the ones we see in Buddhist paintings.

This is how the lovers of night receive the illumination that night offers.[71]

Lu Xun's Afterlives

In 2009 an anonymous online commentator reminisced about first hearing "In Praise of Night" on *Keeping You Company Till Dawn (Xiangban dao liming)*, Shanghai East Radio's late-night talk-back show. This popular (and still running) show had apparently used the following lines as its opening theme in 1997: "Night is a heavenly garment, dark and sublime, woven by providence to envelop the whole of humanity in such warmth and serenity as to cause people unconsciously to shed their artificial masks and clothing; bit by bit, until totally naked, they wrap themselves inside this limitless fabric that resembles dark cotton." The commentator recalled: "Back then, there was no Baidu or Google, so I copied the words down one by one as I listened to the broadcast night after night. For the first time I felt that Lu Xun was not merely abusive; that he had also produced exquisite prose even though all that I knew then were just those few lines."[72]

These remarks illustrate the persistent image of Lu Xun as an aggressive polemicist even during the late 1990s, when "the Lu Xun spirit" of the Maoist years had long been displaced by diverse interpretations of his oeuvre. To some extent, the image of Lu Xun as a polemicist was one that he had actively encouraged. All the same, he would have been dismayed to learn that in death, his polemical writings (which he regarded as evidence of his revolutionary purpose) were first turned into an instrument of political violence and subsequently, in much of post-Maoist scholarship, reduced to an example of mere intellectual factionalism. Indeed, the epithet "the abusive Lu Xun" *(marende Lu Xun),* first used by his critics in the 1930s, remains widely used to this day.

In Deng Xiaoping's New Era, reclamations of Lu Xun's humanism occurred in the context of the "Movement to Liberate Thinking." This officially sponsored campaign, initiated in the late 1970s, sought to rally support among China's intellectual elite for the ambitious economic reforms then newly under way. But it proved so successful in "liberating thinking" that in 1983 the government made haste to rein in the increasingly passionate calls for humanism and individual rights by launching an "Anti–Spiritual Pollution Movement."[73] One concrete outcome of the "Movement to Liberate Thinking" was the revitalization of mainland publishing, which throughout the 1980s saw the release of many new anthologies and compendia of key articles and debates in modern Chinese thought and literature. In the Maoist era such reference materials were rare, and their circulation was highly restricted. Accordingly, their post-Maoist proliferation was enthusiastically greeted in intellectual circles as the return of reason *(lixing),* with the implication of intellectual independence.[74]

Among these types of publications, the 1981 two-volume *Selected Historical Materials on the Debate over "Revolutionary Literature"* became something of a pioneer in the effort to rebuild Lu Xun's critical legacy.[75] In the preface to this anthology, the unnamed editors stated that "the debate over proletarian revolutionary literature in 1928 has special importance in the history of modern Chinese literature," explaining that this was because it had been "subjected to vicious attacks and slander from the reactionary camp in recent times." Echoing the then nascent official posture of accusing Mao's widow, Jiang Qing, her closest supporters, and the disgraced and dead Lin Biao (1907–1971), who had once been Mao's chosen successor, of perpetrating organized terror while avoiding blaming the Chairman himself, they wrote:

For the last decade or so, Lin Biao and the "Gang of Four," motivated by their counterrevolutionary politics of attempting to usurp Party power, have totally distorted the historical facts of the debate over "revolutionary literature." With their talent for obscuring differences between the two kinds of contradictions, they created a serious state of confusion. This posed a grave threat to historical research into modern Chinese literature and educational work. To fully eliminate the poisonous influence of Lin Biao and the "Gang of Four," we have compiled these materials to sum up the lessons of history, to reinstate the historical facts, and to meet the needs of research and teaching. Practice is the sole criterion of truth, and facts will lead to the inevitable destruction of slander and falsehood. We believe that the historical materials contained in this work will restore the truth to studies of modern literature. As long as we proceed from practice, we will be able to evaluate the debate over revolutionary literature from a scientific perspective, based in seeking truth from facts.[76]

Though couched in typically wooden officialese, these editorial remarks marked a clear departure from previous representations of the debate over revolutionary literature. The anthology was clearly designed to reflect the diversity of leftist views during the late 1920s and to locate Lu Xun's polemical writings within the commercial currents of Shanghai publishing. In this process, the editors refrained from delivering a verdict on the debate, merely stating that they had selected 150 of the more notable contributions (mostly published in 1928 and focused on Lu Xun) out of a total of some 300 relevant articles (published between 1926 and 1930). In emulation of Li Helin's 1929 anthology,[77] they singled out the writings of the Crescent Moon Society and the *Contemporary Culture* anarchists as illustrative of "the reactionary camp," placing these separately in an appendix. Notwithstanding this lingering tendency to discern "revolutionary" and "counterrevolutionary" elements in intellectual discourse, the editorial preface's declared "scientific perspective, based in seeking truth from facts," was a decisive negation of the Maoist thesis of class antagonisms.

The year 1981 also saw the publication of *Studies of Lu Xun Outside China, 1960–1981 (Guowai Lu Xun yanjiu lunji)*, edited by Yue Daiyun, who headed the comparative literature program at Peking University. When recalling the anthology in 2000, Chen Pingyuan, literary historian and Yue's colleague, wrote that it proved "such an eye-opener" for mainland scholars that the essays of Sinologists like Patrick Hanan, Milena Dolezelova-Velingerova, and Toramaru Ito featured in the anthology remained frequently cited two decades later.[78]

Meanwhile Zhou Yang, whom Lu Xun had thoroughly despised as an apparatchik and dogmatist in 1936, had evolved by the early 1980s into a leading champion of humanism, specifically of "Marxist humanism."[79] From 1978 onward, Zhou was volubly critical of doctrinalism and, together with Wang Ruoshui, editor of *People's Daily*, and other collaborators, attempted to reconstruct "a genuine ethics of humanism within the ideological confines of Marxism."[80] In this process, when attacking the "Gang of Four" in tacit negation of Mao Zedong Thought, Zhou praised Lu Xun as his inspiration and guide.

In a speech published in the *People's Daily* on 27 February 1980, Zhou as China's newly rehabilitated cultural tsar expressed regret for not having accorded Lu Xun proper respect in the 1930s. Resolving to apply himself even more industriously to studying Lu Xun's writings, he enthused: "The cultural heritage that Lu Xun has bequeathed to us is the encyclopedia of our times. It reflects the vastness of his knowledge, intellect, and wisdom and provides us with a resource from which to draw without end. His singular and biting literary style remains an eternal model of emulation." To this speech Zhou gave the panegyric title: "We study Lu Xun because we want to forge ahead, following in his warrior path."[81] It is worth recalling Zhou's denunciation of Hu Feng to Lu Xun in 1936 if only to note that in September 1980 it was Zhou who visited Hu in hospital to personally confirm the news of Hu's political rehabilitation. By then Hu was mentally deranged: he had endured twenty-five years of disgrace and incarceration under Mao.[82]

These nascent post-Maoist uncouplings of Lu Xun from the Maoist "Lu Xun spirit" were often unintendedly ironic, since they remained heavily reliant on "New China Newspeak" (*Xinhua wenti*, a negatively inflected term that became popular among critically minded Chinese writers in the 1980s).[83] New China Newspeak (sometimes also referred to as Maospeak) was what the modern Chinese language, as *baihua,* became on the mainland, under Chinese Communist tutelage from the 1940s. As Geremie Barmé writes: "In its essence, New China Newspeak was and is used by the Party, its propaganda organs, the media and educators to shape (and circumscribe) the way people express themselves in the public (and eventually private) sphere, and to enable the party-state to inculcate its ideology by means of relentless verbal/written imposition and repetition."[84] Throughout the post-Maoist 1980s, the sloganistic formulations of the Maoist era lingered on in the official discourse; its diction was also plainly evident in the declarations of student leaders at Tiananmen Square in the heady spring of 1989.

By the 1990s, however, frequent pillorying had greatly undermined the authority of this state-controlled language, and the parodic writings of the Beijing-based writer Wang Shuo proved particularly effective in this regard. As Barmé has observed, Wang's novels were often nostalgic recollections of the "opportunities for sexual liberation, playing truant, and the joys of gang warfare" that the Cultural Revolution years offered to him and his adolescent peers. New China Newspeak made a frequent appearance in Wang's work as "a sincere and at the same time ironic revival of Mao."[85] Hence, with ribald wit, Wang lent weight to the official postmortem verdict that the Cultural Revolution had been "ten years of chaos," but in a rebellious streetwise manner that endeared him to the mainland reading public.

The fact that in previous decades Lu Xun's words had been forcibly embedded into Maoist doctrine produced in the 1990s an insistent querying and in some quarters a rejection of his authority. As Maoist discourse became, *pace* Lu Xun, the carapace of what was once (terrifyingly) alive, a desacralization of Lu Xun also got underway. A widely noted moment in this process was the publication in October 1994 of "Impromptu Thoughts about the Humanistic Spirit" by Wang Meng, writer and erstwhile minister of culture in the 1980s.[86] In the essay Wang, a staunch defender of Wang Shuo's novels, berated critics who had accused Wang Shuo of producing "hooligan literature" *(pizi wenxue).* Mocking their rhetoric, Wang Meng wrote that they lacked a "humanistic spirit" and showed distinct signs of "doctrinalism." He then asked sardonically:

> Where would we be if all our writers were to be like Wang Shuo? Of course this would not do. Wang Shuo is just one writer and quite far removed at that from a model writer or some supreme exemplar. If we expect all writers to become role models, then that could only result in the elimination of most. By the same token, would everything be perfect if all our writers were to be like Lu Xun? Absolutely not. To have one Lu Xun on the literary scene is a grand thing indeed, but if we were to have fifty Lu Xuns? Heavens!

Wang then repeated his disdain for Wang Shuo's critics, ending with the snipe: "What humanistic spirit could you possibly have if you lack even the slightest sense of humor?"[87]

The phrase "fifty Lu Xuns" was thereafter heatedly debated in mainland intellectual circles as marking a new irreverence toward Lu Xun. Critics of Wang Meng regarded his valorization of Wang Shuo's bestselling literature as highlighting a crossroads moment in Chinese intellectual life, in which scholarship and literary craftsmanship were under threat once more. They argued that if political "redness" had obliterated intellectual life during the Cultural Revolution years, literary commerce in the 1990s was proving just as corrosive. Moreover, they were deeply angered by Wang's parodic use of their favorite phrase "the humanistic spirit" to ridicule their criticisms of the marketplace.

In this connection, Wang Meng's jocular reference to "fifty Lu Xuns" was not critical of Lu Xun per se. Rather, it was his deft caricature of an entrenched habit among Chinese intellectuals to exalt a distinguished individual (indeed, as Mao did with Lu Xun) in order to demonstrate the nobility of their own cause. Wang's polemic hence deeply offended those who felt they were being personally ridiculed. As Wang's fiercest critics were younger than he, the vitriol they exchanged with their erstwhile culture minister led the acclaimed writer Liu Xinwu to liken the ensuing contretemps to the public quarrel between Lu Xun and his ambitious acolyte Gao Changhong in 1926 and 1927. Liu urged Wang's young critics to beware of becoming like Gao.[88]

When writing about Lu Xun in 2000, Wang Shuo reflected indirectly on this war of words five years earlier. Without mentioning the animus generated by the phrase "fifty Lu Xuns," he wrote that Lu Xun's fate in post-Maoist times was the result of his having been "elevated to the hilt such that he became a mythical personage." Consequently, Wang continues, "Lu Xun is ever surrounded by an aura of superstition and a barbaric force that exert such pressure as to prevent us from seeing him directly." Wang muses that this produced a situation whereby people enjoyed the thrill of saying something profane about Lu Xun once the "Movement to Liberate Thinking" gained momentum. He illustrates this with an example of someone he knew, who shouted in a drunken rant: "What's Lu Xun got! As for ideas, who's he next to Mao Zedong Thought? Mao. . . . at the very least caused the souls of three generations of Chinese to undergo a painful baptism," and so on.[89]

Wang Shuo writes that although he liked many of Lu Xun's stories, like everyone else he had been so thoroughly indoctrinated in the Maoist exaltation of Lu Xun, in which "attacking Lu Xun" was considered a serious crime, that he sympathized with the drunken person's put-down of Lu Xun, noting: "To dispel superstition and liberate our thinking, we need to first allow ourselves to act like jerks for a bit."[90] Reprising this idea toward the end of his essay, he remarks:

> Sometimes the praise heaped on [Lu Xun] from so many quarters leaves us with no freedom to breathe. I don't believe that he's as perfect as they say. There's no such person. . . . In fact, he should become a yardstick. If we're able to criticize him without making a fuss and let him fade from memory, then we'll know we've moved on. China has far too many myths. Mere mortals like me who desire spiritual freedom ought to first put out of our minds the idea of "a spirit of spiritual freedom."[91]

But there were many who found Wang Shuo's lighthearted portrayal of Lu Xun's accidental immortality and subsequent desacralization insufferable. He was denounced for attempting "to overthrow Lu Xun" and for "blaspheming against Lu Xun's revolutionary spirit." Zhu Zhenguo, head of the Writers' Association in Shaoxing (Lu Xun's birthplace), published an open letter in May 2000, rebuking Wang

Shuo among others for "disparaging Lu Xun." The letter was promptly followed by a seminar sponsored by the Lu Xun Studies Association in Shaoxing on the theme of "Opposing the Disparagement of Lu Xun" *(Fandui biansun Lu Xun)*.[92]

Meanwhile the 1990s also saw a surge of scholarly interest in reassessing Lu Xun's critical legacy and his polemical writings in particular. Luxunology was animated by the publication of several books and articles about Lu Xun's verbal wars with the Creation Society, Sun Society, and Crescent Moon Society. There were also numerous anthologies featuring the essays of Lu Xun's adversaries. Of these, Sun Yu's *The Maligned Lu Xun*, first published in 1994, is of particular interest, as Sun had substantially researched Lu Xun's polemics and his anthology featured a wide selection of criticisms and parodies of Lu Xun, including several that were published after his death.

In Sun's editorial preface, he wrote that he had produced the anthology to fulfill the maestro's unrealized wish. Lu Xun had first expressed an interest in publishing a collection of writings that attacked his person and his ideas in April 1932. This appeared in the preface he wrote for *Three Leisures,* his 1932 collection of essays first published between 1927 and 1929, of which the majority were polemical responses to the Creation Society, the Sun Society, and the Crescent Moon Society. Lu Xun wrote that a permanent collection of the negative criticisms he had attracted since the mid-1920s would form a vital complement to *Three Leisures,* and he proposed the title *Under Siege (Weijiao ji)* for this envisaged volume.[93] Lu Xun referred again to this matter in a letter of 15 May 1934 to the editor Yang Jiyun, giving the proposed compilation the modified title *A Decade under Siege*. He told Yang that as "reference material," it would shed light on the "strategies and motivations" of his critics and hence "would not be without benefit for readers of a future time" (using litotes to moderate the anxiety he evidently felt about his posthumous fate).[94]

In *The Maligned Lu Xun,* the majority of the anti–Lu Xun essays date from the period 1925-1930, a time when Lu Xun gave freest rein to his feisty wit, before he became encumbered by the politics of the Left-Wing League. Sun included a variety of other texts. Some were short and nasty rants against Lu Xun published (mostly pseudonymously) in the 1930s by pro-Nationalist writers, in which the main objective appeared to have been to undermine the League by claiming that Lu Xun was, among other things, "a quack selling fake cures," someone "barking mad," and "a traitor" (because of his closeness to the Japanese bookstore owner Uchiyama Kanzō and his fondness for Japanese works).[95] The book also featured Xu Maoyong's two letters to Lu Xun in 1936, the first of which goaded Lu Xun into writing a lengthy rebuttal; the second, a protracted self-defense by Xu, received no reply.

Other essays were by prominent writers of the day such as Shi Zhecun, whom Lu Xun regarded with contempt as antiquarian in outlook and a political conformist. Sun also included three articles by Yang Cunren (1901–1955), a Sun Society cofounder who publicly relinquished his membership of the Communist Party in 1932. Of these, an open letter to Lu Xun by Yang attracted a memorable response from Lu Xun, published in 1933 under the title "An Open Letter to Mr. Yang Cunren's Open Letter" (to which we will return shortly).

As for "malignings" perpetrated close to or after Lu Xun's death, Sun included a famous correspondence between Hu Shi and Su Xuelin (1897–1999), a female writer of note who became Lu Xun's most trenchant critic after 1936, as well as several essays by Zhou Zuoren that have long been suspected of directing a barb or two at Lu Xun. Sun's anthology was eagerly anticipated by mainland readers previously denied access to these texts ; Sun noted in his epilogue that several thousand copies had been ordered before the book's release. For decades, scholars outside the People's Republic had known that Hu Shi, in his letter to Su of 14 December 1936, had chastised her for showing extreme prejudice, noting that although he sympathized with her anger toward Lu Xun for backing the Communists, "there's no need to attack his personal conduct."[96]

Hu wrote that what mattered was critical engagement with Lu Xun's ideas and that a balanced approach was necessary for ascertaining the merits and flaws of his intellectual contributions. Hu also expressed regret about the animosity between Chen Yuan and Lu Xun, noting that it was exacerbated when Chen relied on malicious gossip to wrongly accuse Lu Xun of plagiarism. With a mild barb aimed at countering Lu Xun's numerous insults against the Crescent Moon Society, Hu wrote that Chen ought now to acknowledge his past error publicly because "that 'disgusting posture of the *gentleman*' is well worth adopting." He was of course mimicking Lu Xun's derisive use of "upright gentlemen" to describe the Crescentists. The term "disgusting posture" *(chou jiazi)* was also one that Lu Xun had used in referring to them in 1925.[97] Hence, in this letter Hu did not malign Lu Xun per se but used the occasion both to deflect Lu Xun's criticism and to record his own magnanimity for posterity.

Similarly, Zhou Zuoren's essays bore no malice against Lu Xun but rather expressed tacit regret about his older sibling's decision to become involved in leftist politics. A master of oblique prose, Zhou did not mention Lu Xun's name but left suggestive clues for the informed reader. For instance, he cautioned writers against "becoming so bowled over by literary theory and policy as to become forever unable to write creatively."[98] It was widely known that, with the exception of *Old Tales Retold,* published in 1936, Lu Xun stopped writing fiction by 1927 and devoted himself from then on to producing essays of the "mixed impressions" genre. Sun also included Zhou's famous composition "On Abusive Essays" (written six weeks after Lu Xun's death), in which Zhou did not criticize his brother but rather reprised his remark about being "a ladder."[99] It was undoubtedly out of sympathy for Lu Xun that Zhou coined the term "entrepreneurial abuse" *(jinqude ma)* to disparage those whom he accused of attacking someone famous in order to call attention to themselves.[100]

Occurring in tandem with these new publications about Lu Xun in the 1990s was a deepening of interest in figures like Hu Shi and Zhou Zuoren. Their writings, banned during the Maoist years, had resurfaced in the 1980s and were avidly consumed.[101] Thereafter publications comparing the legacies of Lu Xun and Zhou Zuoren, and of Lu Xun and Hu Shi, became highly popular. Beginning in the late 1990s and particularly in the 2000s, comparisons of Lu Xun and Hu Shi acquired an even greater importance; their names were now being used to defend or attack any number of positions across the political spectrum.[102]

During a brief period of loosened censorship from 1998 to 2000, the term "liberalism" *(ziyouzhuyi)*—once forbidden fare—was openly promoted in mainland intellectual circles, with Hu Shi being publicly hailed as the father of Chinese liberalism. But by 2001 the shutters had come down: the values of liberal democracy could no longer be openly espoused. Hence self-declared liberals resorted once more to a theoretical discourse (as they had done since the 1980s) to advance freedoms of speech and press as integral aspects of China's "market economy." A rift had also opened up in elite intellectual circles between these liberals and those whom they regarded as members of the New Left, who defended socialist values and argued in favor of an achievable social justice under one-Party rule.

As this internal dissension among China's leading academics and intellectuals deepened from the late 1990s into the early 2000s, a heated debate developed around whether it was Hu Shi or Lu Xun who provided the intellectual and moral guidance that China needed. Among scholars of Lu Xun, there were those (like Wang Hui) who affirmed Lu Xun's socialist stance, but there were others (such as Lin Xianzhi) who defended his liberal qualities. Still others (such as the widely revered Li Shenzhi) declared Hu Shi's path to be correct, thereby relegating Lu Xun to a lesser role.[103] Among those of a liberal persuasion, the Nanjing-based scholar Shao Jian warned against specious attempts to "liberal-ize" Lu Xun, and the cautionary phrase he coined in 2003, "Putting Hu [Shi]'s hat on Lu [Xun]" *(Hu guan Lu dai),* gained currency for a time.[104]

Throughout the 2000s Lu Xun remained a prominent presence in mainland public culture. The 120th anniversary of his birth in 2001 saw the staging of five plays (including the musical *Mr. Lu Xun*) based on aspects of his life and his best-known works. Of these, *Mr. Lu Xun* proved particularly contentious, for its director, Zhang Guangtian, well known for his leftist leanings, had chosen to celebrate in revue style not the writer's life but his "revolutionary spirit." Zhang, who had attracted considerable attention and controversy in 2000 with his ensemble theatrical production *Che Guevara,* explained in an interview that he wanted the audience to experience "a Mr. Lu Xun that we had created together." Hence "what appears on stage is most definitely not Lu Xun but rather an aspect of each person's inner sense of justice."[105]

Zhang's critics claimed that the musical not only reduced Lu Xun to an abstract and surreal figure but turned him into banal entertainment.

One critic accused Zhang of producing an incoherent "revolutionary show" redolent of Maoist symbolism yet culturally confused, using the term *geming xiu* (revolutionary show) to imply that Zhang's real interest was not Lu Xun but show business. Another described the musical as exemplifying the "demise of leftist thinking in 1990s China."[106] Nonetheless, Zhang also had plenty of supporters among fellow leftists. Among them, one wrote (in an eclectic mix of registers) that *Mr. Lu Xun* showed that "criticism of capitalism and sympathy for the leftist culture of the masses continue to enjoy a definite box-office value," claiming that this popular demand for Lu Xun furnished evidence that China's maturing market economy was remaining true to its socialist roots.[107]

The various excitements and polemical eruptions presented here constitute some of the "afterlives" of Lu Xun. These are conjurations and invocations of Lu Xun that rely on the appropriation and adaptation, quotation and counterquotation of words, phrases, and whole passages taken from his oeuvre. But more than that, they also reflect the intense emotion that his name and memory arouse. It is as if the mark of a serious engagement with Lu Xun, at least in the mainland Chinese context, lies in the excess of meaning generated. This is an excess characteristically presented as a demonstration of fidelity to the spirit of Lu Xun's language. Not surprisingly, such reverence is volubly expressed by those with an ambition to be publicly regarded as genuine interpreters of Lu Xun. Even Mao Zedong did no less. Although he turned Lu Xun into an integral part of his revolutionary propaganda, Mao attempted, in his own way, to honestly reflect the lessons he had learned from reading Lu Xun. As he told Jiang Qing in 1966, his admiration for Lu Xun was of an intimate nature, for he had experienced "a few tumbles" himself and hence fully appreciated Lu Xun's insight that "it is harder by far to dissect oneself than to dissect others."[108]

At any rate, the transmutation of Mao's admiration for Lu Xun into state-sponsored Luxunology ensured that from the 1950s into the 1970s, no high school or college student could escape the tutelage of "the Lu Xun spirit." Commenting on this schooling, Wang Shuo quips that although he had not the faintest idea of how to explain Lu Xun's intellectual importance *(sixiang)*, he could easily hold forth on the maestro's spiritual significance *(jingshen)*, noting that it would normally consist of such things as "using your pen as a javelin or dagger," "beating a drowning dog," "facing dark forces without the slightest compromise," and so on and so forth. Wang adds that he found quite poignant a remark Lu Xun once made about Sun Yat-sen because Lu Xun's admirers later used it to describe Lu Xun: "A flawed warrior remains a warrior; a perfect fly is only a fly."[109] As these remarks suggest, notwithstanding their enforced communion with Lu Xun's "revolutionary spirit" during the Maoist years, for many mainland readers, Lu Xun's writings nonetheless hold a personal significance.

In contrast to this intensity of engagement with Lu Xun on the mainland, on Taiwan the writings of Lu Xun were banned for more than three decades after 1949. As David Wang observes, censorship was at its most extreme in the 1950s, when the pursuit of "aesthetic hygiene" under Chiang Kai-shek resulted in the total ban of Chinese literature written between 1919 and 1949. He points out that skilled writers in Taiwan ensured that the modern *baihua* legacy survived despite these draconian constraints, noting that Chen Jiying's (1908–1997) 1950 novel, *Fool in the Reeds (Dicun shuang)*, was effectively the retranscription of *The True Story of Ah Q* in an anti-Communist context.[110] Given Lu Xun's profound antipathy to Chiang Kai-shek and the Nationalist party, it was not until the mid- to late 1980s, when Taiwan's democratization under Chiang's son, Chiang Ching-kuo (1910–1988), was well under way, that his writings saw the light of day. Even though Lu Xun was widely read in private during the 1980s, the public release of three separate editions of Lu Xun's collected works in 1989 generated much excitement and discussion in Taiwanese intellectual circles.[111]

But it is in mainland China that Lu Xun's legacy remains most fiercely contested. In 2007, when news spread that *The True Story of Ah Q* was being removed from the literature syllabus for senior high-school students in Beijing, a general hue and cry went up on the Internet. Rumors circulated that Lu Xun's story was being replaced with an excerpt from a martial-arts novel by the acknowledged master of the genre, Jin Yong (pen name of Louis Cha; Zha Liangyong, b. 1924), resulting in widespread bewailing of declining cultural standards together with the frequent refrain that a much-loved modern classic had been replaced by a work of "fast-food culture." Meanwhile, opponents of this view argued that Lu Xun was not only obsolete but also tainted by association with the Maoist past.

The editors of the new high-school textbook reassured the reading public that they had the students' best interests in mind.[112] Among the editors was Kong Qingdong, the controversial Peking University academic who rose to fame with his popular 2006 television series on Lu Xun.[113] Kong explained that the selection from Jin Yong's *kung-fu* novel appeared only in the teachers' reference book and was intended as supplementary material for illustrating the knight-errant tradition in premodern Chinese literature (a tradition on which many of today's *kung-fu* movies are based). Kong hastened to add that although Lu Xun remained integral to the curriculum, the decision to remove *The True Story of Ah Q* from teaching materials was based on a judgment that not everything Lu Xun wrote was of relevance to contemporary China. He and his fellow editors had ensured that works by Lu Xun that addressed "ageless human problems" were retained. *Ah Q*, however, apparently did not belong in this category. Kong claimed that the 1921 story depicted the violence and chaos of a revolutionary age that was utterly alien to the experience of present-day students.[114]

Hence some eighty years after Qian Xingcun declared *Ah Q* dead because he found the story insufficiently revolutionary, Kong and his fellow editors deemed it to be *too* revolutionary for the educational needs of a "harmonious China." The debate has continued to the present (2012), with online commentaries lamenting the absence of *Ah Q* from the high-school curriculum. One highly popular commentary posted on 9 September 2010, "Where one Lu Xun retreats, millions of *Ah Q*'s will grow," warns of the dire consequences that would result from forgetting the moral lessons that *Ah Q* imparts.[115]

In mainland scholarship, the self-evident soundness of asking "what Lu Xun would do if he were alive today" is indicative of the enduring moral authority that his writings command. The question in its various permutations has been posed, and answered, countless times since his death.[116] An early instance is the essay Hu Feng wrote in 1941 titled "If He Were Still Alive" *(ruguo ta hai huozhe)*, in which he mourned the declining influence of Lu Xun's critical style with the rise of patriotic fervor in the War of Resistance against Japan (1937-1945) then under way.[117] When Chairman Mao was asked the question in July 1957, he replied that Lu Xun "would either be in prison and still writing or he would have stopped writing altogether."[118] This was a time when the Anti-Rightist Movement, a nationwide purge of intellectual independence, was gaining momentum. Developed out of the Anti–Hu Feng Movement two years earlier, the Anti-Rightist Movement, which lasted for over a year, resulted in the labeling of "somewhere between 300,000 to 700,000 skilled people" as "rightists" and their removal from their jobs.[119] The majority of these "rightists" were subjected to "labor re-education" (a lesser penalty that included a term of imprisonment) and a minority, perceived as a serious threat to Party rule, served long prison sentences via "labor reform." On this occasion, Mao insinuated that even his personal hero would have to conform to the Party's directives or risk incarceration. Reflecting on the abiding prevalence of this counterfactual question as to what Lu Xun would do, Chen Shuyu, director of the Lu Xun Research Office in Beijing, wrote in 2004 that it has mostly served as a device for assessing China's intellectual, political, and social prospects under Party-state rule.[120]

In 1991 the celebrated writer Zhang Chengzhi, an ethnic Hui Muslim, developed this critical aspect of the question into an impassioned commentary addressed to Lu Xun. He called it "A Letter to the Maestro" *(Zhi xiansheng shu),* using *xiansheng* (teacher) to show reverence for Lu Xun without mentioning his name. To refer to Lu Xun by this honorific term alone (a practice that Zhang helped to popularize in the 1990s) was to imply a disavowal of the state-endorsed "Lu Xun."[121] Zhang highlighted his ethnic minority status when extolling Lu Xun's "fearless and fiercely righteous character" as more "barbarian" *(hu)* than "Han." He wrote that, as a member of a national minority, he could not help holding this bias against the pliancy and corruptibility of Han Chinese culture. He then lamented the commercialism of post-Maoist times, noting that the copy of *Wild Grass* he had bought in 1973 for twenty cents was a work that "any poor person could buy" but that this was now impossible because no publisher in the profit-driven society of 1990s China would deem a work of merely 30,000 words commercially viable.[122]

Some two decades later, in August 2010, the best-selling author Han Han reprised the question of "what Lu Xun would do" but in burlesque contrast to the high seriousness of eulogies produced by solemn devotees of Lu Xun like Zhang. As the world's most popular blogger (attracting more than half a billion hits on his personal blog in June 2011), Han wrote a post listing twenty-six situations in which Lu Xun might find himself "were he still alive today." The first of these noted that as Lu Xun would most likely be incapable of using a computer or going online, he would be confined to waging verbal wars in the magazine *Harvest (Shouhuo)*, which in 2000 was a key vehicle for polemical writings about Lu Xun. Hence, Han wrote, "because his articles would appear monthly like a woman's menstrual cycle, he would have no prospect of victory and would only be laughed at." Han then speculated that Lu Xun's biggest fight would be with the People's Literature Publishing House in Beijing (which enjoys a publishing monopoly on his *Collected Works*). Because Lu Xun had made so much money from speaking on the people's behalf, ordinary folk would be incensed and would form "an anti–Lu Xun coalition" to prevent him from "using us to hype things up"; further, he would inevitably be perceived as belonging to the entertainment scene, and thus serious literary types would consider him unworthy of having his collected works published; and so on and so forth.[123]

Han's irreverent treatment of Lu Xun also reflects his familiarity with (and a desire to demonstrate familiarity with) the better-known particulars of the maestro's life and words. Lu Xun himself had pondered the cost of fame, often in the context of answering his critics, and his open letter to Yang Cunren of 1933 offers a useful perspective on his preferred self-image as a polemicist. He wrote that as there were so many rumors circulating about him, he "can't and won't respond" to reported hearsay. Yang, a founding member of the Sun Society who resigned from the Left-Wing League in January 1933, was regarded by his fellow League members as a defector to the enemy camp because he had joined those who were advocating a neutral "third" position (between left and right). Yang had accused Lu Xun of causing him injury because a newspaper had reported Lu Xun as saying dismissively of Yang's work that it deserved no more than a mere "shoo" *(xu)*. Lu Xun wrote that he had indeed made the belittling utterance, for he disliked what Yang had published as justification for leaving the Communist

Party, but that he had done so in a private discussion, unaware that a reporter would write it up.[124]

Lu Xun then informed Yang that he wrote his polemics reactively because "humans are not saints." He added that it was precisely because "others felt compelled to dissect" him that he could not resist ridiculing them in retaliation. Like everyone else, he had "the right to have a laugh" at his enemy's expense, but, unlike his adversaries, he had never sought to justify what amounted to only personal enmity as an "act of conscience" or as action undertaken on behalf of "the proletarian masses." In an earlier essay, Yang had likened Lu Xun's polemics to a broadsword (dadao) used "to hack and slay indiscriminately," without telling right from wrong.[125] In his letter, Lu Xun answered sarcastically that he was touched by Yang's praise for his martial prowess but that it was quite inappropriate: that all he had was a writing brush and its name was "priceless" (jinbuhuan, "cannot be sold for gold").[126]

He explained that he did all his writing with the eminently disposable "cheap brush" (pianyi bi) he had used since childhood, which cost no more than "five cents apiece." When attacking adversaries like Yang, this was a priceless implement because it was "always ready to hand [xinshou nianlai], like the use of classical allusions, bringing delight as it touches the paper."[127] Thus Lu Xun implied that writing draws on the whole of a person's conduct, learning, and talent and that his own classical learning was so deeply rooted in his being as to afford him the same ease as wielding the writing brush: both were ever at his service.

Here it is worth recalling that Lu Xun called his essays "mixed impressions" (zagan) to highlight the somatic experience of writing. As discussed in Chapter 1, he referred to his zagan as "the singing-crying noise one makes when in a state between grief and joy" (beixi shijiede geku).[128] This remark could easily be read as the modern transposition of a well-known literary phrase, "expressing joy in sorrow and voicing sorrow in joy" (you zhong you le, le zhong you you), which the Song-era poet Su Shi (1037–1101) had used when praising the poem "Southern Stream" by the Tang-era essayist Liu Zongyuan (773–819). Juxtaposing the well-worn contrapuntal symmetry of this classical formulation with the plain-spoken bareness of a "singing-crying noise" yields a sense of Lu Xun's radical project of recoding premodern *wenyan* into something straightforward and accessible.

To recapitulate, Lu Xun's revolution consisted in making war against rote-learned habits of language and opposing the ruling class's monopoly of written Chinese. He found the radical egalitarianism that Communism promised deeply appealing. Hence while he abhorred the repressive politics of both the left and the right, he sought to defend the left as offering the best hope of a just society of fellow humans. Insofar as the essays of his last decade emphasize not only the importance of cultivating empathy through literature but a highly circumspect attitude to the vanguard role of the left, they have something in common with Paulo Freire's 1970s notion of a "humanizing pedagogy." As Freire (1921–1997) put it, this is a style of interaction "in which the revolutionary leadership establishes a permanent relationship of dialogue with the oppressed." Against dogmatic tutelage, Freire argues: "In a humanizing pedagogy, the method ceases to be an instrument by which the teachers (here, the revolutionary leadership) can manipulate the students (the oppressed), because it expresses the consciousness of the students themselves."[129]

In Lu Xun's last decade, as he championed the leftist mission of writing for the masses, he did so in contingent ways, evocative of a humanizing pedagogy, in sharp contrast to the ideological certitudes that prevailed in the Left-Wing League. And while he waged polemic war mostly in reaction to criticism, he clearly delighted (as he pointed out to Yang Cunren) in accusing those whom he perceived as posing a threat to the commonality of *baihua*. He believed he was defending *baihua* as a vehicle of human feeling. Indeed, the relationship between language and feeling was of primary importance to Lu Xun in whichever language he wrote, whether archaic *guwen*, classical *wenyan*, or modern *baihua*. As Wang Hui puts it succinctly, glossing Lu Xun's frequently pejorative use of the word "silence": "what he called 'silence' is the condition of language being separated from feeling."[130]

It is no accident that shortly before his death, Lu Xun wrote two essays about the celebrated classicist and onetime revolutionary Zhang Taiyan, his erstwhile mentor. He completed the first on 9 October 1936;

the second, begun on 17 October, remained unfinished, as he died two days later. These two commemorative essays were suffused with mixed feelings, for he clearly wanted to acknowledge a debt yet also to distance himself from Zhang.[131] On the one hand, he extolled Zhang's polemical writings, describing them as his "greatest and most enduring achievements," and praised his commitment to the cause of revolution in the 1900s and early 1910s. He wrote that Zhang was fearless in denouncing Yuan Shikai's treachery and "remained firm in his revolutionary ideal" despite being repeatedly hunted down and imprisoned; that his conduct showed "the spirit of a true sage, an exemplar for posterity."[132]

On the other hand, he criticized Zhang for abandoning the cause of revolution once Yuan Shikai seized power. He wrote that Zhang's vision "lost any basis in reality" such that he "fell into empty words . . . distanced himself from the masses and grew increasingly dispirited." Lu Xun explained that he wanted to commemorate Zhang's "achievements in the history of China's revolution" precisely because Zhang was being celebrated only for his scholarly accomplishments. He noted with regret that Zhang himself had deliberately omitted his early polemical writings from his collected works, as if to avoid "violating ancient Confucian norms [of restraint and temperateness] for fear of earning the scorn of later scholars."[133]

In the first essay, Lu Xun's discussion of the differences between Zhang and Gorky provides the clearest statement of how he understood his own revolutionary purpose. He wrote that Zhang nursed a "masterful illusion," quoting Zhang's famous statement that "the first task is to foster confidence through religion, to improve the moral conduct of citizens; the second is to use [the ideas of] national essence to arouse a sense of ethnic belonging and to encourage patriotic fervor." Implying that this was an institutional fantasy doomed either to coercion or to failure, Lu Xun argued that Gorky chose the superior path of simply "allowing himself to become so identified with the masses that he fully shared their joy and anger, their pleasures and sorrows."[134]

In the second and unfinished essay, Lu Xun bequeathed an image of himself, reacting with sad incredulity to the news that the failing Chinese Republic was celebrating its twenty-fifth anniversary. He wrote that he rubbed his head in amazement: that this was a reflex action acquired in youth that showed his age because "it was a way of saying 'my queue is well and truly gone' and hence, to begin with, an expression of triumph." He wrote that the young, who had never worn queues, "are incapable of fully sharing this feeling." He repeated his praise for Zhang Taiyan's erudite invective during his revolutionary phase and quoted from the solemnly defiant essay that Zhang had written to mark the cutting of his own queue.[135]

Lu Xun then confessed that, unlike Zhang, he cut off his queue not because he burned with a revolutionary passion but because he found it inconvenient and uncomfortable. To make the point that when queue-cutting grew into a trend, the act generated a frisson but required little courage, Lu Xun used the contrastive example of Huang Xing (1874-1916), whom he commended for showing a true rebelliousness. Huang was a revolutionary leader and loyal supporter of Sun Yat-sen in the 1900s. Before Huang was converted to the revolutionary cause, he "neither cut his queue nor clamored for revolution" but was simply rebellious by temperament. During Huang's prerevolutionary phase as a student in Tokyo, the Japanese dean of studies had forbidden the students to bare their arms. Huang "deliberately stripped to his waist and sauntered across the main compound, carrying his enamel wash-basin from the bathroom to his study."[136]

These two parting images, of Lu Xun rubbing his head and Huang's bare-chested disobedience, convey the sheer vibrancy of Lu Xun's critical practice. They illustrate his genius for turning language into "a fleshly vessel holding human juices" *(renrou jianggang)*.[137] Walter Benjamin's notion of "the virtuoso of empathy" is an apt description of Lu Xun's literary craft. Writing of empathy as *Einfühlung* ("in-feeling" or "feeling into"), Benjamin called it "an insinuation of one's own ego into an alien object."[138] He continued: "The virtuoso of empathy does not in fact step outside himself. His masterstroke consists in having so emptied out his own ego, and made it so free of all ballast of the person, that it feels at home in every mask."[139] Lu Xun was a master in the use of affective imagery *(xing)*, an empathic device in premodern Chinese poetics. As Stephen Owen has pointed out, *"xing* is an image whose primary function is not signification but rather the stirring of a particular affection or mood: *xing* does not 'refer to' that mood; it generates it."[140]

In effect, Lu Xun "entrusted his feelings" *(tuoqing)* to the many affective images that he created in the course of his illustrious and contentious career—from the madman and Ah Q through animal, ghost, and warrior figures, to these final images of Zhang Taiyan, Huang Xing, and himself—emptying his learning and memory into the language he called *baihua*. Benjamin wrote of the gifted empathic writer that "nothing more of the person remains than an unlimited capacity, and often also an unlimited propensity, for entering into the situation of every other in the cosmos, including every animal, every inanimate object."[141] Indeed, it is precisely because of Lu Xun's unique talent for "entering into the situation of every other" that his words, and particularly his polemics, have aroused the passions of readers past and present.

Lu Xun wanted to be remembered for his passions rather than for his scholarship. The soulful reflective essays he wrote as he was close to death indicate that his desire was to be "connected with a countless multitude of people," as he had written just two months earlier.[142] In this, he was posthumously aided by Mao Zedong, for despite the awful travesties committed in the name of "the Lu Xun spirit," the mandated study of Lu Xun from the 1940s did secure his textual permanence. If we heed the sense of "spirit" *(shen)* in Chinese poetics as a sensory power—as opposed to an abstract construct—the countless quotations of Lu Xun circulating in academic, literary, official, and everyday Chinese also present themselves as so many apparitions of the writer. On the Chinese Internet, these apparitions continue to proliferate. In "The Epitaph," Lu Xun presented a speaking corpse whose parting remark was: "When I have turned into dust, you will see my smile!" Now that Lu Xun's words have become digital "dust," adapted and cited in a myriad of ways for a multitude of reasons, there's no mistaking his daemonic "smile," which shines darkly out of the abyss of language, daring us to cut our own paths of words with human feeling.

Notes

Acknowledgments

Index

Notes

Abbreviations of Frequently Cited Works

GWLZ   *"Geming wenxue" lunzheng ziliao xuanbian* (Selected historical materials on the debate over "revolutionary literature"), 2 vols. (Beijing: Renmin wenxue chubanshe, 1981)

LXQJ   *Lu Xun quanji* (The complete works of Lu Xun), 16 vols. (1981; repr., Beijing: Renmin wenxue chubanshe, 1991)

SW   Lu Xun, *Selected Works*, trans. Yang Xianyi and Gladys Yang, 4 vols. (Beijing: Foreign Languages Press, 1985)

Introduction

1. Yu Shicun, *Feichang dao* (Extraordinary sayings) (Hong Kong: Cosmos Books, 2006), 125. Lu Xun makes numerous appearances in Yu's critically acclaimed anthology of anecdotes and quips from twentieth-century intellectual China. Xu Maoyong, who became acquainted with Lu Xun in the 1930s, rose to notoriety when Lu Xun published a lengthy and vitriolic letter against him in 1936, titled "A Reply to Xu Maoyong." Xu tried unsuccessfully to placate Lu Xun. This letter, discussed in Chapter 4, ensured Xu's unfortunate commemoration in mainland scholarship thereafter as the maestro's unworthy adversary.

2. As Mark Gamsa observes, "Lu Xun's translation choices by and large ignored the literature of the Western imperialist powers (though he did

translate a variety of short texts by West European writers), while trusting in Japan as his window to the world, encouraging the translation of the literatures of small and oppressed nations (though he did rather little in that field himself) and reifying Russia." Gamsa, *The Chinese Translation of Russian Literature: Three Studies* (Leiden: Brill, 2008), 154.

3. *Lu Xun Studies,* an extensive and regularly updated bibliography of published scholarship on Lu Xun, appears at http://mclc.osu.edu/rc/lxbib .htm (accessed 16 February 2012).

4. Bonnie S. McDougall, *Love Letters and Privacy in Modern China: The Intimate Lives of Lu Xun and Xu Guangping* (Oxford: Oxford University Press, 2002), 34.

5. A letter from Lu Xun to Xu Shoushang (dated 15 November 1910) is frequently cited as evidence for this inference. Lu Xun confided in Xu that his devotion to archival research was a substitute for "wine and women" (using the archaic phrase *chunjiu furen*), thereby suggesting a life of celibacy. See Zhang Yaojie, *Lu Xun yu Zhou Zuoren* (Lu Xun and Zhou Zuoren)(Taipei: Showwe Information, 2008), 4.

6. Fang Xiangdong, ed., *Huode Lu Xun* (The living Lu Xun) (Shanghai: Shiji chuban jituan, 2001), 276, 282.

7. David E. Pollard, *The True Story of Lu Xun* (Hong Kong: Chinese University Press, 2002), 201.

8. Xu Jilin and Luo Gang, *Qimengde ziwo wajie* (Enlightenment collapsing in on itself) (Beijing: Gulin chuban jituan, 2007), 136.

9. "*Jindai muke xuanji* xiaoyin" (A short foreword to *A Selection of Modern Woodcuts*), *LXQJ* 7:320.

10. "Wenyi yu zhengzhide qitu" (The divergent paths of art and politics), *LXQJ* 7:117.

11. Mao Zedong, *Mao Zedong xuanji* (Selected works of Mao Zedong), vol. 2 (Beijing: Renmin chubanshe), 698; translation partly based on the English translation, Mao Zedong, "On Lu Hsun," *Zhi yue (July)* March 1938. Maoist Documentation Project at http://www.marxists.org/reference/ archive/mao/selected-works/volume-6/mswv6_27.htm (last accessed January 2011).

12. This remark appears in a letter Mao wrote on 8 July 1966 in which he noted that both he and Lu Xun admired the Jin-era scholar-recluse Ruan Ji as an exemplary rebel. Mao Zedong, "Mao Zedong gei Jiang Qingde xin" (Mao Zedong's letter to Jiang Qing), in *"Wenhua dageming" yanjiu ziliao* (Research materials on the "Cultural Revolution") (Beijing: Zhongguo renmin jiefang jun, 1988), 55–56, at *China Elections and Governance,* http://www.chinaelections.org/newsinfo.asp?newsid=134300. An

excerpt is cited and translated in Geremie R. Barmé, *Shades of Mao: The Posthumous Cult of the Great Leader* (Armonk, N.Y.: M. E. Sharpe, 1996), 273.

13. Quoted in Simon Leys, *Broken Images: Essays on Chinese Culture and Politics,* trans. Steve Cox (London: Allison and Busby, 1979), 31.

14. The term remains widely cited in discussions of Lu Xun's legacy. See, for instance, Lin Xianzhi, "Lu Xun san lun" (Three issues about Lu Xun), in *Jujiao "Lu Xun shijian": Jinian Lu Xun xiansheng danchen 120 zhounian* (On "the Lu Xun incident": In commemoration of the 120th anniversary of Lu Xun's birth), ed. Ge Tao and Gu Hongmei (Fuzhou: Fujian jiaoyu chubanshe, 2001), 389-390.

15. "Zhishi guosheng" (A surfeit of knowledge), *LXQJ* 5:224.

16. Li Helin, *Jin ershi nian Zhongguo wenyi sichao lun* (Chinese literary trends of the last twenty years) (Chongqing: Shenghuo shudian, 1939), 523.

17. David Pollard makes this helpful observation: "There are three objective measures of his eminence: the sales of his books, the crowds attracted to his public lectures, and the length of his funeral cortege. The heart of the matter, however, is how far he measured up to the title accorded him by the funeral banner 'the soul of the nation.' . . . All nations are divided and so cannot have one 'soul.' . . . What we are really talking about is having the good of the nation at heart, and consistently and courageously speaking out on matters of conscience, in a way that coincided with the general popular will." *The True Story of Lu Xun,* 203.

18. Immanuel C. Y. Hsu, *The Rise of Modern China* (Oxford: Oxford University Press, 1990), 500.

19. Quoted in Vera Schwarcz, *The Chinese Enlightenment: Intellectuals and the Legacy of May Fourth Movement of 1919* (Berkeley: University of California Press, 1990), 127.

20. See also Eva Shan Chou, "Learning to Read Lu Xun, 1918-1923: The Emergence of a Readership," *China Quarterly* 172 (2002), 1042-1064.

21. Michel Foucault, *Aesthetics, Method and Epistemology,* ed. James Faubion, trans. Robert Hurley et al., vol. 2 (London: Penguin Books, 2000), 217-218.

22. Lin Xianzhi, *Lu Xunde zuihou shi nian* (Lu Xun's final decade) (Beijing: Zhongguo shehui kexue chubanshe, 2003).

23. Xu and Luo, *Qimengde ziwo wajie,* 112.

24. "Xie zai *Fen* houmian" (An epilogue to *The Grave*), *LXQJ* 1:284, translation based on Leys, *Broken Images,* 31.

25. "Xiaopinwende weiji" (The personal essay in crisis), *LXQJ* 4:575.

26. "Random Thoughts (57)—Murderers of the Present," *SW* 2:44.

27. Jon Kowallis points out that of Lu Xun's sixty-four extant poems in the classical style, at least twenty-five include words and images from the ancient *Songs of Chu (Chu ci)*. Jon Eugene von Kowallis, *The Lyrical Lu Xun: A Study of His Classical Style Verse* (Honolulu: University of Hawaii Press, 1996), 6.

28. See for instance "Xiaoyin" (Foreword), *LXQJ* 3:183; "Wode taidu qiliang he nianji" (My attitude, tolerance, and age), *LXQJ* 4:112.

29. *Feng* has been variously translated as "style," "trend," and even "phenomenon." I have chosen to render it as "aura" to retain a trace of the etymological root of *feng* in "wind." David Pollard writes of the short-lived magazine *Lu Xun feng* that it featured very few essays that reflected Lu Xun's "art of invective"; instead there was "a good deal of armchair philosophizing" dominated by "a reedy and merely querulous tone" and unconvincing exhortations. See Pollard, "Lu Xun's *zawen*" in, *Lu Xun and his Legacy,* ed. Leo Ou-Fan Lee (Berkeley: University of California Press, 1985), 86.

30. Cited in Xu and Luo, *Qimengde ziwo wajie,* 128.

31. "'Ti weiding' cao 6-9" (Notes without titles, nos. 6-9), *LXQJ* 6:430. A full but different translation of this essay appears in *SW* 4:242.

32. *LXQJ* 6:432.

33. Ibid.

34. "Notes without Titles, 7, 8, 9," *SW* 4:243.

35. "How I Came to Write Stories," *SW* 3:262.

36. *Heng mei* (literally, "linear brow") appears, among other places, in a classical poem that Lu Xun composed in 1932. It was part of the couplet "Fierce-browed and unperturbed, I face a thousand pointing fingers, yet bow my head gladly to be an ox for the children." These lines were praised by Mao in 1942 and thereafter were frequently cited as an ideal revolutionary disposition.

37. These words are especially prominent in his experimental prose writings in *Wild Grass,* discussed in Chapter 5.

38. George Steiner, *Real Presences* (London: Faber and Faber, 1989), 164.

39. "Preface to the *Works of Li Dazhao,*" *SW* 3:294.

40. "Lici cunzhao 7" (For future reference no. 7), *LXQJ* 6:636.

1. Eyes Wide Open

1. Accounts vary on the numbers of those killed and wounded. Thirteen is the most widely accepted number, based on the *Wusa yundong shiliao* (Historical materials on the May Thirtieth Movement), ed. Shanghai shehui kexueyuan lishi yanjiu suo, vol. 1 (Shanghai: Shanghai shehui

kexueyuan lishi yanjiu suo, 1981), 720–721. Also quoted in Elizabeth J. Perry, *Shanghai on Strike: The Politics of Chinese Labor* (Stanford: Stanford University Press, 1995), 81.

2. "Lun zhengle yan kan" (Seeing with eyes wide open), *LXQJ* 1:237–242.

3. Ibid., 237. Lu Xun referred to the adage *feili wushi* (to avert one's gaze from all that is unseemly) in *The Analects* (12:1) as the source of a cultural habit that made "looking straight ahead" *(zhengshi)* virtually impossible. Over time, he wrote, people went from not daring to look straight ahead, to becoming incapable of facing things squarely, and thereafter to failing to notice that they were no longer able to see properly. Ibid.

4. *LXQJ* 1:241; "On Looking Facts in the Face," *SW* 2:203, punctuation modified.

5. *LXQJ* 1:241.

6. During the 1900s the cultural connotations of "revolution" *(geming)* had become interchangeable with those of "reform" *(gexin; weixin),* but their political connotations remained distinct. Whereas revolution was identified with Sun and his allies who sought to overthrow the Qing dynasty, reform was associated with the cause of modern constitutional monarchy that Kang Youwei espoused. Liang Qichao, discussed in this chapter, was Kang's leading protégé. The latter cause, known as the China Reform Association in English and the Protect the Emperor Society *(bao huang hui)* in Chinese, was greatly weakened by the death in 1908 of the Guangxu emperor, the man who had been the reform movement's raison d'être. With the political objective of "protecting the emperor" gone, the idea of reform merged with that of revolution under the political and cultural mantra of "saving China," and the term "revolution" was thereafter unchallenged.

7. Zhang Xun seized power briefly in late June 1917. With Kang Youwei's support, he restored the last Manchu emperor, Puyi, to the throne on 1 July. On 12 July the leaders of the Beiyang warlord regime, Duan Qirui and Cao Kun, recaptured Beijing and ended the restoration. For details of Sun's political life, see Marie-Claire Bergère, *Sun Yat-sen,* trans. Janet Lloyd (Stanford: Stanford University Press, 1998).

8. Sun Yat-sen, *Prescriptions for Saving China: Selected Writings of Sun Yat-sen,* ed. Julie Lee Wei, Ramon H. Myers, and Donald G. Gillin, trans. Julie Lee Wei, E-Su Zen, and Linda Chao (Stanford, Calif.: Hoover Institution Press, 1994), 202–204.

9. Leo Ou-fan Lee, *Voices from the Iron House: A Study of Lu Xun* (Bloomington: Indiana University Press, 1987), 10.

10. The term "literary revolution" appeared in Liang's essay "On the Relationship between Fiction and the Government of the People," a full

translation of which appears in Kirk A. Denton, ed., *Modern Chinese Literary Thought: Writings on Literature, 1893–1945* (Stanford: Stanford University Press, 1996), 74–81.

11. Zhou Zuoren, *Guanyu Lu Xun (About Lun Xun)*, vol. 2 (Shijiazhuang: Hebei Education Press, 2002), 162.

12. Quoted and discussed in Guo Zhanbo, *Jin wushi nian Zhongguo sixiang shi* (The history of Chinese thought in the last fifty years) (Jinan: Shandong renmin chubanshe, 1997), 226.

13. The warlords were former Qing commanders loyal to Yuan Shikai, whom he rewarded with provincial governorships and other high-ranking positions upon assuming the presidency in 1912. Following Yuan's death in 1916, power contests resulted in the transmutation of these provincial governments into warlord regimes. As the power of the nominal national government seated in Beijing declined, the constitution of the Republic itself came under threat.

14. Conrad Brandt, Benjamin Schwartz, and John K. Fairbank, *A Documentary History of Chinese Communism* (Oxford: Routledge, 2005), 70.

15. Ibid., 72.

16. The development of their relationship is extensively covered in Bonnie S. McDougall, *Love Letters and Privacy in Modern China: The Intimate Lives of Lu Xun and Xu Guangping* (Oxford: Oxford University Press, 2002).

17. Lu Xun first received an invitation by telegram from Zhu Jiahua, one of Sun Yat-sen University's five directors, on 16 October 1926, but it was not until 20 November that he made up his mind to accept the university's offer. See *LXQJ* 11:157, 211.

18. McDougall, *Love Letters and Privacy*, 184–185.

19. Jian Ru, "Huanying le Lu Xun yihou" (After welcoming Lu Xun), in *Lu Xun zai Guangdong* (Lu Xun in Guangdong), ed. Zhong Jingwen (Shanghai: Beixin Publishing House, July 1927), 21. Jian Ru was a pseudonym used by Bi Lei. On Lu Xun's unhappiness with the anthology, see Chapter 3.

20. "Tongxin" (Correspondence), *LXQJ* 3:447. The octopartite composition, or *baguwen*, was an essential part of the imperial examination system in dynastic China, requiring an argument on a set topic to be developed in eight mandated sections. By the 1920s the term had become a derogatory reference for lifeless and rigidly formulaic writing.

21. Roland Felber, "A 'Bloc Within' or a 'Bloc Without'?," in Mechthild Luetner, Roland Felber, M. L. Titarenko, and A. M. Grigoriev, eds., *The Chinese Revolution in the 1920s: Between Triumph and Disaster* (London: Routledge-Curzon, 2002), 55–57.

22. See David P. Barrett, "The Role of Hu Hanmin in the First 'United Front,'" *China Quarterly*, no. 89 (1982), 34-64.

23. Yu Min-ling, "A Reassessment of Chiang Kai-shek and the Policy of Alliance with the Soviet Union, 1923-1927," in Luetner et al., *The Chinese Revolution in the 1920s*, 115.

24. Citing a 1927 eyewitness account of these events, Harold Isaacs reported that Wang wrote to Chiang before he left, "imploring him to keep to the 'revolutionary' path," adding that "if he would only do so, Wang did not mind sacrificing himself." Isaacs, *The Tragedy of the Chinese Revolution* (Stanford: Stanford University Press, 1961), 94.

25. Yu, "A Reassessment of Chiang Kai-shek," 115.

26. Ibid., 114-116.

27. Guo Moruo, "Geming yu wenxue" (Revolution and literature), *GWLZ* 1:3-4.

28. "Fan Ainong," *SW* 1:417.

29. Raymond Geuss, *Philosophy and Real Politics* (Princeton: Princeton University Press, 2008), 24.

30. Guo, "Geming yu wenxue," *GWLZ* 1:5.

31. Ibid., 8.

32. Guo's revolutionary idiom replicates the Mencian dictum that one must know what to adopt *(qu)* and what to discard *(she)*. Ibid., 4, 12.

33. Ibid., 12.

34. "Geming shidaide wenxue," *LXQJ* 3:421; "Literature of a Revolutionary Period," *SW* 2:330-331. Lu Xun frequently referred to Guangzhou, the provincial capital, as Guangdong (the province).

35. Yu, "A Reassessment of Chiang Kai-shek," 102-103.

36. *LXQJ* 3:422; *SW* 2:332-333. Three thousand *mou* is around five hundred acres.

37. "The Other Side of Celebrating the Recovery of Shanghai and Nanjing," *SW* 2:343. The statement was Stalin's but was attributed to Lenin in a speech that was widely known in Chinese intellectual circles. Ibid.

38. Ibid., 344, modified.

39. Figures cited in Isaacs, *The Tragedy of the Chinese Revolution*, 177.

40. Chiang Kai-shek sought assistance from Du Yuesheng, Shanghai's leading gangster, to crush the Communist-led and -organized labor movement in Shanghai. On 13 April, when members and supporters of Shanghai's General Labor Union held a protest march against the slaughter of the previous day, there were further casualties of over 300 killed and even more wounded; ibid., 179-180. The Nationalist Party's relationship

with the Shanghai underworld is examined in Brian G. Martin, *The Shanghai Green Gang: Politics and Organized Crime, 1919–1937* (Berkeley: University of California Press, 1996).

41. "Literature of a Revolutionary Period," *SW* 2:336.

42. "Geming shidaide wenxue," *LXQJ* 3:423; "Literature of a Revolutionary Period," *SW* 2:341, modified.

43. *Wen yi zai dao*, coined by Zhou Dunyi (1017–1073), was frequently used in the late 1890s and the 1900s to affirm the "new prose style" *(xin wenti)* then being promoted by the intellectual activist and entrepreneur Liang Qichao.

44. "Record of a Speech," *SW* 2:300–305. On Lu Xun's translation of *Shevyrev*, see Mark Gamsa, *The Chinese Translation of Russian Literature: Three Studies* (Leiden: Brill, 2008), 116–120, 156–160.

45. Sun, *Prescriptions for Saving China,* 252–266.

46. The admiration was not mutual: although Lenin praised Sun in 1912, he criticized him as "a dreamer and indecisive" in 1913 and in 1921 professed no knowledge of Sun's revolutionary activities in Guangzhou. See Bergère, *Sun Yat-sen,* 307.

47. Sun, *Prescriptions for Saving China,* 279.

48. Tony Saich and Benjamin Yang, eds., *The Rise to Power of the Chinese Communist Party: Documents and Analysis* (Armonk, N.Y.: M. E. Sharpe, 1996), lvi.

49. Lu Xun, *Wild Grass,* trans. Yang Xianyi and Gladys Yang (Beijing: Foreign Languages Press, 1976), 8.

50. Lee, *Voices from the Iron House,* 28.

51. "Yingde gaobie" (The shadow's farewell), *LXQJ* 2:166.

52. Christopher Read, *Lenin: A Revolutionary Life* (Oxford: Routledge, 2005), 27.

53. Gamsa, *The Chinese Translation of Russian Literature,* 159.

54. Yu Dafu, "Guangzhou shiqing" (Guangzhou affairs), in *Yu Dafu wenji* (The works of Yu Dafu), vol. 8 (Hong Kong: Joint Publications, 1984), 22.

55. Ibid., 21. In December 1926, when the Northern Expedition had scored successive victories to occupy a large area of central China, the seat of the revolutionary government was moved from Guangzhou to Wuhan.

56. Mikhail M. Bakhtin, *The Dialogic Imagination: Four Essays,* trans. Cary Emerson and Michael Holquist (Austin: University of Texas Press, 1981), 342.

57. Chang Kuo-tao (Zhang Guotao), *The Rise of the Chinese Communist Party,* vol. 1 (Lawrence: University Press of Kansas, 1971), 547.

58. Robert C. North and Xenia J. Eudin, *M. N. Roy's Mission to China: The Communist-Kuomintang Split of 1927* (Berkeley: University of California Press, 1963), 57.

59. Quoted in Isaacs, *The Tragedy of the Chinese Revolution*, 119.

60. Ibid., 122.

61. Ibid., 103.

62. Leon Trotsky, *Problems of the Chinese Revolution* (Ann Arbor: University of Michigan Press, 1967), 34.

63. Isaacs, *The Tragedy of the Chinese Revolution*, 127.

64. Steve Smith, "Moscow and the Armed Uprisings in Shanghai, 1927," in Leutner et al., *The Chinese Revolution in the 1920s*, 235.

65. Isaacs, *The Tragedy of the Chinese Revolution*, 150. *The Constitutionalist* was the organ of the Constitutional Defence League, an organization of Shanghai's British residents formed in 1926 for the express purpose of countering communism among Chinese workers.

66. Ibid., 120-121.

67. Ibid., 113.

68. A full translation appears in Timothy Cheek, *Mao Zedong and China's Revolutions: A Brief History with Documents* (Boston: Bedford/St. Martin's: 2002), 41-75.

69. Ibid., 47.

70. Quoted in Vera Schwarcz, *The Chinese Enlightenment: Intellectuals and the Legacy of the May Fourth Movement of 1919* (Berkeley: University of California Press, 1990), 147.

71. Quoted in Leo Ou-fan Lee, *The Romantic Generation of Modern Chinese Writers* (Cambridge, Mass.: Harvard University Press, 1973), 97-98.

72. Cheng's rebuttal was published in the 1 March 1927 issue of *Hongshui* (Deluge). An engaging account of Yu's public dispute with his fellow Creationists appears in Zheng Boqi, "Chuangzao she houqide geming wenxue huodong" (Activities concerning revolutionary literature in the late phase of the Creation Society), in *Zhongguo xiandai wenyi ziliao congkan* (Collected materials on modern Chinese literature), vol. 2 (Shanghai: Shanghai wenyi chubanshe, 1962), 3-4.

73. "Kou si zagan" (Mixed impressions on the constraining of *Threads*), *LXQJ* 3:485.

74. David Der-wei Wang offers this helpful insight: "If one of the most important lessons one can learn from modern Chinese literature and history is the tortuous nature of Chinese writers' attempt to grapple with polymorphous reality, this knowledge can be appreciated in full only by a criticism

equally exempt from any form of formulaic and ideological dogmatism." *The Monster That Is History: History, Violence, and Fiction Writing in Twentieth-Century China* (Berkeley: University of California Press, 2004), 10.

75. Sun, *Prescriptions for Saving China*, 214.

76. "Guanyu Zhongguode liang sanjian shi" (Two or three things about China), *LXQJ* 6:9. Lu Xun's view of the "kingly way" as the ancient paradigm that facilitated the spread of Nationalist political tutelage has been taken up in several recent works of Chinese scholarship, including Lin Xianzhi, *Lu Xunde zuihou shi nian* (Lu Xun's last decade) (Beijing: Zhongguo shehui kexue chubanshe, 2003). I have followed the translation of *badao* as the "tyrant's way" in "Two or Three Things Chinese," *SW* 4:29. The use of *badao* to mean "hegemon" is a Soviet practice that postdates Lu Xun's understanding of *badao*.

77. Ibid.

78. "Zhongshan xiansheng shishi hou yi zhounian" (The first anniversary of Mr. Sun Yat-sen's death), *LXQJ* 7:293.

79. Sun, *Prescriptions for Saving China*, 214.

80. Julie Lee Wei, Ramon H. Myers, and Donald G. Gillin, "Introduction," in ibid., xxvii–xxviii, xxix.

81. "Zixu" (Preface), *LXQJ* 1:419. See also *SW* 1:38.

82. Jacques Derrida, *The Politics of Friendship*, trans. George Collins (London: Verso, 2005), 68.

83. "Huanghua jiede zagan" (Mixed impressions during the Yellow Flower Festival), *LXQJ* 3:410.

84. Ibid., 412.

85. Julia Lovell, "Introduction," in *Lu Xun: The Real Story of Ah Q and Other Tales of China* (London: Penguin, 2009), xxi–xxii.

86. Quotations from Yun Daiying and Deng Zhongxia appear in *Wenxue yundong shiliao xuan* (Selected historical materials on literary movements), vol. 1 (Shanghai: Jiaoyu chubanshe, 1979), 394, 398–399. Also quoted in Márian Gálik, *The Genesis of Modern Chinese Literature (1917–1930)* (London: Curzon Press, 1980), 131, 135.

87. Xiao Chunü, "Yishu yu shenghuo" (Art and life), in *Wenxue yundong shiliao xuan*, 1:400. On Xiao's death, see Gálik, *The Genesis of Modern Chinese Literature*, 260.

88. Quoted in Gálik, *The Genesis of Modern Chinese Literature*, 139, published in 1924 as "Gao yanjiu wenxuede qingnian" (Addressed to young students of literature). Li was arrested together with Lu Xun's favorite student, Rou Shi. They were commemorated as two of the "five martyrs" of the League of Left-Wing Chinese Writers who died that day.

89. Schwarcz, *The Chinese Enlightenment*, 154.

90. Wang-chi Wong, *Politics and Literature in Shanghai: The Chinese League of Left-Wing Writers* (Manchester: Manchester University Press, 1991), 13.

91. Guo, "Geming yu wenxue," *GWLZ* 1:10.

92. Cheng Fangwu, "Geming wenxue yu tade yongyuanxing" (Revolutionary literature and its immortality), *GWLZ* 1:16.

93. Ibid., 14. This revelatory impulse frequently invoked in Chinese revolutionary writings was integral to Marxist thinking as a whole. As Walter Benjamin writes, the apocalyptic element in Marxism resides in the idea that "what characterizes revolutionary classes at their moment of action is the awareness that they are about to make the continuum of history explode"; Walter Benjamin, *Selected Writings,* ed. Howard Eiland and Michael W. Jennings, trans. Edmund Jephcott and others, vol. 4: *1938–1940* (Cambridge, Mass.: Harvard University Press, 2003), 395.

94. Cheng, "Geming wenxue yu tade yongyuanxing," *GWLZ* 1:14.

95. Ibid.

96. Xiaoming Chen, *From the May Fourth Movement to Communist Revolution: Guo Moruo and the Chinese Path to Communism* (Albany: State University of New York, 2007), 71–72.

97. George Kateb, *Patriotism and Other Mistakes* (New Haven: Yale University Press, 2006), 128–129.

98. Isaacs, *The Tragedy of the Chinese Revolution,* 296. The Trotskyist Albert Weisbord gives an estimate of 100,000 Communists and workers killed in 1927 and 1928 in his October 1933 pamphlet, *For a New Communist International* (New York: Communist League of Struggle).

99. Feng Xuefeng, *Huiyi Lu Xun* (Remembering Lu Xun) (Beijing: Renmin wenxue chubanshe, 1952), 25.

100. Ibid., 26.

101. "Da Youheng xiansheng" (Reply to Mr. Youheng), *LXQJ* 3:454.

102. "Reply to Mr.Youheng," *SW* 2:348.

103. *LXQJ* 3:453–454.

104. Guo Moruo, "Tuoli Jiang Jieshi yihou" (After leaving Chiang Kai-shek), in *Moruo wenji* (The works of Moruo), vol. 8 (Beijing: Renmin wenxue chubanshe, 1958), 163–164.

105. "Xiao zagan" (Fleeting mixed impressions), *LXQJ* 3:532.

106. "Xiao yin" (Preface), *LXQJ* 3:183.

107. Guo, "Geming yu wenxue," *GWLZ* 1:10.

108. Ibid.

2. The Shanghai Haze

1. "Tan 'jilie'" (On "intensity"), *LXQJ* 3:476.

2. Ibid., 476-480.

3. Ibid., 478-479.

4. "Zenme xie" (How to write), *LXQJ* 4:18-25.

5. Lu Xun relayed this information and expressed his sorrow in a letter of 20 April 1927 to Li Jiye, his former student in Beijing; *LXQJ* 11:540-541.

6. "Zenme xie," *LXQJ* 4:21.

7. Wang Xiaoming, *Wufa zhimiande rensheng: Lu Xun zhuan* (Life that cannot be squarely faced: A biography of Lu Xun) (Shanghai: Shanghai wenyi chubanshe, 2001), 135-136.

8. Lu Xun first met Gu Jiegang, a protégé of Hu Shi's, in Beijing in the early 1920s. Their amicable relationship proved short-lived; Lu Xun had become hostile to Hu Shi and his associates by 1925. Thereafter Lu Xun regarded Gu as an enemy.

9. Gu Mingyuan, Yu Fang, Jin Qiang, and Li Kai, *Lu Xunde jiaoyu sixiang he shijian* (Lu Xun's ideas about education and the things he did) (Beijing: Renmin jiaoyu chubanshe, 1981), 62. See also "Wei-Jin fengdu ji wenzhang yu yao ji jiuzhi guanxi" (The style and prose of the Wei-Jin epoch and their connection with wine and drugs), *LXQJ* 3:517.

10. Fengtian was the name for Liaoning Province from 1907 to 1929.

11. John K. Fairbank and Albert Feuerwerker, eds., *The Cambridge History of China: Republican China*, vol. 12, part 1: *1912–1949* (New York: Cambridge University Press, 1983), 169.

12. S. A. Smith, *Revolution and the People in Russia and China: A Comparative History* (Cambridge: Cambridge University Press, 2008), 34.

13. Bruce A. Elleman, *Moscow and the Emergence of Communist Power in China, 1925–1930: The Nanchang Rising and the Birth of the Red Army* (Abingdon: Routledge, 2009), 145-147; Harold Isaacs, *The Tragedy of the Chinese Revolution* (Stanford: Stanford University Press, 1961), 278-279; Lazlo Ladany, *The Communist Party of China and Marxism, 1921–1985: A Self-Portrait* (Hong Kong: Hong Kong University Press, 1992), 16-17.

14. See Tony Saich and Benjamin Yang, eds., *The Rise to Power of the Chinese Communist Party: Documents and Analysis* (Armonk, N.Y.: M. E. Sharpe, 1996), 277-286. Party policy continued to fluctuate in reaction to changing events and realpolitik considerations such that the message of "national unity" was revived in 1936 in the face of imminent war with Japan.

15. Yu Dafu, "Wuchanjieji zhuanzheng he wuchanjiejiede wenxue" (Dictatorship of the proletariat and proletarian literature), *GWLZ* 1:25.

16. "Kou *Si* zagan" (Mixed impressions on the constraining of *Threads*), *LXQJ* 3:485.

17. "'Zuiyan' zhongde menglong" (The haze of "drunken eyes"), *LXQJ* 4:61–71.

18. Feng Naichao, "Yishu yu shehui shenghuo" (Art and social life), *GWLZ* 1:116. Bonnie S. McDougall notes that Cheng Fangwu and Feng Naichao also sneered at Lu Xun "for having left his wife to start an affair with his student," noting this as a sign of "ideological backwardness"; *Love Letters and Privacy in Modern China: The Intimate Lives of Lu Xun and Xu Guangping* (Oxford: Oxford University Press, 2002), 60.

19. "'Zuiyan' zhongde menglong," *LXQJ* 4:61.

20. Ibid., 61; "Befuddled Woolliness," *SW* 3:16, modified.

21. *LXQJ* 11:191.

22. *LXQJ* 11:582–583.

23. "Tongxin" (Correspondence), *LXQJ* 4:97. In 1927 Cheng was thirty, some sixteen years younger than Lu Xun. The other Creation Society members who attacked Lu Xun in 1928 were even younger.

24. Gong Jimin and Fang Rennian, eds., *Guo Moruo nianpu* (A chronological biography of Guo Moruo), vol. 1 (Tianjin: Tianjin renmin chubanshe, 1982), 176.

25. Arima Takeo, *The Failure of Freedom* (Cambridge, Mass.: Harvard University Press, 1969), 188.

26. Zheng Boqi, "Chuangzao she houqide geming wenxue hudong" (Revolutionary literature in the later phase of the Creation Society), in *Zhongguo xiandai wenyi ziliao congkan* (Collected materials on modern Chinese literature), vol. 2 (Shanghai: Shanghai wenyi chubanshe, 1962), 5.

27. Ibid., 6–10.

28. Guo Moruo, "Li Hu zhiqian" (Before leaving Shanghai), in *Moruo wenji* (The works of Guo Moruo), vol. 8 (Beijing: Renmin wenxue chubanshe, 1958), 257.

29. Zheng, "Chuangzao she houqide geming wenxue hudong," 6–10.

30. Guo Moruo, "Kuazhe donghai" (Crossing the eastern sea), in *Moruo wenji*, 8:289–290. Written in 1947.

31. Wang-chi Wong, *Politics and Literature in Shanghai: The Chinese League of Left-Wing Writers, 1930–1936* (Manchester: Manchester University Press, 1991), 16–17.

32. McDougall, *Love Letters and Privacy*, 34.

33. On the Chinese Internet, articles abound on Wang's romance with Yu Dafu, together with photographic images testifying to her beauty as "Miss Hangzhou" *(Hangzhou diyi meiren)*. Details of Wang's and Yu's

relationship are examined in Sang Fengkang, *Yu Dafu Wang Yingxia* (Beijing: Zhongguo qingnian chubanshe, 1995).

34. *Lu Xun nianpu* (A chronological biography of Lu Xun), ed. Lu Xun Nianpu Editorial Committee of Fudan University, Shanghai Normal University, Shanghai Normal College, 2 vols. (Hefei: Anhui renmin chubanshe, 1979), 1:66–67. See also Xu Shoushang, *Wang you Lu Xun yinxiang ji* (Impressions of my departed friend Lu Xun) (Shanghai: Emei chubanshe, 1947), 60.

35. McDougall, *Love Letters and Privacy*, 58. Zhu An's unhappy marriage remains a topic of interest to this day. In 2002 a blogger using the moniker Xieyang xilou published the online story "Lu Xunde gushi," in which Zhu An is given, in fiction, the loving attention from Lu Xun that she never received in life. See Ge Tao, "2002 niande wangluo Lu Xun" (Cyber-Lu Xun in 2002), in Zheng Xinsen, Sun Yu, and Liu Zengren, eds., *2002 nian Lu Xun yanjiu nian jian* (2002 yearbook of Lu Xun Studies) (Beijing: Renmin wenxue chubanshe, 2002), 146.

36. Discussed in McDougall, *Love Letters and Privacy*, 57–58; Leo Ou-fan Lee, *The Romantic Generation of Modern Chinese Writers* (Cambridge, Mass.: Harvard University Press, 1973), 101–102.

37. Discussed in McDougall, *Love Letters and Privacy*, 59. McDougall also notes that Yu Dafu's 1940 essay "Remembering Lu Xun" includes a comment about the changed man Yu found himself socializing with in Shanghai from the abstemious Lu Xun he had first met in Beijing; ibid.

38. This period in the lives of Lu Xun and Xu Guangping is discussed in ibid.

39. *Lu Xun nianpu*, 1:363.

40. Ibid., 364.

41. "Wei-Jin fengdu ji wenzhang yu yao ji jiuzhi guanxi," *LXQJ* 3:517.

42. Ibid.

43. *Lu Xun nianpu*, 1:343, 348, 355.

44. "Wei-Jin fengdu ji wenzhang yu yao ji jiuzhi guanxi," *LXQJ* 3:517.

45. James Reeve Pusey, *Lu Xun and Evolution* (Albany: State University of New York, 1998), 109.

46. "Wei-Jin fengdu ji wenzhang yu yao ji jiuzhi guanxi," *LXQJ* 3:513.

47. "Xuyan" (Preface), *LXQJ* 4:4.

48. As David R. Knechtges observes, modern scholarship has confirmed the "Seven Worthies" to be a fictional construct of Wei-Jin enthusiasts from a later date. See Knechtges, "From the Eastern Han through the Western Jin (25–317)," in *The Cambridge History of Chinese Literature*, ed. Kang-I

Sun Chang and Stephen Owen, vol. 1 (to 1375) (Cambridge: Cambridge University Press, 2010), 177.

49. "Wei-Jin fengdu ji wenzhang yu yao ji jiuzhi guanxi," *LXQJ* 3:510-513.

50. "Tongxin," *LXQJ* 4:97-98.

51. After living with Lu Xun and Xu Guangping in Guangzhou, Xu Shoushang went to Nanjing at Cai's invitation to work at the academy. For sources, see Tsi-An Hsia, *The Gate of Darkness: Studies on the Leftist Literary Movement in China* (Seattle: University of Washington Press, 1968), 179. In Chinese-language scholarship, Xu Shoushang is frequently praised as a loyal friend to Lu Xun and described as a model of moral constancy. See, for instance, the discussion of these events in Sun Yu, *Deng xia xian tan* (Casual chats by lamplight) (Fuzhou: Fujian jiaoyu chubanshe, 1999), 138.

52. Discussed in Timothy B. Weston, *The Power of Position: Beijing University, Intellectuals, and Chinese Political Culture, 1898–1929* (Berkeley: University of California Press, 2004), 126.

53. Chen Mingyuan, *Wenhua rende jingji shenghuo* (The economic life of China's cultural figures) (Shanghai: Wenhui chubanshe, 2005), 200-201; Gu et al., *Lu Xunde jiaoyu sixiang he shijian*, 29-30; Hsia, *The Gate of Darkness*, 179. Hsia notes that Lu Xun used this salary to establish his personal library in Shanghai; ibid.

54. Feng, "Yishu yu shehui shenghuo," *GWLZ* 1:302.

55. "Dengxia man bi" (Lamplit scribbles), *LXQJ* 1:213.

56. "'Zuiyan' zhongde menglong," *LXQJ* 4:61.

57. "Wei-Jin fengdu ji wenzhang yu yao ji jiuzhi guanxi," *LXQJ* 3:502-503.

58. Ibid., 505-506.

59. Ibid., 512.

60. On these developments, see I. C. Y. Hsu, *The Rise of Modern China* (Oxford: Oxford University Press, 1975), 635-639, 652-653.

61. Ibid., 638. The accident was an explosion reported to have been rigged by Zhang Zuolin's Japanese sponsors.

62. Ch'i Hsi-Sheng, *Warlord Politics in China, 1916–1928* (Stanford: Stanford University Press, 1976), 97, 125, 201.

63. Jay Taylor, *The Generalissimo: Chiang Kai-shek and the Struggle for Modern China* (Cambridge, Mass.: Harvard University Press, 2009), 84.

64. "Wei-Jin fengdu ji wenzhang yu yao ji jiuzhi guanxi," *LXQJ* 3:513-514.

65. Constantine Tung, "The Search for Order and Form: The Crescent Moon Society and the Literary Movement of Modern China, 1928-1933" (Ph.D. diss., Claremont Graduate School, 1971), 48-49.

66. Ibid., 55–57; for details of the incident and correspondence between Lu Xun and Xu Guangping during this period, see McDougall, *Love Letters and Privacy*, 17, 32–34.

67. "Nü xiaozhangde nannüde meng" (The headmistress's dreams about men and women), *LXQJ* 7:290–291.

68. On the involvement of Peking University faculty in this protest, see Weston, *The Power of Position*, 238–239. Lu Xun's animosity toward Chen is most evident in the three essays he wrote between June and November 1925 under the common title "Bingfei xianhua" (No mere casual chat). The title flatly repudiates Chen's regular column "Causeries." See *LXQJ* 3:75–79, 123–125, 148–153. An English translation of the third essay appears in *SW* 2:205–211.

69. "Bingfei xianhua 3," *LXQJ* 3:152; *SW* 2:205. The "Royal Highness" in question was Zhang Shizhao and, by implication, Duan Qirui himself.

70. "Yidian biyu" (A bit of metaphor), *LXQJ* 3:217.

71. Chen Xiying, "Xianhuade xianhuazhi xianhua yinchude jifeng xin" (Letters concerning casual chats caused by casual chats about "Causeries"), *Chenbao fukan*, 30 January 1926. Reprinted in Sun Yu, ed., *Bei xiedude Lu Xun* (The maligned Lu Xun) (Beijing: Qunyan chubanshe, 1994), 4.

72. Lu Xun wrote in 1934 that even before his quarrel with Chen Yuan, he had made an enemy of Xu Zhimo in 1924 by mocking his style of poetry and his talent for self-promotion in print. See "Xuyan," *LXQJ* 7:4–5.

73. Lawrence Wang-chi Wong, "Lions and Tigers in Groups: The Crescent Moon School in Modern Chinese Literary History," in *Literary Societies of Republican China*, ed. Kirk A. Denton and Michel Hockx (Lanham, Md.: Lexington Books, 2008), 280.

74. Ibid., 302.

75. Ibid., 302–303.

76. *LXQJ* 11:682.

77. Jerome B. Grieder, *Hu Shih and the Chinese Renaissance: Liberalism in the Chinese Revolution, 1917–1937* (Cambridge, Mass.: Harvard University Press, 1970), 224, 226.

78. Zhang Yaojie, *Lu Xun yu Zhou Zuoren* (Lu Xun and Zhou Zuoren) (Taipei: Showwe Information, 2008), 176.

79. "Preface to *The Works of Li Dazhao*," *SW* 3:295, modified.

80. Quoted in Wong, *Politics and Literature in Shanghai*, 154.

81. The couplet is widely understood in Chinese scholarship as an expression of Lu Xun's gratitude to Qu for understanding the significance of his polemical writings. See, for example, Zhu Jing, *Lu Xun huozhe* (Lu Xun lives) (Beijing: Wenhua yishu chubanshe, 2005), 170.

82. *Lu Xun nianpu*, 2:377.

83. *LXQJ* 12:606; Hsia, *The Gate of Darkness*, 114. Yang Jiyun edited Lu Xun's 1935 *Anthology of Uncollected Works (Ji wai ji)*.

84. "Tongxin," *LXQJ* 4:84; "Correspondence," *SW* 3:27-28.

85. "Tongxin," *LXQJ* 4:84.

86. Feng Xiaoxiong, ed., "Feng Xuefeng tan Zuolian" (Feng Xuefeng discusses the League of Left-Wing Chinese Writers), *Xin wenxue shiliao*, 1 (1980), 1.

87. "Wiping Out the Reds—A Great Spectacle," *SW* 3:46. I have translated "Chan Gong da guan" more literally as "The Prospect of Purging the Communists."

88. On the political uses of Prospect Garden, see Geremie R. Barmé, "Beijing, a Garden of Violence," *Inter-Asia Cultural Studies*, 9, no. 4 (2008), 612-639.

89. "Wiping Out the Reds—A Great Spectacle," *SW* 3:46, punctuation modified; "Chan Gong da guan," *LXQJ* 4:105-106.

90. *SW* 3:47. On the symbolic complexity of beheadings presented in Chinese literature, see David Der-Wei Wang, *The Monster That Is History: History, Violence, and Fiction Writing in Twentieth-Century China* (Berkeley: University of California Press, 2004), 15-40.

91. "Sheng wu" (Sagely and martial), *LXQJ* 1:355; "Martial and Sagacious," *SW* 2:50.

92. "Liumangde bianqian" (The evolution of hooligans), *LXQJ* 4:155-156.

93. In Lu Xun's use of the term *ru* there is a distinct echo of the explication, provided by his mentor Zhang Binglin, of *ru* as referring to "an elite corps of priests, shamans, and sorcerers" before the time of Confucius. See Lionel M. Jensen, *Manufacturing Confucianism: Chinese Traditions and Universal Civilization* (Durham, N.C.: Duke University Press, 1997), 160-161.

94. "Liumangde bianqian," *LXQJ* 4:155.

95. Ibid., 156.

96. Ibid.

97. Ibid.

98. On Zhang Ziping, see Jianmei Liu, *Revolution plus Love: Literary History, Women's Bodies, and Thematic Repetition in Twentieth-Century Chinese Fiction* (Honolulu: University of Hawaii Press, 2003), 152-156.

99. The Sun Society was established under instructions from the Party leadership (Qu Qiubai, Deng Zhongxia, and Li Lisan), but throughout 1928 its members made their own publishing decisions. It was only in late 1928 that the Party leadership became more directly involved in intellectual

publishing. On the Chinese Communist Party's relationship with this organization in the late 1920s, see Wu Taichang, ed., "A Ying yi Zuolian" (A Ying's recollections of the Left-Wing League), *Xin wenxue shiliao*, no. 1 (1980), 12–20; Yi Xinding, "Lun Taiyang she" (About the Sun Society), *Wenxue pinglun*, no. 6 (1984), 40.

100. Wu, "A Ying yi Zuolian," 14.

101. Guo's reply appears as the foreword *(faduan)* to his book *Chuangzao shinian* (The Creation Society: A decade), first published in 1932. Guo wrote that the unjustified attacks on the Creation Society in Lu Xun's 1931 lecture inspired him to write the book in the first place. He noted, among other things, that while the Creationists' literary endeavors were not without flaws, their conscientious efforts at translating foreign works appeared "to have been undeserving of even 'a cursory look' from the great eyes of Mr. Lu Xun"; *Guo Moruo quanji* (The collected works of Guo Moruo), vol. 12 (Beijing: Renmin wenxue chubanshe, 1992), 26.

102. "Shanghai wenyizhi yipie" (A cursory look at Shanghai literature), *LXQJ* 4:303.

103. Ibid., 291–292. An English translation appears in *SW* 3:127–141.

104. "Shanghai wenyizhi yipie," 292. Here Lu Xun alludes to the frequent appearance in Shanghai's "revolutionary literature" of prostitutes (cast as candidates for revolutionary transformation, with a notable number depicted as victims of venereal disease). Of this literature, David Wang writes: "Revolution and romance—punctuated by frequent outbreaks of disease—constitute major phenomena in the literary etiology of the First Chinese Communist Revolution of 1927"; *The Monster That Is History*, 79.

105. "Shanghai wenyizhi yipie," *LXQJ* 4:297–298.

106. Ibid.,297.

107. Ibid.

108. Ibid., 298; "A Glance at Shanghai Literature," *SW* 3:135.

109. In the early to mid-1910s, Liu Bannong was a writer of romantic fiction in Shanghai, a fact that he sought to obscure following his conversion to New Culture after 1916. For an overview of the New Culture elite's disparagement of Shanghai romantic fiction, see Chen Sihe, "Lun Haipai wenxuede chuantong" (On the literary tradition of the Shanghai School), *Hangzhou shifanxueyuan xuebao*, no. 1 (2002), 1–6.

110. Zhao Cong, *Wu Si wenxue nizhua* (The tracks of May Fourth literature) (Taipeh: Shibao shuxi, 1980), 46.

111. In his memoirs Mao Dun recounts the attempts of the Commercial Press's chief editor, Wang Yunwu, to boost revenue by including some "new-style" writings in the press's popular "old-style" fiction magazines.

New Culture advocates promptly denounced the ploy in print, in defense of their own literary wares. See Mao Dun, "Fuza er jinzhangde shenghuo, xuexi yu douzheng" (Living, studying, and struggling in complex and anxious times), Part 1, *Xin wenxue shiliao*, no. 40 (1979), 13–15. On the rivalry of "old" and "new," see Michel Hockx, "The Chinese Literary Association," in Denton and Hockx, *Literary Societies of Republican China*, 89.

112. The term "modern print capitalism" is Christopher Reed's, in *Gutenberg in Shanghai: Chinese Print Capitalism. 1876–1937* (Vancouver: University of British Columbia Press, 2004), 238.

113. Xueqing Xu, "The Mandarin Duck and Butterfly School," in Denton and Hockx, *Literary Societies of Republican China*, 61. Bao and Zhou were co-signatories with Lu Xun of an important 1936 public statement: "A Manifesto of Fellows in the Literary Realm, United against Foreign Aggression and in Defense of Free Speech" ("Wenyijie tongren wei tuanjie yuwu yu yanlun ziyou xuanyan"), *Wenxue* 7, no. 40 (1 October 1936).

114. Examples of the business acumen of Shanghai's leading publishers are discussed in Reed, *Gutenberg in Shanghai*, 217–223.

115. Mao Dun, "Fuza er jinzhangde shenghuo, xuexi yu douzheng," 14–15.

116. See, for instance, Hu Shi's account of the *baihua* movement in "Dao yan" (Introduction), in *Zhongguo xin wenxue daxi* (Compendium of modern Chinese literature), ed. Zhao Jiabi, vol. 1 (Shanghai: Liangyou, 1935), 1.

117. Lu Xiangyuan, *Gaochou zenyang jiaodong wentan* (How manuscript fees caused a stir in the literary scene) (Beijing: Hongqi chubanshe, 1998), 190.

118. Chen, *Wenhua rende jingji shenghuo*, 87–88. Chinese silver dollars were the closest to a standard currency in early Republican China; ibid., 334.

119. In mid-1926 Lu Xun wrote an essay detailing the bureaucratic morass involved in claiming a partial (one-third) salary payment. See "Ji 'fa xin'" ("Getting paid": A record), *LXQJ* 3:349–354.

120. Wang Jianhui, "Shanghai Shangwu yinshuguan: Bianji xinshui he zuozhe gaochou wenti" (The Commercial Press in Shanghai: On editors' salaries and manuscript fees), *Chuban faxing yanjiu*, no. 8 (2002), 70; Chen, *Wenhua rende jingji shenghuo*, 54.

121. Reed, *Gutenberg in Shanghai*, 206–211. Reed makes the important point that these publishers "now embraced the semiregulated marketplace and patronage of the Nationalist party-state," thus paving the way for state-run publishing after 1937; ibid., 205–206.

122. Xu Zhimo et al., "*Xinyuede* taidu" (The attitude of the Crescent Moon), *GWLZ* 2:1034–35.

123. Ibid., 1035.

124. Ibid., 1034.

125. Ibid., 1033.

126. Ibid.

127. Ibid., 1036-37.

128. "Some Thoughts on Our New Literature," *SW* 3:52.

129. Ibid., 51-52.

130. In his lectures from 1924 to 1927, Lu Xun made extensive use of his translations of Kuriyagawa's work. See Huang Dezhi, "Chuchuanbaichun zai xiandai Zhongguode yijie yu chuanbo" (Translation and dissemination of Kuriyagawa's work in China), *Journal of Changshu Institute of Technology (Philosophy and Social Sciences)*, no. 9 (September 2008), 78, 80.

131. On Lu Xun's translations of Russian literature, see Mark Gamsa, *The Chinese Translation of Russian Literature* (Leiden: Brill, 2008), 181-189.

132. "Xuyan," *LXQJ* 4:6.

133. "Tongxin," *LXQJ* 4:96-97; "Two Letters," *SW* 3:36, modified.

134. Chen, *Wenhua rende jingji shenghuo*, 200-201. An account of this dispute appears in *LXQJ* 15:420-421.

135. Chen, *Wenhua rende jingji shenghuo*, 122-123. The same survey is cited in Hanchao Lu, *Beyond the Neon Lights: Everyday Shanghai in the Early Twentieth Century* (Berkeley: University of California Press, 1999), 60.

136. Fang Xiangdong, ed., *Huode Lu Xun* (The living Lu Xun) (Shanghai: Shiji chuban jituan, 2001), 288-289.

137. "Shanghai wenyizhi yipie," *LXQJ* 4:298.

138. Zhang Kejia, "Lu Xun xiansheng yu bianji chuban gongzuo" (Lu Xun's role in editing and publishing), in *Zhongguo xiandai chuban shiliao* (Materials on publishing in China), ed. Zhang Jinglu, vol. 2 (Beijing: Zhonghua shuju, 1959), 260.

139. See *LXQJ* 15:420; Chen, *Wenhua rende jingji shenghuo*, 114; Chen Shuping, "Tianrande mengyou yu 'duikangxin lianmeng': Lun Lu Xun yu Beixin shujude shizhong" (Natural allies and "a union of resistance": On Lu Xun's relations with Beixin Publishing House), *Shanxi shifandaxuebao (shehui kexue ban)*, 35, no. 5 (2008), 52.

140. As tallied in Chen, *Wenhua rende jingji shenghuo*, 202.

141. "Zai Shanghaide Lu Xun qishi" (A notice from the [real] Lu Xun in Shanghai), *LXQJ* 4:75.

142. "The History of My Connection with the *Tatler*," *SW* 3:70; "Wo he *Yuside* shizhong" (*Threads of Talk* and me: A full account), *LXQJ* 4:171.

143. Kuang Xinnian, *1928: Geming wenxue* (1928: Revolutionary literature) (Jinan: Shandong jiaoyu chubanshe, 1998), 288.

144. "On Seeing Shaw and Those Who Saw Shaw," *SW* 3:252.

145. Discussed in Jonathan Hutt, *"La Maison d'Or:* The Sumptuous World of Shao Xunmei," *East Asian History,* no. 21 (2001), 119–123.

146. Ibid., 124–125; "Deng long shu shiyi" (The art of quick success: A supplement), *LXQJ* 5:274–275.

147. Jonathan Hutt, "Changing Minds: Intellectual Anxiety and the Shanghai Style" (Ph.D. diss., Australian National University, 2003), 159.

148. The patronage of influential Japanese-educated Chinese intellectuals made Neishan one of Shanghai's best-known bookstores. As Hanchao Lu writes: "[Uchiyama] operated his bookstore in a Barnes and Noble-type fashion: the bookstore was fitted with full-wall open stacks and a set of seven or eight rattan-framed sofas and chairs encircling a small table known as the 'chatting corner' *(mantanxi)* and free tea was served"; *Beyond the Neon Lights,* 176.

149. Shu-Mei Shi, *The Lure of the Modern: Writing Modernism in Semi-Colonial China, 1917–1937* (Berkeley: University of California Press, 2001), 141.

150. Quoted in Wang Qiong and Wang Junke, "Kafeiguan: Shanghai ershi shiji chude xiandaixing xiangxiang kongjian" (Cafés: Modern imaginary spaces in early twentieth-century Shanghai), *Yue hai feng,* no. 4 (2006), at http://www.yuehaifeng.com.cn/YHF2006/yhf2006-04-15.htm (accessed 20 December 2011).

151. Ti Jima, *Lu Xun he tade tong shidai ren* (Lu Xun and his contemporaries) (Shenyang: Chunfeng wenyi chubanshe, 1985), 43.

152. "Geming kafeidian" (Revolutionary café), *LXQJ* 4:116.

153. Cheng Fangwu, "Cong wenxue geming dao geming wenxue" (From literary revolution to revolutionary literature), *GWLZ* 1:137.

154. "Geming kafeidian," *LXQJ* 4:116–117.

155. Wang and Wang, "Kafeiguan," at http://www.yuehaifeng.com.cn/YHF2006/yhf2006-04-15.htm (accessed 20 December 2011).

156. *LXQJ* 14:810, 812.

157. Wong, *Politics and Literature in Shanghai,* 51.

158. "Two Letters," *SW* 3:38.

159. See Brian G. Martin, *The Shanghai Green Gang: Politics and Organized Crime, 1919–1937* (Berkeley: University of California Press, 1996), 141–149.

160. Ibid., 141.

161. The observations Lu Xun made in "The Evolution of Hooligans" were reprised in several other essays and speeches he produced in the 1930s.

162. The quote appears in "Zuiyan zhongde menglong," *LXQJ* 4:61. What Lu Xun wrote was "few are foolish enough to forget who actually wields the commander's sword."

3. Guns and Words

1. Paul Virilio, *Speed and Politics: An Essay on Dromology* (New York: Columbia University Press, 1986), 98.

2. Bruce D. Porter, *The USSR in Third World Conflicts: Soviet Arms and Diplomacy in Local Wars* (London: Cambridge University Press, 1984), 10.

3. Quoted in Hsi-sheng Chi, *Warlord Politics in China, 1916–1928* (Stanford: Stanford University Press, 1976), 122.

4. Patrick Cavendish, "The 'New China' of the Kuomintang," in *Modern China's Search for a Political Form,* ed. Jack Gray (London: Oxford University Press, 1969), 147.

5. "An Unrevolutionary Eagerness for Revolution," *SW* 3:100; "Fei gemingde jijin geming lun zhe," *LXQJ* 4:227.

6. *SW* 3:100–102; *LXQJ* 4:227–228.

7. Yu Dafu, "Guangzhou shiqing" (Guangzhou affairs), in *Yu Dafu wenji* (The works of Yu Dafu), vol. 8 (Hong Kong: Joint Publications, 1984), 17.

8. Ibid.

9. Quoted in Cavendish, "The 'New China' of the Kuomintang," 147.

10. Deng returned to China in 1930 to form the "Third Party" as a political organization opposed to both the Nationalists and the Communists. Shortly after his return, he was arrested in Shanghai by the French authorities and handed over to the Nationalist government. He was executed under orders from Chiang Kai-shek. Harold Isaacs, *The Tragedy of the Chinese Revolution* (Stanford: Stanford University Press, 1961), 271.

11. "Xiao zagan," *LXQJ* 3:530; "Odd Fancies," *SW* 2:356–357.

12. Fang Xiangdong, ed., *Huode Lu Xun* (The living Lu Xun) (Shanghai: Shiji chuban jituan, 2001), 283.

13. "Geming wenxue" (Revolutionary literature), *LXQJ* 3:554.

14. "Wenyi yu zhengzhide qitu" (The divergence between the arts and politics), *LXQJ* 7:119.

15. Lu Xun, however, was familiar with Artsybashev's 1912 work *At the Brink* and his depiction of an epidemic of suicides among Russian intellectuals. See Mark Gamsa, *The Chinese Translation of Russian Literature* (Leiden: Brill, 2008), 185.

16. Lu Xun, "The Divergence of Art and Politics," trans. Donald Holoch and Shu-ying Tsau, in *Modern Chinese Literary Thought: Writings on Literature,*

1893–1945, ed. Kirk A. Denton (Stanford: Stanford University Press, 1996), 331.

17. Ibid., 334, modified.
18. "Wenyi yu zhengzhide qitu," *LXQJ* 7:120.
19. In 1928 Lu Xun's antagonists in the Creation and Sun Societies took particular delight in mocking him as a laggard not least because his reputation as China's foremost modern writer was bound up with the idea of "speed."
20. "Kuangren riji," *LXQJ* 1:432; "A Madman's Diary," *SW* 1:51.
21. Walter Benjamin, *Selected Writings,* ed. Howard Eiland and Michael W. Jennings, trans. Edmund Jephcott and others, vol. 4: *1938–1940* (Cambridge, Mass.: The Belknap Press of Harvard University Press, 2003), 405.
22. "Suigan lu 48" (Impromptu notes no. 48), *LXQJ* 1:336.
23. "Gu *Xueheng*" (Reviewing *Critical Review*), *LXQJ* 1:377.
24. "Suigan lu 48," *LXQJ* 1:336.
25. The work appeared in several editions in the early 1920s. A final revised edition was produced in 1931. Reprinted in *LXQJ* 9:1–297.
26. John Y. C. Wang, "Lu Xun as a Scholar of Traditional Chinese Literature," in *Lu Xun and His Legacy,* ed. Leo Ou-fan Lee (Berkeley: University of California Press, 1985), 92–99.
27. As Lu Xun put it, paeans were the work of "progressive writers" extolling "the destruction of the old and the construction of the new," while dirges issued from those "unable to change overnight into new people" who mourned "the good old days and hanker after the old society"; "Literature of a Revolutionary Period," *SW* 2:338.
28. The *Zuo Commentary* describes Ji Zha, a prince of the state of Wu, as undertaking a moral taxonomy of musical renditions of the *Book of Odes (Shi Jing),* both to assess the various states of his time and to imbibe the virtues of the well-governed ones.
29. "Literature of a Revolutionary Period," *SW* 2:339.
30. "Reply to Mr. Youheng," *SW* 2:347; "Da Youheng xiansheng," *LXQJ* 3:454.
31. "Xiezai *Fen* houmian" (An epilogue to *The Grave*), *LXQJ* 1:286.
32. "Wenyi yu zhengzhide qitu," *LXQJ* 7:118.
33. "Yijue," *LXQJ* 2:223; "The Awakening," *SW* 1:363–364.
34. *LXQJ* 2:223.
35. "In Memory of Miss Liu Hezhen," *SW* 2:272.
36. "Kou si zagan" (Mixed impressions on the constraining of *Threads*), *LXQJ* 3:485.
37. Ibid., 489, n. 12.

38. *LXQJ* 11:176.

39. On Lu Xun's support of young writers, see Howard Goldblatt, "Lu Xun and Patterns of Literary Sponsorship," in Lee, *Lu Xun and His Legacy,* 199-215.

40. *LXQJ* 11:176.

41. "Yi Wei Suyuan jun" (In memory of Mr. Wei Suyuan), *LXQJ* 6:64.

42. "Suowei 'sixiangjie xianquzhe' Lu Xun qishi" (A notice on the so-called "intellectual pioneer" Lu Xun), *LXQJ* 3:391; *LXQJ* 11:176. See also Goldblatt, "Patterns of Literary Sponsorship," 209.

43. Bonnie S. McDougall, *Love Letters and Privacy in Modern China: The Intimate Lives of Lu Xun and Xu Guangping* (Oxford: Oxford University Press, 2002), 168, 184.

44. Leo Ou-Fan Lee, *Voices from the Iron House: A Study of Lu Xun* (Bloomington: Indiana University Press, 1987), 179.

45. "Yibiao zhi wai" (Beyond appearances), *LXQJ* 3:496.

46. "Wo he *Yusi*de shizhong" (*Threads of Talk* and me: A full account), *LXQJ* 4:164-175; a full English translation appears in *SW* 3:62-71.

47. Vera Schwarcz, *The Chinese Enlightenment: Intellectuals and the Legacy of the May Fourth Movement of 1919* (Berkeley: University of California Press, 1990), 134-135, 152-153.

48. "The History of My Connection with the *Tatler,*" *SW* 3:66.

49. Mark Miller, "The Yusi Society," in *Literary Societies of Republican China,* ed. Kirk A. Denton and Michel Hockx (Lanham, Md.: Lexington Books, 2008), 184-187.

50. *A Brief History (Zhongguo xiaoshuo shilue)* was first published by New Tide in 1923 and 1924 as a two-volume work. Beixin published a one-volume edition in 1925, with a revised edition appearing in 1931. *A Call to Arms* first appeared under the New Tide imprint in 1923. Beixin published the work's third reprint in 1926. Details appear in *LXQJ* 9:2, 1:414.

51. Chen Shuping, "Tianrande mengyou yu 'duikangxin lianmeng': Lun Lu Xun yu Beixin shujude shizhong" (Natural allies and "a union of resistance": On Lu Xun's relations with Beixin Publishing House), *Shanxi shifandaxuebao (shehui kexue ban),* 35, no. 5 (2008), 52-53.

52. "The History of My Connection with the *Tatler,*" *SW* 3:70.

53. Ibid., 68.

54. Ibid., 66, 70-71.

55. Ibid., 68-69.

56. McDougall, *Love Letters and Privacy,* 24-25.

57. Lee, *Voices from the Iron House,* 90.

58. Ibid.

59. Ibid., 62.

60. The reference appears in Mao's January 1940 speech "On New Democracy," at http://www.marxists.org/reference/archive/mao/selected-works /volume-2/mswv2_26.htm (accessed 20 December 2011).

61. Lu Xun's reference to "Jiang Guang X" was a jibe at Jiang for changing the revolutionary name he had chosen for himself, Guangchi ("radiantly red") to Guangci ("radiantly compassionate") to avoid attracting suspicion from the Nationalist government. The quotation "echoes his younger brother in saying beautiful things" is from Feng Naichao's attack on Lu Xun and Zhou Zuoren in a January 1928 essay. "Wentande zhanggu" (Tales from the literary scene), *LXQJ* 4:122.

62. Xu Guangping, *Lu Xun huiyi lu* (Remembering Lu Xun) (Wuhan: Changjiang wenyi chubanshe, 2010), 192.

63. Of the prominent intellectuals who went to Guangzhou in 1926 and 1927, Lu Xun alone was honored with a Festschrift celebrating his role in the revolution's headquarters.

64. "Tongxin" (Correspondence), *LXQJ* 3:447. Li complied with two of these requests. *Lu Xun zai Guangdong* was duly revised and published under the name of its editor, Zhong Jingwen (then a student in Guangzhou who later achieved eminence as a literary scholar), and Lu Xun's letter was published in *Threads of Talk*. But Li evidently chose to ignore Lu Xun's first request: an extant copy of the revised book features Lu Xun's four lectures in the appendix.

65. "Guanyu zhishijieji" (On the intelligentsia), *LXQJ* 8:188.

66. Quoted in Zeev Sternhell, with Mario Sznajder and Maia Asheri, *The Birth of Fascist Ideology: From Cultural Rebellion to Political Revolution,* trans. David Maisel (Princeton: Princeton University Press, 1994), 28–29. On futurism in 1920s China, see Chen Sihe, "Shilun 'Wu Si' xinwenxue yundongde xianfengxing" (Avant-garde aspects of the May Fourth New Literature Movement), *Fudan xuebao (shehui kexue ban),* no. 6 (2005), 1–17.

67. As translated in Yu-shih Chen, *Realism and Allegory in the Early Fiction of Mao Dun* (Bloomington: Indiana University Press, 1986), 74.

68. Qian Xingcun, "Cong Dongjing huidao Wuhan" (From Tokyo to Wuhan), in *Xiandai Zhongguo wenxue zuojia* (Modern Chinese writers), ed. Qian Xingcun, vol. 2 (Shanghai: Taidong shudian, 1930), 70.

69. On Jiang Guangci's style of revolutionary romanticism, see David Derwei Wang, *The Monster That Is History: History, Violence, and Fiction Writing in Twentieth-Century China* (Berkeley: University of California Press, 2004), 86–93.

70. Quoted in Kuang Xinnian, *1928: Geming wenxue* (1928: Revolutionary literature) (Jinan: Shandong jiaoyu chubanshe, 1998), 96.
71. Hsia added that "each printing of Jiang's books probably did not exceed 2,000 copies" but the multiple print runs gave Jiang a good source of income from publishing royalties. Hsia, *The Gate of Darkness: Studies on the Leftist Literary Movement in China* (Seattle: University of Washington Press, 1968), 63.
72. Hua Xili, "Lun xin jiu zuojia yu geming wenxue" (On new and old writers and revolutionary literature), *GWLZ* 1:251. This was published under one of Jiang's pen names, a transliteration of Vasily.
73. Jiang Guangci, "Xiandai Zhongguo wenxue yu shehui shenghuo" (Contemporary Chinese literature and social life), *GWLZ* 1:85.
74. "'Hard Translation' and the 'Class Character of Literature,'" *SW* 3:94–95; "'Ying yi' yu 'wenxuede jiejixing,'" *LXQJ* 4:211.
75. First published as Guangci, "Lu Xun xiansheng" (Mr. Lu Xun), *Haishen Fortnightly,* January 1929; quoted in Shi Huige, "Bu jiqi yeba, pian jiqi" (We might as well remember this), *Jinan jiaoyu xueyuan xuebao,* no. 4 (2002), 55.
76. Quoted in Hsia, *The Gate of Darkness,* 55.
77. See ibid., 213–215.
78. Isaacs, *The Tragedy of the Chinese Revolution,* 330–333.
79. Hsia, *The Gate of Darkness,* 55–57; Wang, *The Monster That Is History,* 93.
80. Quoted in Hsia, *The Gate of Darkness,* 57–58, 63–64.
81. "'Hard Translation' and the 'Class Character of Literature,'" *SW* 3:95.
82. Shi, "Bu jiqi yeba, pian jiqi," 56.
83. Quoted in Kuang, *1928: Geming wenxue,* 95.
84. Ibid., 105.
85. "Literature and Revolution," *SW* 3:27.
86. Li Chuli, "Zenyangde jianshe geming wenxue" (How to construct revolutionary literature), *GWLZ* 1:166.
87. Ibid., 163. Liang Qichao and Zhang Taiyan, who in the 1900s were revered as revolutionary visionaries, were by the 1920s regularly derided in radical circles as men of obsolete views.
88. Ibid., 164–166.
89. "Befuddled Woolliness," *SW* 3:16.
90. Ibid., 20–21; "'Zuiyan' zhongde menglong," *LXQJ* 4:65.
91. *SW* 3:21–22, modified.
92. "Literature and Revolution," *SW* 3:26; "Wenxue yu geming," *LXQJ* 4:83.
93. This was the Communists' attempt to regain power in Guangzhou, encouraged by Moscow, in December 1927. At six A.M. on 11 December a

small group of activists occupied Guangzhou's police headquarters and proclaimed the start of a Soviet government, encouraging workers to join them. By midmorning the Nationalist troops struck back, and on 13 December the uprising was decisively put down. The Japanese-run newspaper *Shuntian shibao* reported that Communist casualties were enormous, and the massacre was particularly gruesome: "The corpses lying stiff in their blood stank horribly . . . I saw three trucks piled high with corpses. . . . There were mournful shrieks and in the distance there still seemed to be shooting going on." Quoted in Isaacs, *The Tragedy of the Chinese Revolution*, 288–291.

94. "Some Thoughts on Our New Literature," *SW* 3:54; "Xianjinde xin wenxuede gaiguan," *LXQJ* 4:135.

95. Xu Jie, "Kanke daolushangde zuji" (Footprints on the long hard path), Part 6, *Xinwenxue shiliao*, no. 2 (1984), 61.

96. The work in question was *Dafu daibiao zuo* (The representative works of Yu Dafu), discussed in Lou Shiyi, "Huiyi Dafu" (Remembering Yu Dafu), *Xin wenxue shiliao*, no. 2 (1984), 116. By the late 1920s Yu was receiving between 100 to 200 dollars per month in royalty payments alone. He had several other sources of income, including fees received for his manuscripts and editorial work.

97. Wu Taichang, ed., "A Ying yi Zuolian" (A Ying's recollections of the Left-Wing League), *Xin wenxue shiliao*, no. 1 (1980), 18.

98. Meng Yue, *Shanghai and the Edges of Empire* (Minneapolis: University of Minnesota Press, 2006), 226; Shi Shuping, *Zhishifenzide gangwei yu zhuiqiu: Wenxue yanjiu hui yanjiu* (The position and pursuit of intellectuals: A study of the Chinese Literary Association) (Shanghai: Dongfang chuban zhongxin, 2006), 116.

99. Wu, "A Ying yi Zuolian," 18.

100. In 1923 Zheng involved Hu Shi in negotiating a truce between the Creation Society and the Chinese Literary Association. Hu Shi noted in a diary entry of October 1923 that he was a guest at the dinner that Zheng hosted in Shanghai to make peace with Guo Moruo. See Gong Jimin and Fang Rennian, "Hu Shi and Zheng Zhenduo," *Chinese Studies in History*, 39, no. 4 (2006), 12. The Creationists regarded the association as both an object of envy and its chief adversary. In a 1922 polemic against the association, Guo wrote: "What we detest the most is an organized collective, because a collective is already a form of violence. It may commit all sorts of bizarre deeds in the name of its number and might." See Xiaobing Tang with Michel Hockx, "The Creation Society (1921–1930)," in Denton and Hockx, *Literary Societies of Republican China*, 110.

101. Wu, "A Ying yi Zuolian," 14.

102. Ibid.

103. "'Zuiyan' zhongde menglong," *LXQJ* 4:61; "Befuddled Woolliness," *SW* 3:15-16.

104. Yang Xianru, "Zuoyi zuojia zai Shanghai Yida," *Xin wenxue shiliao,* 1 (1980), 87-89.

105. Cheng Fangwu, "Cong wenxue geming dao gemingwenxue," *GWLZ* 1:133.

106. Yang, "Zuoyi zuojia zai Shanghai Yida," 87. Michel Hockx observes that the popularity of the Creation Society's publications enabled it to be reorganized as a shareholding company in 1926 (at five dollars per share) with its own publishing house and bookshop. By 1927 the Creation Society had 397 listed shareholders and sufficient capital not only to publish a wide range of books and journals but to set up branch offices in other cities that served as both distribution outlets and places to recruit new shareholders. Hockx, "Playing the Field: Aspects of Chinese Literary Life in the 1920s," in *The Literary Field in Twentieth- Century China,* ed. Hockx (Richmond: Curzon Press, 1999), 73-75.

107. Qian Xingcun, "Tingkan xuanyan" (On the cessation of *Sun Monthly:* A declaration), *GWLZ* 1:524.

108. Li Modeng, "Guomindang fandongpai chajin baokan mulu" (A list of newspapers and periodicals banned by the reactionary Nationalist Party), in *Zhongguo xiandai chuban shiliao* (Source materials on modern publishing in China), ed. Zhang Jinglu, 4 vols. (Beijing: Zhonghua shuju, 1959), 2:153-176.

109. Xu Baimin, "Shanghai Shudian huiyi lu" (Recollections of the Shanghai Bookstore), ibid., 1:61-65; Yang Jincheng, "'Siyier'-'yierba' qijian chubande Shanghai gongren he qita jizhong gongren baokan" (*The Shanghai Worker* and other worker publications in the period from 12 April 1927 to 29 January 1931), ibid., 4:105-109.

110. In 1932 the scale of the ban led forty-nine of Shanghai's leading publishing companies to protest formally against unreasonable constraints on freedom of speech in the newly introduced censorship laws. A copy of the petition appears under the title "Shanghai chubanye fandui Guomindang fandong zhengfu shixing chubanfa qingyuanshu" (A petition by the Shanghai publishing industry in protest against the reactionary Nationalist government's censorship laws), ibid., 4 Part 2: 412-414.

111. Chen, "Tianrande mengyou yu 'duikangxin lianmeng,'" 53-56. Chen names *A Selection of Lu Xun's Mixed Impressions (Lu Xun zagan xuanji),* ed-

ited by Qu Qiubai, published in July 1933, as his last book with Beixin. This is incorrect as Beixin released *Essays on False Freedom* in October 1933. By then Beixin had changed its name to Qingguang Publishing House following the company's brief suspension of operations again in late 1932 when it attracted unwanted state attention for publishing a book that Chinese Muslims found offensive; ibid.

112. Lin Xianzhi, *Lu Xunde zuihou shi nian* (Lu Xun's final decade) (Beijing: Zhongguo shehui kexue chubanshe, 2003), 98.

113. "Houji" (Afterword), *LXQJ* 5:382.

114. *LXQJ* 13:332; quoted in Lin, *Lu Xunde zuihou shi nian*, 98.

115. Meng, *Shanghai and the Edges of Empire*, 226.

116. See Hanchao Lu, *Beyond the Neon Lights: Everyday Shanghai in the Early Twentieth Century* (Berkeley: University of California Press, 1999), 175–177.

117. Cao Juren, *Lu Xun pingzhuan* (A biography of Lu Xun) (Shanghai: Dongfang chubanshe, 1999), 100.

118. Ibid.

119. Wu, "A Ying yi Zuolian," 15.

120. The number of people arrested that evening remains unclear. Rou Shi's letter from prison (quoted by Lu Xun) indicates that he was moved to Longhua Prison on 23 January 1931 with thirty-five others, including seven women. See Lu Xun, "Written for the Sake of Forgetting," *SW* 3:242. Rumors were rife that those arrested had been betrayed by a rival Communist faction. It was a time of deepening hostility among rival groups within the underground Party. See Hsia, *The Gate of Darkness*, 205–233; Tony Saich and Benjamin Yang, eds., *The Rise to Power of the Chinese Communist Party: Documents and Analysis* (Armonk, N.Y.: M. E. Sharpe, 1996), 286–288.

121. Quoted in Hsia, *The Gate of Darkness*, 168.

122. Cavendish, "The 'New China' of the Kuomintang," 154.

123. See Wen-hsin Yeh, *Shanghai Splendor: Economic Sentiments and the Making of Modern China, 1843–1949* (Berkeley: University of California Press, 2008), 44–45. In an earlier work, Yeh notes: "The slogan *danghua jiaoyu* (partification of education) first appeared in the mid-1920s, when the Central Executive Committee of the Guomindang in Guangzhou turned its attention to schools and students in the wake of the May Thirtieth Movement. Like so many other concepts employed by the Party at this time, including the Three Principles of the People, the meaning of *danghua jiaoyu* was subject to a number of interpretations, and it was surrounded by endless controversies as the Guomindang

moved from the First United Front towards the Purification Campaign of 1927. For a brief time in 1928, the government even abandoned the phrase *danghua jiaoyu* and insisted that it be replaced by 'education of the Three Principles of the People' *(sanmin zhuyi jiaoyu)*. The adoption of a new phrase in 1928 was undoubtedly motivated by a desire to deflect public criticism. The liberals in particular [including members of the Crescent Moon Society] had loudly decried the attempt to *danghua* and characterized the Party's educational policies as a display of unprincipled partisan control of university appointments and stifled academic freedom." Wen-hsin Yeh, *The Alienated Academy: Culture and Politics in Republican China, 1919–1937* (Cambridge, Mass.: Harvard East Asian Monographs, 2000), 173-174.

124. Jon Eugene von Kowallis, *The Lyrical Lu Xun: A Study of His Classical Style Verse* (Honolulu: University of Hawaii Press, 1996), 35.
125. Feng Xuefeng, *Huiyi Lu Xun* (Remembering Lu Xun) (Beijing: Renmin wenxue chubanshe, 1952), 118.
126. Ibid., 131-132.
127. Ibid., 132.
128. "Suigan lu 56: 'Laile'" (Impromptu notes no. 56: "It's here"), *LXQJ* 1:348.
129. "Suigan lu 59: 'Shengwu'" (Impromptu notes no. 59: "Sagely and martial"), *LXQJ* 1:355.
130. Lu Xun, "Toward a Refutation of Malevolent Voices" ("Po e sheng lun"), trans. Jon Eugene von Kowallis, *boundary 2*, 38, no. 2 (2011), 58-59.
131. *LXQJ* 11:629, as translated in Theodore Huters, "Hu Feng and the Critical Legacy of Lu Xun," in Lee, *Lu Xun and His Legacy*, 137.
132. Lee, *Voices from the Iron House*, 141, 158.
133. *LXQJ* 12:273.
134. "On 'Going into Battle' and 'Running Away,'" *SW* 3:225-226.
135. "Lun 'punan' he 'taonan'" (On "going into battle" and "running away"), *LXQJ* 4:473.
136. Sun Yu, "Ersu wenhua yingzi xiade Lu Xun" (The influence of Soviet Russian culture and film on Lu Xun), in *2003 Lu Xun yanjiu nianjian* (2003 annual review of Lu Xun research), ed. Zheng Xinmiao, Sun Yu, and Liu Zengren (Beijing: Renmin wenxue chubanshe, 2005), 357.
137. "Zai zhonglou shang" (In the belfry), *LXQJ* 4:33.
138. Ibid., 30; "In the Belfry," *SW* 2:369.
139. "The Critics We Need," *SW* 3:109.
140. Ibid.; "Women yao pipingjia," *LXQJ* 4:240.
141. *LXQJ* 4:240-241; *SW* 3:109-110.
142. Quoted in Hsia, *The Gate of Darkness*, 179-180.
143. Quoted in Kuang, *1928: Geming wenxue*, 117.

144. Lee, *Voices from the Iron House*, 181.

145. Yang Dongping, *Chengshi jifeng: Beijing he Shanghai de wenhua jingshen* (Urban monsoon: The cultural spirit of Beijing and Shanghai) (Beijing: Dongfang chubanshe), 142.

146. As Bonnie McDougall points out, Lin Yutang ostensibly meant that Lu Xun was distinct from "the ordinary run of grey elephants" but would have nonetheless known the pejorative connotation of "white elephant" as meaning "a burdensome or costly possession given by the kings of Siam to obnoxious courtiers in order to ruin them." McDougall notes that it remains unclear whether Lu Xun and Xu Guangping understood the barb that Lin intended. Lu Xun also referred to his unborn son with her as "our Little White Elephant." Lin never elaborated on his reasons for using the term. See McDougall, *Love Letters and Privacy*, 59.

147. *LXQJ* 16:23.

148. *LXQJ* 11:395; quoted in Cao, *Lu Xun pingzhuan*, 98.

149. *LXQJ* 11:293.

150. "On 'Going into Battle' and 'Running Away,'" *SW* 3:226.

151. "Weile wangquede jinian" (Remembering in order to forget), *LXQJ* 4:481.

152. Ibid., 483–484; "Written for the Sake of Forgetting," *SW* 3:240. Rou Shi had decided to write political novels instead of realist short stories. Lu Xun regarded him as a paragon of persistence and noted that even in jail Rou Shi "had not changed," for "he was eager to study German and work harder than ever"; *SW* 3:242.

153. "Weile wangquede jinian," *LXQJ* 4:484–485.

154. *The Complete Works of Zhuangzi*, trans. Burton Watson (New York: Columbia University Press, 1968), 80.

155. "Written for the Sake of Forgetting," *SW* 3:245–246, modified; "Weile wangquede jinian," *LXQJ* 4:488.

4. Debating Lu Xun

1. Quoted in Simon Leys, *Broken Images: Essays on Chinese Culture and Politics,* trans. Steve Cox (London: Allison and Busby, 1979), 31; "Xie zai *Fen* houmian" (An epilogue to *The Grave*), *LXQJ* 1: 284; "Scholars Scorn Each Other (1)," *SW* 4:176. *Thus Spoke Zarathustra,* in which the phrase "preachers of death" appears, was well known to Lu Xun. He translated it from the German original in 1920.

2. "Scholars Scorn Each Other (7)," *SW* 4:233.

3. Wang Zhihui, "Lun 'geming wenxue' yundong zhongde zongpaizhuyi" (On factionalism in the movement for "revolutionary literature"), *Hainan shifan xueyuan xuebao (shehui kexueban),* 16, no. 5 (2003), 23.

4. "Befuddled Woolliness," *SW* 3:21, modified; "'Zuiyan' zhongde menglong" (The haze of 'drunken eyes'), *LXQJ* 4:66.

5. Cheng Fangwu, "Wancheng womende wenxue geming" (Complete our literary revolution), *GWLZ* 1:20.

6. This remark of Sun Yat-sen's was quoted in an essay by a Creation Society member, Pan Zinian (writing as Ruo Shui), and requoted sardonically here by Lu Xun.

7. Here Lu Xun quotes from Ruo Shui's defense of the Creation Society. See Ruo Shui, "Tan xianzai Zhongguode wenxue jie" (On China's literary world today), *GWLZ* 1:281.

8. "Wode taidu, qiliang he nianji" (My attitude, tolerance, and age), *LXQJ* 4:112.

9. Guo Moruo, "Geming yu wenxue" (Revolution and literature), *GWLZ* 1:10.

10. Cheng Fangwu, "Cong wenxue geming dao geming wenxue" (From literary revolution to revolutionary literature), *GWLZ* 1:132–133, 136.

11. Ibid., 136, 132.

12. Ibid., 136.

13. Gino K. Piovesanai, *Recent Japanese Philosophical Thought, 1936–1996: A Survey* (with a new survey [1963-1996] by Naoshi Yamawaki) (Surrey: Curzon, Japan Library, 1997), 176.

14. Ibid.

15. Cheng, "Wancheng womende wenxue geming," 22. "Rhythm" appears in English.

16. Cheng, "Cong wenxue geming dao geming wenxue," *GWLZ* 1:135.

17. "Tongxin" (Correspondence), *LXQJ* 4:96.

18. "'Zuiyan' zhongde menglong," *LXQJ* 4:64.

19. Ibid.

20. See also Kuang Xinnian, *1928: Geming wenxue* (1928: Revolutionary literature) (Jinan: Shandong jiaoyu chubanshe, 1998), 60–64. Cheng Fangwu also set out the Creation Society's goals in a March 1928 essay titled "The Necessity of a Totalizing Critique" ("Quanbude pipanzhi biayao"), *GWLZ* 1:178–179.

21. Cheng Fangwu, "Zhuci" (Congratulatory words), *GWLZ* 1:112.

22. "'Zuiyan' zhongde menglong," *LXQJ* 4:64.

23. David E. Apter and Tony Saich, *Revolutionary Discourse in Mao's Republic* (Cambridge, Mass.: Harvard University Press, 1994), 68.

24. "'Zuiyan' zhongde menglong," *LXQJ* 4:63.

25. Ibid., 62.

26. "Yaowen jiaozi" (Chewing and gnawing on words), *LXQJ* 3:9–10. An early appearance of *yaowen jiaozi* is in the Yuan-era (1279-1368) *zaju* or variety

play *Sha gou quan fu* (Killing the dog to convince the husband). The phrase also occurs in the ribald eighteenth-century novel *He dian* (Which classic?), for which Lu Xun wrote a foreword in 1926.

27. Lu Xun's remarks were derisively quoted in the essays of Feng Naichao, Li Chuli, and Peng Kang.

28. Feng Naichao, "Rendaozhuyizhe zenyangde fangweizhe ziji?" (How does a humanist defend himself?), *GWLZ* 1:302-303.

29. Ibid., 302.

30. Li Chuli, "Qing kan women Zhongguode Don Quixote de luanwu" (Look at the wild dance of our Chinese Don Quixote), *GWLZ* 1:291.

31. Ibid., 293-294.

32. Feng Naichao, "Yishu yu shehui shenghuo" (Art and social life), *GWLZ* 1:121-123. As Feng had mocked Lu Xun's praise of Tolstoy's humanism earlier in this essay, the comment about Don Quixote was clearly directed against Lu Xun.

33. Li, "Qing kan women Zhongguode Don Quixote de luanwu," *GWLZ* 1:288-289. "The Diary of a Madman," Lu Xun's first story in *baihua,* appeared in the anthology *Na han.*

34. See, for instance, the essays by Cheng Fangwu and Feng Naichao at *GWLZ* 1:112, 303.

35. Li, "Qing kan women Zhongguode Don Quixote de luanwu," *GWLZ* 1:292-293.

36. Peng Kang, "'Chudiao' Lu Xunde 'chudiao'" (Let's eliminate Lu Xun's "eliminate"), *GWLZ* 1:307.

37. Ibid.

38. Ruo Shui, "Tan xianzai Zhougguode wenxue jie," *GWLZ* 1:281.

39. Fangwu, "Dafa tamen qu" (Send them away), *GWLZ* 1:152.

40. "Wode taidu, qiliang he nianji," *LXQJ* 4:109.

41. Ibid.

42. On the connotations of "Shaoxing legal clerk", see Li Jiao, *Zhongguode shiye* (China's legal clerks) (Shanghai: Shangwu yinshuguan, 1995), 26. In 1949 Zhou Zuoren wrote the essay "Guanyu Shaoxing shiye" (Concerning Shaoxing legal clerks) against this regional slur, 5 April 1949, *Ziyou luntan wanbao* (Free speech forum evening news).

43. Li, "Qing kan women Zhongguode Don Quixote de luanwu," *GWLZ* 1:300.

44. "Xuyan" (Preface), *LXQJ* 4:4. Of these insults, it was Cheng Fangwu and Li Chuli who referred to Lu Xun as "rich and idle," Cheng (using the pseudonym Hou Sheng) who denounced him as moribund, and Guo Moruo (writing as Du Quan) who called him "the dregs of feudalism" and a fascist. Ibid., 8.

45. It was only in the 1980s that mainland scholars were able to ascertain Du Quan's identity. See Wang-chi Wong, *Politics and Literature in Shanghai: The Chinese League of Left-Wing Writers, 1930–1936* (Manchester: Manchester University Press, 1991), 22.

46. Xu Qingquan, "Du Quan (Guo Moruo): Jing dong gaocengde yitiao zhushi" (DU Quan [Guo Moruo]: A startling revelation for those at the top, *Guangming wang*, http://www.gmw.cn/CONTENT/2004-09/07 /content_95078.htm (accessed 30 January 2012).

47. "Two Letters," *SW* 3:35.

48. "Tongxin," *LXQJ* 4:96.

49. "Two Letters," *SW* 3:40-41.

50. Ibid., 41.

51. Apter and Saich, *Revolutionary Discourse in Mao's Republic,* 134.

52. Ibid., 64.

53. "Two Letters," *SW* 3:39-40, modified.

54. "Wenyi yu zhengzhide qitu" (The divergence between the arts and politics), *LXQJ* 7:118.

55. Ibid.

56. Peng, "'Chudiao' Lu Xunde 'chudiao,'" *GWLZ* 1:313.

57. "Wenyi yu zhengzhide qitu," *LXQJ* 7:115.

58. Ibid.

59. Wang Furen, *Zhongguo wenhuade shouyeren: Lu Xun* (Night watchman of Chinese culture: Lu Xun) (Beijing: Renmin wenxue chubanshe, 2002), 24. According to Wang, Lu Xun's approach, as a modern synthesis of Confucian benevolence and Western humanism, presents individual autonomy as an egalitarian "life force" *(shengming huoli)* based in mutual respect; ibid., 114-115. In the 1980s and 1990s, Wang's valorization of Lu Xun's cosmopolitan humanism was highly influential in undermining the revolutionary paragon of state-guided Luxunology.

60. *Lun Yu* 12.22.

61. "Guanyu zhishijiejie" (On the intelligentsia), *LXQJ* 8:190-191. These remarks predate his clashes with the Creation Society and Sun Society.

62. Qian Xingcun, "Siquliaode A Q shidai" (The dead era of Ah Q), *GWLZ* 1:180. A full English translation by Paul Foster and Shelly Mou appears as "The Bygone Age of Ah Q" in *Modern Chinese Literary Thought: Writings on Literature, 1893–1945,* ed. Kirk A. Denton (Stanford: Stanford University Press, 1996), 276-288.

63. Ibid., 186.

64. Ibid., 182.

65. Paul B. Foster, *Ah Q Archaeology: Lu Xun, Ah Q, Ah Q Progeny and the National Character Discourse in Twentieth-Century China* (Lanham, Md.: Lexington Books, 2006), 190, 253.

66. "How *The True Story of Ah Q* Was Written," *SW* 2:316.

67. Foster, *Ah Q Archaeology,* 182.

68. *SW* 2:317, modified.

69. "Da *Xi zhoukan* bianzhe xin" (My reply to a letter from the editor of *Theatre Weekly*), *LXQJ* 6:145.

70. Qian, "Siquliaode A Q shidai," *GWLZ* 1:192. The term "Baudon," appearing in Roman letters, was a transliteration of the Chinese word *baodong,* meaning a revolt or uprising.

71. Liu Dajie became a leading literary historian whose 1941 survey account of Chinese literature, *Zhongguo wenxue fazhan shi* (The historical development of Chinese literature), shaped the periodization of Chinese literature thereafter. Liu, *"Nahan yu Panghuang yu Yecao"* (On *A Call to Arms, Wandering,* and *Wild Grass*), *GWLZ* 1:435.

72. Gan Ren, "Laza yipian da Li Chuli jun" (A jumbled response to Mr. Li Chuli), *GWLZ* 1:407.

73. Ibid., 409.

74. Qian, "Siquliaode A Q shidai," *GWLZ* 1:183.

75. "Wenyi yu zhengzhide qitu," *LXQJ* 7:119.

76. Qian, "Siquliaode A Q shidai," *GWLZ* 1:184.

77. "Taiping gejue" (Ditties on universal peace), *LXQJ* 4:103–104. The Mausoleum was completed in 1929.

78. Ibid., 103.

79. Ibid., 104.

80. Ke Xing (Fang Kexing), "Xiaozichan jiejie wenyi lun zhi miuwu" (The errors of the petty-bourgeois discourse on the arts), *GWLZ* 2:750.

81. Qian, "Siquliaode A Q shidai," *GWLZ* 1:193.

82. "Wenxuede jiejixing" (The class character of literature), *LXQJ* 4:127. Trotsky wrote: "Emancipated man will want to attain a greater equilibrium in the work of his organs and a more proportional developing and wearing out of his tissues, in order to reduce the fear of death to a rational reaction of the organism towards danger. There can be no doubt that man's extreme anatomical and physiological disharmony, that is, the extreme disproportion in the growth and wearing out of organs and tissues, give the life instinct the form of a pinched, morbid and hysterical fear of death, which darkens reason and which feeds the stupid and humiliating fantasies about life after death." Trotsky, *Literature and*

Revolution, trans. Rose Strunsky (New York: Russell & Russell, 1957), archived at http://www.marxists.org/archive/trotsky/1924/lit_revo/ch08 .htm.

83. Lu Xun coined the term "hard translation" in 1929 when describing his approach to translating Lunacharsky.

84. *Ying yi* can also be translated as "stiff" or "tough" translation; I have retained "hard translation" because it has long been the conventional, and literal, English translation and because it best reflects the ambiguity that Lu Xun intended.

85. Liang Shiqu, "Lun Lu Xun xianshengde 'ying yi'" (On Mr. Lu Xun's "hard translation"), *Xinyue yuekan,* 2, no. 6 (1929).

86. "'Ying yi' yu 'wenxuede jiejixing'" ("Hard translation" and "the class character of literature"), *LXQJ* 4:200.

87. Ibid., 195-197.

88. Ibid., 204. Liang's argument appears in "Wenxue shiyou jiejixingde ma?" (Does literature have a class character?), *GWLZ* 2:1090.

89. "'Ying yi' yu 'wenxuede jiejixing,'" *LXQJ* 4:204-205.

90. Ibid., 206.

91. The quotation appears in Qian Xingcun, "Huanmie dongyao shidaide tuidong lun" (Moving on from the age of disillusionment and vacillation), *GWLZ* 2:832.

92. "'Hard Translation' and the 'Class Character of Literature'," *SW* 3:89.

93. Ibid.; "'Ying yi' yu 'wenxuede jiejixing,'" *LXQJ* 4:206.

94. *LXQJ* 4:207-208.

95. "Thoughts on the League of Left-Wing Writers," *SW* 3:105-106, modified; "Duiyu Zuoyi zuojia lianmengde yijian," *LXQJ* 4:235-236.

96. *LXQJ* 4:235.

97. Lu Xun's admirers frequently praised his "objective" portrayals of social reality. See, for instance, Gan Ren, "Zhongguo xin wenyide jianglai yu qi zijide renshi" (On the future of China's New Literature and its identity), *GWLZ* 1:61.

98. Li Chuli, "Ziran shengzhangxing yu mudi yishixing" (Natural development and purposive consciousness), *GWLZ* 2:647.

99. "'Hard Translation' and the 'Class Character of Literature'," *SW* 3:91, modified.

100. "'Ying yi' yu 'wenxuede jiejixing,'" *LXQJ* 4:209.

101. "Duiyu Zuoyi zuojia lianmengde yijian," *LXQJ* 4:236. Lu Xun used the term *kong cheng ji,* or "the empty city stratagem," attributed to the military strategist Zhuge Liang (181-234). Zhuge allegedly deceived enemy

troops into thinking they were approaching a well-garrisoned city when he lacked the troops to defend it.

102. Ibid.

103. "Women yao pipingjia" (We need critics) *LXQJ* 4:240–241; "The Critics We Need," *SW* 3:110. *Da chuang* lends itself to being read as a double entendre, as it carries the dual connotation of a "serious wound" and "great originality."

104. Qian Xingcun, "Lu Xun," *GWLZ* 2:957.

105. *LXQJ* 12:8. *Qie hua se* (literally, "the color of aubergine flowers") has the connotation in Zhejiang dialect of being unremarkable, hence useless.

106. David Pollard, *The True Story of Lu Xun* (Hong Kong: Chinese University Press, 2002), 144.

107. Ibid., 144–145.

108. T. A. Hsia, *The Gate of Darkness: Studies on the Leftist Literary Movement in China* (Seattle: University of Washington Press, 1968), 101.

109. Katerina Clark, *The Soviet Novel: History as Ritual* (Bloomington: Indiana University Press, 2000), 31–32.

110. As James Goodwin points out, there was no "hard line" in Soviet cultural matters before 1928. A progressive hardening occurred between 1928 and 1932 in which the Party-state became directly involved in controlling the arts. RAPP, having served its purpose during this crucial period of cultural narrowing, was summarily dissolved in 1932. Goodwin, *Eisenstein, Cinema, and History* (University of Illinois Press, 1993), 141.

111. These statements were extensively reproduced in the afterword Lu Xun wrote for *A Policy on the Arts,* his 1930 anthology of Soviet works translated from Japanese. "*Wenyi zhengce* houji" (Afterword to *A Policy on the Arts*), *LXQJ* 10:306–307.

112. Ibid. On Lu Xun's noncommittal approach to Soviet literary policy and practice, see Leo Ou-Fan Lee, *Voices from the Iron House: A Study of Lu Xun* (Bloomington: Indiana University Press, 1987), 154–158.

113. "*Wenyi zhengce* houji," *LXQJ* 10:309.

114. Liang Shiqiu, "Suowei 'wenyi zhengce' zhe" (About the so-called "Policy on the Arts"), *Xinyue yuekan,* 3, no. 3 (May 1930), reproduced at http://www.tianyabook.com/luxun/001/001.htm (accessed 30 November 2011).

115. Wong, *Politics and Literature in Shanghai,* 153.

116. "On the 'Third Category,' " *SW* 3:189, modified.

117. On the connotations of this term and the debate it generated, see Sean Macdonald, " 'Modernism' in Modern Chinese Literature: The 'Third

Type of Person' as a Figure of Autonomy," *Canadian Review of Comparative Literature,* June–September 2002, 289-315.

118. "Lun 'disan zhong ren'" (On the third type of person), *LXQJ* 4:439-440; "On the 'Third Category,'" *SW* 3:189.

119. *LXQJ* 4:441.

120. "A Reply to *International Literature,*" *SW* 4:35.

121. Quoted in C. T. Hsia, *A History of Modern Chinese Fiction* (Indiana University Press, 1999), 594-595, slightly modified.

122. See Mark Selden, *China in Revolution: The Yenan Way Revisited* (Armonk, N.Y.: M. E. Sharpe, 1995), 86-88.

123. See Theodore Huters, "Hu Feng and the Critical Legacy of Lu Xun"; David Holm, "Lu Xun in the Period of 1936-1949: The Making of a Chinese Gorki"; and Merle Goldman, "The Political Uses of Lu Xun in the Cultural Revolution and After," in *Lu Xun and His Legacy,* ed. Leo Ou-fan Lee (Berkeley: University of California Press, 1985), 139, 154-155, 184-185.

124. As Wang-Chi Wong points out, before the League's dissolution, Lu Xun frequently attacked Zhou Yang in his private correspondence; *Politics and Literature in Shanghai,* 205.

125. Feng Xuefeng, *Huiyi Lu Xun* (Remembering Lu Xun) (Beijing: Renmin wenxue chubanshe, 1952), 132.

126. T. A. Hsia, *The Gate of Darkness,* 121.

127. Leo Ou-fan Lee offers the helpful observation that the "battle of the two slogans" in which Lu Xun became embroiled in the remaining months of his life "seemed to give the impression that, in matters of literary policy, the dictatorial Zhou Yang argued for more liberality whereas the anti-authoritarian opposition opted for more rigidity." He explains that "in matters of literary practice, the situation was just the reverse": "Lu Xun and Mao Dun insisted on creative freedom for the revolutionary writer while Zhou Yang considered it 'a dangerous illusion.' Veiled in their conflicting slogans was therefore a basic difference in the outlook between the literary commissar and the creative writer. For Zhou Yang, the literary commissar *par excellence,* the party policy of the united front took precedence over everything else, including artistic creation. As writers, Lu Xun and Mao Dun placed more value on creative writing for the goals of revolution: they were obstinate in their belief that conscientious artists should never compromise their personal integrity or lose their creative prerogatives. They strongly resented the imposition of this new *partiinost* by a self-appointed party spokesman." Lee, "Literary Trends: The Road to Revolution, 1927-1949," in *The Cambridge History of China,* ed. John K. Fairbank and Albert Feuerwerker, vol. 13, pt. 2: *Repub-*

lican China, 1912–1949 (Cambridge: Cambridge University Press, 1986), 442.

128. See Holm, "Lu Xun in the Period of 1936–1949," 154.

129. See Huters, "Hu Feng and the Critical Legacy of Lu Xun," 139.

130. Lu Xun published Xu's letter together with his reply. Xu's letter is reproduced in *LXQJ* 6:526–528.

131. Mu Mutian, a League member formerly of the Creation Society, was arrested by the Nationalist government in July 1934. Upon his release in September 1936, he resigned from the League. It was widely rumored that he had betrayed his fellow League members. In recent decades his resignation has been more sympathetically explained as an attempt to protect the League, since he was under close surveillance by the Nationalist secret police. See Wang Hongzhi, *Lu Xun yu "Zuo lian"* (Lu Xun and the Left-Wing League) (Beijing: Xinxing chubanshe, 2006), 286.

132. "Da Xu Maoyong bing guanyu kang Ri tongyi zhanxian wenti" (A reply to Xu Maoyong and remarks on the issue of a united front in resistance to Japan), *LXQJ* 6:534–535.

133. Ibid., 529–530.

134. Hsia, *The Gate of Darkness*, 144–145.

135. *LXQJ* 6:530.

136. Ibid. See also Huters, "Hu Feng and the Critical Legacy of Lu Xun," 141.

137. *LXQJ* 6:532.

138. Chiu-yee Cheung, *Lu Xun: The Chinese "Gentle" Nietzsche* (Frankfurt am Main: Peter Lang, 2001), 124.

139. T. A. Hsia observes that Guo was off by some 4,000 characters; the essay runs to about 6,000; *The Gate of Darkness*, 136.

140. Huters, "Hu Feng and the Critical Legacy of Lu Xun," 142.

141. Li Helin, the pseudonym of Li Zhunian, established his literary reputation through editing this 1929 "revolutionary literature" anthology. In the newly formed People's Republic of 1951, he was a member of the national committee (together with Lao She, Cai Yi, and Wang Yao) responsible for drafting the "Outline for Teaching the History of Modern Chinese Literature."

142. Li Helin, ed., *Zhongguo wenyi lunzhan* (A literary debate in China) (Shanghai: Beixin shudian, 1929), 2–3.

143. Ibid., 2.

144. See Li Helin, "Wode wenxue yanjiu yu jiaoxue shengya" (My literary research and teaching career), in *Li Helin quan ji* (The complete works of Li Helin), vol. 1 (Hebei Jiaoyu chubanshe, 2003), 12.

145. Li, *Zhongguo wenyi lunzhan*, 3.

146. The pseudonym Hua Shi ("artist's studio") points to the avant-garde leftist image that Feng, then already a prominent Communist operative, sought to project. On *Trackless Train,* see Leo Ou-fan Lee, *Shanghai Modern: The Flowering of a New Urban Culture in China, 1930–1945* (Cambridge, Mass.: Harvard University Press, 1999), 129–133, 191.

147. Feng Xuefeng, "Geming yu zhishijieji" (Revolution and the intellectual class), *GWLZ* 2:659–660.

148. Ibid, 659.

149. Feng, *Huiyi Lu Xun,* 3.

150. Ibid., 13.

151. Li Helin, *Jin ershi nian Zhongguo wenyi sichao lun* (Chinese literary trends of the last twenty years) (Chongqing: Shenghuo shudian, 1939), 243.

152. Ibid., 221–223.

153. Qian Liqun, "Wo duiyu Li Helin xianshengde xueshu gongxiande liang-dian kanfa" (Two comments on the scholarly contributions of Mr. Li Helin), *Lu Xun yanjiu yuekan,* no. 10 (2004), 4–12.

154. Li, *Jin ershi nian Zhongguo wenyi sichao lun,* 523–526.

155. Holm, "Lu Xun in the Period of 1936-1949," 167.

156. Ibid.

157. Ibid.

158. Ibid., 170.

159. Hsia, *The Gate of Darkness,* 144.

160. Xu Maoyong's words remain widely known and are posted at numerous Chinese-language websites on Lu Xun. See, for instance, "Xu Maoyong lun Lu Xun" (Xu Maoyong on Lu Xun), at http://www.eywedu.com/luxun/plo2o.htm (accessed 20 November 2011).

161. Quoted and discussed in Hsia, *The Gate of Darkness,* 138–139.

162. Ibid., 143–144.

163. Holm, "Lu Xun in the Period of 1936-1949," 170–172, 175.

164. Goldman, "The Political Uses of Lu Xun," 183–184.

165. Ibid., 184.

166. Wang Youqin, "1966: Xuesheng da laoshide geming" (1966: A revolution in which students beat their teachers), *Ershiyi shiji,* August 1995, now available at http://www.tianya.cn/publicforum/content/books/1/102869.shtml (accessed 30 November 2011).

167. Shi Housheng (a pseudonym of Cheng's), "Bijing shi 'zuiyan taoran' bale" (Just a case of "drunken euphoria"), *GWLZ* 1:375.

168. "A Glance at Shanghai Literature," *SW* 3:134, modified; "Shanghai weny-izhi yipie," *LXQJ* 4:297.

169. "Xu Guangping zai 'Wenge' zhong weiceng dian Cheng Fangwude ming" (Xu Guangping did not name Cheng Fangwu during the Cultural Revolution), *Lu Xun yanjiu yuekan,* no. 12 (1996), 11 (unattributed).

170. Mu Xin, "Guo Moruo zai Wenge zhongde jienan" (The tribulations of Guo Moruo during the Cultural Revolution), *Yanhuang chunqiu,* no. 7 (1998), 44-45, 47.

171. Chen and Hu served the Nationalist government as diplomats: Chen went to London in 1944 to head up the Sino-British Cultural Association; Hu was China's ambassador to the United States from 1938 to 1942. After 1949 Hu lived in New York before going to Taiwan in 1958. Liang went to Taiwan in 1949, when the Communist victory was imminent.

172. Quoted in Simon Leys, *Broken Images: Essays on Chinese Culture and Politics,* trans. Steve Cox (London: Allison and Busby, 1979), 17.

173. Wang Jing, Zhu Songmei, and Ren Yan, "Cheng Fangwu: 'Wo meiyou yijian': Ting Liu Peicheng laoshi huiyi sanshinian qiande yiduan wangshi" (On Cheng Fangwu's "I Have No Opinion": The recollections of our teacher, Liu Peicheng, on a thirty-year-old incident), *Shandong daxue xiaobao,* 28 November 2008, at www.view.sdu.edu.cn/news/news/sdrw/2008-11-28/1227860392.html (accessed 15 December 2011).

174. Quoted in Holm, "Lu Xun in the Period of 1936-1949," 166.

175. Wu Jiarong, "Wenge zhongde A Ying" (A Ying [Qian Xingcun] during the Cultural Revolution), *Jianghuai wenshi,* no. 1 (2002), 40; Joseph W. Esherick, Paul G. Pickowicz, and Andrew G. Walder, *The Chinese Cultural Revolution as History* (Stanford: Stanford University Press, 2006), 76.

176. Holm, "Lu Xun in the Period of 1936-1949," 165-166.

177. Quoted in "Lun fei'e bolai' yinggai yuanxing" (On deferring "fair play"), *LXQJ* 1:277. It was Zhou Zuoren who first described "fair play" as "Don't beat a drowning dog." See Yu Tang (Lin Yutang), "Chalun *Yusi* de wenti: Yinjian, maren yu fei'erpolai" (An intervention regarding the style of *Threads of Talk:* On firmness, abuse, and fair play), was published in *Yu Si,* no. 57 (14 December 1925), 3-6.

178. "Lun fei'e bolai' yinggai yuanxing," *LXQJ* 1:271-272.

179. "Da Tuoluosiji paide xin" (A reply to the Trotskyists), *LXQJ* 6:587-589; see Gregor Benton, "Lu Xun, Leon Trotsky, and the Chinese Trotskyists," *East Asian History,* no. 7 (1994), 93-104.

180. "'Ying yi' yu 'wenxuede jiejixing,'" *LXQJ* 4:197.

181. "Notes after Reading (3)," *SW* 4:101.

182. "Ban xia xiao ji" (A short midsummer anthology), *LXQJ* 6:597.

183. Ibid.

5. Lu Xun's Revolutionary Literature

1. "Preface to *Letters between Two*," *SW* 3:207, modified.

2. See for instance Sun Yushi, Ye cao *yanjiu* (A study of *Wild Grass*) (Beijing: Beijing daxue chubanshe, 2007), 43–44. The first edition of this work, which appeared in 1982, was regarded by many mainland academics as a watershed moment in post-Maoist scholarship on Lu Xun.

3. Qian Liqun, *Yu Lu Xun xiangyu: Beida yanjianglu 2* (An encounter with Lu Xun: Lectures at Beida part 2) (Beijing: Sanlian shudian, 2003), 290.

4. Feng Xuefeng, *Huiyi Lu Xun* (Remembering Lu Xun) (Beijing: Renmin wenxue chubanshe, 1952), 14–15.

5. Ibid., 14–15, 19.

6. "Xie zai *Fen* houmian" (An epilogue to *The Grave*), *LXQJ* 1:286. Ban Wang, quoting the Lu Xun scholar Wang Hui, reads Lu Xun's figure of "in-betweenness" (*zhongjianwu*) as signifying the "historical impasse" that Lu Xun and his contemporaries experienced as they actively promoted an alien "modernity" over a familiar "tradition." See Wang, *Illuminations from the Past: Trauma, Memory, and History in Modern China* (Stanford: Stanford University Press, 2004), 34–35. Here Lu Xun was making the general observation that we are each an "intermediate entity," speaking and writing in ways expressive of our time.

7. "Xie zai *Fen* houmian," *LXQJ* 1:286.

8. The anthology was first published in March 1927 by the Yet to Be Named Society, cofounded by Lu Xun's disciples with his assistance.

9. "Xie zai *Fen* houmian," *LXQJ* 1:286. On Lu Xun's use of these varieties of literary Chinese, see Leo Ou-fan Lee, "Tradition and Modernity in the Writings of Lu Xun," in *Lu Xun and His Legacy*, ed. Lee (Berkeley: University of California Press, 1985), 1–31.

10. "Moluo shi li shuo," *LXQJ* 1:63–100. An excerpt appears as "On the Power of Mara Poetry," trans. Shu-ying Tsau and Donald Holoch, in *Modern Chinese Literary Thought: Writings on Literature, 1893–1945*, ed. Kirk A. Denton (Stanford: Stanford University Press, 1996), 96–109.

11. "Silent China," *SW* 2:332.

12. Ibid., 333.

13. "Zai lun 'wenren xiangqing'" (Further words on "mutual contempt among the lettered"), *LXQJ* 6:336; "Scholars Scorn Each Other (2)," *SW* 4:200.

14. Michel Foucault, *The Hermeneutics of the Subject: Lectures at the Collège de France, 1981–1982*, ed. Frédéric Gros, trans. Graham Burchell (New York: Picador, 2006), 15.

15. "Buman" (Dissatisfaction), *LXQJ* 1:358.

16. Ibid.
17. Ibid.
18. "Pushed," *SW* 3:304, modified.
19. "Jingyan" (Experience), *LXQJ* 4:540.
20. "Xiaopinwende weiji" (The personal essay in crisis), *LXQJ* 4:576-577.
21. "Hei'an Zhongguode wenyi jiede xianzhuang" (The present situation of the literary scene in dark China), *LXQJ* 4:285-290, the essay he wrote in 1931 for the American magazine *New Masses*. There is no extant copy of the essay in English. A translation of the Chinese essay appears as "The Present Condition of Art in Darkest China" in *SW* 3:122-126.
22. Sonia Orwell and Ian Angus, eds., *The Collected Essays, Journalism, and Letters of George Orwell*, vol. 3, *As I Please: 1943-1945* (New York: Harcourt, Brace and World, 1968), 7.
23. "A ton of TNT" was Cheng Fangwu's phrase; "machine guns and trench mortars" appeared in an essay by Li Chuli and "gonnon" in an essay by Guo Moruo. See Cheng, "Cong wenxue geming dao geming wenxue," *GWLZ* 1:135; Li, "Zenyangde jianshe geming wenxue," *GWLZ* 1:166; Mai Ke'ang (Guo's pseudonym), "Yingxiong shu," *GWLZ* 1:76.
24. "Da Youheng xiansheng" (A reply to Mr. Shi Youheng), *LXQJ* 3:454.
25. "Tongxin" (Correspondence), *LXQJ* 4:97; "Two Letters," *SW* 3:36-37.
26. "'Ying yi' yu 'wenxuede jiejixing'" ("Hard translation" and "the class character of literature"), *LXQJ* 4:209.
27. "Fuchou" (Revenge) and "Fuchou II," *LXQJ* 2:172-175. The writing in *Wild Grass* defies classification. Lu Xun referred to the individual pieces as "short compositions" that could be "more pretentiously called prose poetry." Quoted in Leo Ou-fan Lee, *Voices from the Iron House: A study of Lu Xun* (Bloomington: Indiana University Press, 1987), 91.
28. This sentiment echoes the statement he made in his 1923 essay "What Happens after Nora Leaves Home?" that the only way to save this crowd "is to give them no drama to watch"; *SW* 2:93.
29. "Fuchou," *LXQJ* 2:172-173.
30. As translated in Simon Leys, *Broken Images: Essays on Chinese Culture and Politics,* trans. Steve Cox (London: Allison and Busby, 1979), 28.
31. "Tici" (Preface), *LXQJ* 2:159; Lu Hsun, *Wild Grass*, trans. Yang Xianyi and Gladys Yang (Peking: Foreign Languages Press, 1976), 3.
32. "Tici," *LXQJ* 2:159.
33. "Waiting for a Genius," *SW* 2:96.
34. Martin Heidegger, *Discourse on Thinking: A Translation of Gelassenheit,* trans. John M. Anderson and E. Hans Freund (New York: Harper and Row, 1966), 53.

35. *LXQJ* 12:381, discussed in John Wang, "Lu Xun as a Scholar of Traditional Chinese Literature," in Lee, *Lu Xun and His Legacy*, 92.

36. Lu Xun's portrait of Laozi is discussed later in this chapter. Of Confucius, he wrote in 1935 that once when he was traveling on a rough road in Shandong, he was suddenly reminded of "that forbidding-looking sage jolting along in a rickety cart as he hurried about his business here in the old days"; "Confucius in Modern China," *SW* 4:182.

37. Wang, "Lu Xun as a Scholar," 99.

38. Leys, *Broken Images*, 27.

39. "Sudden Notions," *SW* 2:181.

40. "Zheyangde zhanshi" (Such a warrior), *LXQJ* 2:215.

41. Ibid., 214; "Such a Fighter," *SW* 1:354

42. *LXQJ* 2:215.

43. "Yingde gaobie" (The shadow's farewell), *LXQJ* 2:165-166; "The Shadow's Leave-Taking," *SW* 1:320-321.

44. Lee, *Voices from the Iron House*, 124.

45. Quoted in Leys, *Broken Images*, 31, modified; "Xie zai *Fen* houmian," *LXQJ* 1:285.

46. Leys, 18, modified; "Xie zai *Fen* houmian," *LXQJ* 1:285.

47. "Wo hai buneng 'daizhu'" (I'm still unable to "hold my tongue"), *LXQJ* 3:244.

48. The term "softer knives" derives from a work by the late Ming early Qing poet Jia Fuxi (1589-1675) that refers to "demons carrying soft knives" catching people unawares and killing them. Also used in Lu Xun's preface to *The Grave*, *LXQJ* 1:4.

49. (Untitled), *LXQJ* 3:365.

50. "Tici" (Preface), *LXQJ* 3:407.

51. J. M. Coetzee, *Doubling the Point: Essays and Interviews*, ed. David Atwell (Cambridge, Mass.: Harvard University Press, 1992), 60.

52. "Xie zai *Fen* houmian," *LXQJ* 1:284.

53. "Xiaopinwende weiji," *LXQJ* 4:575.

54. Discussed in David Pollard, *The True Story of Lu Xun* (Hong Kong: Chinese University Press, 2002), 173-174.

55. Zhou Zuoren, "In Praise of Anesthesia," modified, in *Zhou Zuoren: Selected Essays*, trans. David Pollard (Hong Kong: Chinese University of Hong Kong Press, 2006), 254.

56. Ibid., 255.

57. "Xiaopinwende weiji," *LXQJ* 4:575, 576.

58. Lee, *Voices from the Iron House*, 92. Lu Xun not only praised Kuriyagawa's work as "highly original" but described his theoretical text as "a kind of

creative work that offers a wealth of unique and penetrating insights";
LXQJ 10:232. As Wendy Larson points out, Lu Xun shared Kuriyagawa's
interest in exploring the anguish resulting from the injustice of "unfavourable social conditions." See Larson, *From Ah Q to Lei Feng: Freud and Revolutionary Spirit in Twentieth-Century China* (Stanford: Stanford University Press, 2009), 68.

59. Quoted in Lee, *Voices from the Iron House*, 92.
60. Ibid., 94.
61. My reading here draws on Lee's analysis in ibid., 94-95.
62. "Daoshi" (The mentor), *LXQJ* 3:56.
63. "Qingnian bidu shu" (Must-read books for the young), *LXQJ* 3:12.
64. "Haishang tongxin" (A letter written at sea), *LXQJ* 3:401-402.
65. "A Letter Written at Sea," *SW* 2:323-324.
66. *LXQJ* 11:184. Also quoted and discussed in Pollard, *The True Story of Lu Xun*, 110.
67. "A Layman's Remarks on Writing," *SW* 4:123-124.
68. Wang Hui, *Zixuan ji* (Selected works) (Nanning: Guangxi shifan daxue chubanshe, 1997), 310.
69. "The Classics and the Vernacular," *SW* 2:248.
70. Leys, *Broken Images*, 26.
71. An English translation appears in *SW* 1:52-57. "Kong Yiji," *LXQJ* 1: 434-439.
72. "Silent China," *SW* 2:333.
73. Sun, *Ye cao yanjiu*, 23.
74. "Guoke" (The wayfarer), *LXQJ* 2:190-191. Translated as "The Passer-by" in *SW* 1:336-341.
75. Quoted in Sun, *Ye cao yanjiu*, 29.
76. "Guoke," *LXQJ* 2:188-194.
77. "Zixu" (Preface), *LXQJ* 1:419.
78. "Guoke," *LXQJ* 2: 190.
79. An account of Lu Xun's involvement in the "Latinization" movement appears in Pollard, *The True Story of Lu Xun*, 182-188.
80. Tang Tao, *Lu Xun lunji* (Essays on Lu Xun) (Beijing: Wenhua yishu chubanshe, 1991), 46-47.
81. "Guoke," *LXQJ* 2:194.
82. "Xiaopinwende weiji," *LXQJ* 4:574-575. On intellectual syncretism during the Ming, see John B. Henderson, "Strategies in Neo-Confucian Heresiography," in *Imagining Boundaries: Changing Confucian Doctrines, Texts, and Hermeneutics*, ed. Kai-wing Chow, On-cho Ng, and John B. Henderson (Albany: State University of New York Press, 1999), 107-120.

83. Sun, Ye cao *yanjiu,* 9.
84. Lu Xun, *Dawn Blossoms Plucked at Dusk,* trans. Yang Xianyi and Gladys Yang (Peking: Foreign Language Press, 1976), 68. In an earlier version of this story, published on 9 September 1919 under the pseudonym Shen Fei, the narrator accuses his nanny of making him shout at his father. The narrator then states that when his own end is near, he would never allow his child to shout in his ear. See *LXQJ* 8:95.
85. "Tuibai xiande zhandong" (The tremor of debased lines), *LXQJ* 2:204.
86. Ibid., 205. A full translation appears in Lu Hsun, *Wild Grass,* 46-49. Lu Xun was evidently fond of figuring emotional intensity as "stonelike" or "statuelike." Four months after completing "The Tremor of Debased Lines," he wrote a short story, "The Loner" *(guduzhe),* in which the protagonist, the biology teacher Wei Lianshu, expresses his grief for his dead grandmother "like a wounded wolf howling in the wilderness" while standing "motionless as an iron statue." *SW* 1:228, translated as "The Misanthrope."
87. *LXQJ* 2:206.
88. Lu Hsun, *Wild Grass,* 46.
89. *LXQJ* 2:206.
90. "My Old Home," *SW* 1:97.
91. J. M. Coetzee, *Giving Offense: Essays on Censorship* (Chicago: University of Chicago Press, 1996), 160.
92. Lu Hsun, "Foreword," *Wild Grass,* 3; "Tici," *LXQJ* 2:159.
93. Lu Hsun, "Foreword," *Wild Grass,* 4; "Tici," *LXQJ* 2:159-160.
94. Martin Heidegger, *On the Way to Language,* trans. Peter D. Hertz (New York: Harper and Row, 1971), 107.
95. Ibid., 423.
96. "Yingde gaobie," *LXQJ* 2:166.
97. Quoted in Lee, *Voices from the Iron House,* 89.
98. Feng, *Huiyi Lu Xun,* 20.
99. Ibid., 14-15.
100. "Silent China," *SW* 2:330.
101. "Da *Beidou* zazhishe wen" (In response to questions put by *The Dipper*), *LXQJ* 4:364-365. Lu Xun expanded on several of these points in the 1933 essay "How I Came to Write Short Stories," in which he wrote that he "inevitably turned toward Eastern Europe" when he embarked on his literary career, favoring in particular the works of Nikolai Gogol and Henryk Seinkiewicz as well as the Japanese authors Soseki Natsume and Ogai Mori. He noted, among other things: "When I could not find suitable vernacular expressions I used classical ones, hoping some read-

ers would understand"; "While writing, I paid no attention to any criticism whatsoever because if Chinese writers were childish in those days, Chinese critics were even more so...I often read foreign critical essays...and although they wrote of other authors, there were many judgments which I could apply to myself"; *SW* 3:262-265.

102. "Shigu san mei" (In perfect awareness of being worldly wise), *LXQJ* 4:592.

103. "Ying yiben *Duanpian xiaoshuo xuanji* zixu" (An author's preface to the English translation of *A Selection of Short Stories*), *LXQJ* 7:390.

104. "Experience," *SW* 3:306.

105. "Nalaizhuyi" (Appropriatism), *LXQJ* 6:39.

106. On Lu Xun's *pingdan* aesthetics, see David Pollard, "Lu Xun's *zawen*," in Lee, *Lu Xun and His Legacy*, 82.

107. "Xie zai *Fen* houmian," *LXQJ* 1:285.

108. "Wei-Jin fengdu ji wenzhang yu yao ji jiuzhi guanxi" (The style and prose of the Wei-Jin epoch and their connection with wine and drugs), *LXQJ* 3:502, discussed in Chapter 2.

109. Tang, *Lu Xun lunji*, 112. Also quoted in Pollard, "Lu Xun's *zawen*," 72.

110. "What Is Satire?," *SW* 4:190.

111. Translated as "Leaving the Pass" in Lu Xun, *Old Tales Retold*, trans. Yang Xianyi and Gladys Yang (Peking: Foreign Languages Press, 1972), 96-108.

112. "Chu guan" (Exit from the pass), *LXQJ* 2:442.

113. George Steiner, *Real Presences* (London: Faber and Faber, 1989), 53.

114. Among other things, Zhou Zuoren defined *quwei* as follows: "I have to confess that I prize *quwei* very highly. I believe that it is beautiful and good and that to be without it is calamitous. It includes many things, such as dignity (*ya* [usually rendered 'elegance']), lack of artifice *(zhuo)*, honesty *(pu)*, lack of glibness *(se* ['tartness']), steadfastness *(zhonghou)*, clarity *(qinglang)*, depth of understanding about human affairs *(tongda)*, moderation *(zhongyong)*, discrimination *(you bieze)*. What is contrary to these lacks *quwei (mei quwei)*." Quoted in Susan Daruvala, *Zhou Zuoren and an Alternative Chinese Response to Modernity* (Cambridge, Mass.: Harvard East Asian Monographs, 2000), 149.

115. Foucault, *Hermeneutics of the Subject*, 239-240.

116. "Women yao pipingjia" (We need critics), *LXQJ* 4:240.

117. "The Present Condition of Art in Darkest China," *SW* 3:125, intended for publication in the American magazine *New Masses*.

118. "Kuangren riji" (The diary of a madman), *LXQJ* 1:432.

119. "Medicine," *SW* 1:58-67.

120. The analogy is even more striking given the two aphorisms preceding this most famous maxim: "Beasts feed; man eats: the man of intellect alone knows how to eat"; "The fate of nations hangs upon their choice of food." Jean-Anthelme Brillat-Savarin, *The Physiology of Taste,* trans. Fayette Robinson (New York: Dover, 2002), 3.

121. "Three Summer Pests," *SW* 2:134–135.

122. "Tiji" (Prologue), *LXQJ* 3:3.

123. "Tiji" (Prologue), *LXQJ* 1:4.

124. "Lusuo he weikou," *LXQJ* 3:552–553; "Rousseau and Appetite," *SW* 2:379.

125. Lu Hsun, *Wild Grass,* 44, modified.

126. "Mujiewen" (The epitaph), *LXQJ* 2:202.

127. Lu Xun composed "The Epitaph" while a clamor still raged over the May Thirtieth Movement, and a month before he completed his essay "On Seeing with Eyes Wide Open" (discussed in Chapter 1).

128. C. G. Jung, *The Collected Works of C. G. Jung: Mysterium Coniunctionis; An Inquiry into the Separation and Synthesis of Psychic Opposites in Alchemy,* vol. 14, ed. Michael Fordham and Gerhard Adler, trans. R. F. C. Hull (New York: Pantheon, 1970), 365.

129. C. G. Jung, *Psychology and Alchemy,* trans. R. F. C. Hull (Princeton: Princeton University Press), 372.

130. "Mujiewen," *LXQJ* 2:202.

131. Ibid., 202–203.

132. Quoted and discussed in Jacques Derrida, *Negotiations: Interventions and Interviews, 1971–2001,* trans. Elisabeth Rottenberg (Stanford: Stanford University Press, 2002), 268.

133. Ibid., 274–275.

134. Ibid., 275–276.

135. Harald Weinrich, *On Borrowed Time: The Art and Economy of Living with Deadlines,* trans. Steven Rendall (Chicago: Chicago University Press, 2008), 54.

136. *The Analects of Confucius,* trans. Simon Leys (New York: W. W. Norton, 1997), 76 (15.20).

137. On the axiom's present-day relevance, see Gloria Davies, *Worrying about China: The Language of Chinese Critical Inquiry* (Cambridge, Mass.: Harvard University Press, 2007), 230–231.

138. "Xiaoyin" (Preface), *LXQJ* 2:229; Lu Xun, *Dawn Blossoms Plucked at Dusk,* 1–2.

139. "Zhe ye shi shenghuo" (This too is life), *LXQJ* 6:601.

140. Ibid., 602. A different English translation appears in *SW* 4:308–309.

141. Quoted in Coetzee, *Giving Offense,* 106.

142. Quoted in Edel Lancashire, "Popeye and the Case of Guo Yidong: Alias Bo Yang," *China Quarterly,* no. 92 (December 1982), 675–676.
143. "Ye song" (In praise of night), *LXQJ* 5:193–194.
144. Ibid.
145. "Buzhi rou wei he buzhi shui wei" (Forgetting the taste of meat and not knowing the taste of water), *LXQJ* 6:111–113; "Forgetting Meat and Forgetting Water," *SW* 4:126–128.
146. *Lun Yu* 7.14. Simon Leys translates the passage: "When the Master was in Qi, he heard the Coronation Hymn of Shun. For three months, he forgot the taste of meat. He said: 'I never imagined that music could reach such a point.'" *The Analects of Confucius,* 30. *Shao* music "celebrated the coronation of Shun, the mythical early ruler who attained supreme power through the most civilized process: the wise ruler Yao, having noticed his superior virtue, abdicated in his favor." Ibid., 129.
147. *LXQJ* 6:112.
148. Ibid.
149. This chapter was completed when China was in the grip of a massive drought that affected the entire Yangtze area in the early months of 2011. The drought in May was followed by an equally devastating flood in June. Photographic images of both natural disasters were published in *The Atlantic* on 20 June 2011 at http://www.theatlantic.com/infocus/2011/06/floods-follow-drought-in-china/100090/ (accessed 30 June 2011).

6. Raising Revolutionary Specters

1. Quoted in Simon Leys, *The Burning Forest: Essays on Culture and Politics in Contemporary China* (London: Paladin Grafton Books, 1988), 206, translation modified; *LXQJ* 3:532.
2. "Menwai wen tan" (Discussing writing from the outside), *LXQJ* 6:92.
3. Walter Benjamin, *Selected Writings,* ed. Howard Eiland and Michael W. Jennings, trans. Edmund Jephcott and others, vol. 4: *1938–1940* (Cambridge, Mass.: The Belknap Press of Harvard University Press, 2003), 392.
4. "'Ying yi' yu 'wenxuede jiejixing'" ("Hard translation" and "the class character of literature"), *LXQJ* 4:201. See also "The Critics We Need," *SW* 3:109, in which this comparison is explicitly stated.
5. "Random Thoughts (59)," *SW* 2:50, modified.
6. "'Ti weiding' cao 6–9" (Notes without titles, nos. 6–9), *LXQJ* 6:425–430.
7. Quoted in ibid., 427. Qu Yuan and Ruan Ji were among Lu Xun's favorite ancient poets. Lu Xun scholars have also identified the influence of Li Bai and Du Fu on his poetry.

8. Ibid., 427-428; an alternative English translation appears at *SW* 4:239.

9. Umberto Eco, *Travels in Hyper-Reality*, trans. William Weaver (London: Picador, 1987), 34.

10. Ibid.

11. "'Ti weiding' cao 6-9," *LXQJ* 6:426.

12. "Rival Schools of Reading," *SW* 4:156.

13. Zhou Zuoren, "On Closing One's Door and Getting Down to Studying," in Zhou, *Selected Essays*, trans. David Pollard (Hong Kong: Chinese University of Hong Kong Press, 2006), 112.

14. "Women xianzai zenyang zuo fuqin?" (How should we be as fathers today?), *LXQJ* 1:130, 140; "What Is Required of Us as Fathers Today?," *SW* 2:71.

15. T. A. Hsia, *The Gate of Darkness: Studies on the Leftist Literary Movement in China* (Seattle: University of Washington Press, 1968), 146.

16. "Custom and Reform," *SW* 3:98.

17. "Weile wangquede jinian" (Remembering in order to forget), *LXQJ* 4:482. On Fang, see Benjamin A. Elman, "The Formation of 'Dao Learning' as Imperial Ideology during the Early Ming Dynasty," in *Culture and State in Chinese History: Conventions, Accommodations and Critiques*, ed. Theodore Huters, R. Bin Wong, and Pauline Yu (Stanford: Stanford University Press, 1997), 58-59.

18. Jacques Derrida, *Specters of Marx: The State of the Debt, the Work of Mourning and the New International*, trans. Peggy Kamuf (London: Routledge, 2006), 153.

19. Ibid., 163.

20. This is a quotation from Chen Yuan's famous open letter to Xu Zhimo (dated 26 January 1926), in which he presented Lu Xun as irascible, arrogant, and small-minded.

21. "Wu Chang," *LXQJ* 2:269-270. In 1926 and 1927 Lu Xun frequently mentioned Chen Yuan's open letter to Xu Zhimo in his essays. He was evidently wounded by Chen's highly unflattering portrait of him.

22. Ibid., 273.

23. Ibid., 272.

24. On the significance and Confucian treatment of the Maudgalyāyana story in Chinese folk culture, see Qitao Guo, *Ritual Opera and Mercantile Lineage: The Confucian Transformation of Popular Culture in Late Imperial Huizhou* (Stanford: Stanford University Press, 2005), 89-102.

25. "Wu Chang," *LXQJ* 2:272.

26. "A Layman's Remarks on Writing," *SW* 4:122, modified.

27. "Menwai wen tan," *LXQJ* 6:95.

28. This was a reference to the twenty-eight Latin letters of Esperanto, in which Lu Xun had an abiding interest.
29. *LXQJ* 6:97.
30. Ibid., 96.
31. Ibid., 97-98.
32. "Ren hua" (Human language), *LXQJ* 5:73-74.
33. Ibid., 74.
34. Ibid.
35. Ibid.
36. "Da Youheng xiansheng" (In reply to Mr. Shi Youheng), *LXQJ* 3:454.
37. "'Ying yi' yu 'wenxuede jiejixing,'" *LXQJ* 4:203-204.
38. "Shengmingde lu" (The road of life), *LXQJ* 1:368-369; an alternative translation appears in *SW* 2:54-55.
39. Discussed in Roger T. Ames and David L. Hall, *Daodejing: "Making This Life Significant," A Philosophical Translation* (New York: Ballantine Books, 2003), 84-85, 206.
40. "Xie zai *Fen* houmian" (An epilogue to *The Grave*), *LXQJ* 1:284.
41. *LXQJ* 11:274.
42. "Nü diao" (The hanged woman), *LXQJ* 6:614.
43. Ibid., 614-615.
44. Ibid., 616-618.
45. Ibid., 618-619.
46. "Si" (Death), *LXQJ* 6:610.
47. "Nü diao," *LXQJ* 6:614.
48. "Si," *LXQJ* 6:612.
49. "Nü diao," *LXQJ* 6:614.
50. "Fuchou II," *LXQJ* 2:175; "Revenge II," *SW* 1:325.
51. "Fengzheng" (The kite), *LXQJ* 2:182-184.
52. Ibid., 184. An earlier version of this story was published pseudonymously in 1919; see *Lu Xun quanji* (Complete works of Lu Xun), vol. 8 (Beijing: Renmin wenxue chubanshe, 2005), 119-120.
53. *The True Story of Ah Q*, *SW* 1:152-153; *A Q zhengzhuan*, *LXQJ* 1:526.
54. *LXQJ* 1:527.
55. "What Happens after Nora Leaves Home?" *SW* 2:92-93; "Nala zou hou zenyang," *LXQJ* 1:163-164.
56. "Si," *LXQJ* 6:609.
57. "Xieyu shenye li," *LXQJ* 6:502; "Written in Deep Night," *SW* 4:266.
58. *LXQJ* 6:502.
59. "'Da xue fen fei'" (Snow everywhere, swirling in profusion), *LXQJ* 5:552-553.

60. Ibid., 553.

61. Ibid.

62. Quoted and discussed in David Pollard, "Lu Xun's zawen," in *Lu Xun and His Legacy*, ed. Leo Ou-fan Lee (Berkeley: University of California Press, 1985), 85.

63. Xu Guangping, *Lu Xun huiyi lu* (Recollections of Lu Xun) (Wuhan: Changjiang wenyi chubanshe, 2010), 163.

64. "Zhe yeshi shenghuo," *LXQJ* 6:600–601; "This, Too, Is Life," *SW* 4:307.

65. *LXQJ* 6:601.

66. Ibid.

67. "Da Xu Maoyong bing guanyu kang Ri tongyi zhanxian wenti" (A reply to Xu Maoyong and remarks on the issue of a united front in resistance to Japan), *LXQJ* 6:529.

68. "Zhe yeshi shenghuo," *LXQJ* 6:601.

69. Jorge Luis Borges, *In Praise of Darkness*, trans. Norman Thomas di Giovanni (New York: Dutton, 1974), 57.

70. "Zhe yeshi shenghuo," *LXQJ* 6:601.

71. "Ye song" (In praise of night), *LXQJ* 5:193.

72. "Lu Xun 'Ye song' de xiezuo beijing" (Background notes on Lu Xun's "In Praise of Night"), *Baidu zhidao*, 22 March 2009, at http://zhidao.baidu.com/question/90551208.html?fr=qrl&cid=170&index=5 (accessed 2 January 2011).

73. On the intellectual ramifications of this movement, see Jing Wang, *High Culture Fever: Politics, Aesthetics, and Ideology in Deng's China* (Berkeley: University of California Press, 1996), 9–36.

74. The hopes invested in the publishing enterprises of the 1980s are amply detailed in Chen Fong-Ching and Jin Guantao, *From Youthful Manuscripts to River Elegy: The Chinese Popular Cultural Movement and Political Transformation, 1979–1989* (Hong Kong: Chinese University Press, 1997).

75. *"Geming wenxue" lunzheng ziliao xuanbian* (Selected historical materials on the debate over "revolutionary literature"), 2 vols. (Beijing: Renmin wenxue chubanshe, 1981).

76. Ibid., 1:2.

77. Li Helin, ed., *Zhongguo wenyi lunzhan* (A literary debate in China) (Shanghai: Beixin shudian, 1929).

78. Chen Pingyuan, *Xuezhede renjian qinghuai* (The human concerns of scholars) (Beijing: SDX Joint Publishing, 2007), 206.

79. Zhou was chairman of the All-China Federation of Literary and Art Circles and deputy director of the Propaganda Department from 1978 to 1983.

80. This is Jing Wang's succinct description of their tortuous project. See *High Culture Fever*, 11.

81. On Zhou's speech and its revision by Hu Qiaomu, the leading Party propagandist, see Xu Qingquan, "Xin faxiande Hu Qiaomu zhi Zhou Yang xinba" (A newly discovered letter from Hu Qiaomu to Zhou Yang), first published in *Guangming Ribao*, 26 April 2004, at http://www.people.com.cn/GB/wenhua/1088/2468371.html (accessed 20 November 2011).

82. Kwok-sing Li, *A Glossary of Political Terms of the People's Republic of China*, trans. Mary Lok (Hong Kong: Chinese University Press, 1995), 168.

83. Geremie R. Barmé, "New China Newspeak *Xinhua Wenti*," *China Heritage Quarterly*, no. 29 (2012), at http://www.chinaheritagequarterly.org/glossary.php?searchterm=029_xinhua.inc&issue=029 (accessed 1 April 2012).

84. Ibid.

85. Geremie R. Barmé, *Shades of Mao: The Posthumous Cult of the Great Leader* (Armonk, N.Y.: M. E. Sharpe, 1996), 224.

86. Wang Meng, "Renwen jingshen wenti ougan" (Impromptu thoughts about the humanistic spirit), in *Renwen jingshen xunsi lu* (In search of the humanistic spirit), ed. Wang Xiaoming (Shanghai: Wenhui chubanshe, 1996), 106-119. The phrase "the loss of the humanistic spirit" *(renwen jingshende shiluo)* had enjoyed great currency in the elite intellectual circles of Shanghai and Beijing in the early to mid-1990s.

87. Quoted in Xu Jilin and Luo Gang, *Qimengde ziwo wajie* (Enlightenment collapsing in on itself) (Beijing: Gulin chuban jituan, 2007), 113-114.

88. Ibid., 115.

89. Wang Shuo, "Wo kan Lu Xun" (How I see Lu Xun), in *Shijimo de Lu Xun lunzheng* (A fin-de-siècle debate over Lu Xun), ed. Gao Xudong (Beijing: Dongfang chubanshe, 2001), 8-9.

90. Ibid., 9.

91. Ibid., 12.

92. Xu and Luo, *Qimengde ziwo wajie*, 126-127.

93. "Xuyan" (Preface), *LXQJ* 4:4-5.

94. *LXQJ* 12:409-410. Quoted in Sun Yu, "Xu" (Preface), in *Bei xiedude Lu Xun* (The maligned Lu Xun), ed. Sun (Beijing: Qunyan chubanshe, 1994), 1.

95. Five articles of this type are included in ibid., 131-136, 149, and 164-166.

96. Hu Shi and Su Xuelin, "Guanyu dangqian wenhua dongtaide taolun" (A discussion about recent cultural developments), in ibid., 180.

97. In Hu's letter the word "gentleman" appears in English; ibid., 180-181.

98. Zhou Zuoren, "'Wa'de jiaoxun" (The lesson of *The Frog*), in ibid., 198.

99. Ibid.; Zhou Zuoren, "Lun maren wenzhang" (On abusive essays), in ibid., 203.

100. Zhou Zuoren, "Lun maren wenzhang," 203.

101. Zhou died in 1967 "confined to a shed in appalling conditions" after being severely beaten by Red Guards months earlier. See Susan Daruvala, *Zhou Zuoren and an Alternative Chinese Response to Modernity* (Cambridge, Mass.: Harvard East Asian Monographs, 2000), 4.

102. See, for instance, Xie Yong, ed., *Hu Shi haishi Lu Xun* (Hu Shi or Lu Xun) (Beijing: Zhongguo gongren chubanshe, 2003); Sun Yu, *Lu Xun yu Hu Shi* (Lu Xun and Hu Shi) (Wuchang: Changjiang wenyi chubanshe, 2007); Shao Jian, *Ershishijide liangge zhishifenzi: Hu Shi yu Lu Xun* (Two intellectuals of the twentieth century: Hu Shi and Lu Xun) (Taipei: Showwe Information, 2008).

103. Li Shenzhi, "Huigui 'Wu Si' xuexi minzhu" (Learning democracy *via* a return to "May Fourth"), *Shuwu*, no. 5 (2001), also at http://www.yuedu. org/review/review-225573506.htm (accessed 20 January 2012).

104. Quoted in Xu and Luo, *Qimengde ziwo wajie*, 122, http://www.duping.net /XHC/show.php?bbs=10&post=544788 (accessed 20 January 2012).

105. Zhang Guangtian, "Lu Xun xiansheng shi yangei Wang Shuo Qian Liqun tamen kande" (*Mr. Lu Xun* is performed for the likes of Wang Shuo and Qian Liqun), *Beijing wanbao*, 5 May 2001, at http://news.sohu .com/62/08/news145070862.shtml (accessed 20 January 2012).

106. Jie Xizhang, "Zhang Guangtiande 'geming xiu': Ping 'Lu Xun xiansheng'" (Zhang Guangtian's "revolutionary show": A review of *Mr. Lu Xun*), *Nanfang Zhoumo*, 11 May 2001, at http://ent.sina.com.cn/r/m/42863.html (accessed 20 January 2012); and Kuang Xinnian, quoted in Xu and Luo, *Qimengde ziwo wajie*, 135.

107. Quoted in Xu and Luo, *Qimengde ziwo wajie*, 134–135.

108. Mao Zedong, "Mao Zedong gei Jiang Qingde xin" (Mao Zedong's letter to Jiang Qing), at China Elections and Governance, http://www.chinaelec tions.org/newsinfo.asp?newsid=134300 (accessed 30 November 2011).

109. Wang Shuo, "Wo kan Lu Xun," 10.

110. David Wang, *The Monster That Is History: History, Violence, and Fiction Writing in Twentieth-Century China* (Berkeley: University of California Press, 2004), 157.

111. Chen Shuyu, *Juan yan mengleng ji: Chen Shuyu xueshu suibi zixuan ji* (The haze of tired eyes: Chen Shuyu's selected essays) (Fuzhou: Fujian jiaoyu chubanshe, 2000), 97. Chen is a leading curator and editor of Lu Xun's oeuvre in the People's Republic.

112. The controversy attracted official media reports such as "A Textbook Case—Revisions in Mainland Literary Selections Cause a Stir," Xinhua

News Agency, 30 November 2007, http://china.org.cn/english/China /233945.htm (accessed 2 February 2010).

113. Kong, an ardent nationalist with a large following in mainland China, attracted global media attention in January 2012 when in a webcast interview he stated that it was the duty of every Chinese person to learn Putonghua and in this context berated people in Hong Kong who defend their local Cantonese culture as thoroughly colonized "running dogs of the British," "bastards," and "thieves." Kong also called them *Xi zi* (Western lackeys), a demeaning term made famous by Lu Xun. A copy of the interview with English subtitles is available at http://shanghaiist .com/2012/01/20/kong-qingdong-hk-bastards-dogs.php (accessed 22 January 2012). Lu Xun had used *Xi zi* in a lecture of May 1929 to disparage his Crescent Moon rivals as "lackeys" *(zi)* living off the words of Western *(Xi)* writers and thinkers. See "Xianjinde xin wenxuede gainian," *LXQJ* 4:133; "Some Thoughts on Our New Literature," *SW* 3:51. In June 1935 he explained that by *Xi zi* he meant Chinese people of a particular ilk who use their knowledge of or connections with the West to bully fellow Chinese yet see themselves as culturally superior to Westerners. "Weiti cao (1-3)" (Untitled notes 1-3), *LXQJ* 6:352-355.

114. Ceng Yu, "Beijing 9 quxian gaozhong yuwen 'huanxue' Ah Q zhengzhuan deng mingpian beishan" (A "change of blood" for Chinese-language curriculum in 9 Beijing districts and counties: The removal of *The True Story of Ah Q* and other well-known works), *Zhongguo xinwen wang*, 30 August 2007, reposted at http://lib.360doc.com/07/0830/09/23974_704421.shtml (accessed 2 February 2010).

115. Diaoxin liuyun, "Yige Lu Xun chetui, qianwange A Q chengzhangle," *Tianya shequ*, 9 September 2010, at http://www.tianya.cn/publicforum /content/news/1/182123.shtml (accessed 30 November 2011).

116. See also Howard Goldblatt, "Lu Xun and Patterns of Literary Sponsorship," in Lee, *Lu Xun and His Legacy*, 211-213.

117. Discussed in Theodore D. Huters, "Hu Feng and the Critical Legacy of Lu Xun," in ibid., 148-149.

118. Chen Zongying, "Wo qinling Luo Jinan yu Mao Zedong duihua" (The conversation between Luo Jinan and Mao Zedong that I heard), in *Jiaru Lu Xu huozhe* (If Lu Xun were still alive), ed. Chen Mingyuan (Shanghai: Wenhui chubanshe, 2003), 92.

119. John King Fairbank and Merle Goldman, *China: A New History*, 2nd enlarged ed. (Cambridge, Mass.: The Belknap Press of Harvard University Press, 2006), 365.

120. Chen Shuyu, *Dianfu yu chuancheng: Lun Lu Xunde dangdai yiyi* (Inversion and transmission: On the contemporary significance of Lu Xun) (Fuzhou: Fujian jiaoyu chubanshe, 2006), 287.

121. Luo Xingping, "Lu Xun jingshen zai dangdai wenxue zhongde fuhuo" (The revival of the Lu Xun spirit in present-day Chinese literature), in *2002 Lu Xun yanjiu nian jian* (2002 yearbook of Lu Xun Studies), ed. Zheng Xingsen, Sun Yu, and Liu Zengren (Beijing: Remin wenxue chubanshe, 2002), 223-224.

122. Zhang Chengzhi, "Zhi xiansheng shu" (A letter to the maestro), first published in 1991 and included in Zhang's 1994 anthology of essays, *Huangwu yingxiong lu* (The hero's desolate path), is now widely available on the Internet. See http://www.chinese-thought.org/ddpl/006354.htm (10 December 2010).

123. Han Han, "Ruguo Lu Xun huodao xianzai" (If Lu Xun were still alive), first posted on 25 July 2007 and, for reasons unknown, subsequently removed from Han's blog. The post appears on numerous other websites, including http://tieba.baidu.com/f?kz=699161680 (10 December 2010).

124. "Da Yang Cunren xiansheng gongkai xinde gongkai xin" (An open letter in reply to Mr. Yang Cunren's open letter), *LXQJ* 4:625-627.

125. Quoted in ibid., 628, 632.

126. Ibid., 629.

127. Ibid.

128. "Xiao yin" (Preface), *LXQJ* 3:183.

129. Paulo Freire, *Pedagogy of the Oppressed* (Harmondsworth: Penguin Books, 1972), 44.

130. Wang Hui, "The Voices of Good and Evil: What Is Enlightenment? Rereading Lu Xun's 'Toward a Refutation of Malevolent Voices,'" *boundary 2*, 38, no. 2 (2011), 88.

131. "Guanyu Taiyan xiansheng er san shi" (Two or three things about Mr. Zhang Taiyan), *LXQJ* 6:545-547; "Yin Taiyan xiansheng er xiangqide er san shi" (Two or three things that came to mind because of Mr. Zhang Taiyan), ibid., 556-559. English translations appear in *SW* 4:322-326, 327-332. See also Wang Hui's discussion of both essays in "Dead Fire Rekindled," *boundary 2*, 34, no. 3 (2007), 3.

132. *LXQJ* 6:545-546; *SW* 4:324.

133. *LXQJ* 6:546-547.

134. Ibid., 546.

135. *LXQJ* 6:556, 559; *SW* 4:327, 331.

136. *SW* 4:332, modified.

137. "Ye song" (In praise of night), *LXQJ* 5:194.

138. Peter Buse, Ken Hirschcop, Scott McCracken, and Bertrand Taithe, *Benjamin's Arcades: An unGuided Tour* (Manchester: Manchester University Press, 2005), 71; Walter Benjamin, *On Hashish,* ed. and trans. Howard Eiland (Cambridge, Mass.: Harvard University Press, 2006), 142.

139. Benjamin, *On Hashish,* 142.

140. Stephen Owen, *Readings in Chinese Literary Thought* (Cambridge, Mass.: Council of East Asian Studies, Harvard University, 1992), 46.

141. Benjamin, *On Hashish,* 142–143.

142. "Zhe yeshi shenghuo," *LXQJ* 6:601.

Acknowledgments

I have called this book *Lu Xun's Revolution* to evoke not only his literary powers but also the times in which he lived and his complex afterlife in the politics and literature of the People's Republic of China. The writing was fraught from the outset with all the difficulties that accompany any attempt to make new sense of the formidable corpus that is *The Collected Works of Lu Xun,* of which so much has been written and over which so many quarrels have persisted. Thus, first and foremost, I must acknowledge the many scholars of Lu Xun whose valuable insights have informed the account presented here.

I am indebted to my husband, M. E. Davies, for his generous gifts of criticism, insight, and wit and for inspiring me to persevere with the writing whenever my heart grew faint. He has encountered Lu Xun with me while reading and commenting on the many draft versions of this work.

I must thank my dear friend Geremie Barmé for his very helpful comments on an early draft chapter and for inviting me to publish some of my ideas about Lu Xun in the *China Heritage Quarterly* as the writing progressed. I am also grateful to Lindsay Waters for his valuable advice in thinking about this book and to Lindsay and Paul Bové for encouraging me to develop my initial views on Lu Xun's language into two essays. Both were subsequently published in *boundary 2*.

Grateful thanks go to Wu Guanjun for his generous assistance in locating photographic images and articles about Lu Xun. Claire Roberts, Bick-har Yeung and Warren Sun must also be thanked for sharing useful information. I am grateful to Wang Yan and the Lu Xun Memorial Hall in Shanghai for allowing me to use images of Lu Xun from their collections.

I thank the two anonymous reviewers for their encouraging and insightful comments. I am very grateful to Shanshan Wang at Harvard University Press and Barbara Goodhouse at Westchester Publishing Services for their assistance with the technical production of this book. My copyeditor, Ann Hawthorne, must be thanked for her indispensable advice.

Study leave in the latter half of 2008 (under the auspices of the Outside Study Program, Faculty of Arts, Monash University) gave me an initial space of time in which to reread Lu Xun closely. Part of the research, on Lu Xun's present-day relevance, was funded by an Australian Research Council Discovery Grant (DP0985781).

I first read Lu Xun seriously when I was pregnant with my son, John. I now dedicate this book to him and his partner, Jessie.

Index

Class struggle *(continued)*

international, 174, 192; Li on, 146, 217-218; Lu Xun on, 187, 198, 224, 234-235, 236-237, 266; as revolutionary focus, 50, 63-64, 70, 83, 151-152; Stalin on, 46-47; Trotsky on, 46

Clear-sightedness, 24, 33, 52

Coetzee, J. M., 245, 258-259

Comintern. *See* Soviet Comintern

Commercial Press, 150-151

Communist Party, Chinese. *See* Chinese Communist Party

Communist Party, Japanese. *See* Japanese Communist Party

Communist Party, Soviet. *See* Soviet Communist Party

"Complete Our Literary Revolution" (Cheng), 172, 176

Confucianism: altruism of, 61-62; benevolence of, 190; criticism of, 50, 133-134, 299; on educated elite, 61, 126; humanism of, 189-190, 197; on immorality, 274-275; on immortality, 274-275; morality, 10, 16, 85-86, 91, 189-190, 280, 332; on obedient reverence, 88; state, 39-40, 59; on "unseemly," 23

Confucius, 97, 142, 190, 231, 240, 265-266, 279-280

Contemporary Culture (journal), 217, 317

Contemporary Review (journal), 91

Cosmopolitanism, 90, 108, 113, 114, 127, 250

Cowley, Malcolm, 157

Creation Society: and *baihua*, 175; criticism of, 149; debate with, 217; Feng on, 219; as geniuses+hooligans, 100-103, 142; on Lu Xun, 76-77, 85, 174, 181-182; Lu Xun on, 12, 73-75, 95, 99, 101, 102-103, 115, 142-149, 153, 171, 205, 241; and Marxism, 76-77, 83, 99, 146, 174, 178-179; periodicals, 72; on petty bourgeoisie, 203-204; reconciliation

with Lu Xun, 99-100; on revolutionary literature, 57, 101, 141, 145-147, 152; on romantic writing, 32, 149

Creation Weekly (journal), 75, 76

Crescent Moon Monthly (journal), 91-92, 106-107, 154

Crescent Moon Society: and cosmopolitan sophistication, 108; debate with, 217; on Lu Xun, 90; Lu Xun on, 12, 89-93, 171, 209, 223, 322-323; as reactionary, 316; on revolutionary literature, 12, 92-93, 106-108; Xu on, 106

Critical Review (journal), 126-127

Criticism, literary. *See* Literary criticism

Cultural Critique (journal), 95, 153-154, 178-179, 183, 219

Cultural Revolution, 7, 222, 223-224, 318, 319

Dai Kechong. *See* Su Wen

Dao, 39, 59, 233, 266

Daoist magic, Lu Xun on, 13, 164, 282-283, 284, 288

Dawn Blossoms Plucked at Dusk (Lu Xun), 68, 275-276

Debate over Chinese Literature, A (Li Helin, ed.), 216-218

Deluge (journal), 51

Deng Xiaoping, 315

Deng Yanda, 121-122

Derrida, Jacques, 55, 273, 290

"Diary of a Madman" (Lu Xun), 10, 125, 231, 268

Dipper, The (journal), 262

"Discussing Writing from the Outside" (Lu Xun), 292-293

"Dissatisfaction" (Lu Xun), 234

"Ditties on Universal Peace" (Lu Xun), 196-197

"Divergence between the Arts and Politics, The" (Lu Xun lecture), 187-188

Shao Jian, 324

Shao Xunmei, 113-114

Shen bao (newspaper), 41, 113, 114, 277

Shen Yanbing. *See* Mao Dun

Shen Yinmo, 83

Sheng Peiyu, 113

Shenyun. See under Aura

Shi Youheng, 60-61, 185

Shi Zhecun, 322

Shiwu bao (newspaper), 26, 41

Short Story Monthly (journal), 217

Shu-mei Shih, 114

Sima Yi, 81

Sinclair, Upton, 145, 201

Slogans: belief in, 52-53; Maoist, 7; of revolutionary literature, 44, 153, 163, 174, 182, 201, 212-213, 216, 224

"Snow Everywhere, Swirling in Profusion" (Lu Xun), 309

Sobol, Andrei, 123, 129, 190, 197

Social sciences, rise of, 164

Soong Ching-ling, 121-122

Soul of the nation, Lu Xun as, 8-9

Soviet Comintern: aid of, 6, 31; Chinese Communist loyalty to, 49; vs. Chinese Nationalist campaign, 69-70; on Fukumoto, 175-176; and officers' land, 49-50; and Stalin, 46-47

Soviet Communist Party: influence on Nationalist Party, 27-28; translations of works, 42

Soviet intellectual circles, 207-208

Speed: of change, 12, 25, 121-125, 191; Lu Xun on, 159-169

Spirit: defined, 232; fighting, 6-7, 16-17, 229; humanistic, 318-319; influence of, 325-326, 334; Maoist, 314-315, 317; revolutionary, 65, 153, 196, 198, 200, 219, 222, 225, 228, 320, 324, 332; of spiritual freedom, 320; of struggle, 221; use of term, 17, 290, 334; as *Zeitgeist,* 35, 58. *See also* Aura

Stalin, Joseph, 46-49, 207

Steiner, George, 20, 266

"Story of Hair, The" (Lu Xun), 44

Strange Tales from the Tang and Song Epochs (Lu Xun), 68, 173

Strikes. *See* Labor strikes

Student activism, 88-89

Studies of Lu Xun Outside China, 1960-1981, 317

"Style and Prose of the Wei-Jin Epoch and Their Connection with Wine and Drugs, The" (Lu Xun lectures), 80, 265

Su Shi, 330

Su Wen, 209-210

Su Xuelin, 322

"Such a Warrior" (Lu Xun), 241-242, 243

Sun Fuxi, 151

Sun Fuyuan, 132-135, 151, 192-193

Sun Monthly (journal), 153

Sun Society: Lu Xun on, 12, 95, 153, 171; periodicals, 72; on petty bourgeoisie, 203-204; reconciliation with Lu Xun, 99-100; revolutionary literature of, 152; support for, 150

Sun Yat-sen: and Chiang Kai-shek, 36, 59, 88; on illiteracy, 231; Lu Xun on, 53-55, 326; on Nationalists, 48; and Northern Expedition, 29; on one-party rule, 40, 42; as Party-builder, 11; on political obedience, 43-44; on political tutelage, 41-42, 48; as president, 25; on revolutionary construction, 25-26, 52-54; Three Principles, 26, 58, 81, 87, 232; unfinished revolution, 28, 30, 40, 119

Sun Yu, 162, 321

Sun Yushi, 229

Tai Jingnong, 79, 94, 132

Taiwan. *See* Republic of China (Taiwan)

Tan Pingshan, 47

Tang Tao, 254, 265

Tao Xisheng, 164

Tao Yuanming, 285, 287

www.ingramcontent.com/pod-product-compliance
Lightning Source LLC
Chambersburg PA
CBHW021830090426
42811CB00032B/2103/J